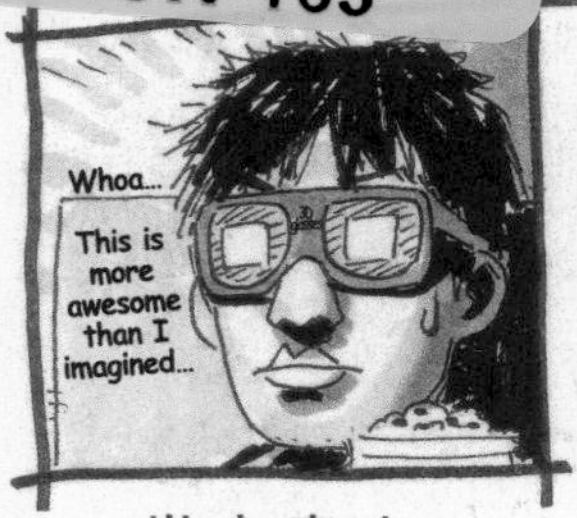
Whoa...
This is more awesome than I imagined...

岸本斉史

You know, there's something that I think is really confusing: The term "3-D" has been real popular lately, right? But that word has existed for a long time, from back when video games, anime and movies first started using polygons and CG. But now, 3-D refers to three-dimensional images that appear to leap out at you, like 3-D films or 3-D live animation. I mean, I understand...I really do understand... My only question is, what should we now call what used to be called 3-D? 2.5-D? Or perhaps we should call the current stuff super-3D?

—Masashi Kishimoto, 2010

Author/artist Masashi Kishimoto was born in 1974 in rural Okayama Prefecture, Japan. After spending time in art college, he won the Hop Step Award for new manga artists with his manga **Karakuri** (Mechanism). Kishimoto decided to base his next story on traditional Japanese culture. His first version of **Naruto**, drawn in 1997, was a one-shot story about fox spirits; his final version, which debuted in **Weekly Shonen Jump** in 1999, quickly became the most popular ninja manga in Japan.

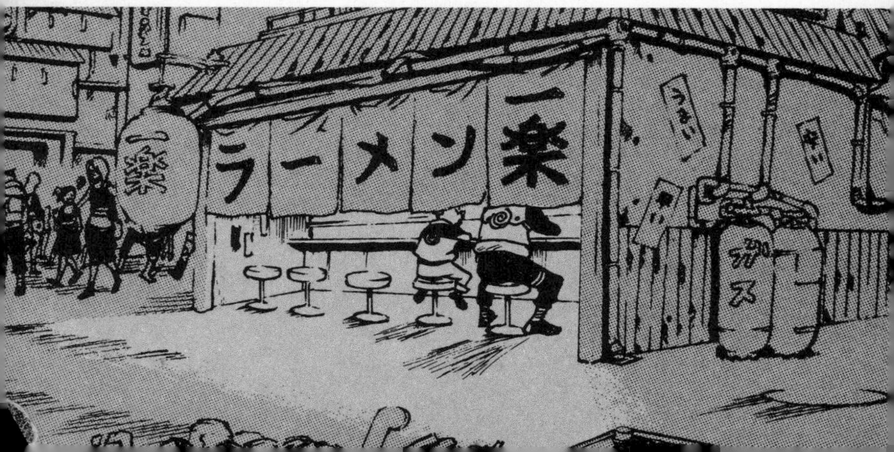
ラーメン一楽
一楽

NARUTO VOL. 51
SHONEN JUMP Manga Edition
This graphic novel contains material that was originally published in English in SHONEN JUMP #91–94. Artwork in the magazine may have been slightly altered from that presented here.

STORY AND ART BY MASASHI KISHIMOTO

Translation/Mari Morimoto
Series Touch-up Art & Lettering/Inori Fukuda Trant
Additional Touch-up Art & Lettering/Sabrina Heep
Design/Sam Elzway
Series Editor/Joel Enos
Graphic Novel Editor/Megan Bates

Printed in the U.S.A.

Published by VIZ Media, LLC
P.O. Box 77010
San Francisco, CA 94107

10 9 8 7 6 5 4 3 2 1
First printing, June 2011

viz media
www.viz.com

RATED T FOR TEEN

PARENTAL ADVISORY
NARUTO is rated T for Teen and is recommended for ages 13 and up. This volume contains realistic and fantasy violence.
ratings.viz.com

NARUTO

VOL. 51
SASUKE VS. DANZO!!

CONTENTS

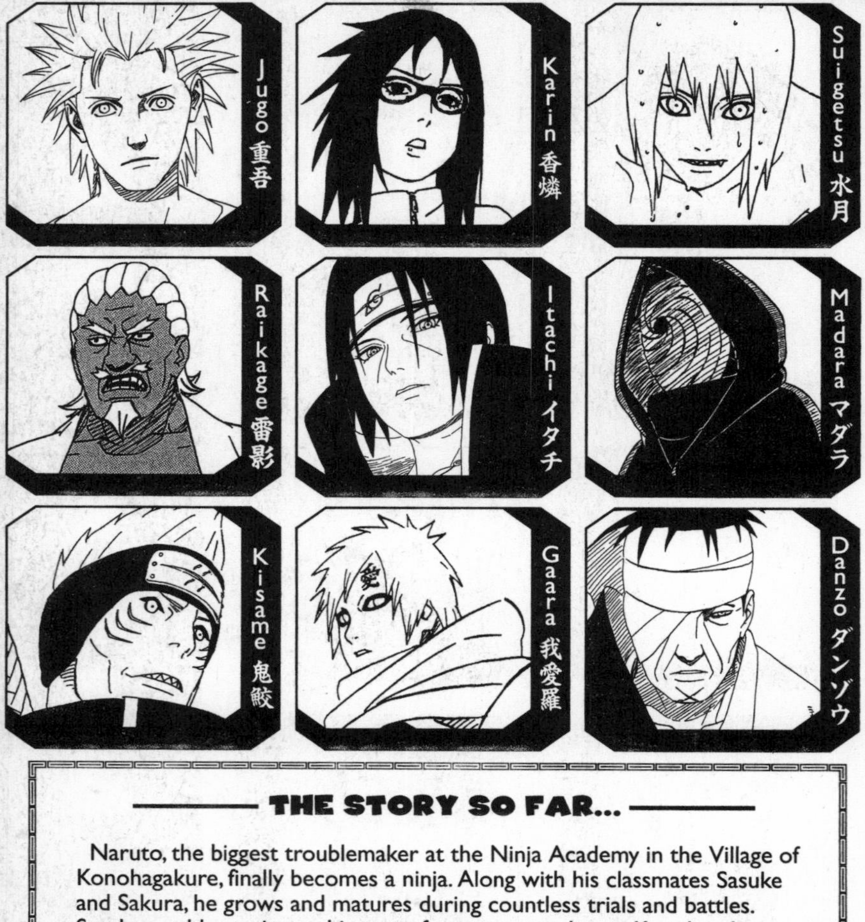
Jugo 重吾
Karin 香燐
Suigetsu 水月
Raikage 雷影
Itachi イタチ
Madara マダラ
Kisame 鬼鮫
Gaara 我愛羅
Danzo ダンゾウ

THE STORY SO FAR...

Naruto, the biggest troublemaker at the Ninja Academy in the Village of Konohagakure, finally becomes a ninja. Along with his classmates Sasuke and Sakura, he grows and matures during countless trials and battles. Sasuke, unable to give up his quest for vengeance, leaves Konohagakure to seek the renegade ninja Orochimaru, from whom he hopes to gain immense power.

Two years pass. Naruto battles against the Tailed Beast-targeting Akatsuki. Elsewhere, after winning the epic battle against his brother Itachi, Sasuke learns the truth about Itachi's perceived betrayal of their clan. He allies with the Akatsuki and sets out to destroy Konoha.

Sasuke invades the Gokage Summit convened to deal with the Akatsuki. Danzo manages to escape and Sasuke's assault ends in failure, but after Madara declares war on the Shadow leaders, an Allied Shinobi Force is formed! Meanwhile, Sai reappears before Naruto, who is still confused by Sakura's unexpected confession...

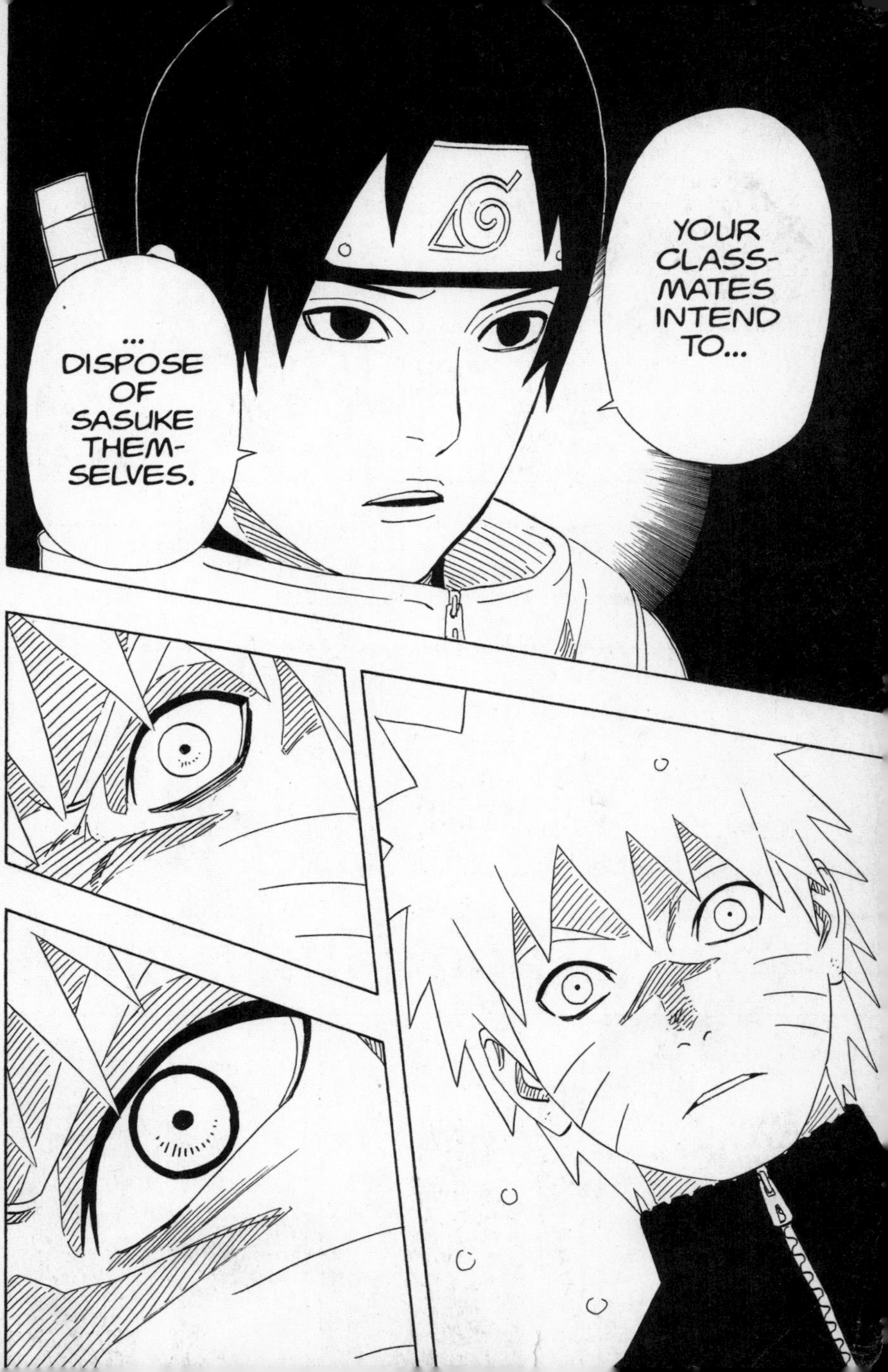
YOUR CLASS-MATES INTEND TO...
... DISPOSE OF SASUKE THEM-SELVES.

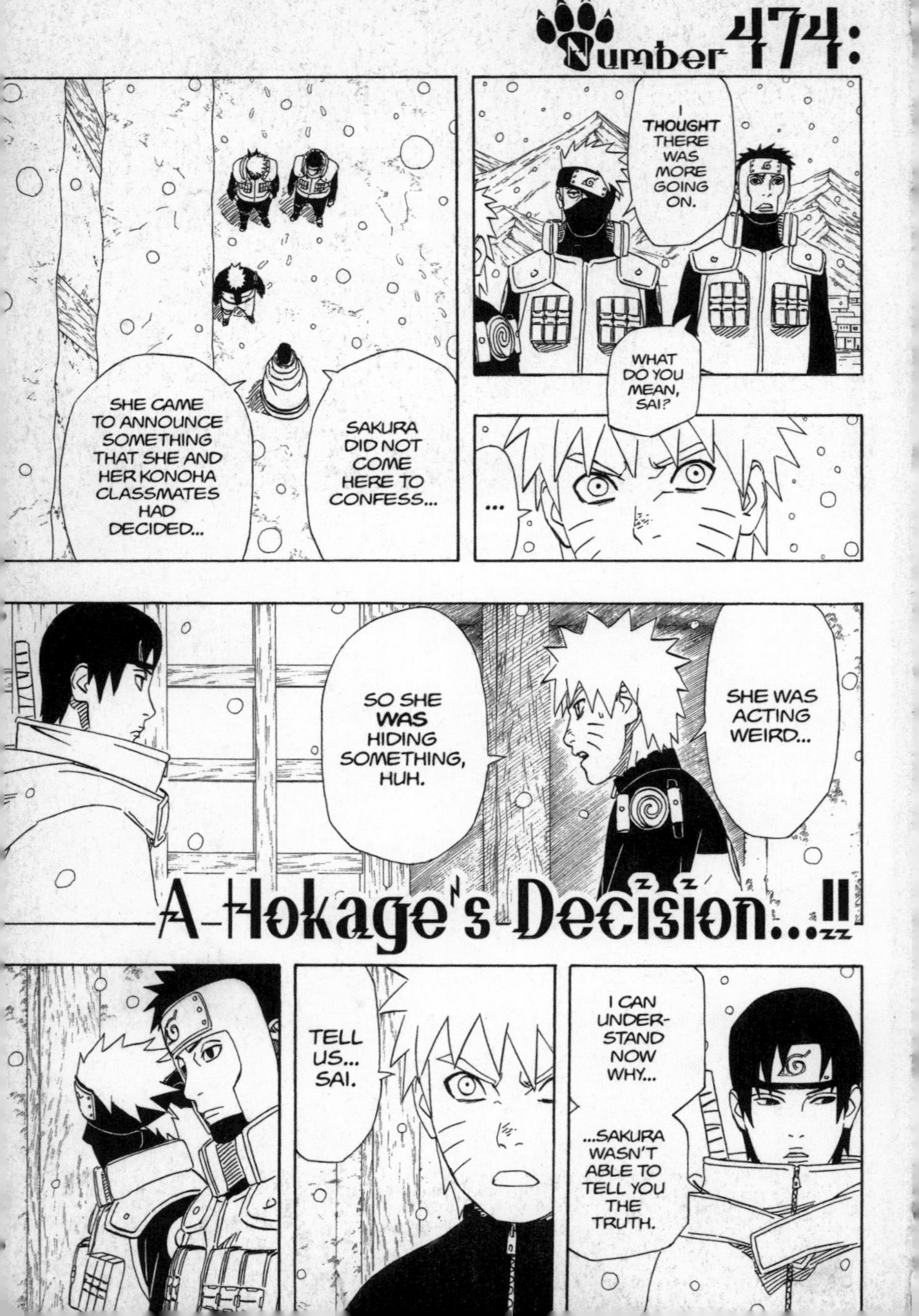
Number 474:
A Hokage's Decision...!!
I THOUGHT THERE WAS MORE GOING ON.
WHAT DO YOU MEAN, SAI?
...
SAKURA DID NOT COME HERE TO CONFESS...
SHE CAME TO ANNOUNCE SOMETHING THAT SHE AND HER KONOHA CLASSMATES HAD DECIDED...
SHE WAS ACTING WEIRD...
SO SHE WAS HIDING SOMETHING, HUH.
I CAN UNDER-STAND NOW WHY...
...SAKURA WASN'T ABLE TO TELL YOU THE TRUTH.
TELL US... SAI.

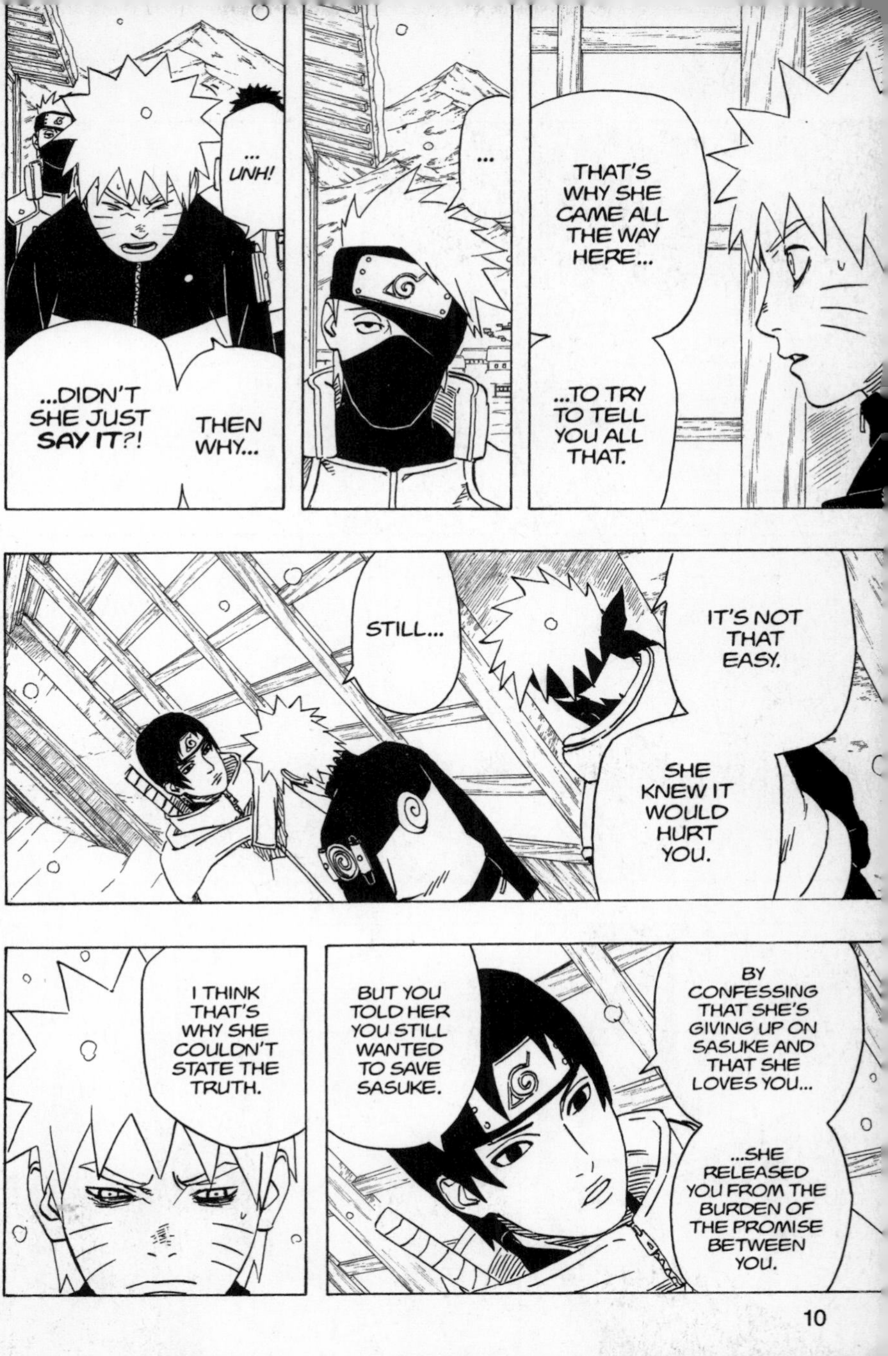
THAT'S WHY SHE CAME ALL THE WAY HERE...
...TO TRY TO TELL YOU ALL THAT.
...
... UNH!
THEN WHY...
...DIDN'T SHE JUST SAY IT?!
IT'S NOT THAT EASY.
SHE KNEW IT WOULD HURT YOU.
STILL...
BY CONFESSING THAT SHE'S GIVING UP ON SASUKE AND THAT SHE LOVES YOU...
...SHE RELEASED YOU FROM THE BURDEN OF THE PROMISE BETWEEN YOU.
BUT YOU TOLD HER YOU STILL WANTED TO SAVE SASUKE.
I THINK THAT'S WHY SHE COULDN'T STATE THE TRUTH.

READ THIS WAY

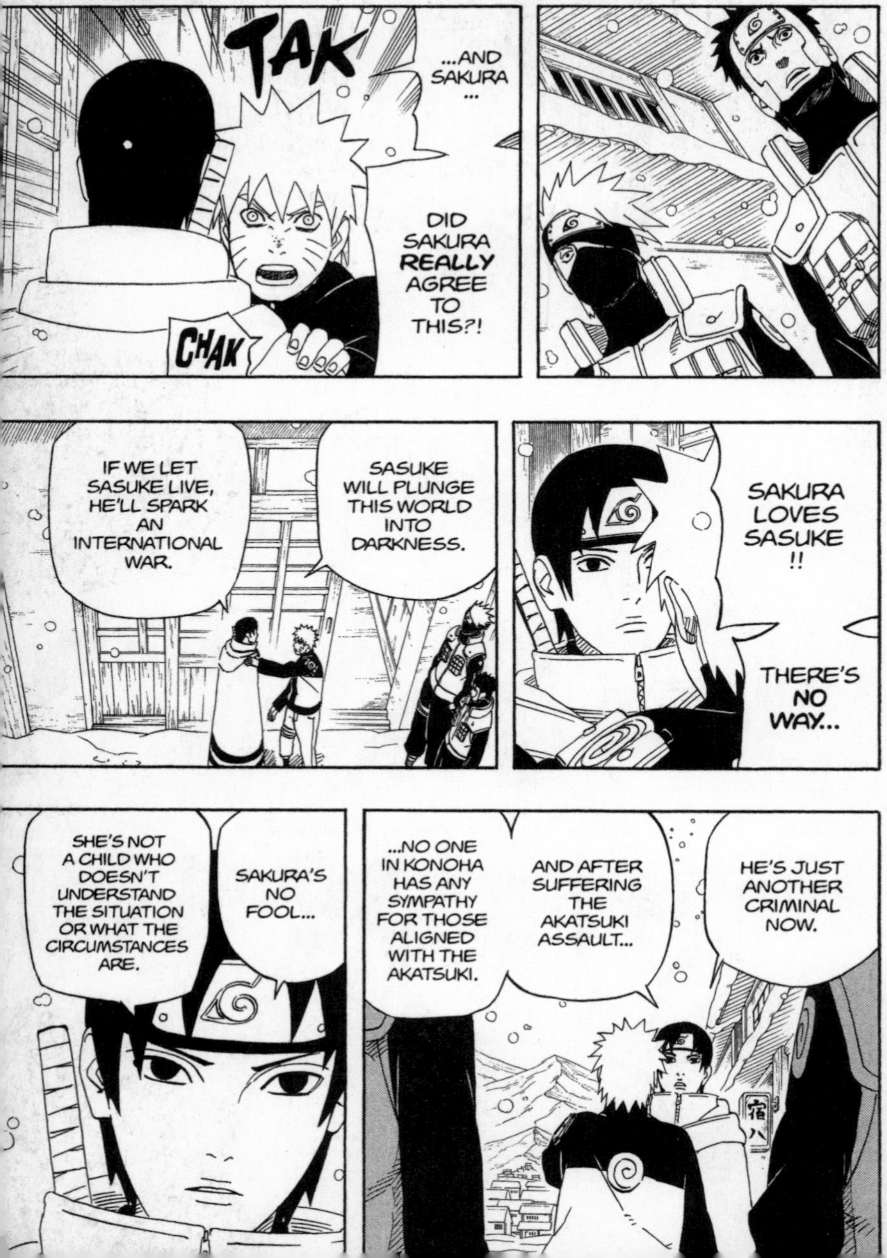
TAK
...AND SAKURA ...
DID SAKURA REALLY AGREE TO THIS?!
CHAK
SAKURA LOVES SASUKE !!
THERE'S NO WAY...
SASUKE WILL PLUNGE THIS WORLD INTO DARKNESS.
IF WE LET SASUKE LIVE, HE'LL SPARK AN INTERNATIONAL WAR.
HE'S JUST ANOTHER CRIMINAL NOW.
AND AFTER SUFFERING THE AKATSUKI ASSAULT...
...NO ONE IN KONOHA HAS ANY SYMPATHY FOR THOSE ALIGNED WITH THE AKATSUKI.
SAKURA'S NO FOOL...
SHE'S NOT A CHILD WHO DOESN'T UNDERSTAND THE SITUATION OR WHAT THE CIRCUMSTANCES ARE.

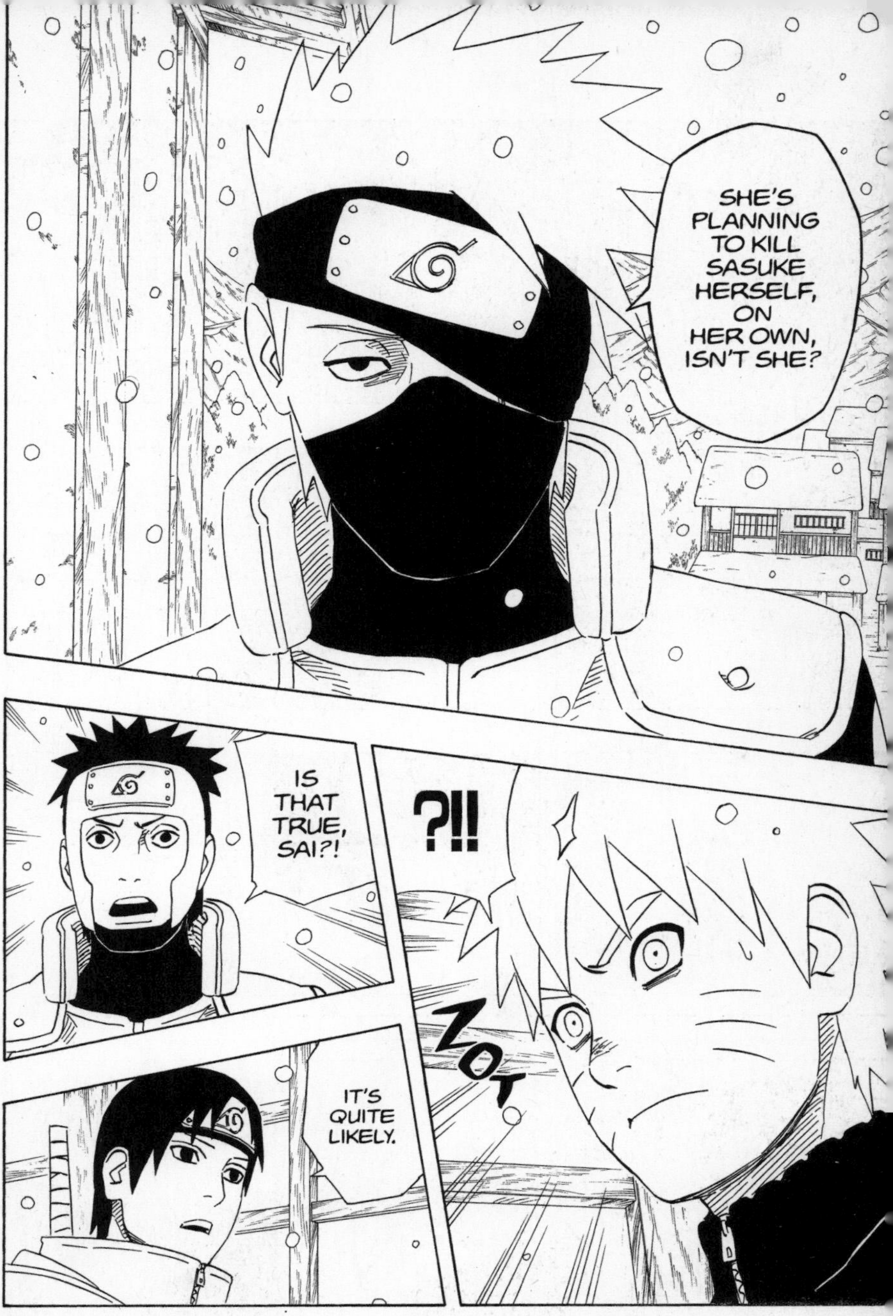
SHE'S PLANNING TO KILL SASUKE HERSELF, ON HER OWN, ISN'T SHE?
IS THAT TRUE, SAI?!
?!!
IT'S QUITE LIKELY.
ZOT

READ THIS WAY

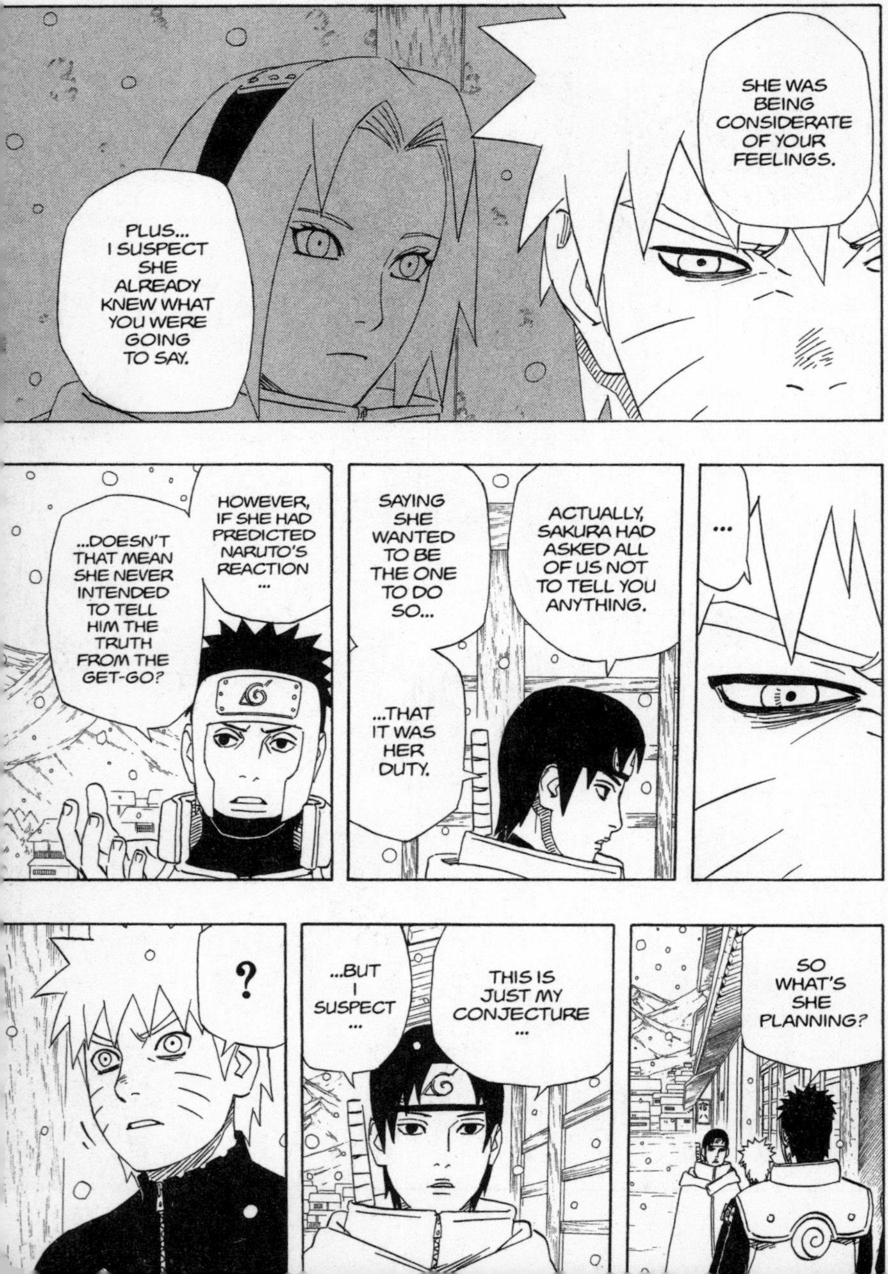

SHE WAS BEING CONSIDERATE OF YOUR FEELINGS.
PLUS... I SUSPECT SHE ALREADY KNEW WHAT YOU WERE GOING TO SAY.
...
ACTUALLY, SAKURA HAD ASKED ALL OF US NOT TO TELL YOU ANYTHING.
SAYING SHE WANTED TO BE THE ONE TO DO SO...
...THAT IT WAS HER DUTY.
HOWEVER, IF SHE HAD PREDICTED NARUTO'S REACTION ...
...DOESN'T THAT MEAN SHE NEVER INTENDED TO TELL HIM THE TRUTH FROM THE GET-GO?
SO WHAT'S SHE PLANNING?
THIS IS JUST MY CONJECTURE ...
...BUT I SUSPECT ...
?

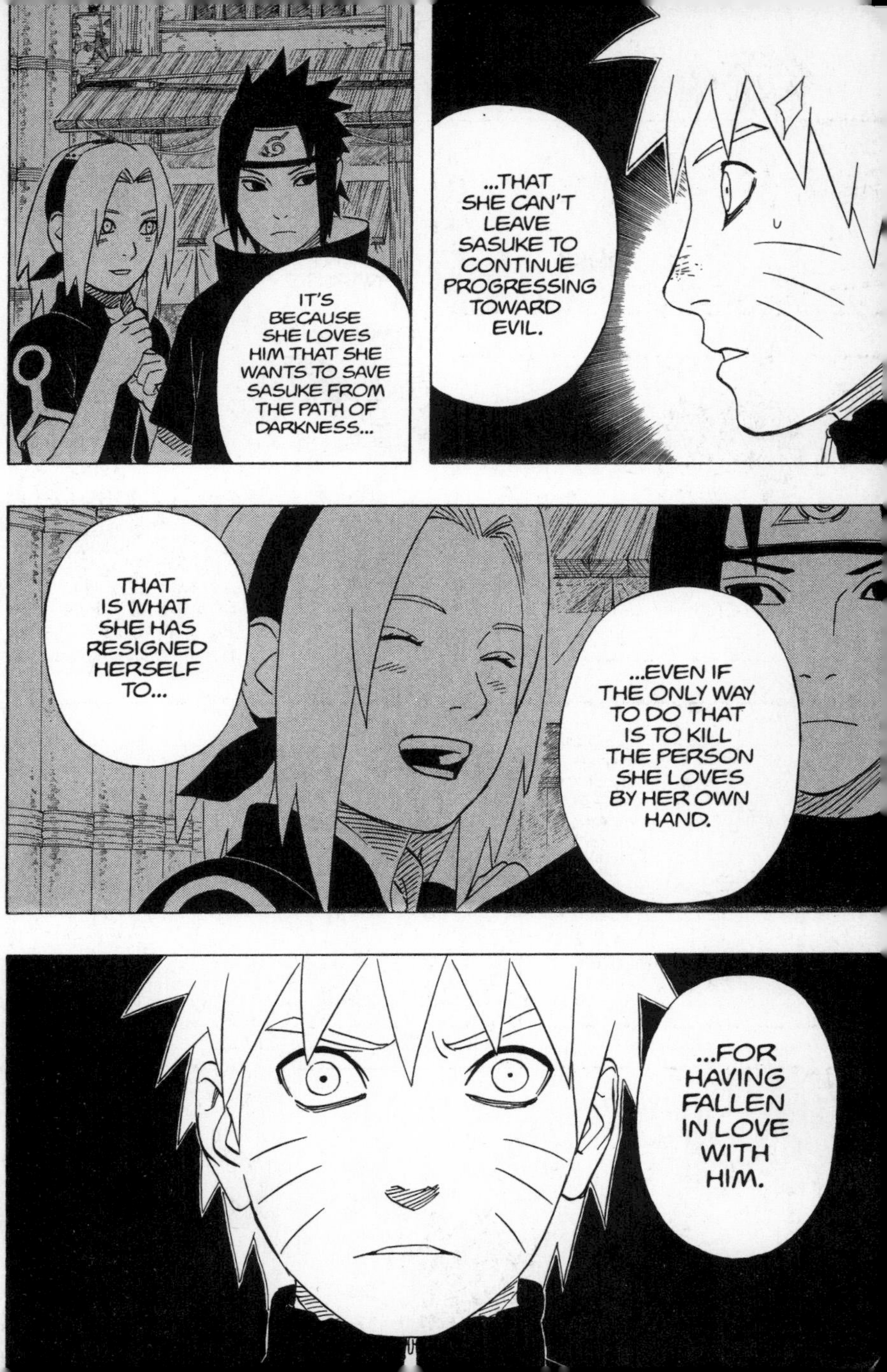
IT'S BECAUSE SHE LOVES HIM THAT SHE WANTS TO SAVE SASUKE FROM THE PATH OF DARKNESS...
...THAT SHE CAN'T LEAVE SASUKE TO CONTINUE PROGRESSING TOWARD EVIL.
THAT IS WHAT SHE HAS RESIGNED HERSELF TO...
...EVEN IF THE ONLY WAY TO DO THAT IS TO KILL THE PERSON SHE LOVES BY HER OWN HAND.
...FOR HAVING FALLEN IN LOVE WITH HIM.

READ THIS WAY

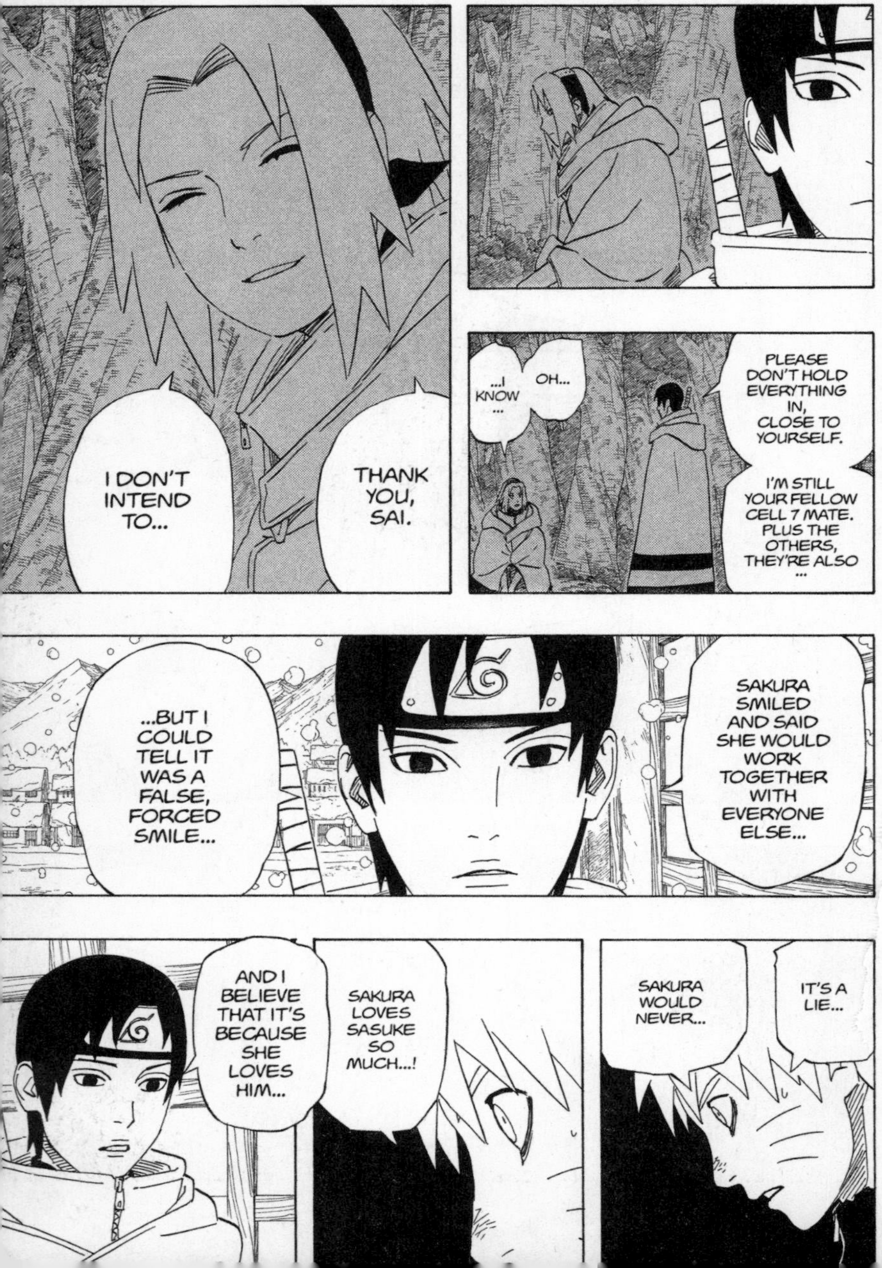
PLEASE DON'T HOLD EVERYTHING IN, CLOSE TO YOURSELF.
I'M STILL YOUR FELLOW CELL 7 MATE. PLUS THE OTHERS, THEY'RE ALSO ...
OH...
...I KNOW ...
THANK YOU, SAI.
I DON'T INTEND TO...
SAKURA SMILED AND SAID SHE WOULD WORK TOGETHER WITH EVERYONE ELSE...
...BUT I COULD TELL IT WAS A FALSE, FORCED SMILE...
IT'S A LIE...
SAKURA WOULD NEVER...
SAKURA LOVES SASUKE SO MUCH...!
AND I BELIEVE THAT IT'S BECAUSE SHE LOVES HIM...

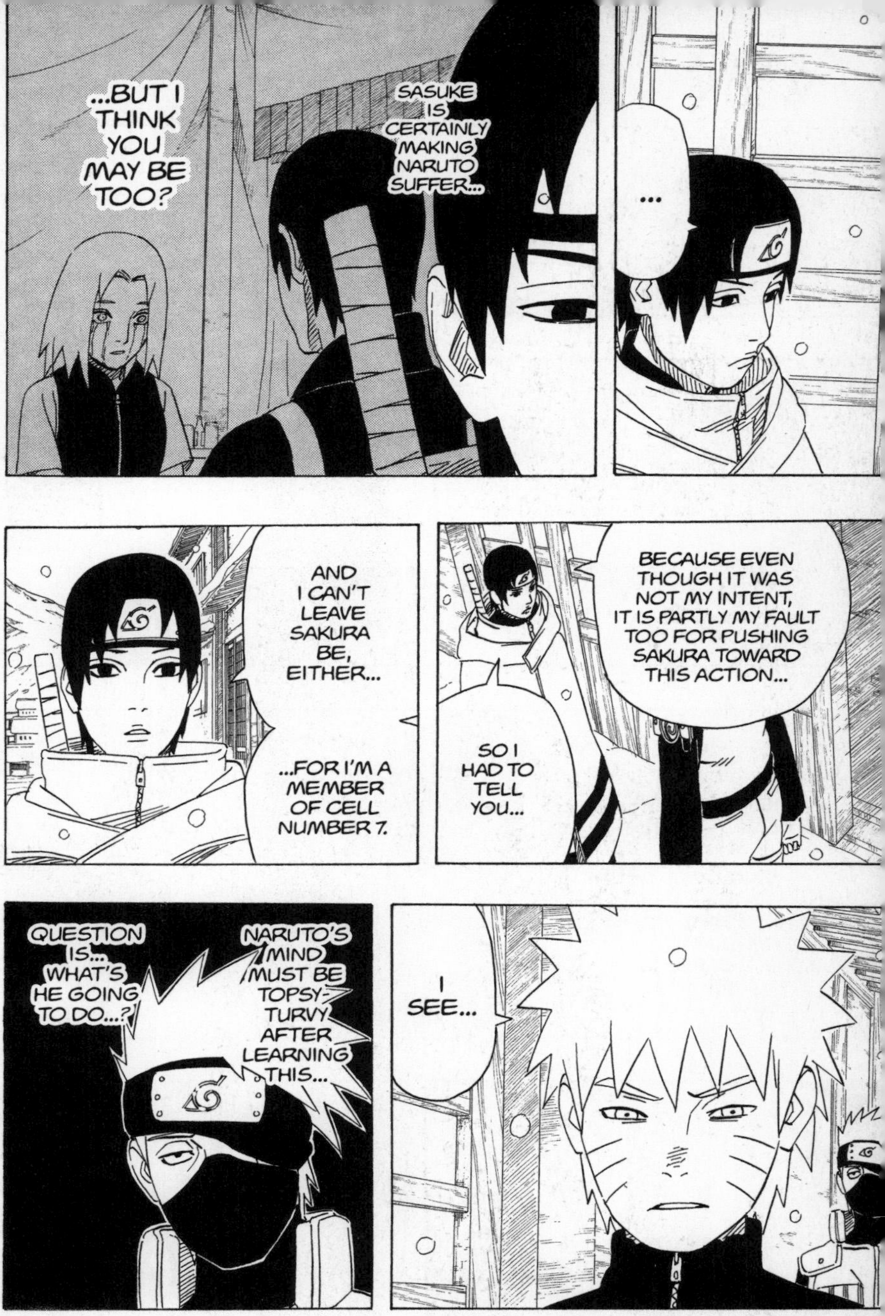
SASUKE IS CERTAINLY MAKING NARUTO SUFFER...
...BUT I THINK YOU MAY BE TOO?
...
AND I CAN'T LEAVE SAKURA BE, EITHER...
...FOR I'M A MEMBER OF CELL NUMBER 7.
BECAUSE EVEN THOUGH IT WAS NOT MY INTENT, IT IS PARTLY MY FAULT TOO FOR PUSHING SAKURA TOWARD THIS ACTION...
SO I HAD TO TELL YOU...
NARUTO'S MIND MUST BE TOPSY-TURVY AFTER LEARNING THIS...
QUESTION IS... WHAT'S HE GOING TO DO...?
I SEE...

READ THIS WAY

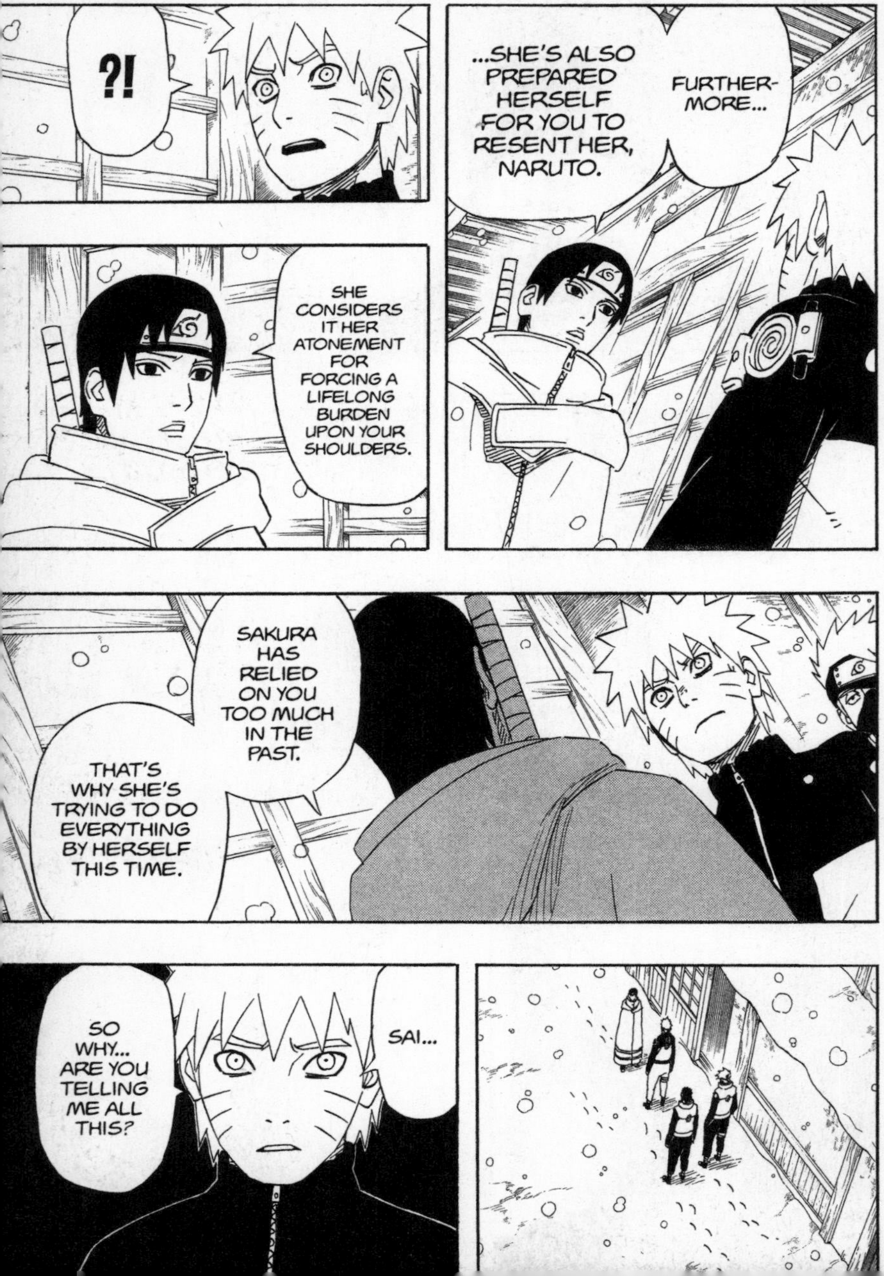
FURTHER-MORE...
...SHE'S ALSO PREPARED HERSELF FOR YOU TO RESENT HER, NARUTO.
?!
SHE CONSIDERS IT HER ATONEMENT FOR FORCING A LIFELONG BURDEN UPON YOUR SHOULDERS.
SAKURA HAS RELIED ON YOU TOO MUCH IN THE PAST.
THAT'S WHY SHE'S TRYING TO DO EVERYTHING BY HERSELF THIS TIME.
SAI...
SO WHY... ARE YOU TELLING ME ALL THIS?

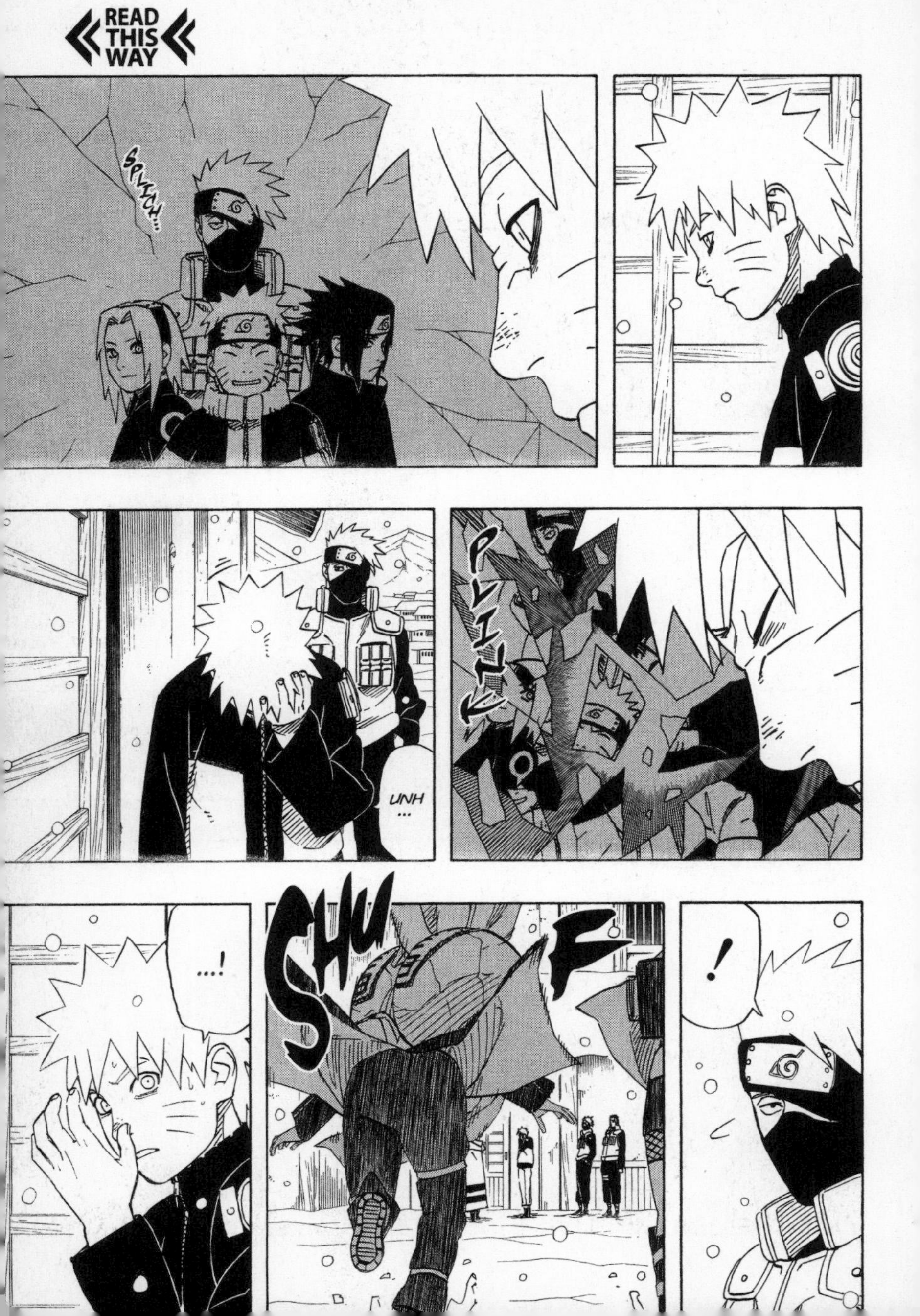
READ THIS WAY
SPLICH...
PLIIIK
UNH ...
!
SHU F
...!

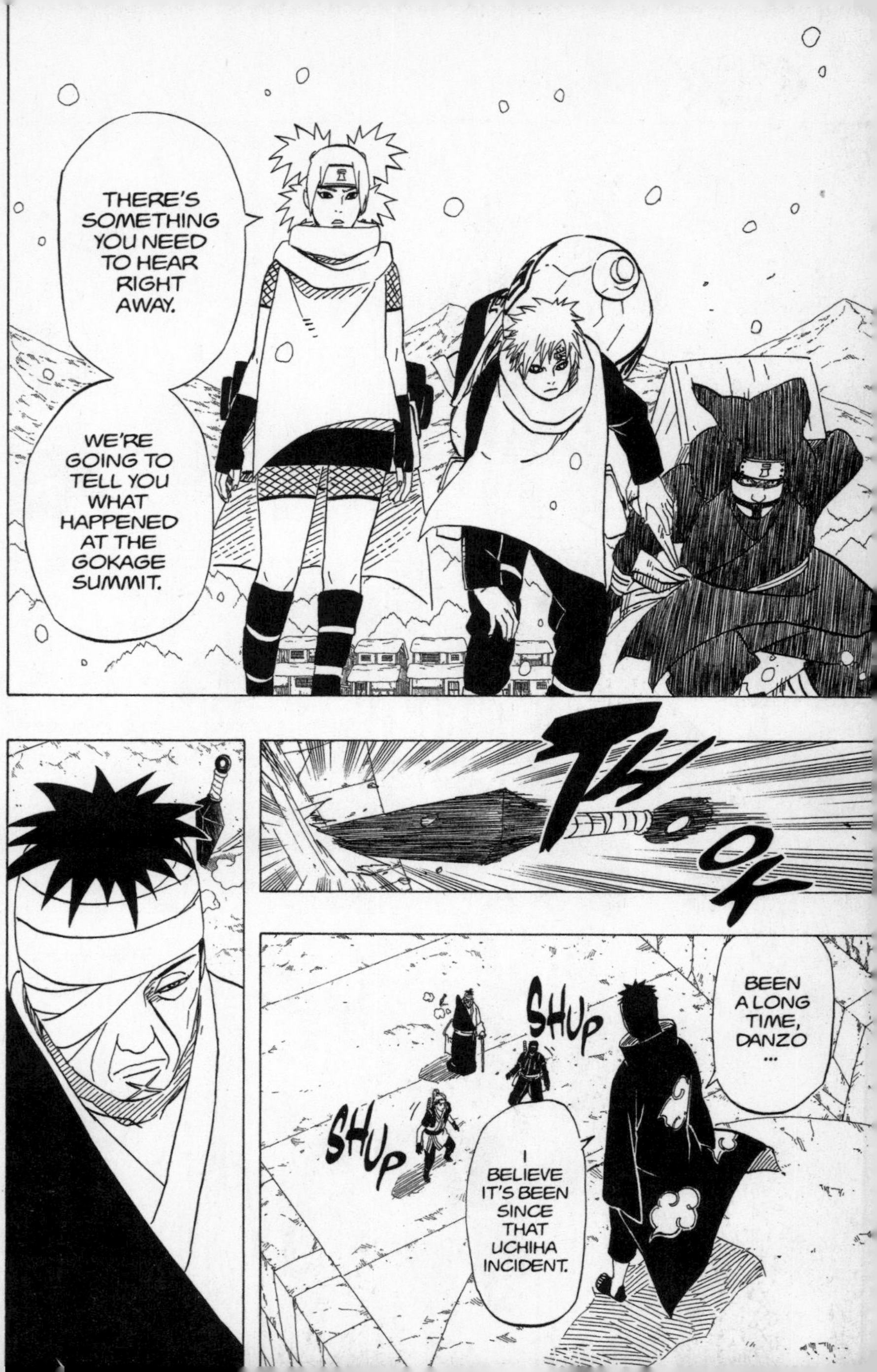
THERE'S SOMETHING YOU NEED TO HEAR RIGHT AWAY.
WE'RE GOING TO TELL YOU WHAT HAPPENED AT THE GOKAGE SUMMIT.
THOOK
BEEN A LONG TIME, DANZO ...
SHUP
SHUP
I BELIEVE IT'S BEEN SINCE THAT UCHIHA INCIDENT.

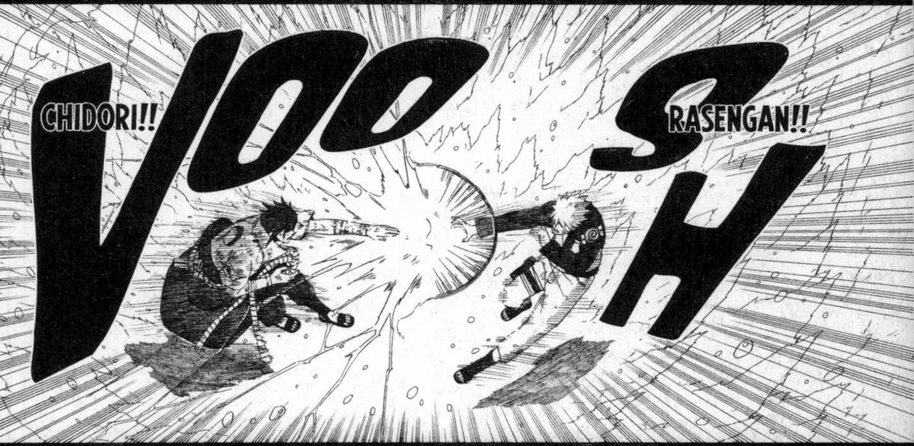
CHIDORI!!
VOOSH
RASENGAN!!

IN THE NEXT VOLUME...

CELL SEVEN REUNION!!

Sasuke, Sakura and Naruto finally meet, as the former classmates' complicated past gives way to a violent and unsure future. Naruto realizes he must eventually battle Sasuke one-on-one...to the death! But with Sasuke and his dark allies bent on complete destruction, and political intrigue in the villages, will the powerful Allied Shinobi Forces allow the two "friends" to meet in battle?!

AVAILABLE OCTOBER 2011!
READ IT FIRST IN SHONEN JUMP MAGAZINE!

READ THIS WAY

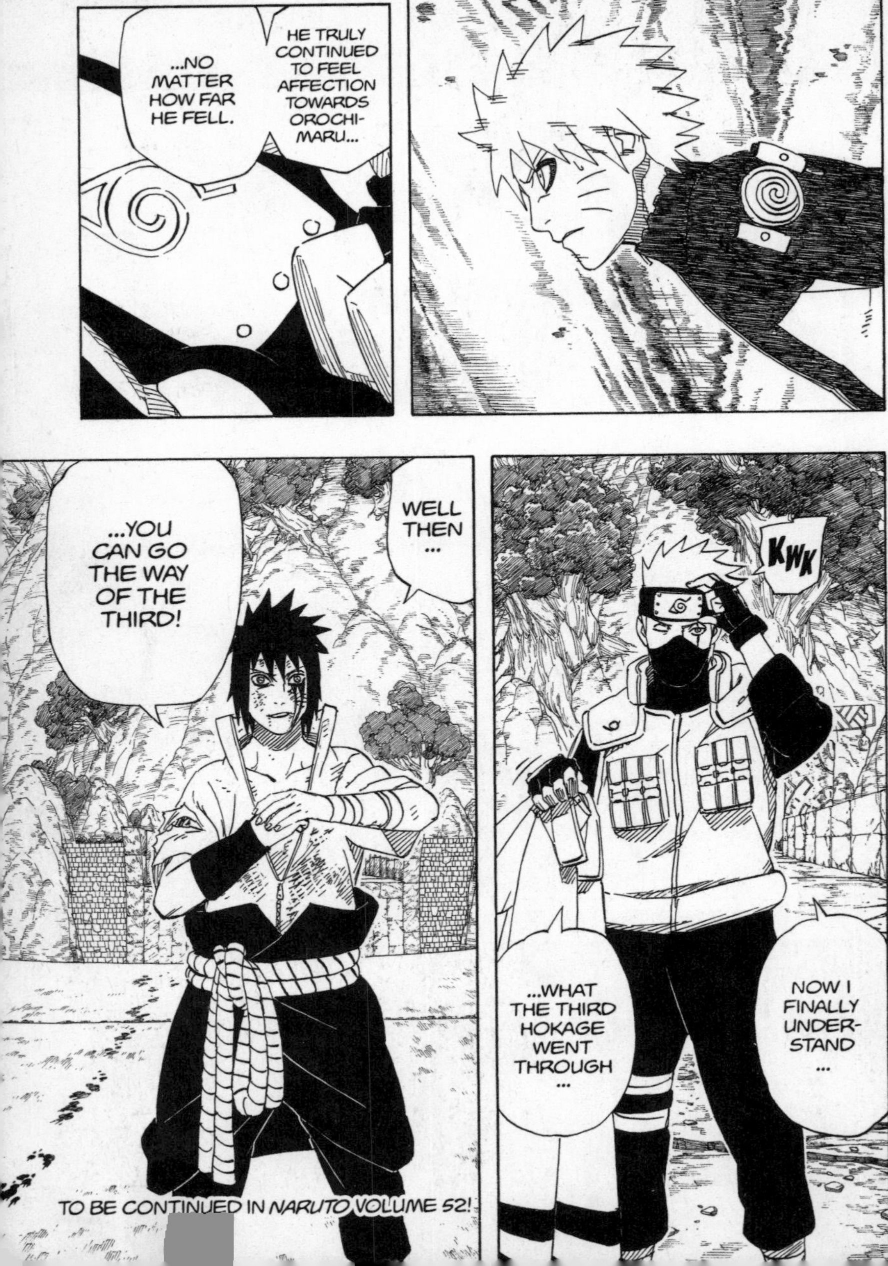
HE TRULY CONTINUED TO FEEL AFFECTION TOWARDS OROCHI-MARU...
...NO MATTER HOW FAR HE FELL.
KWK
NOW I FINALLY UNDER-STAND...
...WHAT THE THIRD HOKAGE WENT THROUGH...
WELL THEN...
...YOU CAN GO THE WAY OF THE THIRD!
TO BE CONTINUED IN NARUTO VOLUME 52!

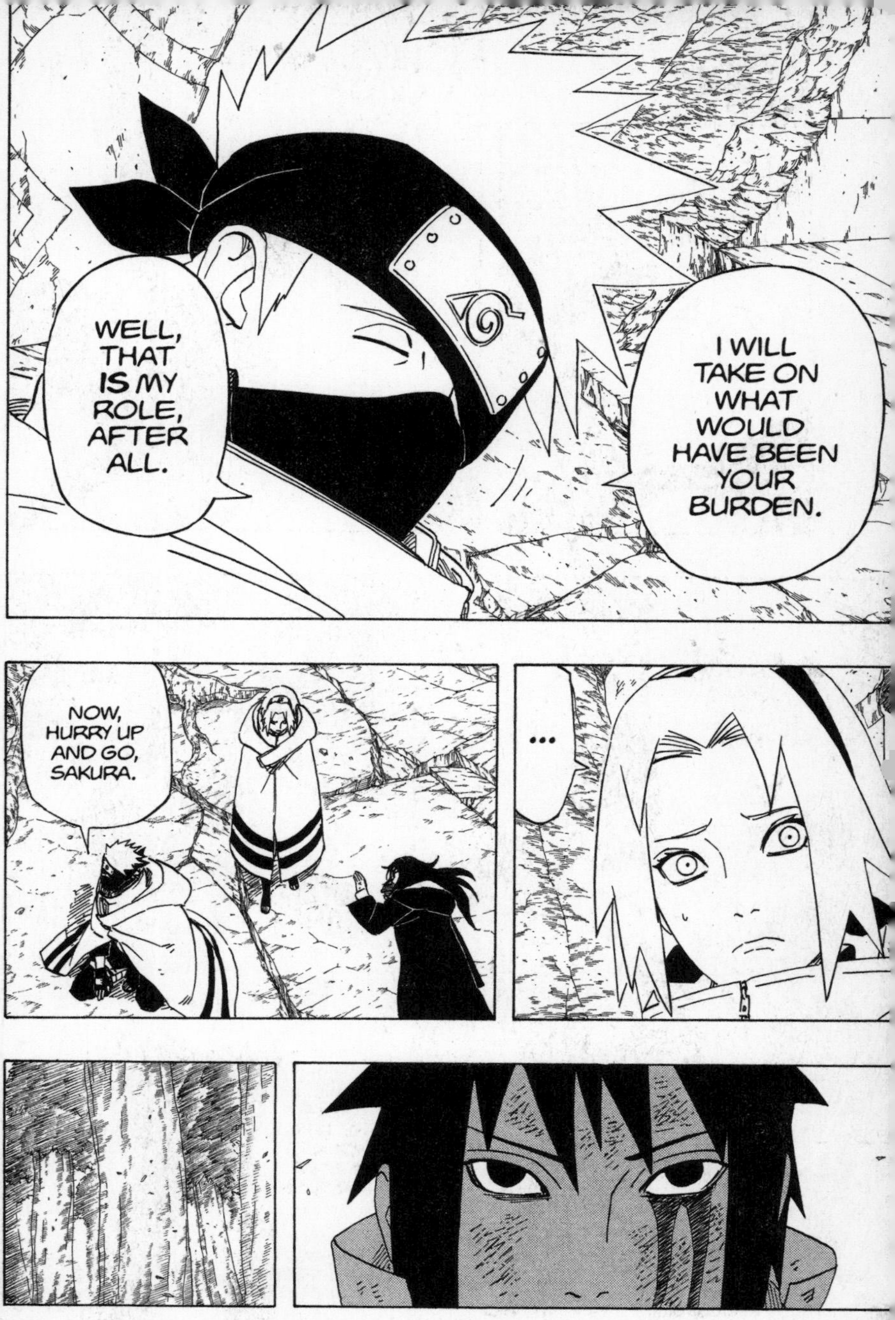
I WILL TAKE ON WHAT WOULD HAVE BEEN YOUR BURDEN.
WELL, THAT IS MY ROLE, AFTER ALL.
...
NOW, HURRY UP AND GO, SAKURA.

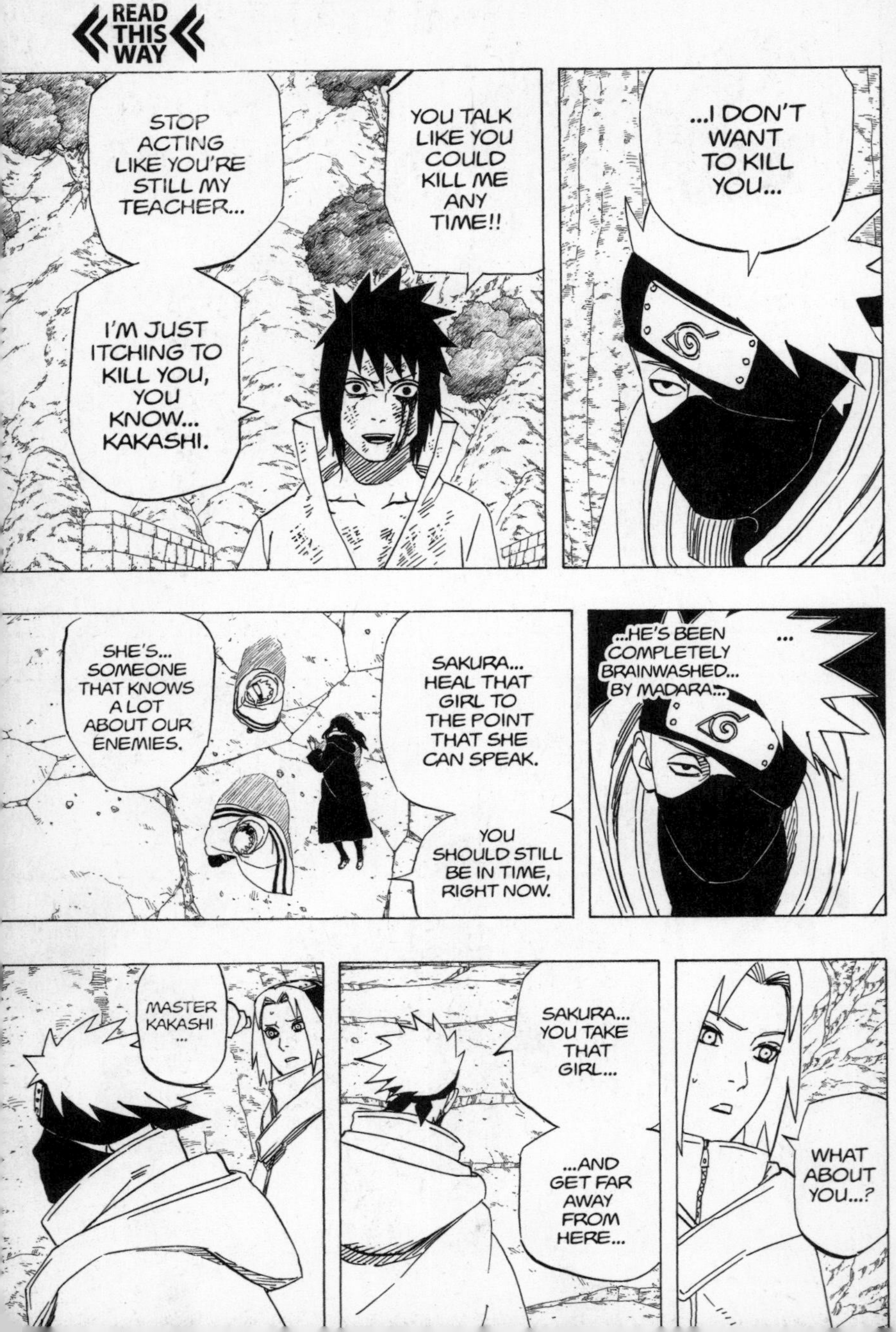
READ THIS WAY
...I DON'T WANT TO KILL YOU...
YOU TALK LIKE YOU COULD KILL ME ANY TIME!!
STOP ACTING LIKE YOU'RE STILL MY TEACHER...
I'M JUST ITCHING TO KILL YOU, YOU KNOW... KAKASHI.
...
...HE'S BEEN COMPLETELY BRAINWASHED... BY MADARA...
SAKURA... HEAL THAT GIRL TO THE POINT THAT SHE CAN SPEAK.
YOU SHOULD STILL BE IN TIME, RIGHT NOW.
SHE'S... SOMEONE THAT KNOWS A LOT ABOUT OUR ENEMIES.
WHAT ABOUT YOU...?
SAKURA... YOU TAKE THAT GIRL...
...AND GET FAR AWAY FROM HERE...
MASTER KAKASHI ...

SH

NARUTO

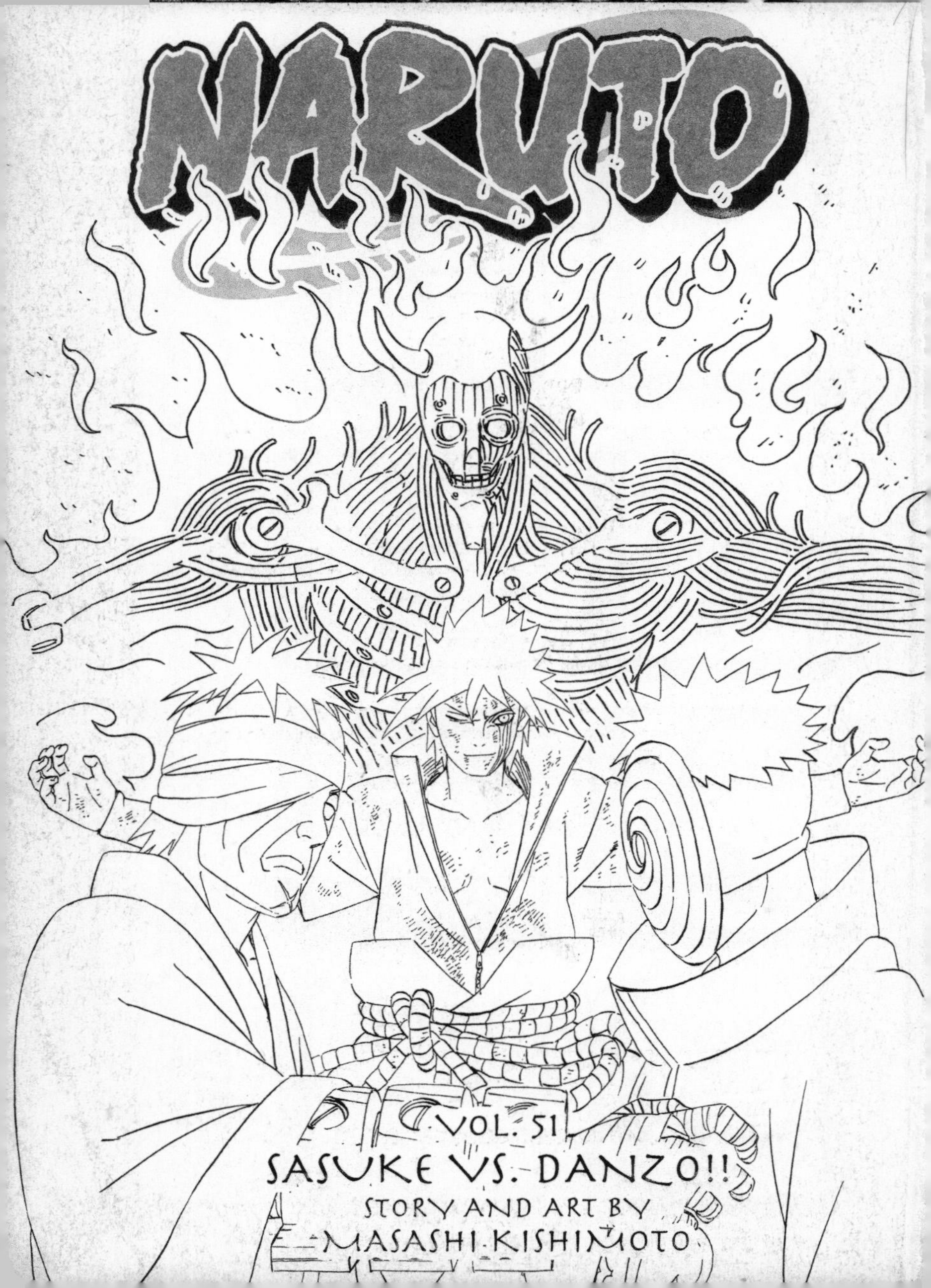

VOL. 51

SASUKE VS. DANZO!!

STORY AND ART BY
MASASHI KISHIMOTO

CHARACTERS

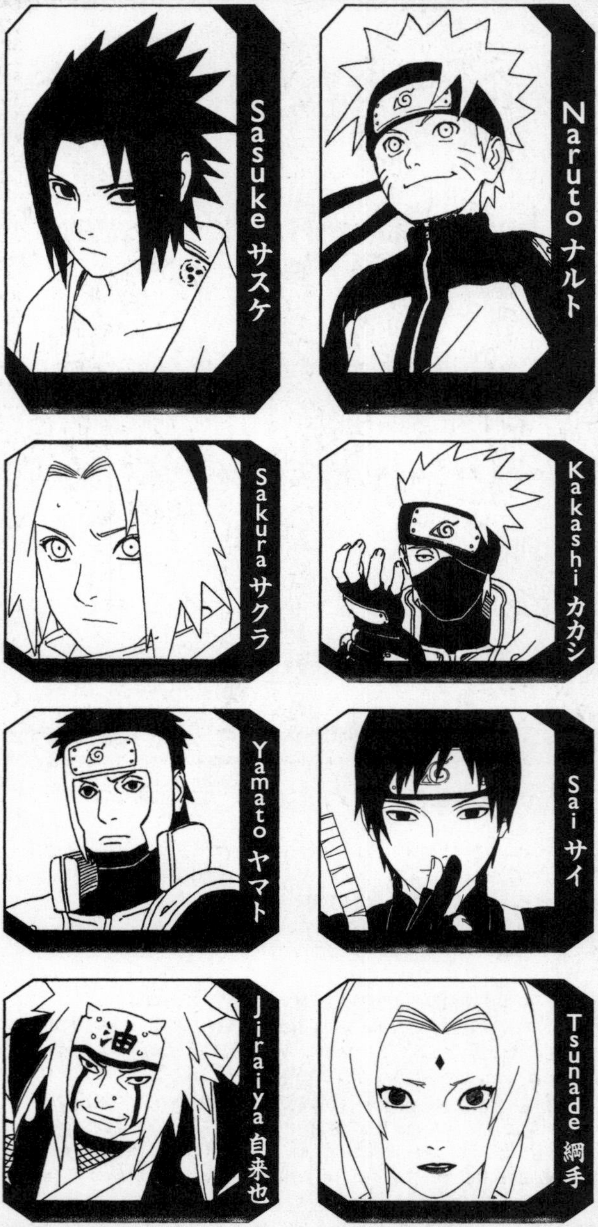
Naruto ナルト
Sasuke サスケ
Kakashi カカシ
Sakura サクラ
Sai サイ
Yamato ヤマト
Tsunade 綱手
Jiraiya 自来也

READ THIS WAY

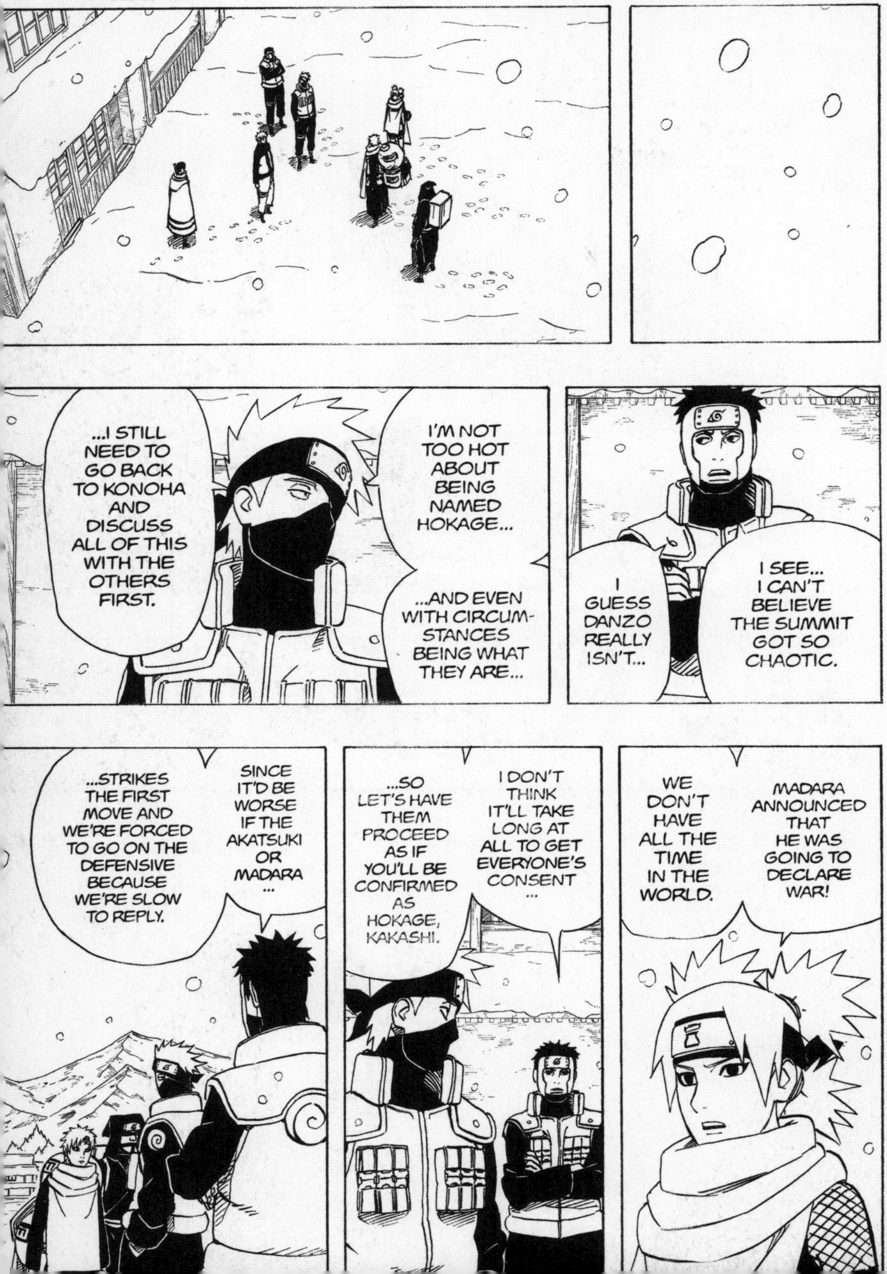
I SEE... I CAN'T BELIEVE THE SUMMIT GOT SO CHAOTIC.
I GUESS DANZO REALLY ISN'T...
I'M NOT TOO HOT ABOUT BEING NAMED HOKAGE...
...AND EVEN WITH CIRCUMSTANCES BEING WHAT THEY ARE...
...I STILL NEED TO GO BACK TO KONOHA AND DISCUSS ALL OF THIS WITH THE OTHERS FIRST.
MADARA ANNOUNCED THAT HE WAS GOING TO DECLARE WAR!
WE DON'T HAVE ALL THE TIME IN THE WORLD.
I DON'T THINK IT'LL TAKE LONG AT ALL TO GET EVERYONE'S CONSENT...
...SO LET'S HAVE THEM PROCEED AS IF YOU'LL BE CONFIRMED AS HOKAGE, KAKASHI.
SINCE IT'D BE WORSE IF THE AKATSUKI OR MADARA...
...STRIKES THE FIRST MOVE AND WE'RE FORCED TO GO ON THE DEFENSIVE BECAUSE WE'RE SLOW TO REPLY.

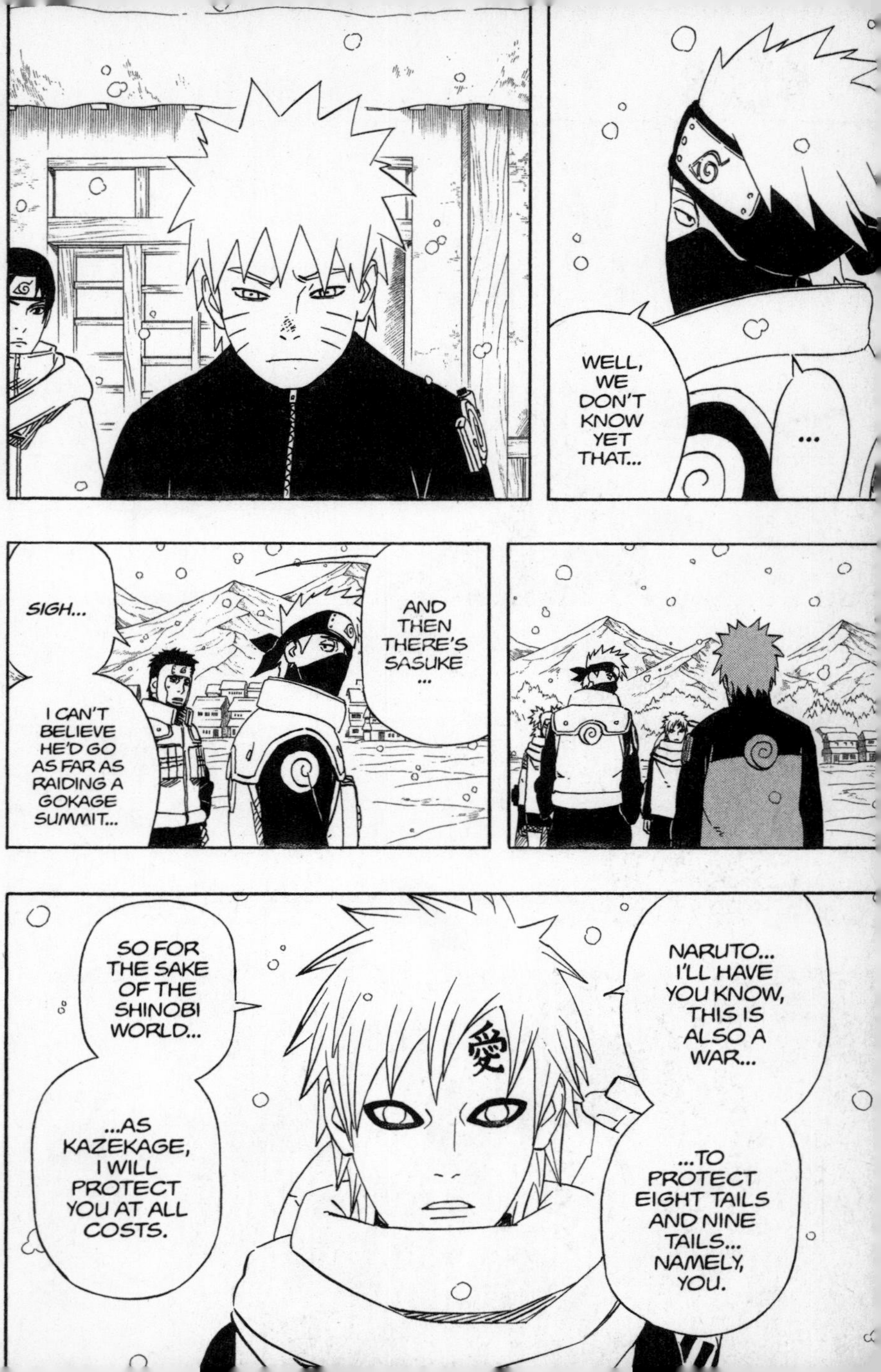
...
WELL, WE DON'T KNOW YET THAT...
AND THEN THERE'S SASUKE ...
SIGH...
I CAN'T BELIEVE HE'D GO AS FAR AS RAIDING A GOKAGE SUMMIT...
NARUTO... I'LL HAVE YOU KNOW, THIS IS ALSO A WAR...
...TO PROTECT EIGHT TAILS AND NINE TAILS... NAMELY, YOU.
SO FOR THE SAKE OF THE SHINOBI WORLD...
...AS KAZEKAGE, I WILL PROTECT YOU AT ALL COSTS.

READ THIS WAY

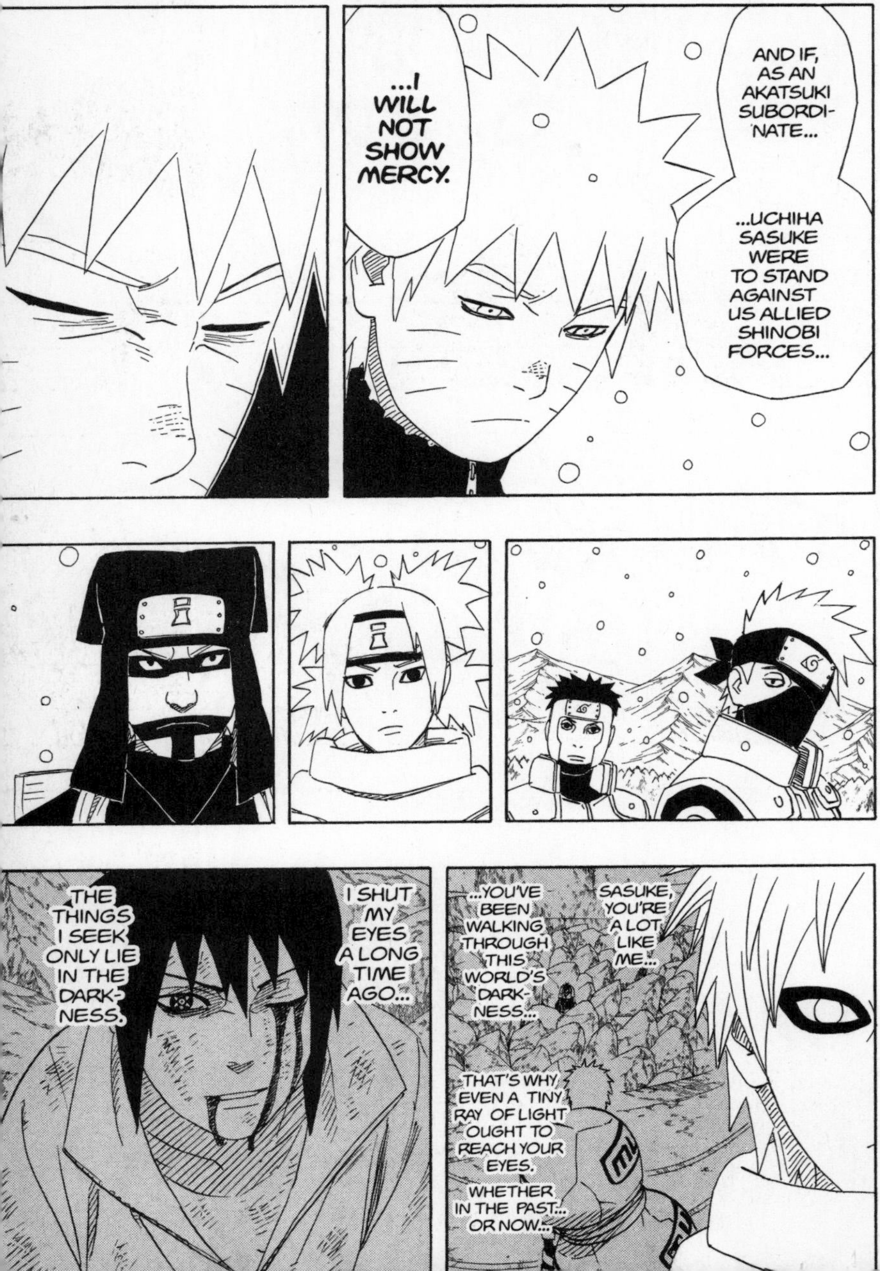
AND IF, AS AN AKATSUKI SUBORDINATE...
...UCHIHA SASUKE WERE TO STAND AGAINST US ALLIED SHINOBI FORCES...
...I WILL NOT SHOW MERCY.
SASUKE, YOU'RE A LOT LIKE ME...
...YOU'VE BEEN WALKING THROUGH THIS WORLD'S DARKNESS...
THAT'S WHY EVEN A TINY RAY OF LIGHT OUGHT TO REACH YOUR EYES.
WHETHER IN THE PAST... OR NOW...
I SHUT MY EYES A LONG TIME AGO...
THE THINGS I SEEK ONLY LIE IN THE DARKNESS.

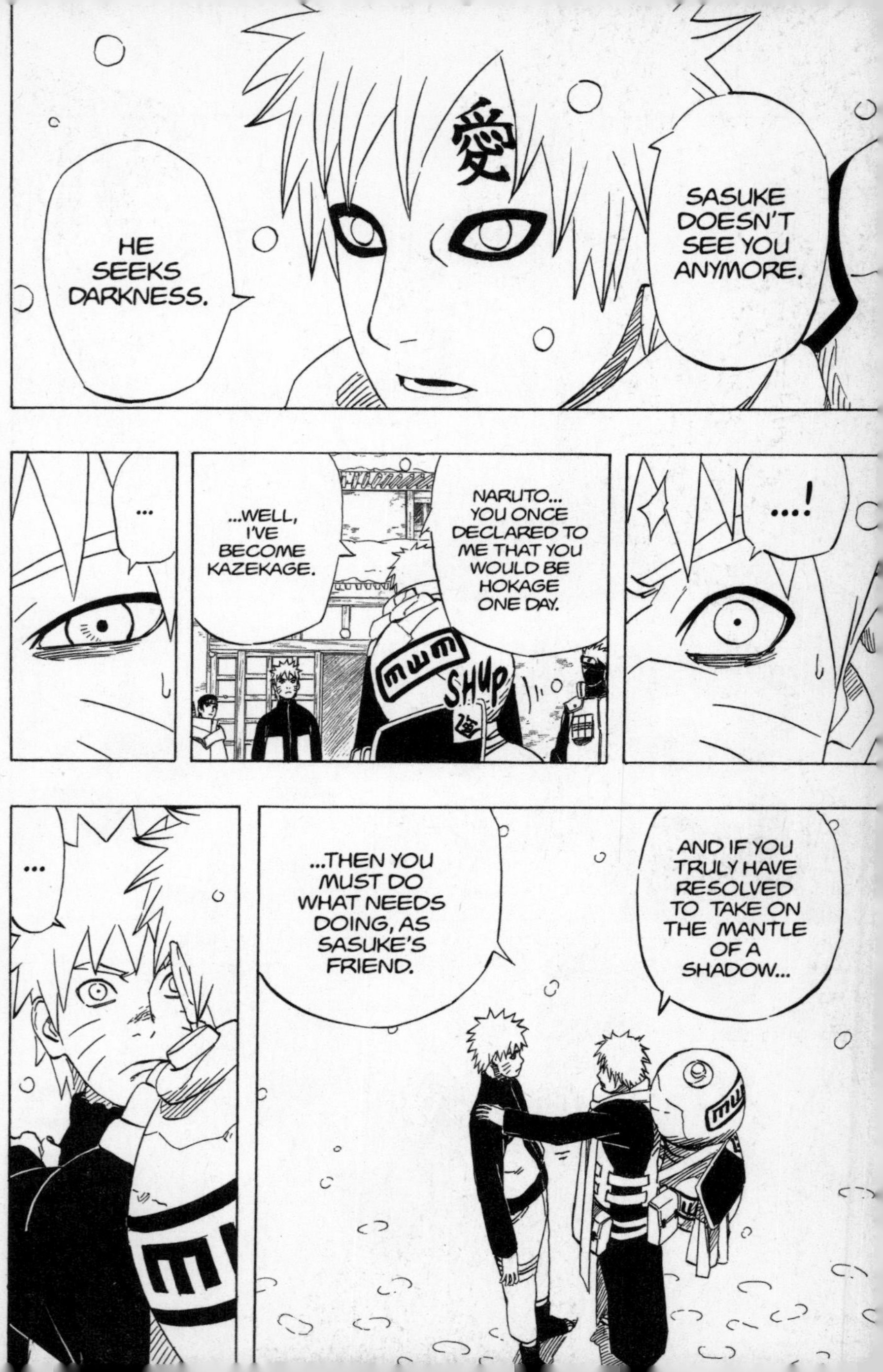
SASUKE DOESN'T SEE YOU ANYMORE.
HE SEEKS DARKNESS.
...!
NARUTO... YOU ONCE DECLARED TO ME THAT YOU WOULD BE HOKAGE ONE DAY.
SHUP
...WELL, I'VE BECOME KAZEKAGE.
...
AND IF YOU TRULY HAVE RESOLVED TO TAKE ON THE MANTLE OF A SHADOW...
...THEN YOU MUST DO WHAT NEEDS DOING, AS SASUKE'S FRIEND.
...

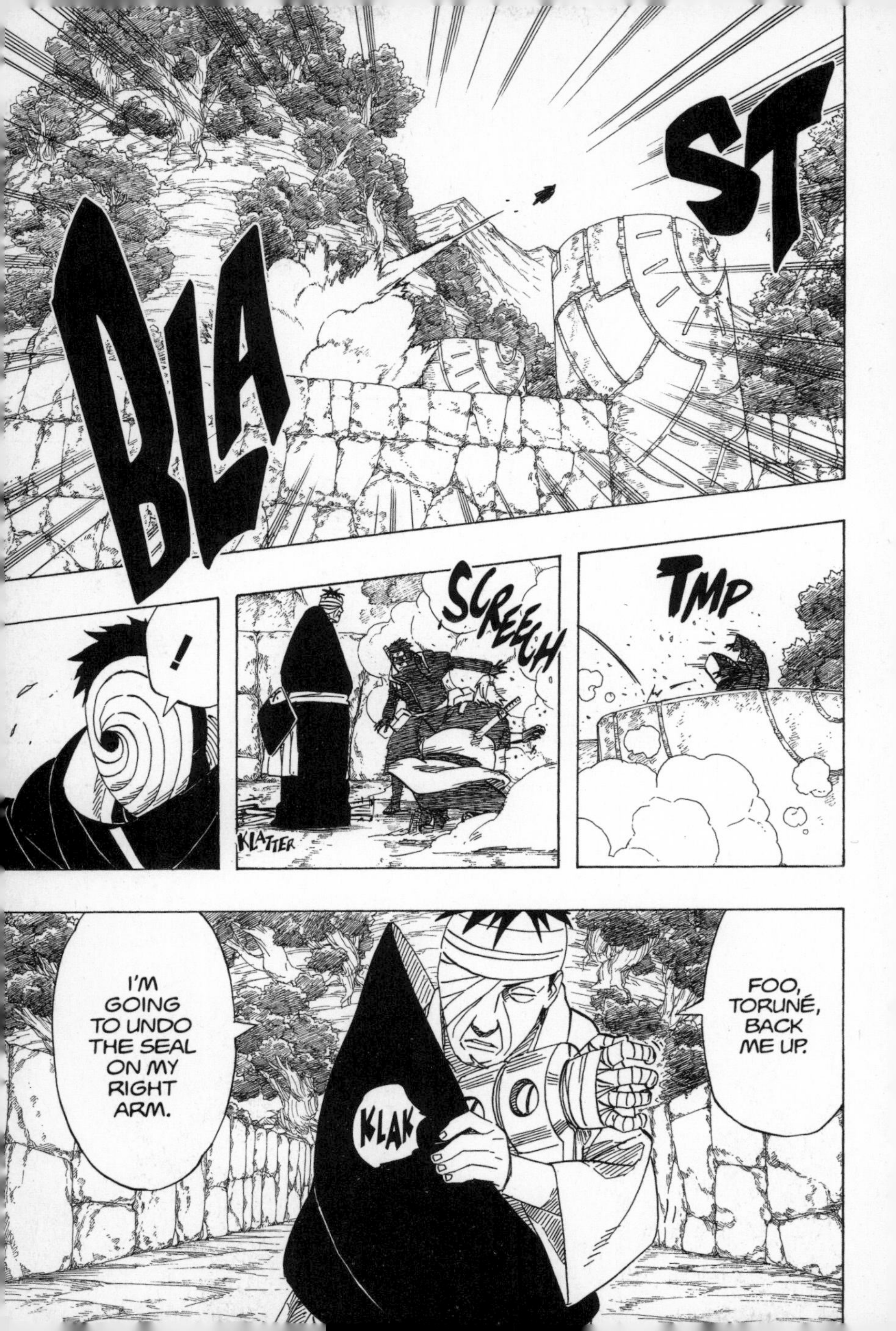
BLAST
TMP
SCREECH
KLATTER
!
FOO, TORUNÉ, BACK ME UP.
KLAK
I'M GOING TO UNDO THE SEAL ON MY RIGHT ARM.

Number 475: Madara's True Worth!!

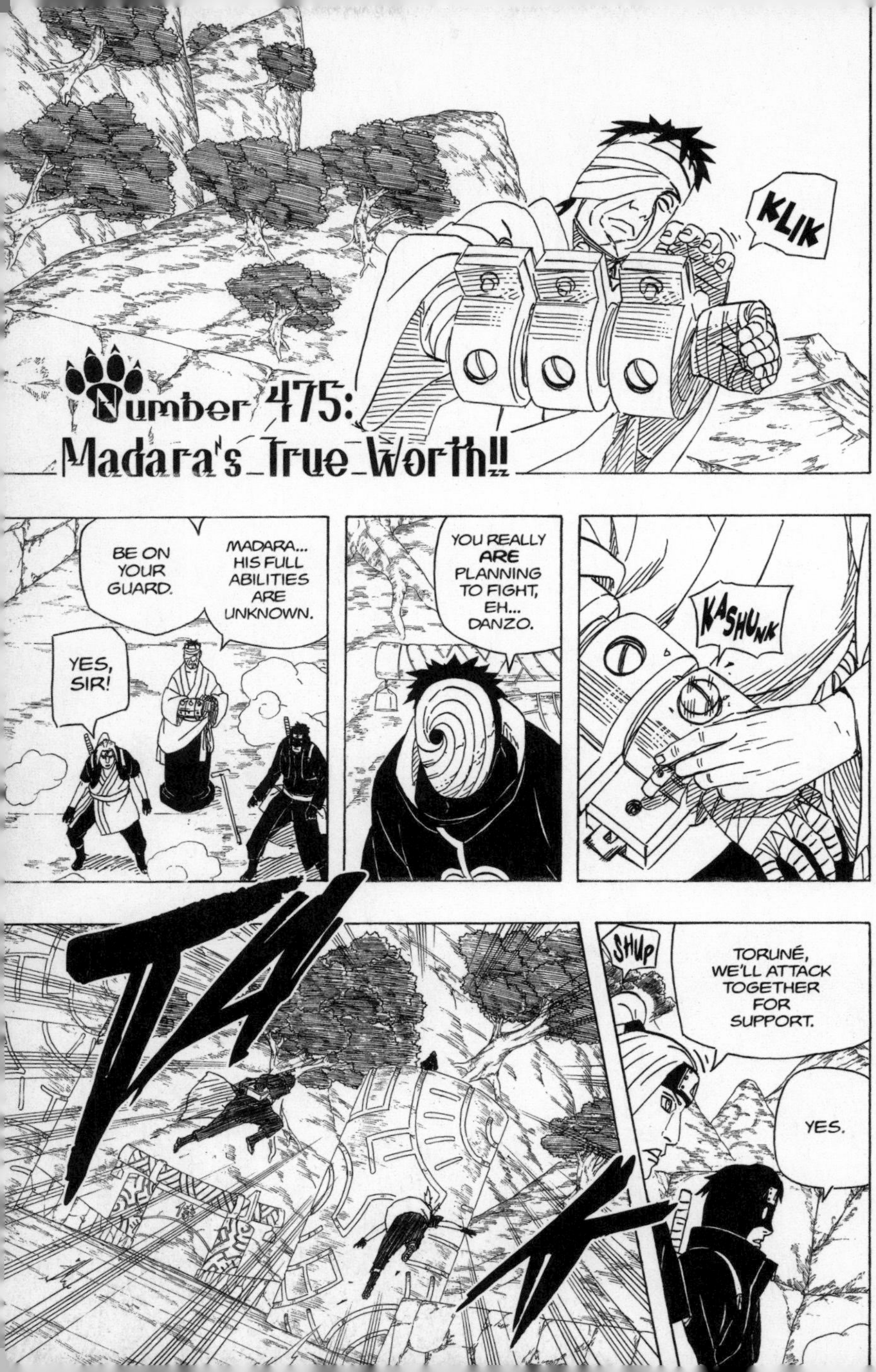
KLIK
KASHUNK
YOU REALLY ARE PLANNING TO FIGHT, EH... DANZO.
MADARA... HIS FULL ABILITIES ARE UNKNOWN.
BE ON YOUR GUARD.
YES, SIR!
SHUP
TORUNÉ, WE'LL ATTACK TOGETHER FOR SUPPORT.
YES.

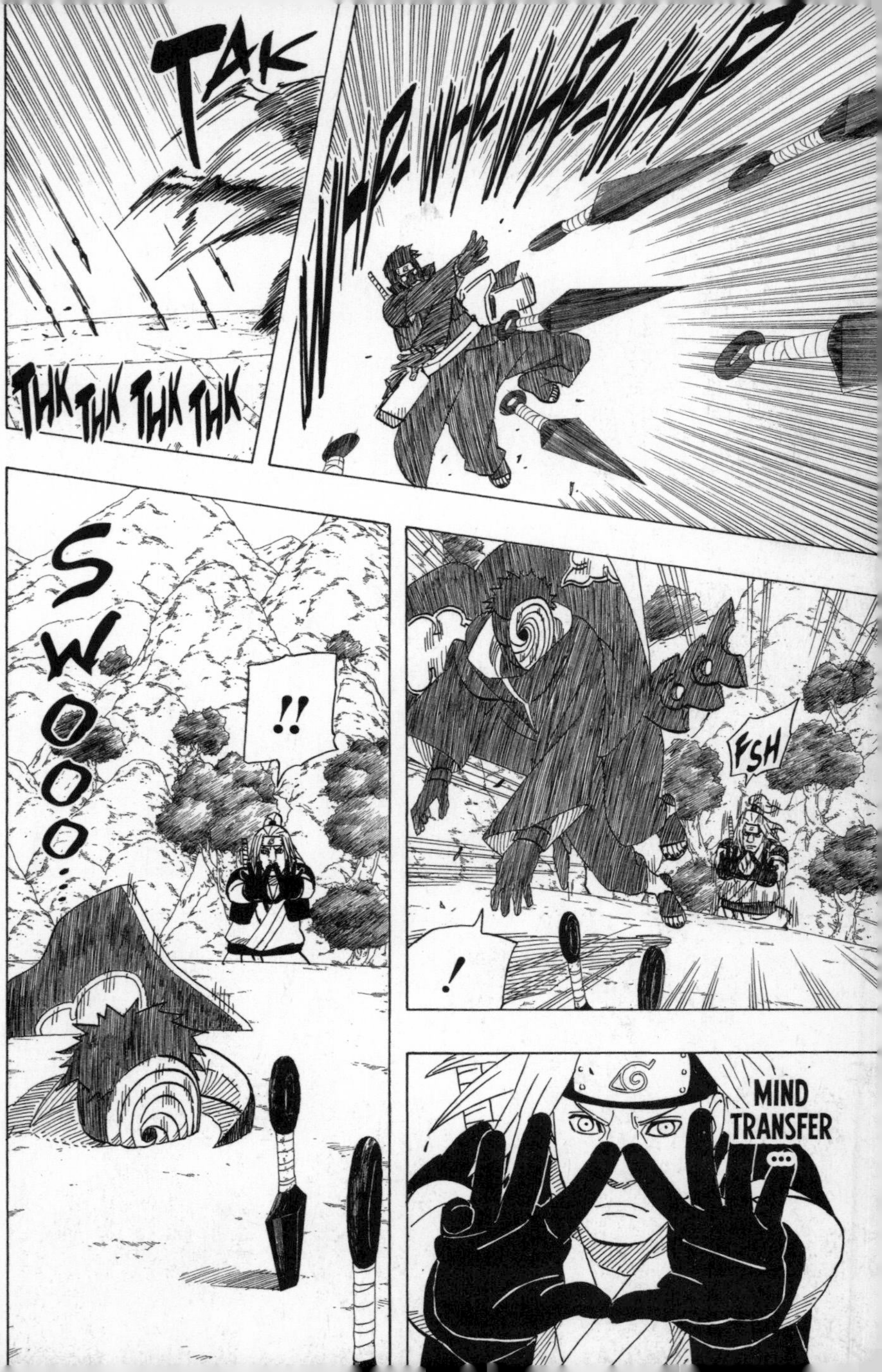

TAK
WHAP WHAP WHAP WHAP
THK THK THK THK
SWOOOO...
!!
FSH
!
MIND TRANSFER
...

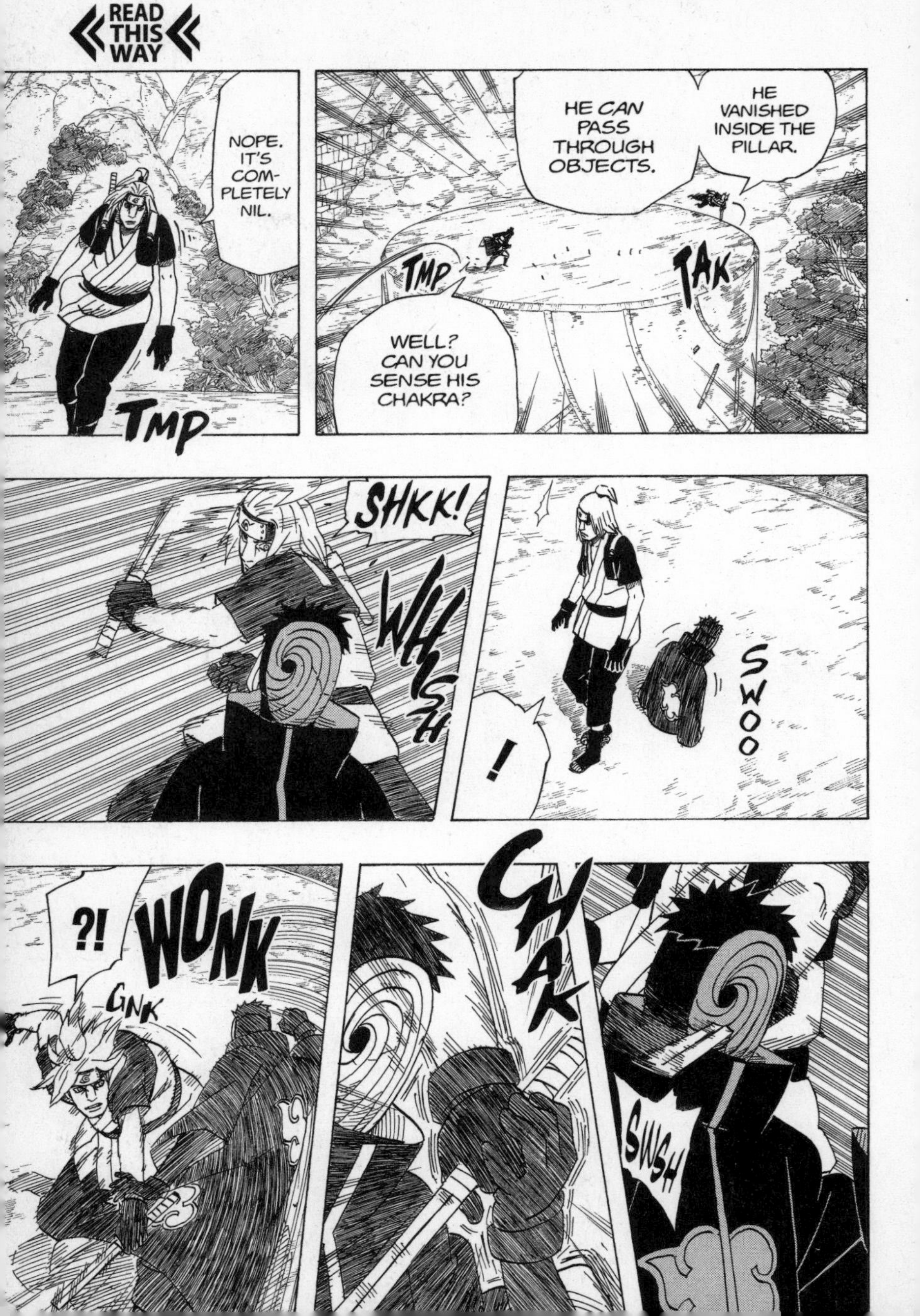
READ THIS WAY
HE VANISHED INSIDE THE PILLAR.
HE CAN PASS THROUGH OBJECTS.
TAK
TMP
WELL? CAN YOU SENSE HIS CHAKRA?
NOPE. IT'S COM-PLETELY NIL.
TMP
SWOO
!
SHKK!
WHASH
CHAK
SWSH
?!
WONK
GNK

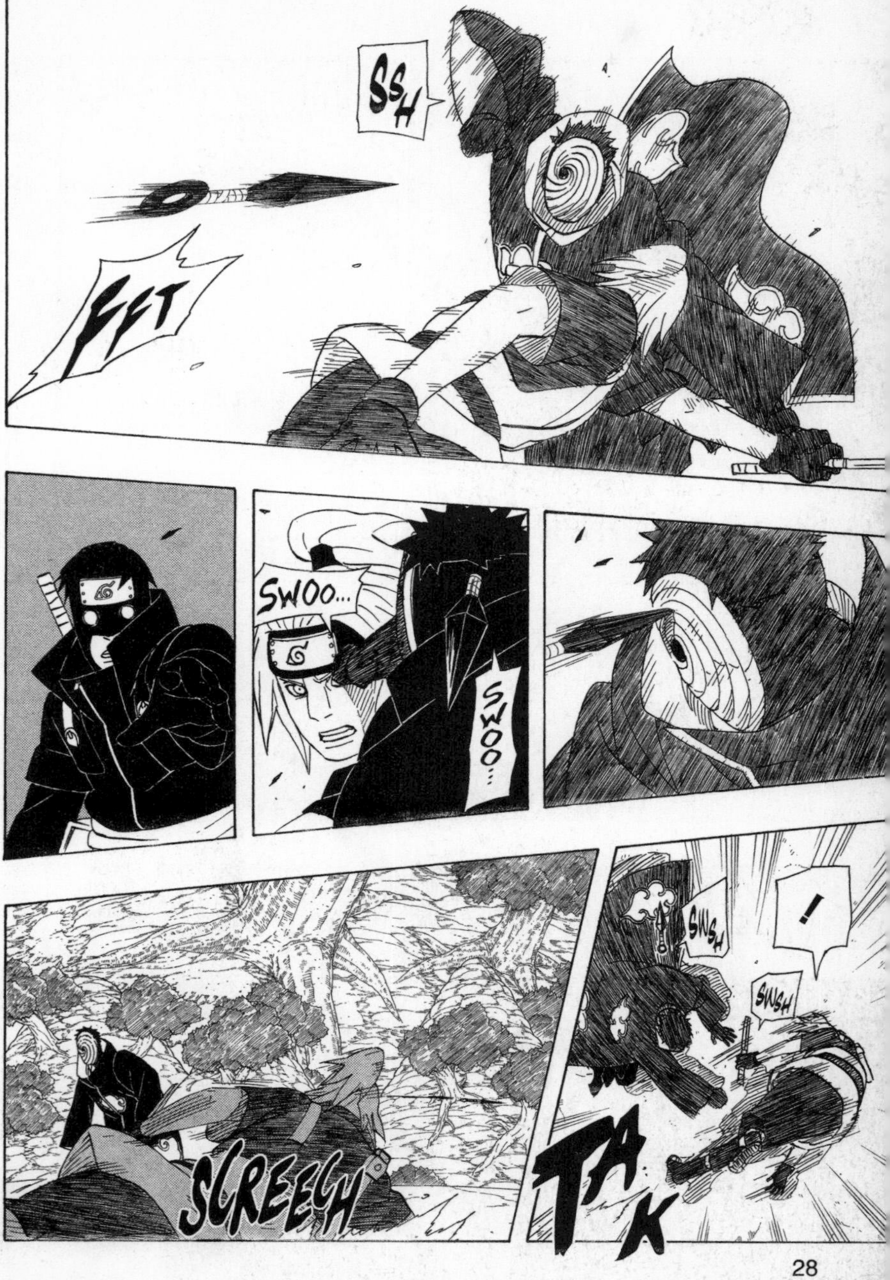

SSH
FFT
SWOO...
SWOO...
!
SWSH
SWSH
TAK
SCREECH

READ THIS WAY

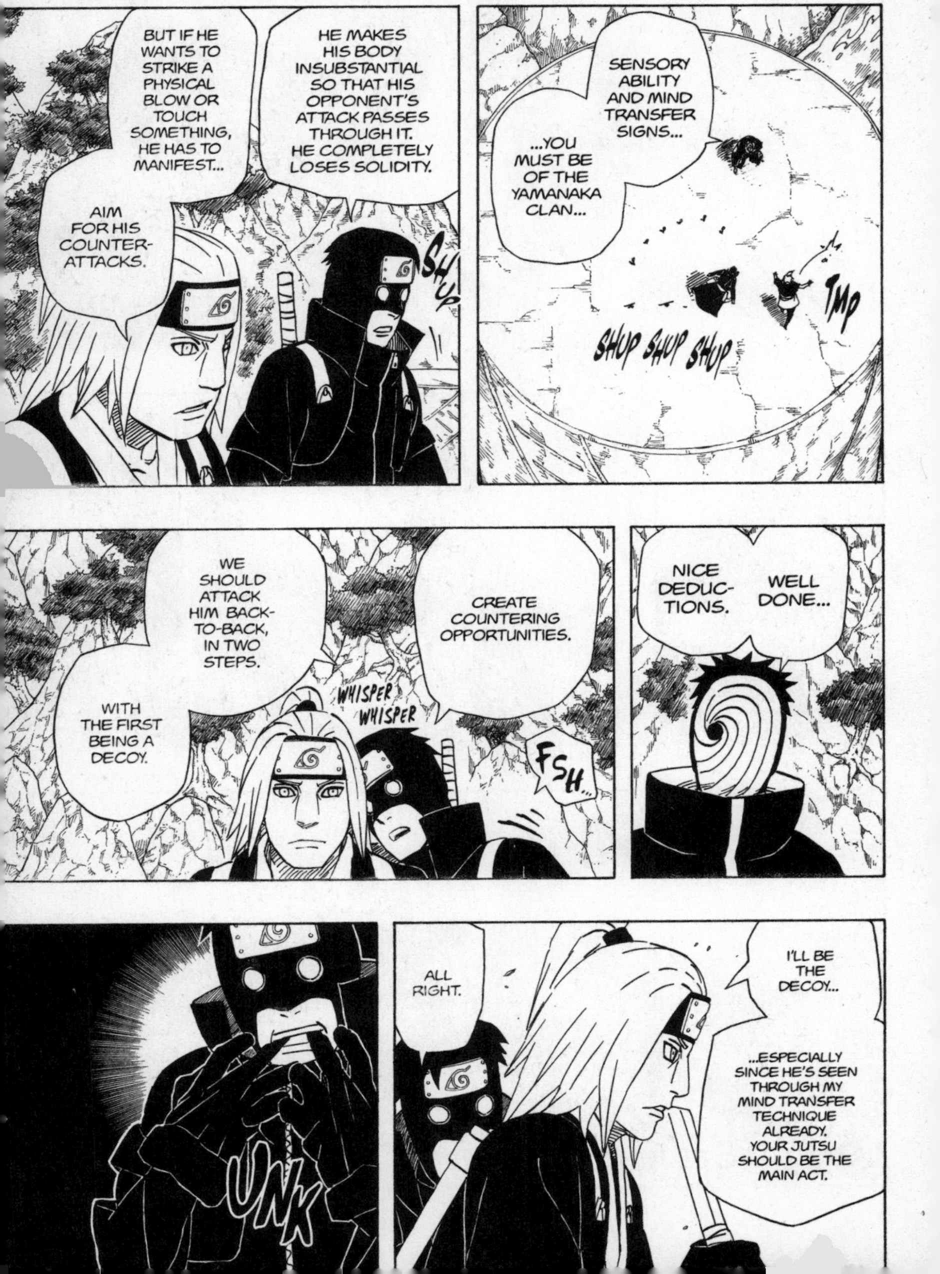
SENSORY ABILITY AND MIND TRANSFER SIGNS...
...YOU MUST BE OF THE YAMANAKA CLAN...
SHUP SHUP SHUP
TMP
HE MAKES HIS BODY INSUBSTANTIAL SO THAT HIS OPPONENT'S ATTACK PASSES THROUGH IT. HE COMPLETELY LOSES SOLIDITY.
BUT IF HE WANTS TO STRIKE A PHYSICAL BLOW OR TOUCH SOMETHING, HE HAS TO MANIFEST...
AIM FOR HIS COUNTER-ATTACKS.
SHUP
WELL DONE...
NICE DEDUCTIONS.
CREATE COUNTERING OPPORTUNITIES.
FSH...
WHISPER WHISPER
WE SHOULD ATTACK HIM BACK-TO-BACK, IN TWO STEPS.
WITH THE FIRST BEING A DECOY.
I'LL BE THE DECOY...
...ESPECIALLY SINCE HE'S SEEN THROUGH MY MIND TRANSFER TECHNIQUE ALREADY. YOUR JUTSU SHOULD BE THE MAIN ACT.
ALL RIGHT.
UNK

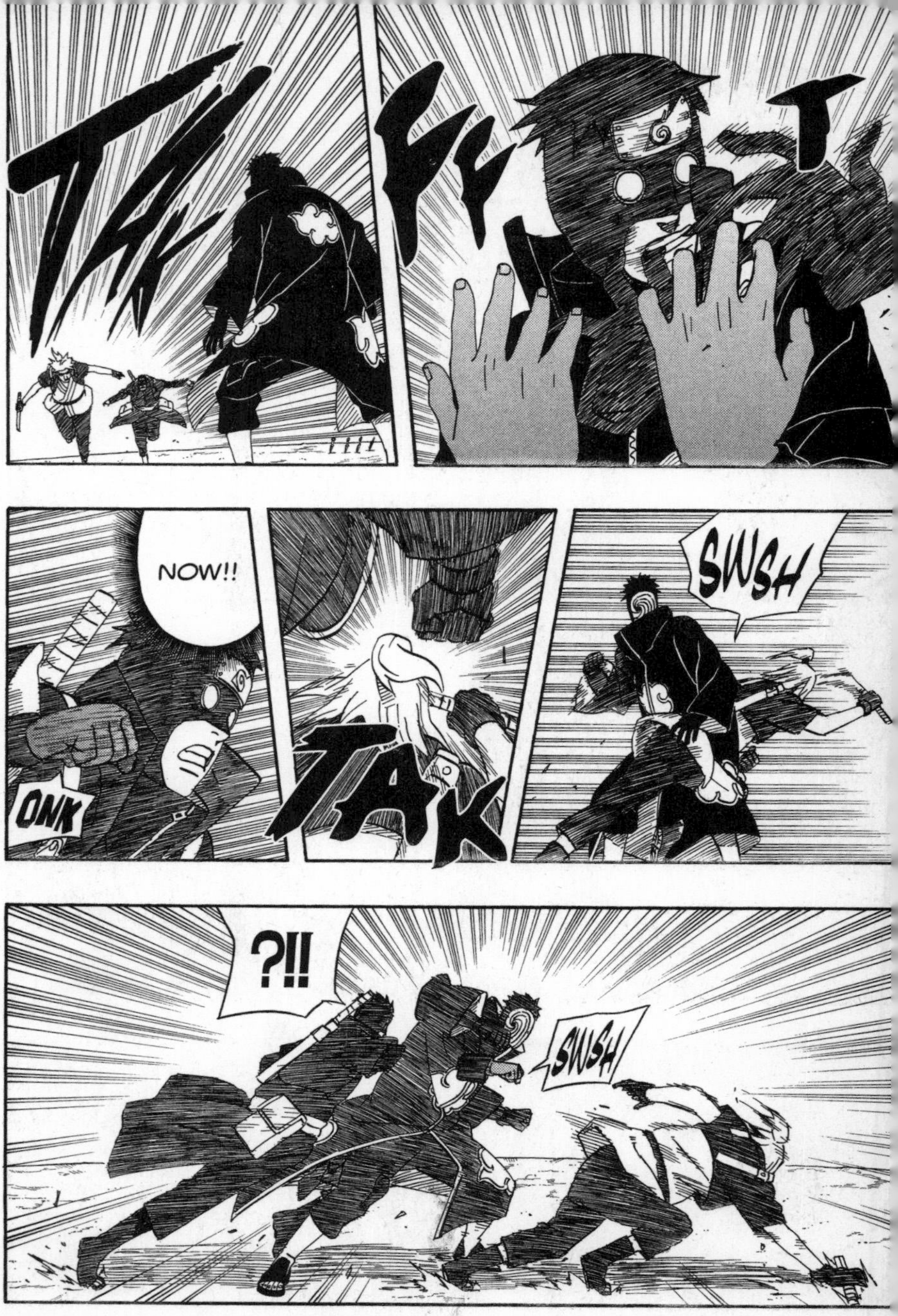
TAK
SWSH
NOW!!
ONK
TAK
?!!
SWSH

READ THIS WAY

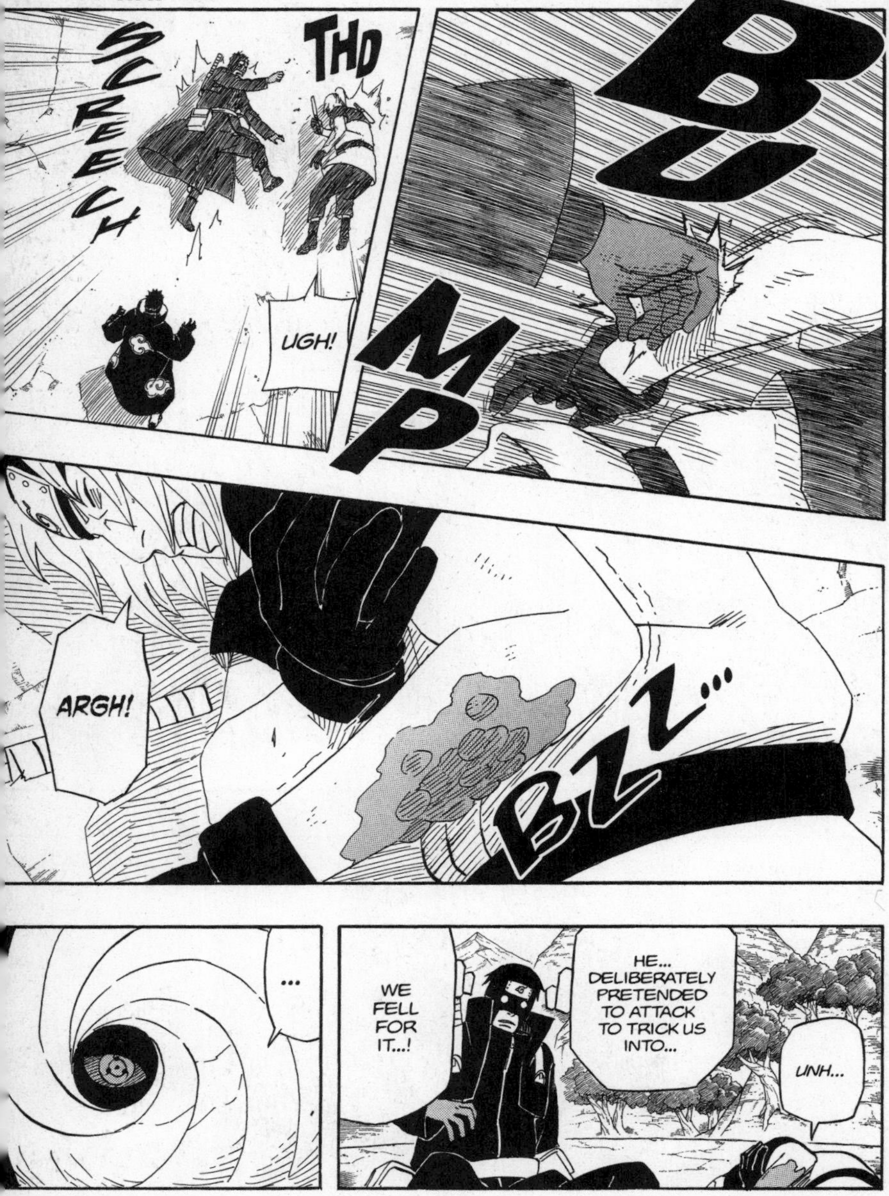
BUMP
THD
SCREECH
UGH!
ARGH!
BZZ...
UNH...
HE... DELIBERATELY PRETENDED TO ATTACK TO TRICK US INTO...
WE FELL FOR IT...!
...

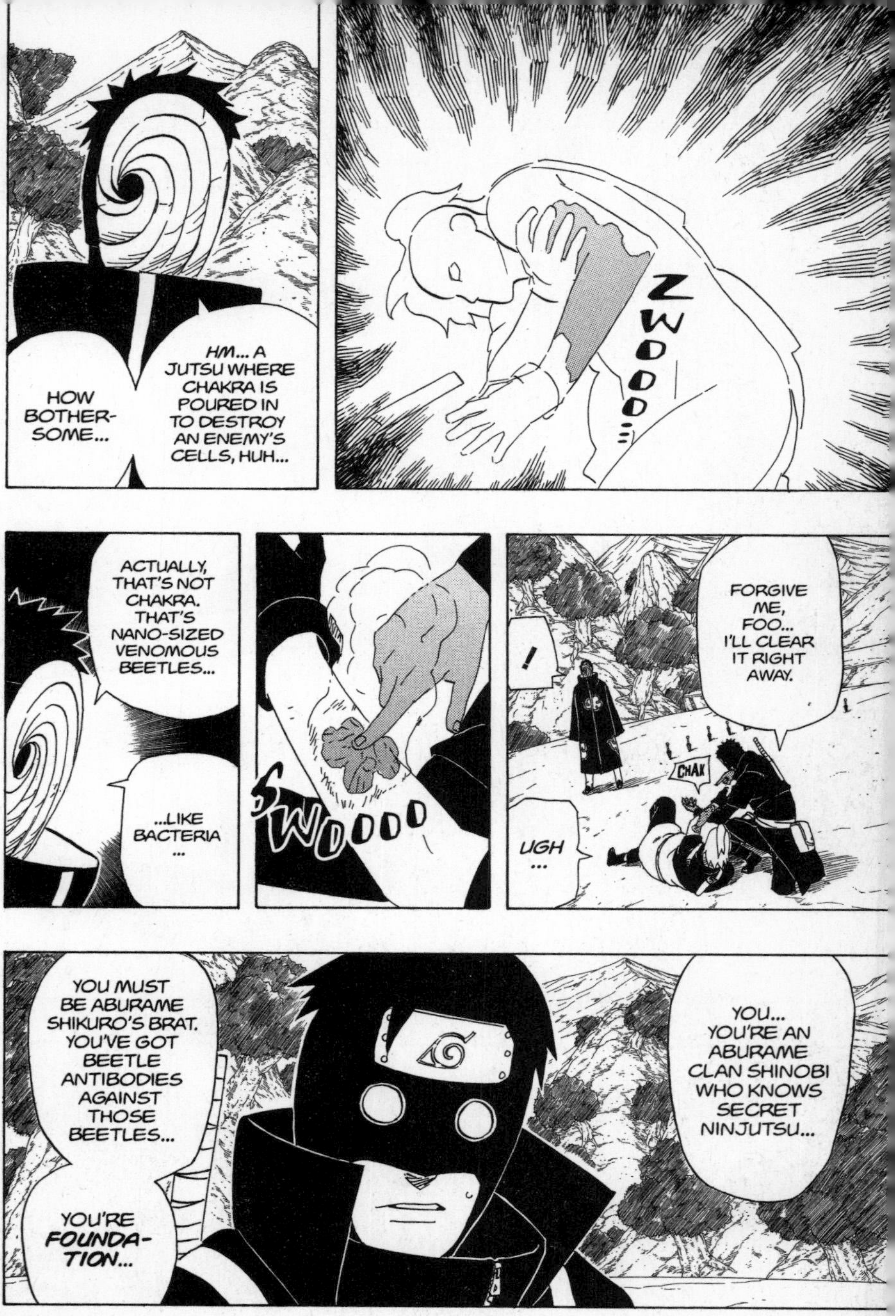
ZWOOO...
HM... A JUTSU WHERE CHAKRA IS POURED IN TO DESTROY AN ENEMY'S CELLS, HUH...
HOW BOTHER-SOME...
FORGIVE ME, FOO... I'LL CLEAR IT RIGHT AWAY.
!
CHAK
UGH...
SWOOOO
ACTUALLY, THAT'S NOT CHAKRA. THAT'S NANO-SIZED VENOMOUS BEETLES...
...LIKE BACTERIA...
YOU... YOU'RE AN ABURAME CLAN SHINOBI WHO KNOWS SECRET NINJUTSU...
YOU MUST BE ABURAME SHIKURO'S BRAT. YOU'VE GOT BEETLE ANTIBODIES AGAINST THOSE BEETLES...
YOU'RE *FOUNDA-TION*...

READ THIS WAY

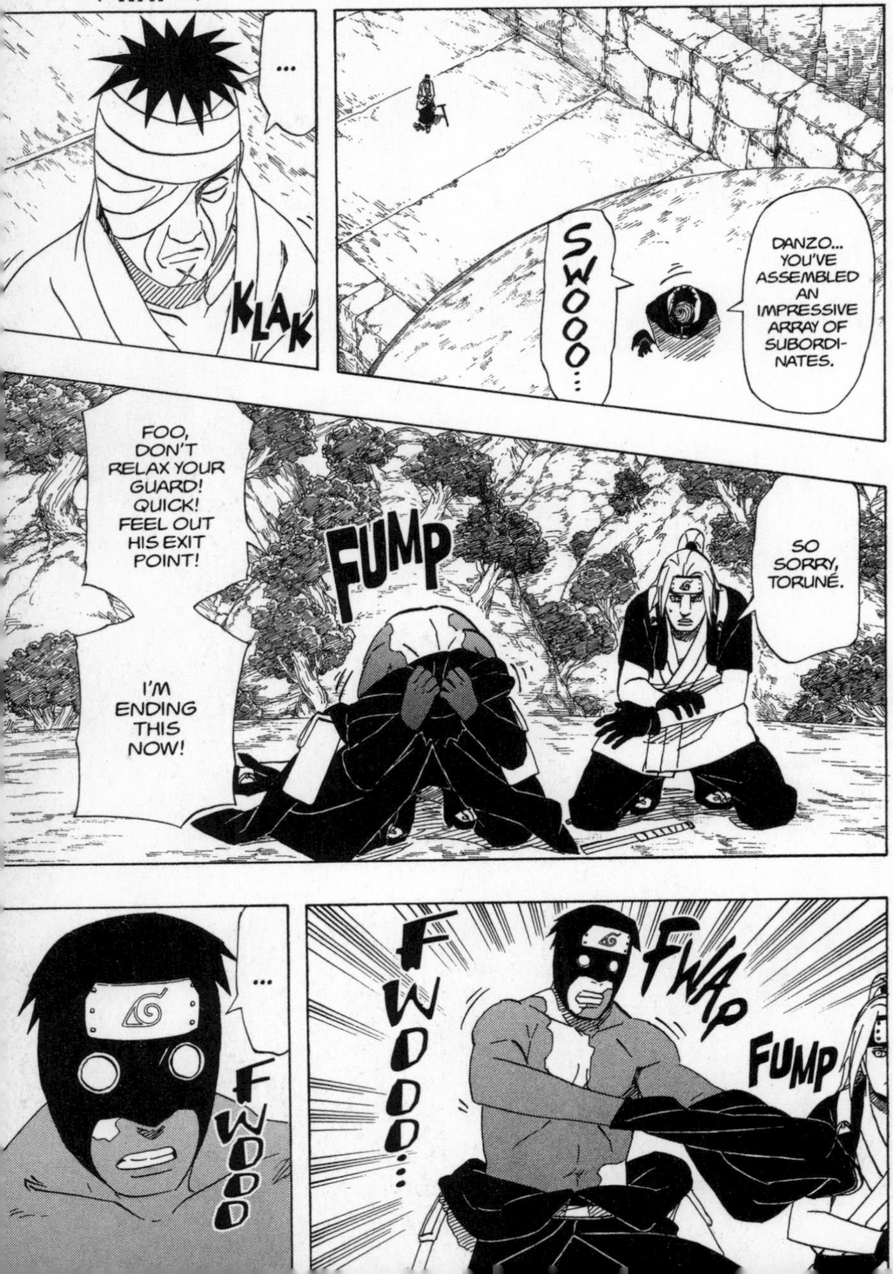

SWOOO...
DANZO... YOU'VE ASSEMBLED AN IMPRESSIVE ARRAY OF SUBORDI-NATES.
...
KLAK
SO SORRY, TORUNÉ.
FUMP
FOO, DON'T RELAX YOUR GUARD! QUICK! FEEL OUT HIS EXIT POINT!
I'M ENDING THIS NOW!
FUMP
FWAP
FWDDD...
...
FWDDD

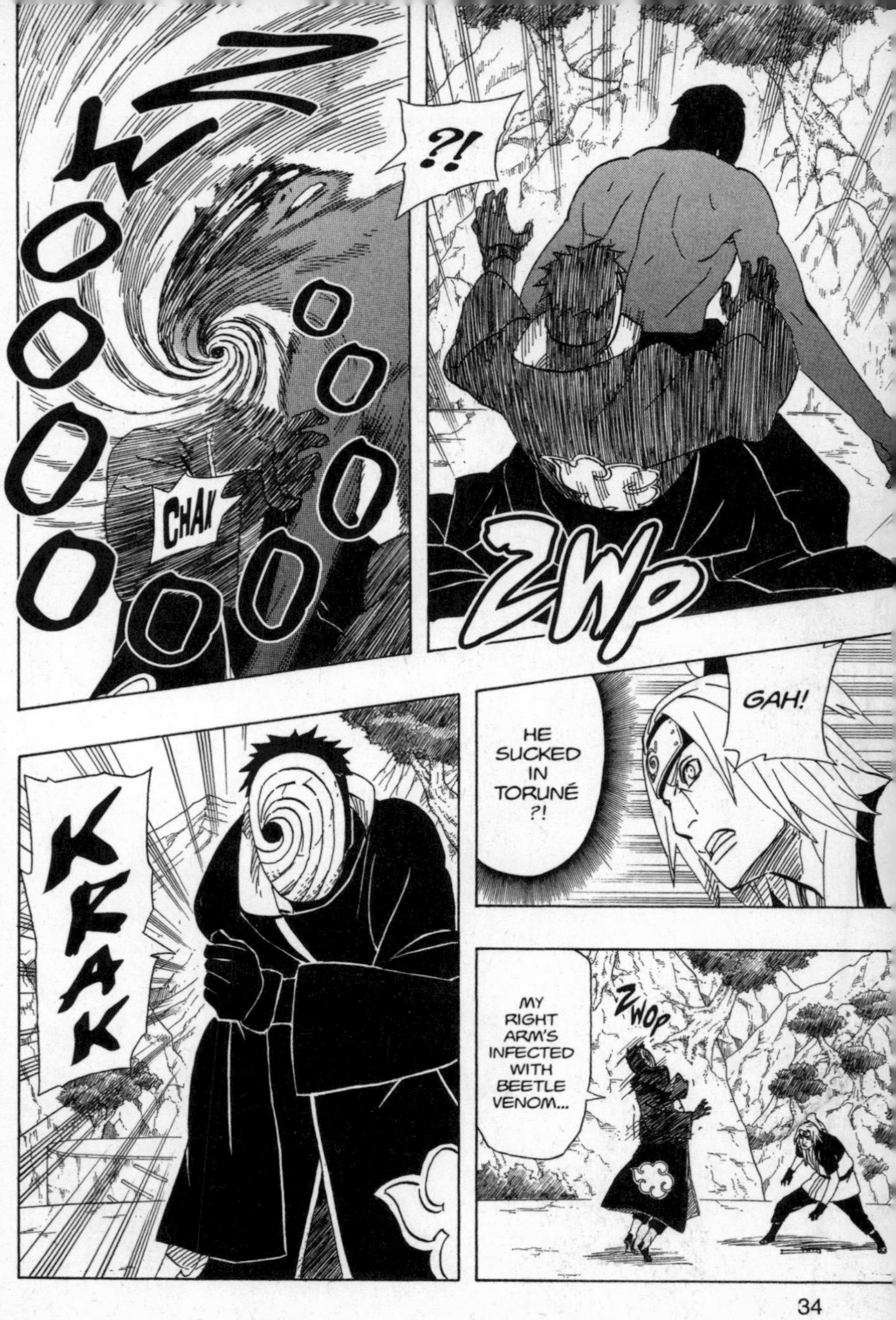
?!
ZWP
ZWOOOOOOOO
CHAK
GAH!
HE SUCKED IN TORUNÉ?!
KRAK
MY RIGHT ARM'S INFECTED WITH BEETLE VENOM...
ZWOP

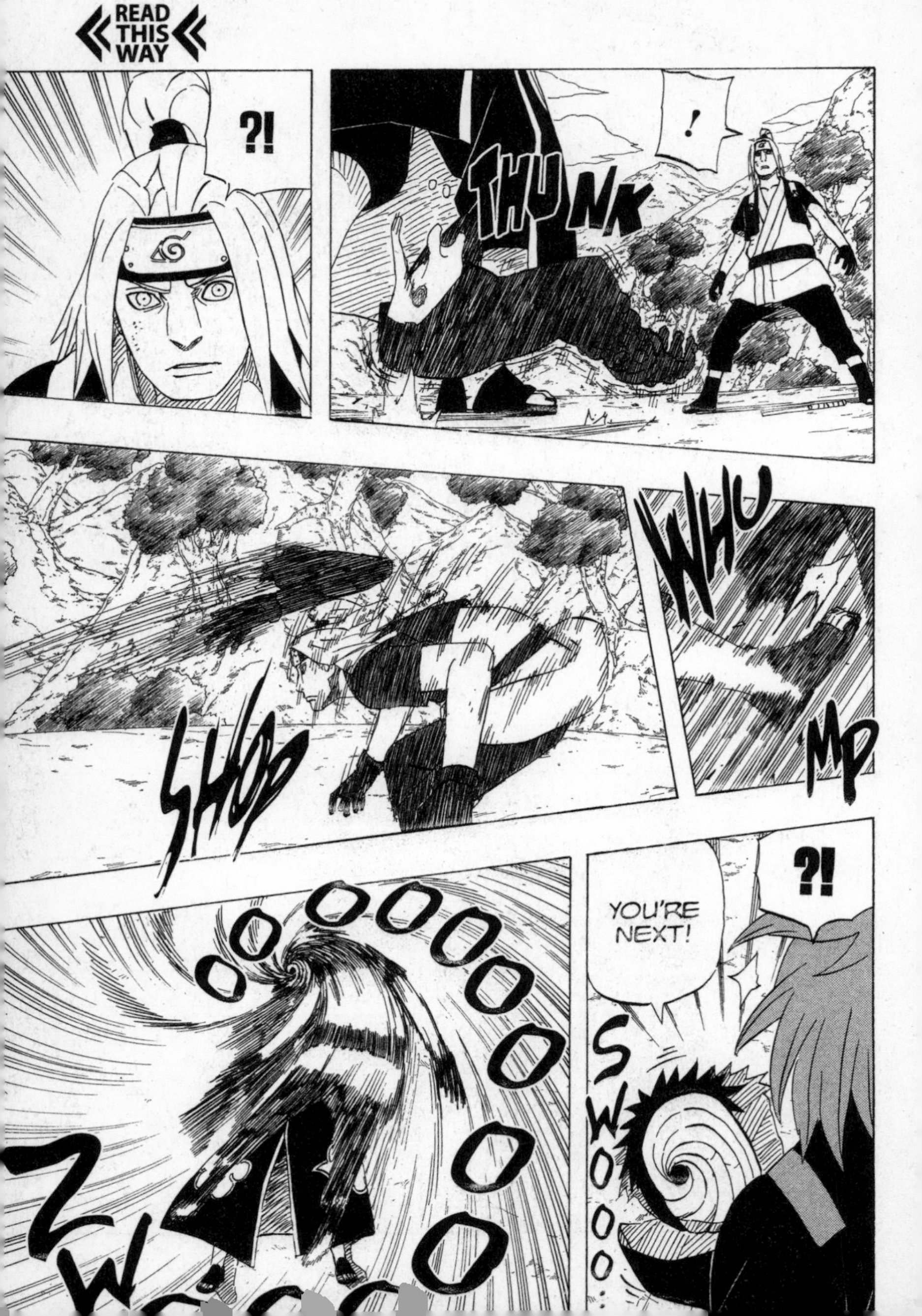
READ THIS WAY
!
THUNK
?!
WHUMP
SHOB
?!
YOU'RE NEXT!
SWOOOO...
ZWOOOOOOOOOOOOO

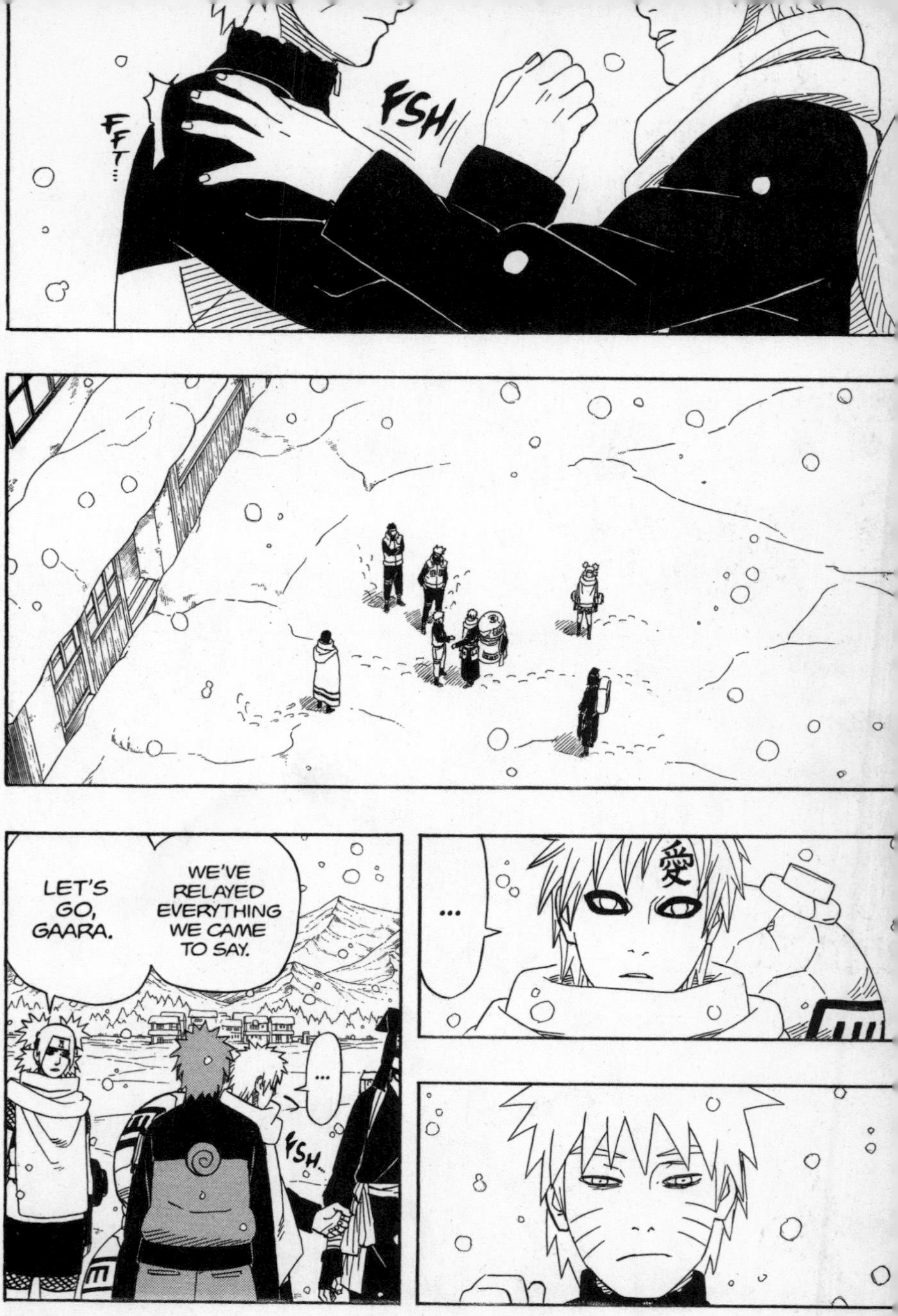
FSH
FFT...
...
WE'VE RELAYED EVERYTHING WE CAME TO SAY.
LET'S GO, GAARA.
...
FSH..

READ THIS WAY

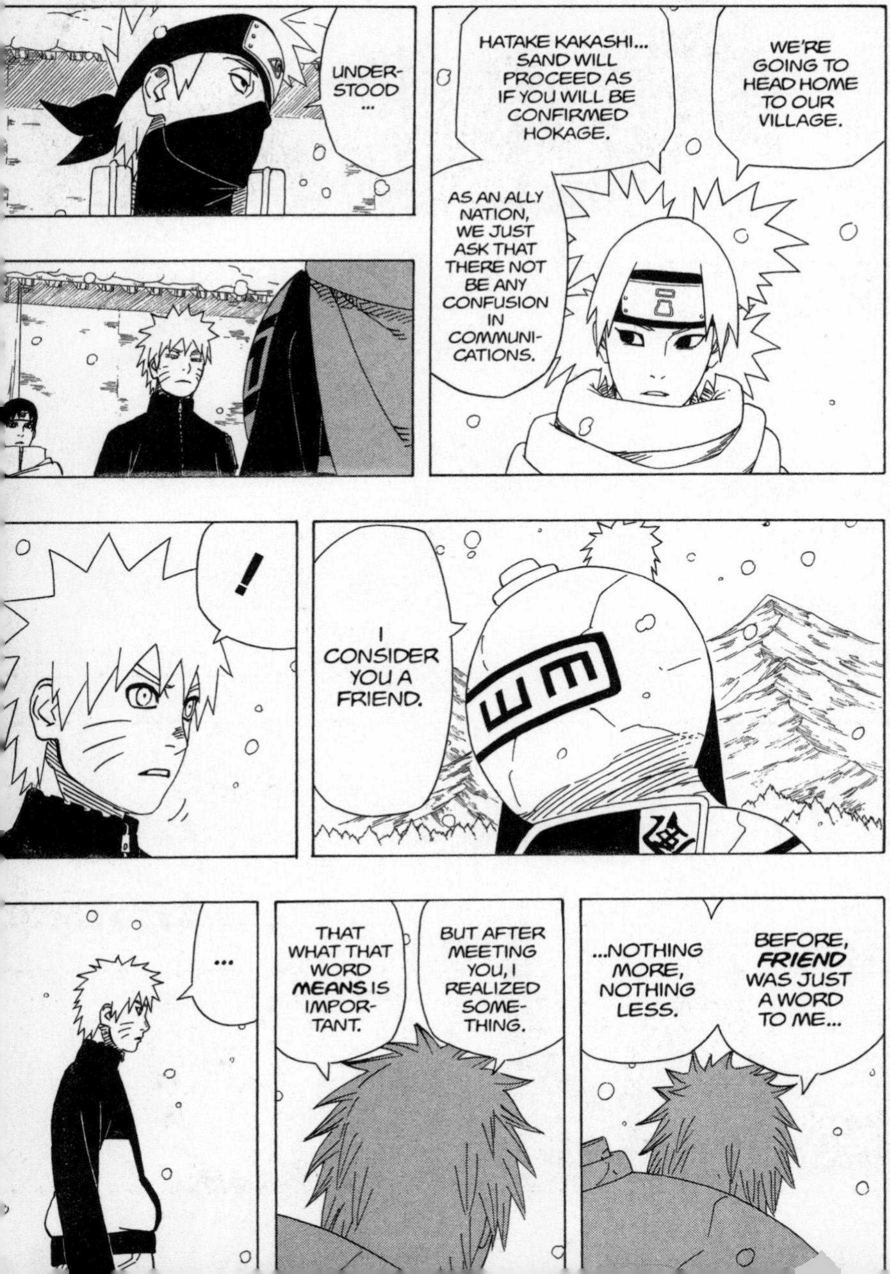

WE'RE GOING TO HEAD HOME TO OUR VILLAGE.
HATAKE KAKASHI... SAND WILL PROCEED AS IF YOU WILL BE CONFIRMED HOKAGE.
AS AN ALLY NATION, WE JUST ASK THAT THERE NOT BE ANY CONFUSION IN COMMUNICATIONS.
UNDERSTOOD ...
I CONSIDER YOU A FRIEND.
!
BEFORE, FRIEND WAS JUST A WORD TO ME...
...NOTHING MORE, NOTHING LESS.
BUT AFTER MEETING YOU, I REALIZED SOMETHING.
THAT WHAT THAT WORD MEANS IS IMPORTANT.
...

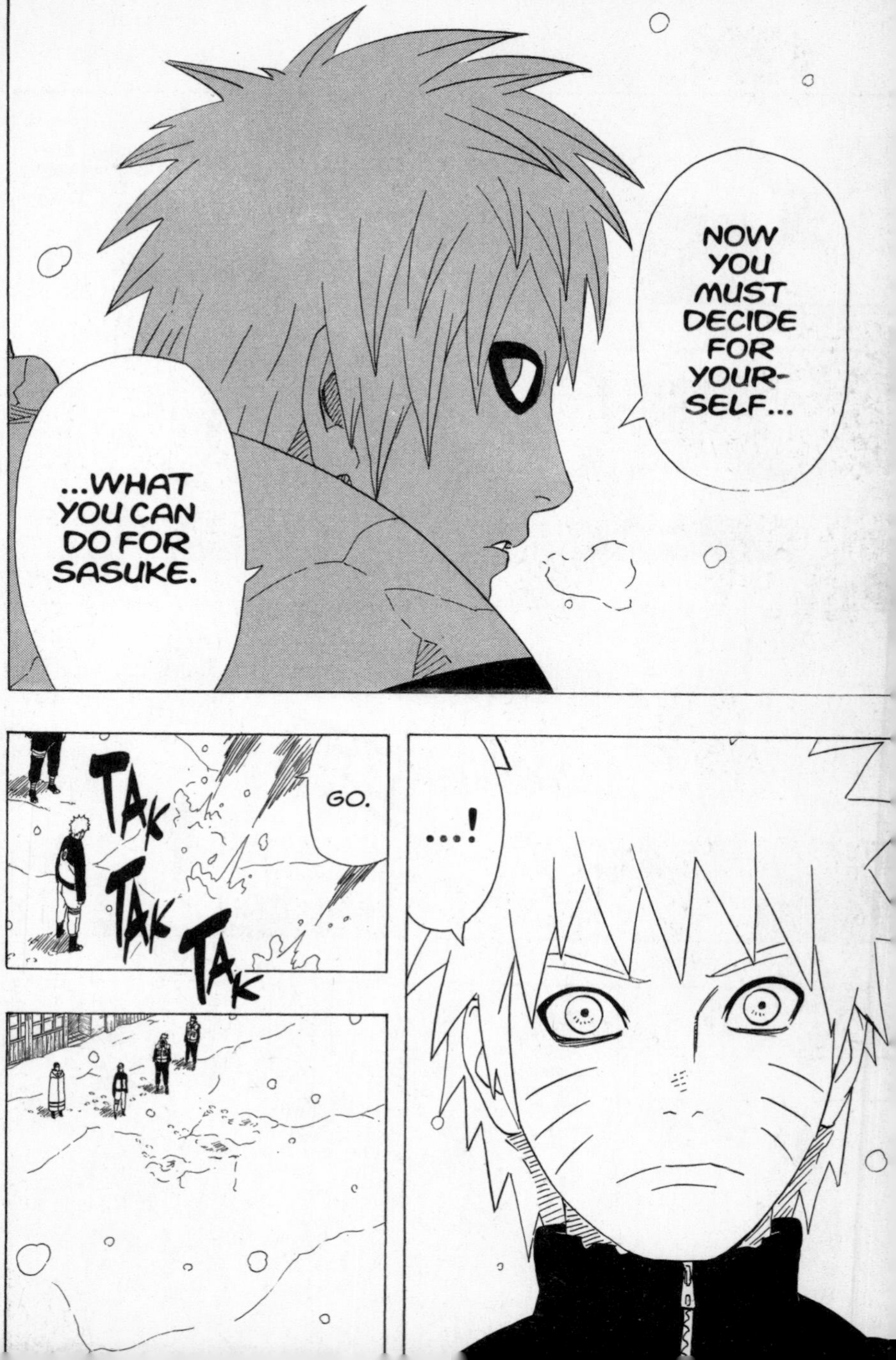
NOW YOU MUST DECIDE FOR YOURSELF...
...WHAT YOU CAN DO FOR SASUKE.
...!
GO.
TAK
TAK
TAK

READ THIS WAY

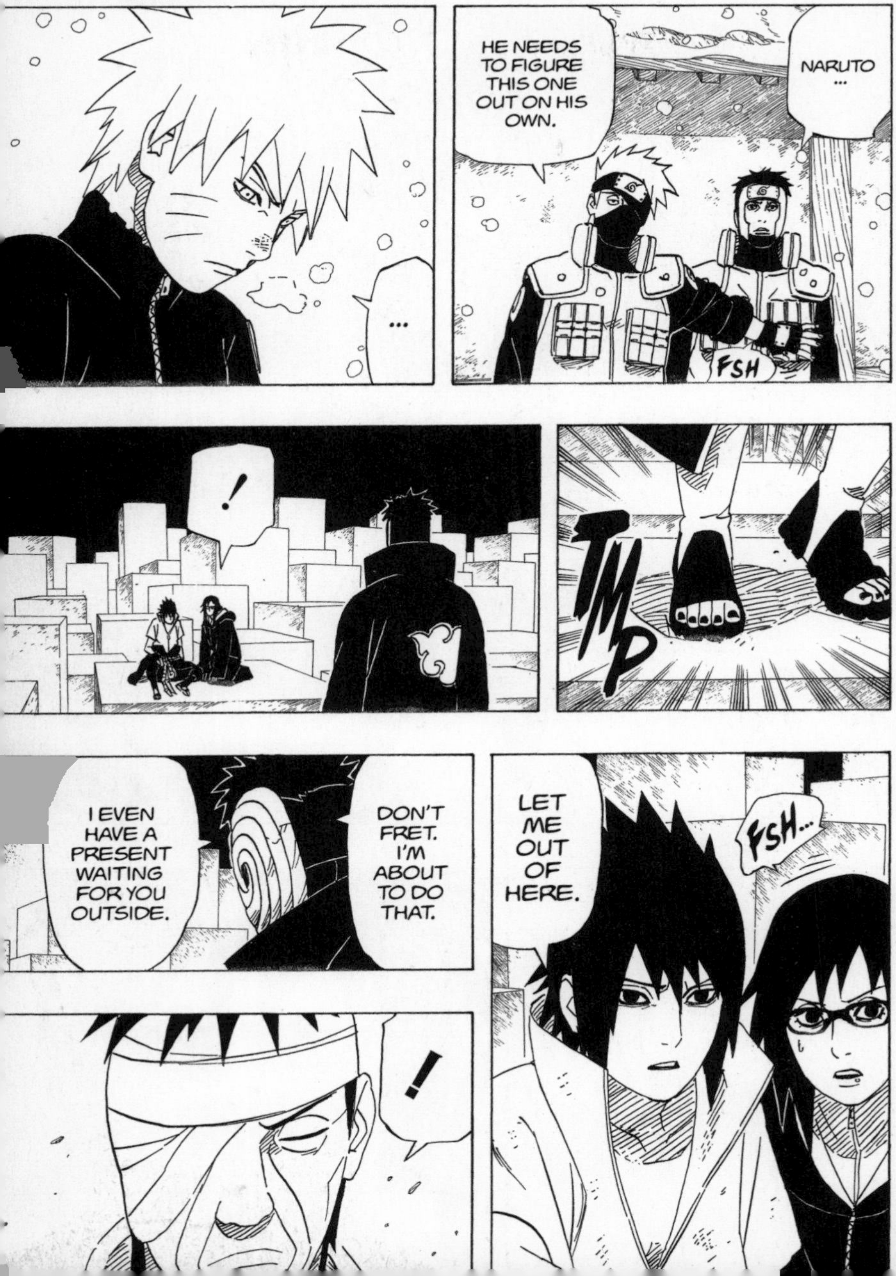
NARUTO ...
HE NEEDS TO FIGURE THIS ONE OUT ON HIS OWN.
FSH
...
TMP
!
FSH...
LET ME OUT OF HERE.
DON'T FRET. I'M ABOUT TO DO THAT.
I EVEN HAVE A PRESENT WAITING FOR YOU OUTSIDE.
!

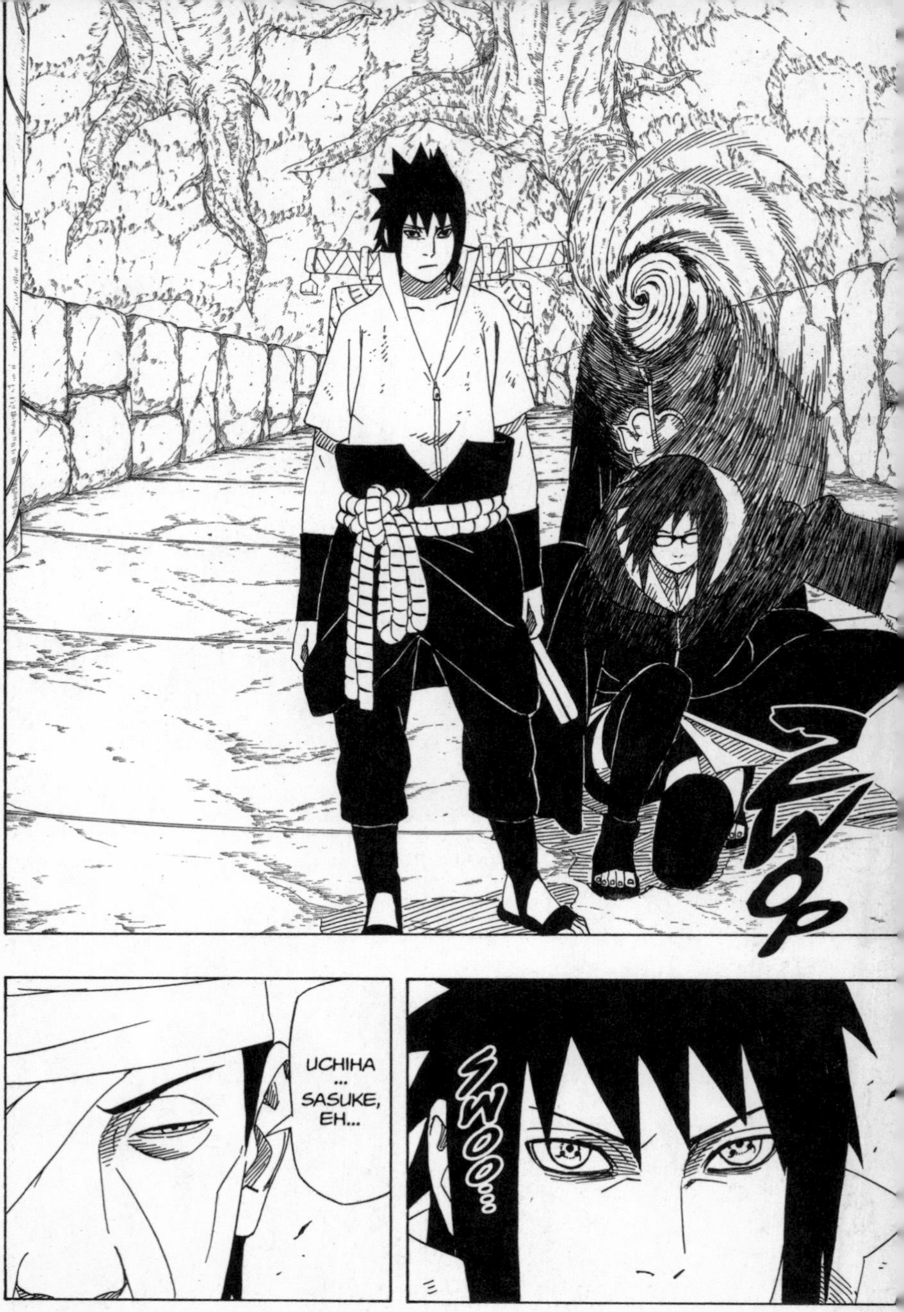
ZWOP
UCHIHA ... SASUKE, EH...
SWOO...

YOU'LL DIE IF YOU GET CAUGHT UP IN THIS.

YOU STAY BACK...

....!

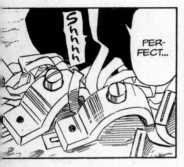

Shhhh

PER-FECT...

TMP

TAK

I CAN TAKE *BOTH* YOUR SHARINGAN.

NARUTO

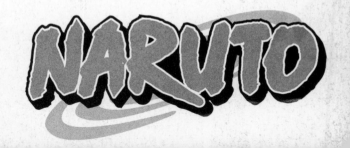

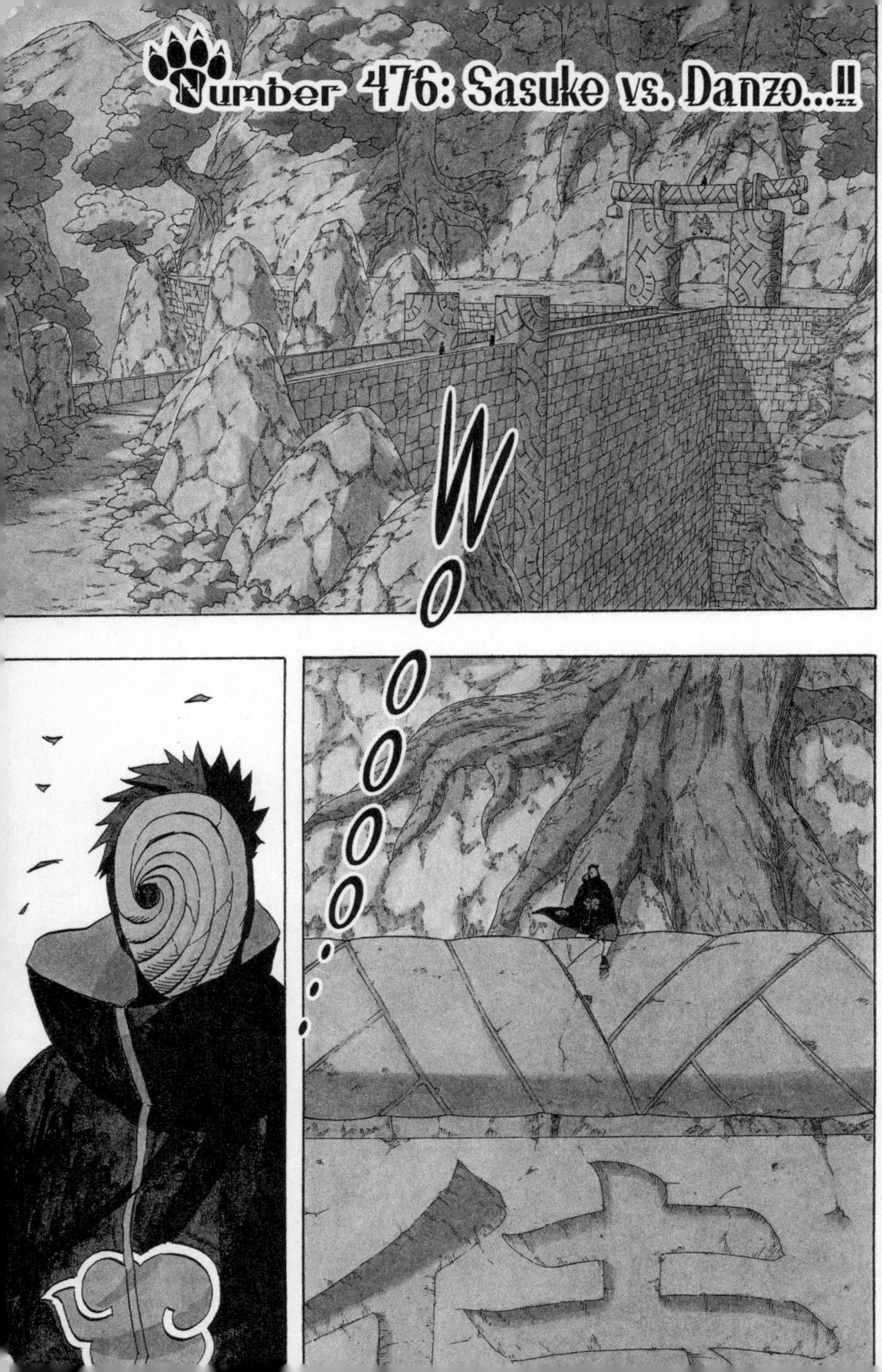
Number 476: Sasuke vs. Danzo...!!
WOOOOOO...

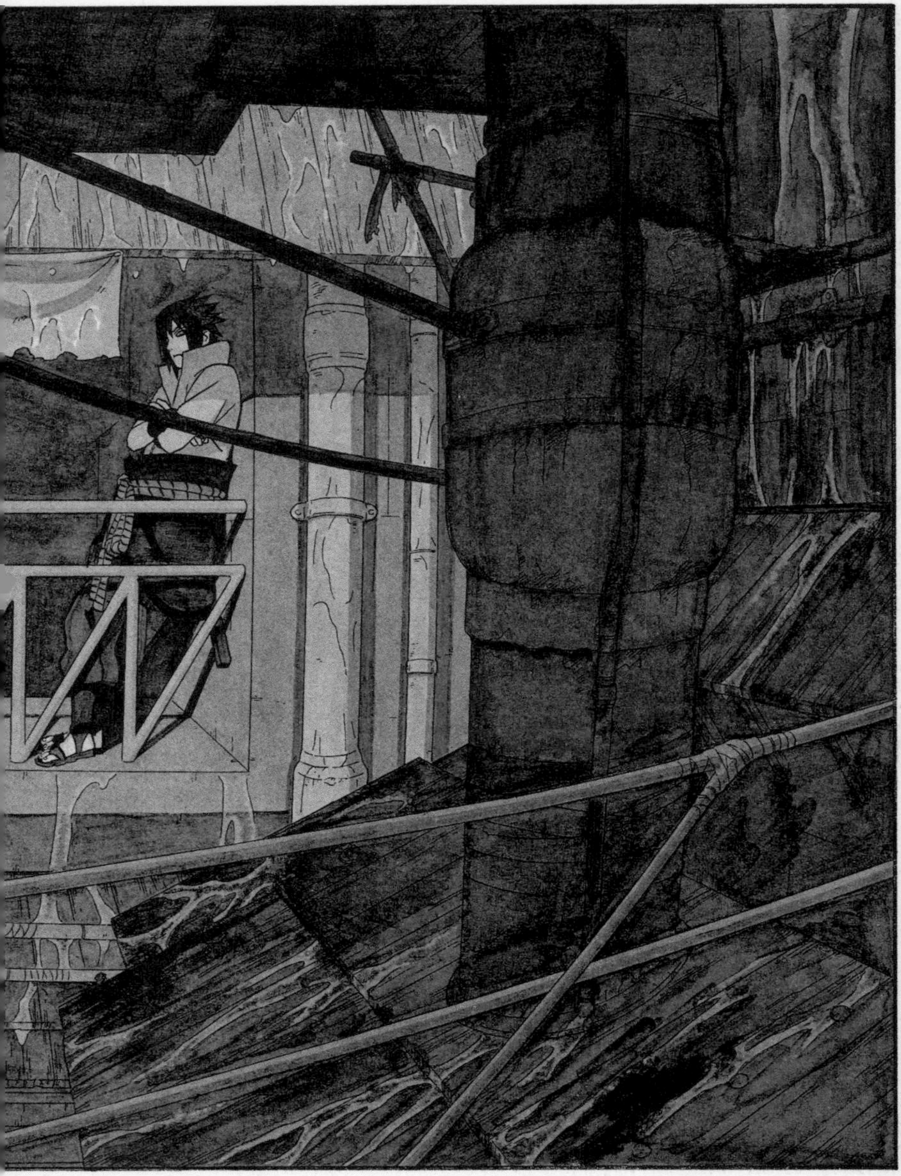

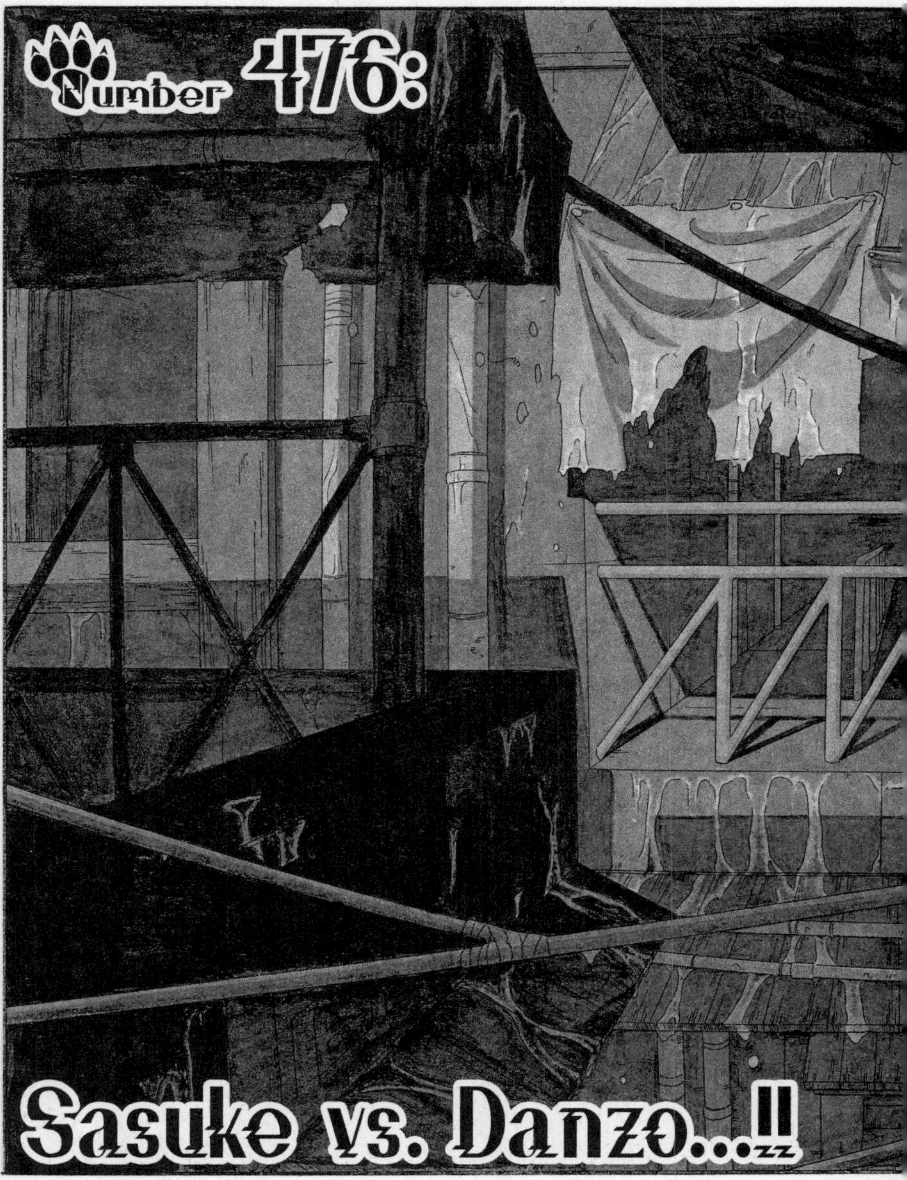
Number 476:
Sasuke vs. Danzo...!!

NARUTO

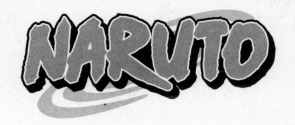

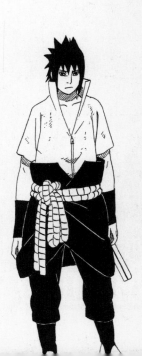

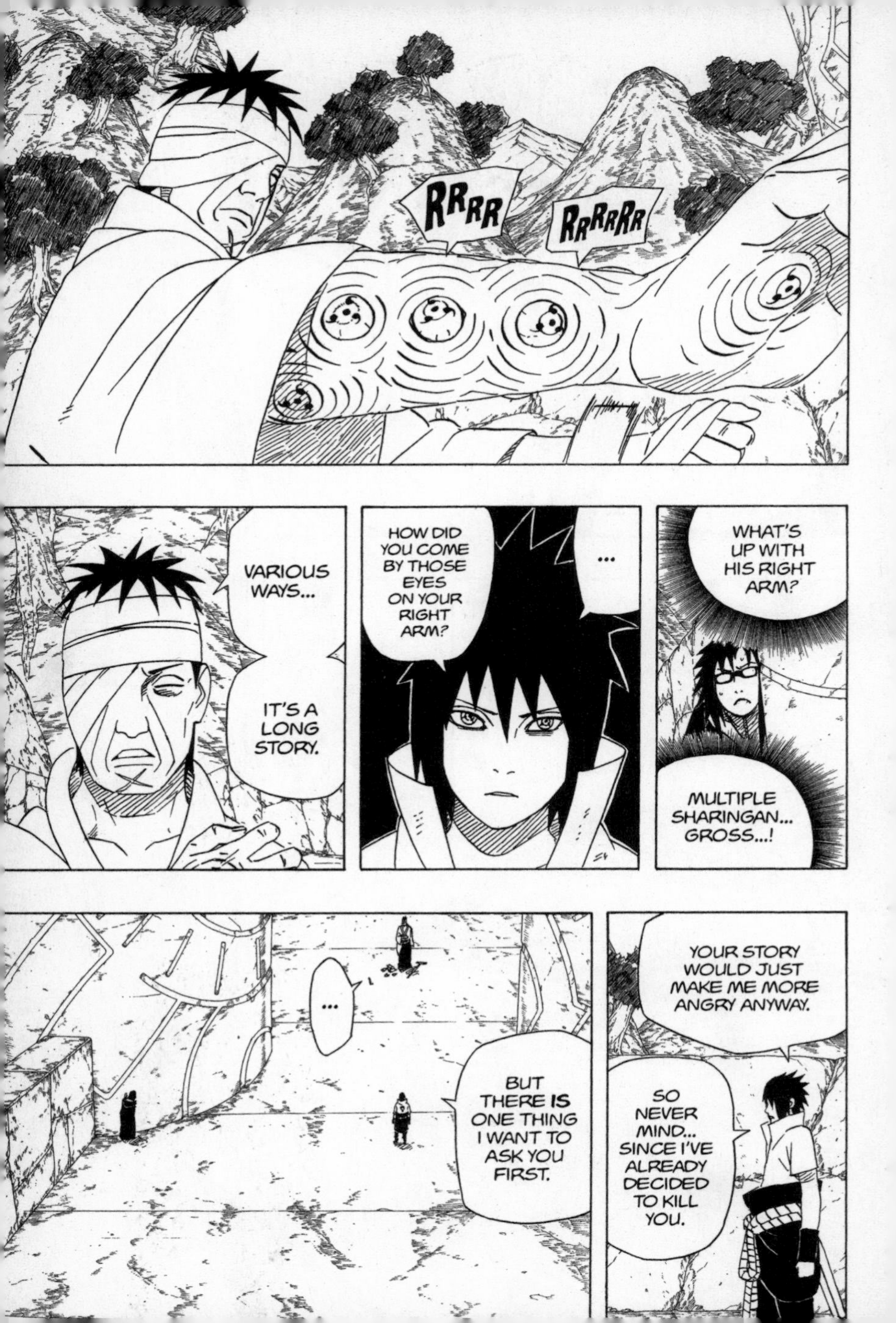
RRRR
RRRRRR
WHAT'S UP WITH HIS RIGHT ARM?
MULTIPLE SHARINGAN... GROSS...!
...
HOW DID YOU COME BY THOSE EYES ON YOUR RIGHT ARM?
VARIOUS WAYS...
IT'S A LONG STORY.
YOUR STORY WOULD JUST MAKE ME MORE ANGRY ANYWAY.
SO NEVER MIND... SINCE I'VE ALREADY DECIDED TO KILL YOU.
BUT THERE **IS** ONE THING I WANT TO ASK YOU FIRST.
...

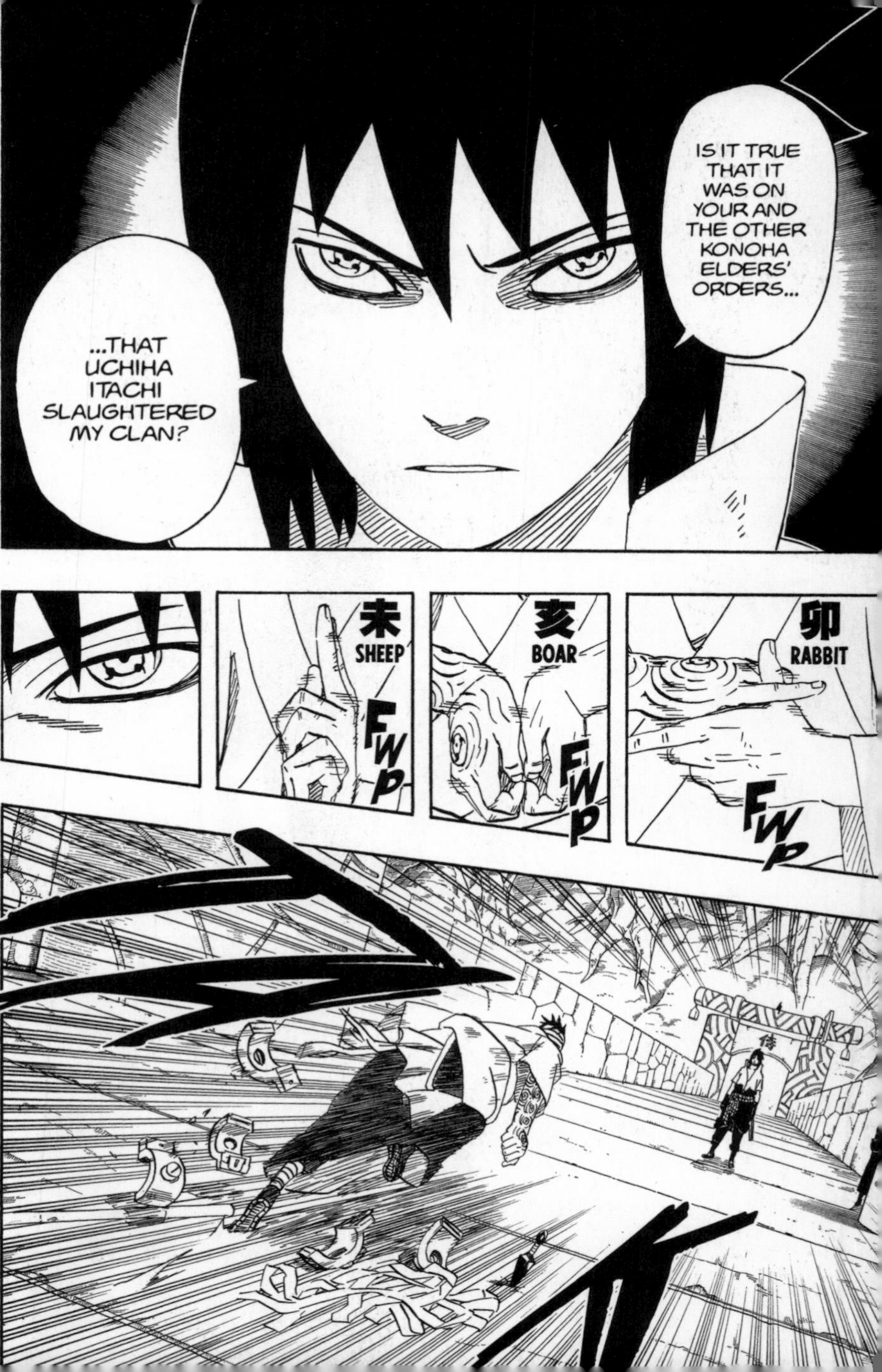
IS IT TRUE THAT IT WAS ON YOUR AND THE OTHER KONOHA ELDERS' ORDERS...
...THAT UCHIHA ITACHI SLAUGHTERED MY CLAN?
卯 RABBIT
FWP
亥 BOAR
FWP
未 SHEEP
FWP

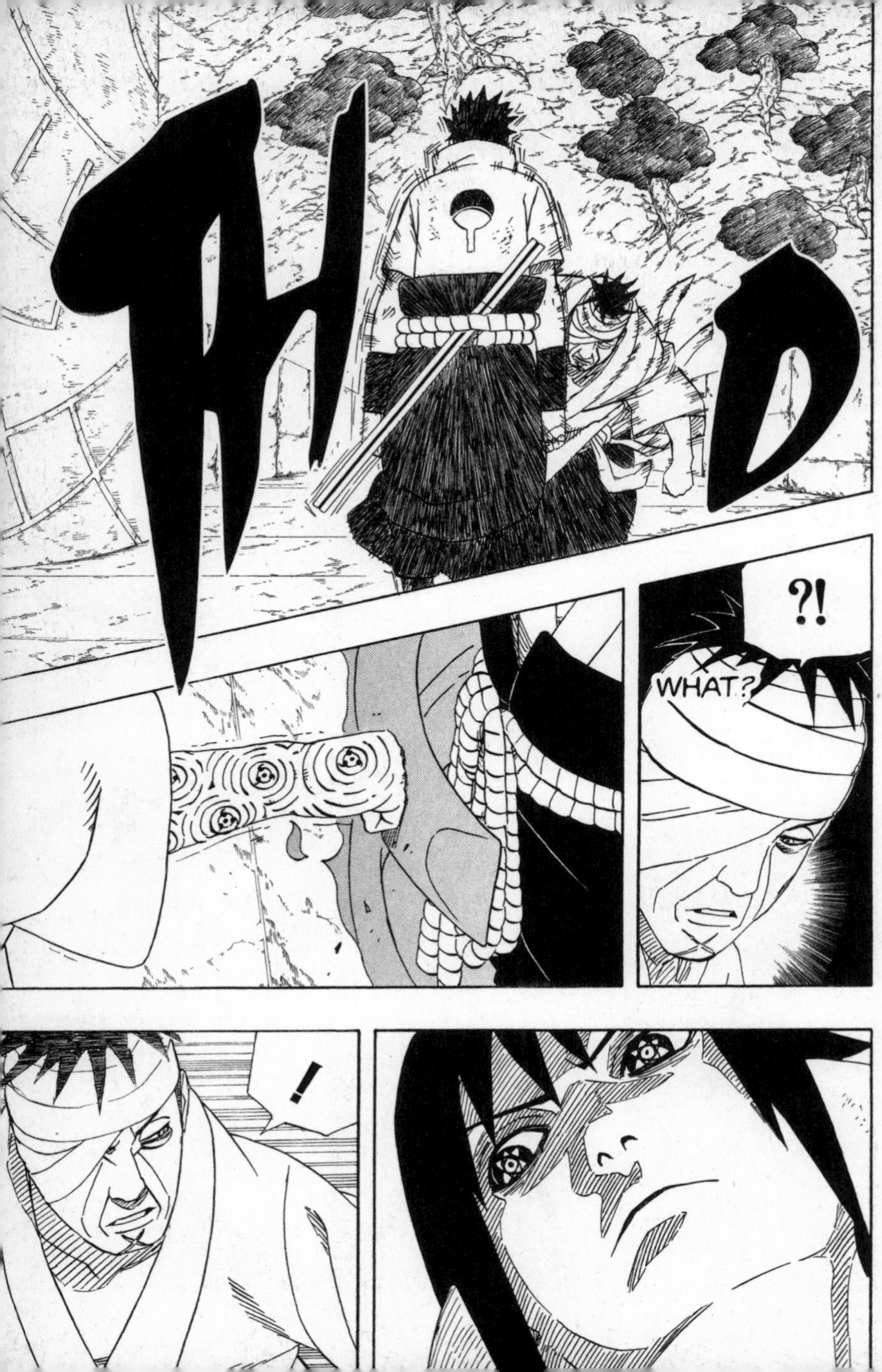
?!
WHAT?
!

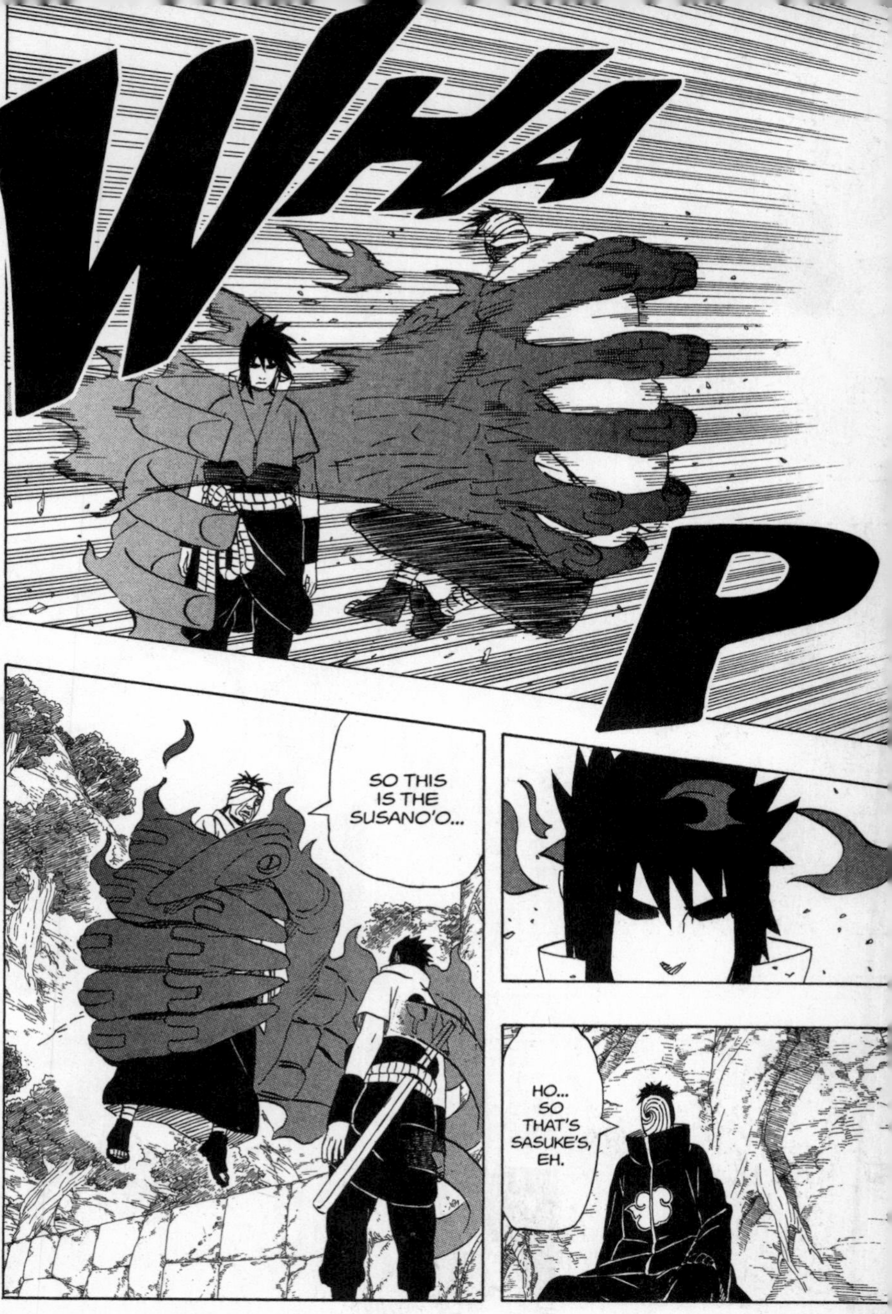
WHAP
SO THIS IS THE SUSANO'O...
HO... SO THAT'S SASUKE'S, EH.

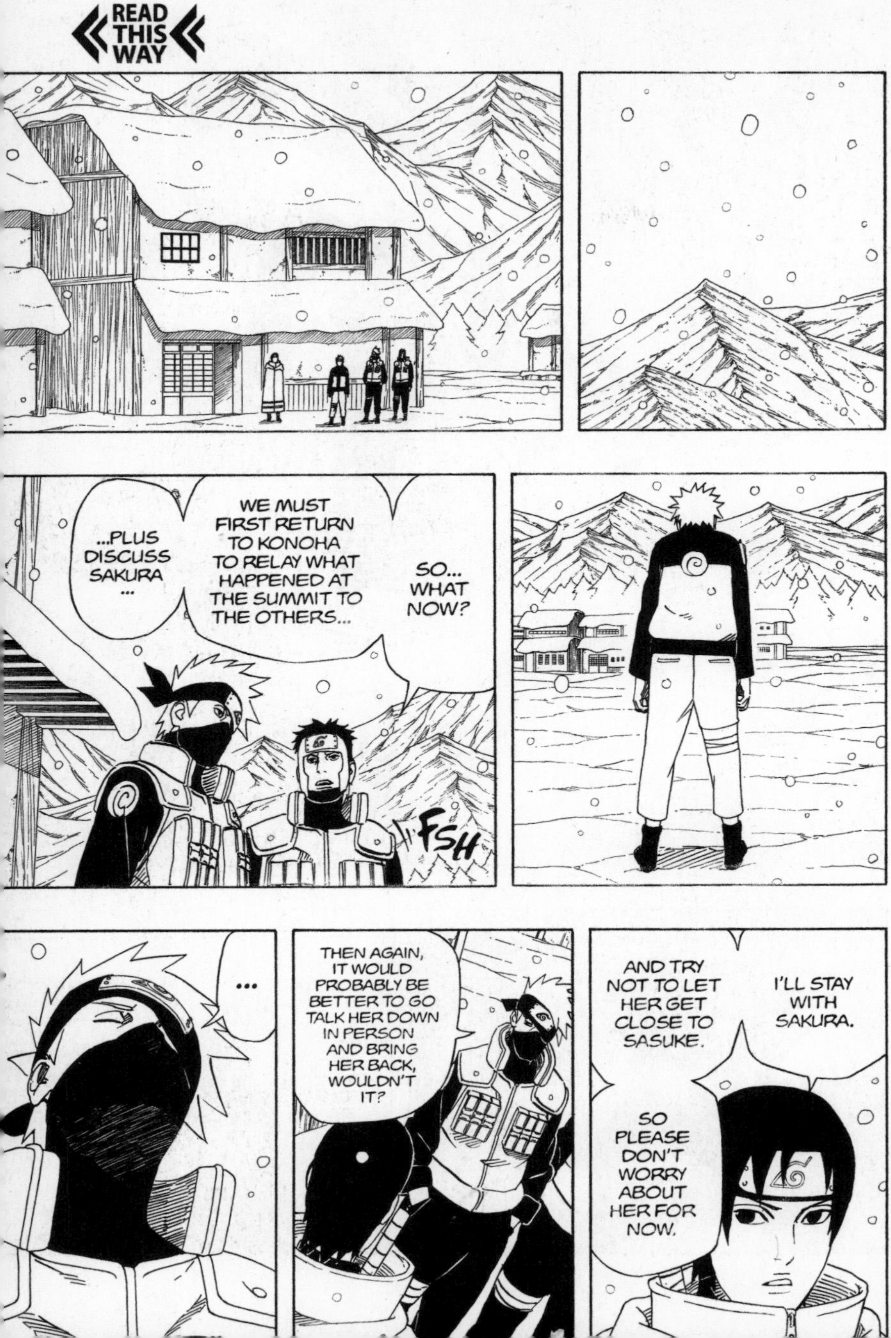
READ THIS WAY
SO... WHAT NOW?
WE MUST FIRST RETURN TO KONOHA TO RELAY WHAT HAPPENED AT THE SUMMIT TO THE OTHERS...
...PLUS DISCUSS SAKURA ...
FSH
I'LL STAY WITH SAKURA.
AND TRY NOT TO LET HER GET CLOSE TO SASUKE.
SO PLEASE DON'T WORRY ABOUT HER FOR NOW.
THEN AGAIN, IT WOULD PROBABLY BE BETTER TO GO TALK HER DOWN IN PERSON AND BRING HER BACK, WOULDN'T IT?
...

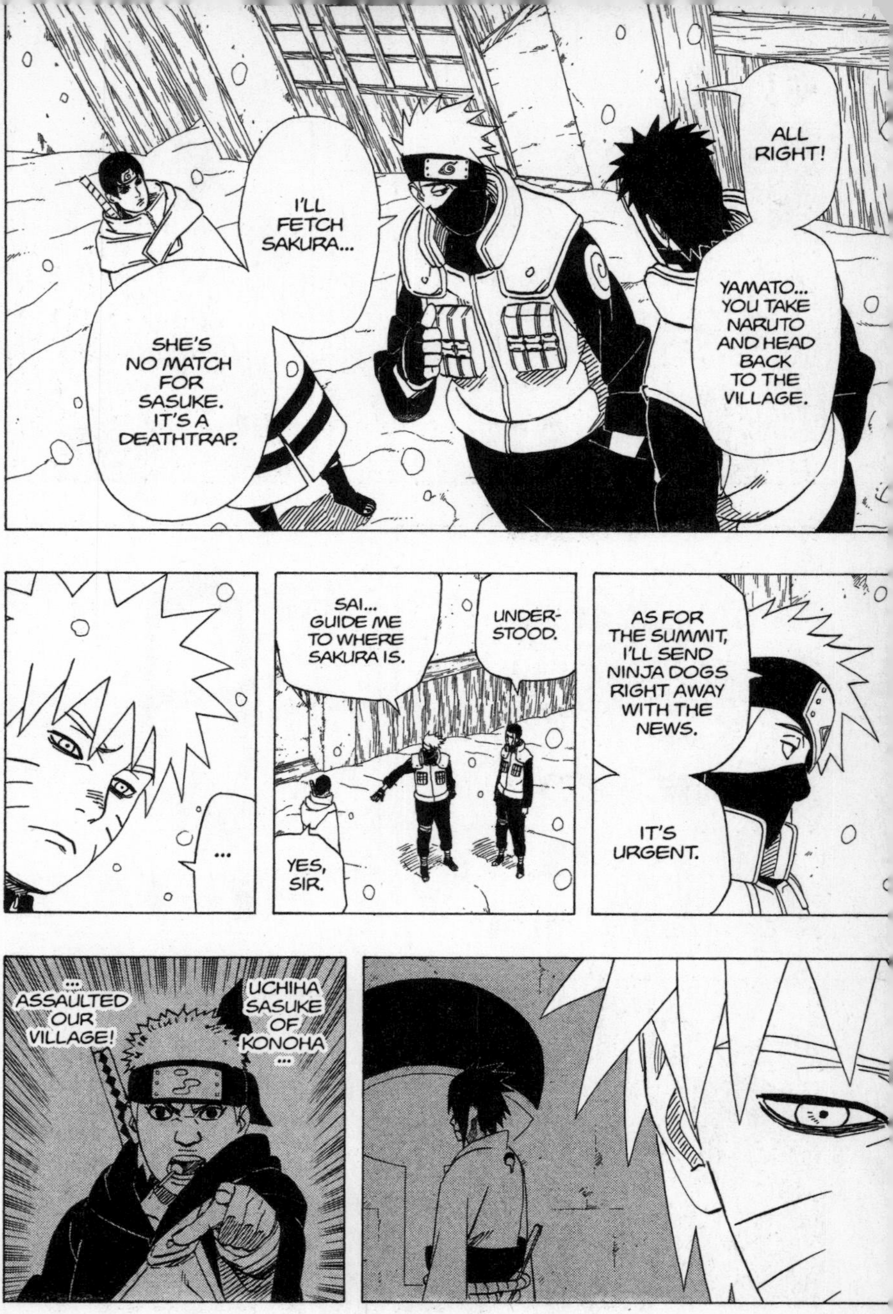
YAMATO... YOU TAKE NARUTO AND HEAD BACK TO THE VILLAGE.
ALL RIGHT!
I'LL FETCH SAKURA...
SHE'S NO MATCH FOR SASUKE. IT'S A DEATHTRAP.
AS FOR THE SUMMIT, I'LL SEND NINJA DOGS RIGHT AWAY WITH THE NEWS.
IT'S URGENT.
UNDER-STOOD.
SAI... GUIDE ME TO WHERE SAKURA IS.
YES, SIR.
...
UCHIHA SASUKE OF KONOHA ...
... ASSAULTED OUR VILLAGE!

READ THIS WAY

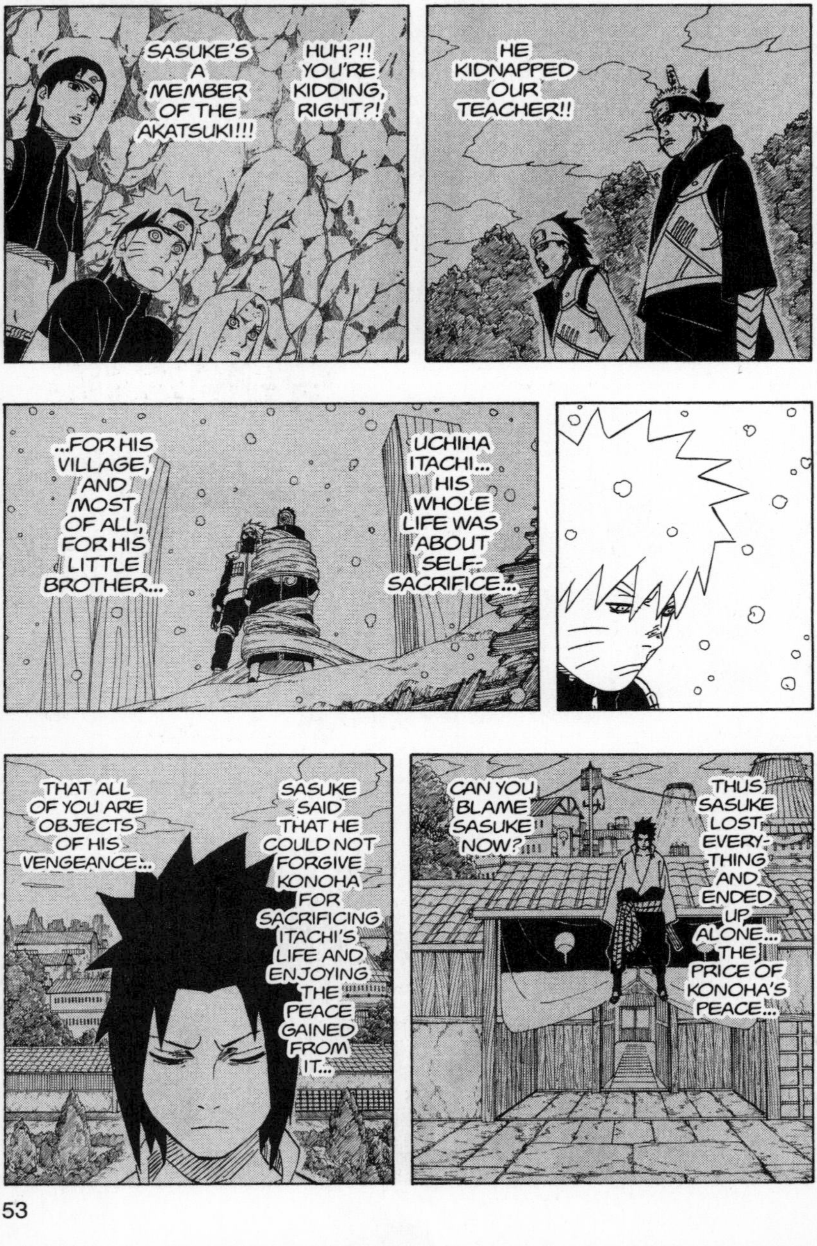
HE KIDNAPPED OUR TEACHER!!
HUH?!! YOU'RE KIDDING, RIGHT?!
SASUKE'S A MEMBER OF THE AKATSUKI!!!
UCHIHA ITACHI... HIS WHOLE LIFE WAS ABOUT SELF-SACRIFICE...
...FOR HIS VILLAGE, AND MOST OF ALL, FOR HIS LITTLE BROTHER...
THUS SASUKE LOST EVERY-THING AND ENDED UP ALONE... THE PRICE OF KONOHA'S PEACE...
CAN YOU BLAME SASUKE NOW?
SASUKE SAID THAT HE COULD NOT FORGIVE KONOHA FOR SACRIFICING ITACHI'S LIFE AND ENJOYING THE PEACE GAINED FROM IT...
THAT ALL OF YOU ARE OBJECTS OF HIS VENGEANCE...

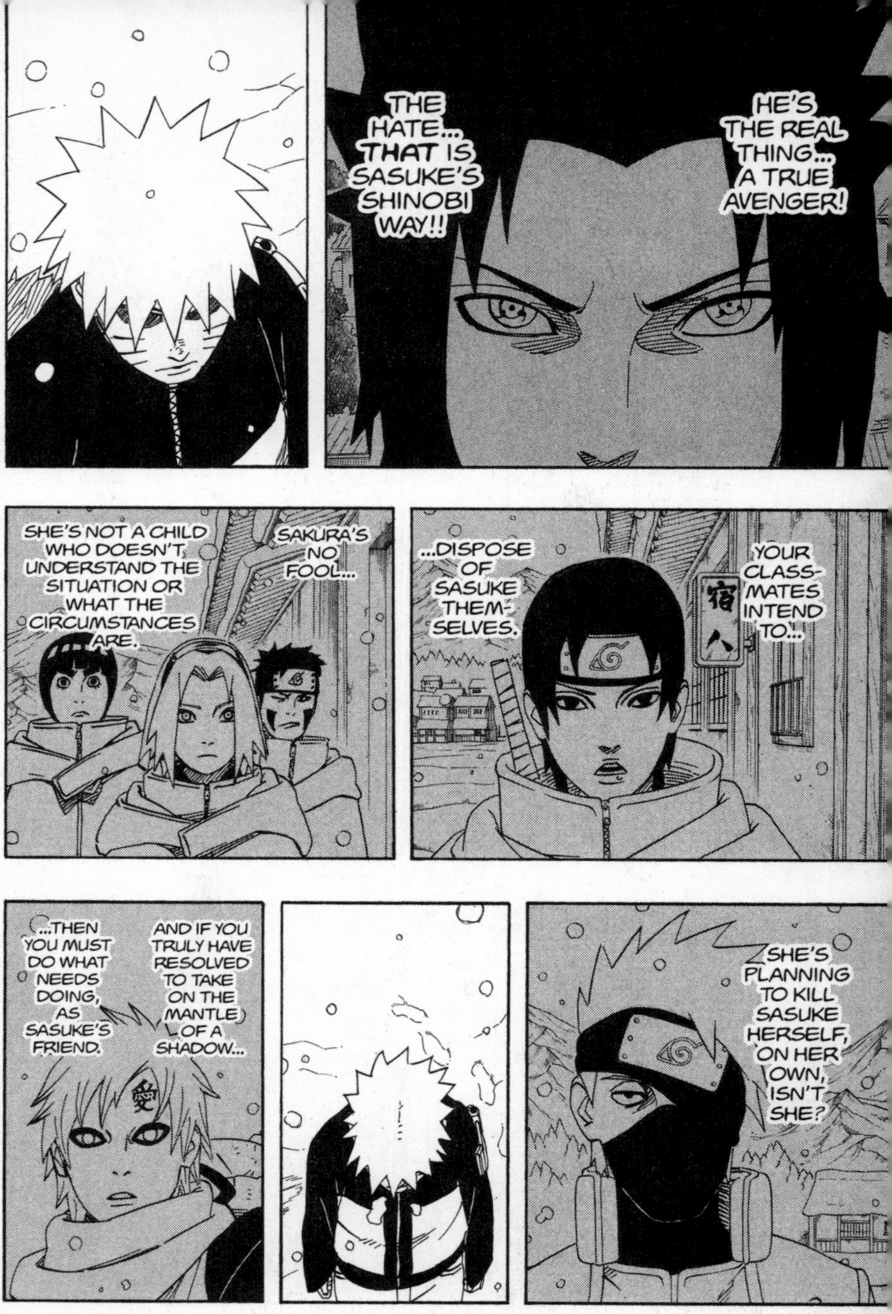
HE'S THE REAL THING... A TRUE AVENGER!
THE HATE... THAT IS SASUKE'S SHINOBI WAY!!
YOUR CLASSMATES INTEND TO...
...DISPOSE OF SASUKE THEMSELVES.
SAKURA'S NO FOOL...
SHE'S NOT A CHILD WHO DOESN'T UNDERSTAND THE SITUATION OR WHAT THE CIRCUMSTANCES ARE.
SHE'S PLANNING TO KILL SASUKE HERSELF, ON HER OWN, ISN'T SHE?
AND IF YOU TRULY HAVE RESOLVED TO TAKE ON THE MANTLE OF A SHADOW...
...THEN YOU MUST DO WHAT NEEDS DOING, AS SASUKE'S FRIEND.

READ THIS WAY

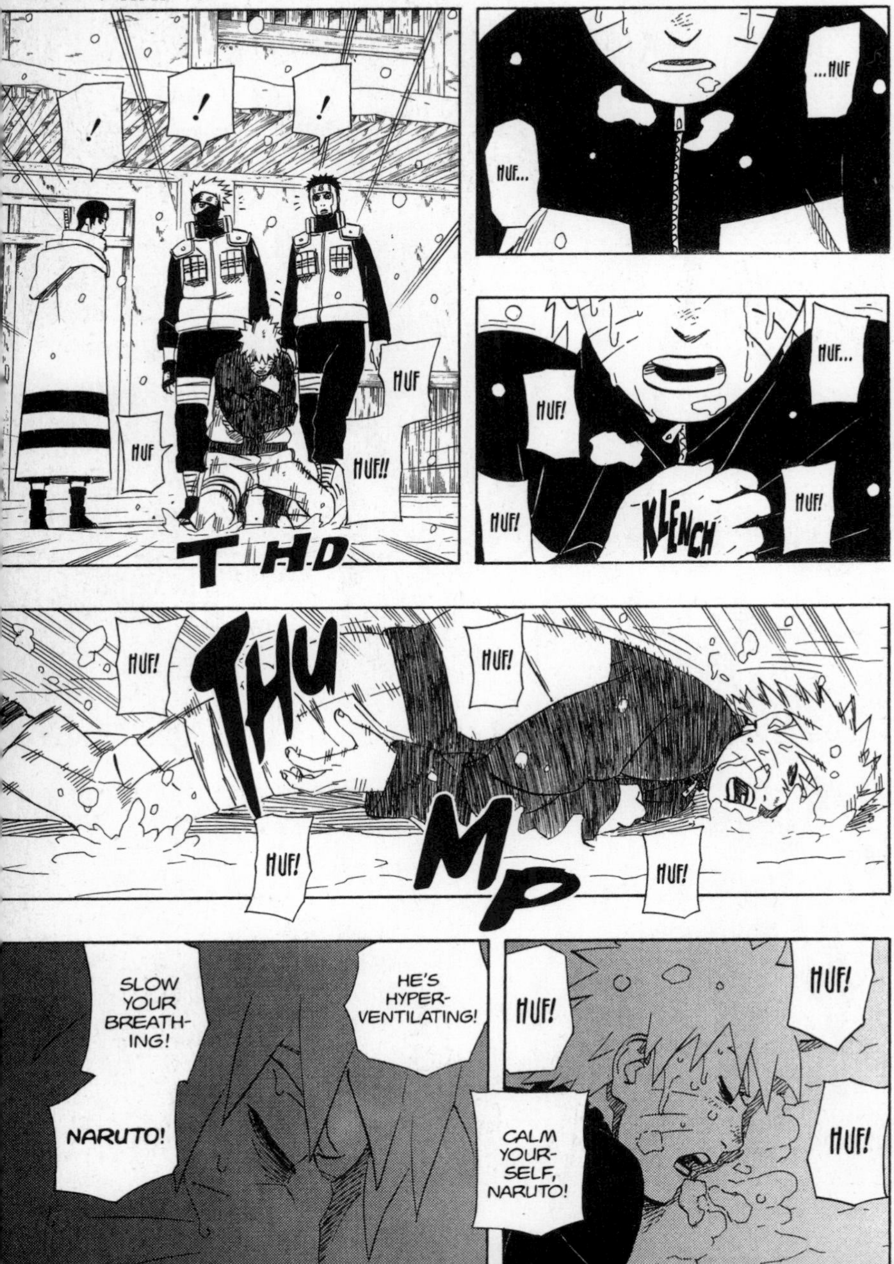

...HUF
HUF...
HUF...
HUF!
HUF!
KLENCH
HUF!
!
!
!
HUF
HUF
HUF!!
THD
HUF!
HUF!
THUMP
HUF!
HUF!
HUF!
HUF!
CALM YOURSELF, NARUTO!
HUF!
HE'S HYPERVENTILATING!
SLOW YOUR BREATHING!
NARUTO!

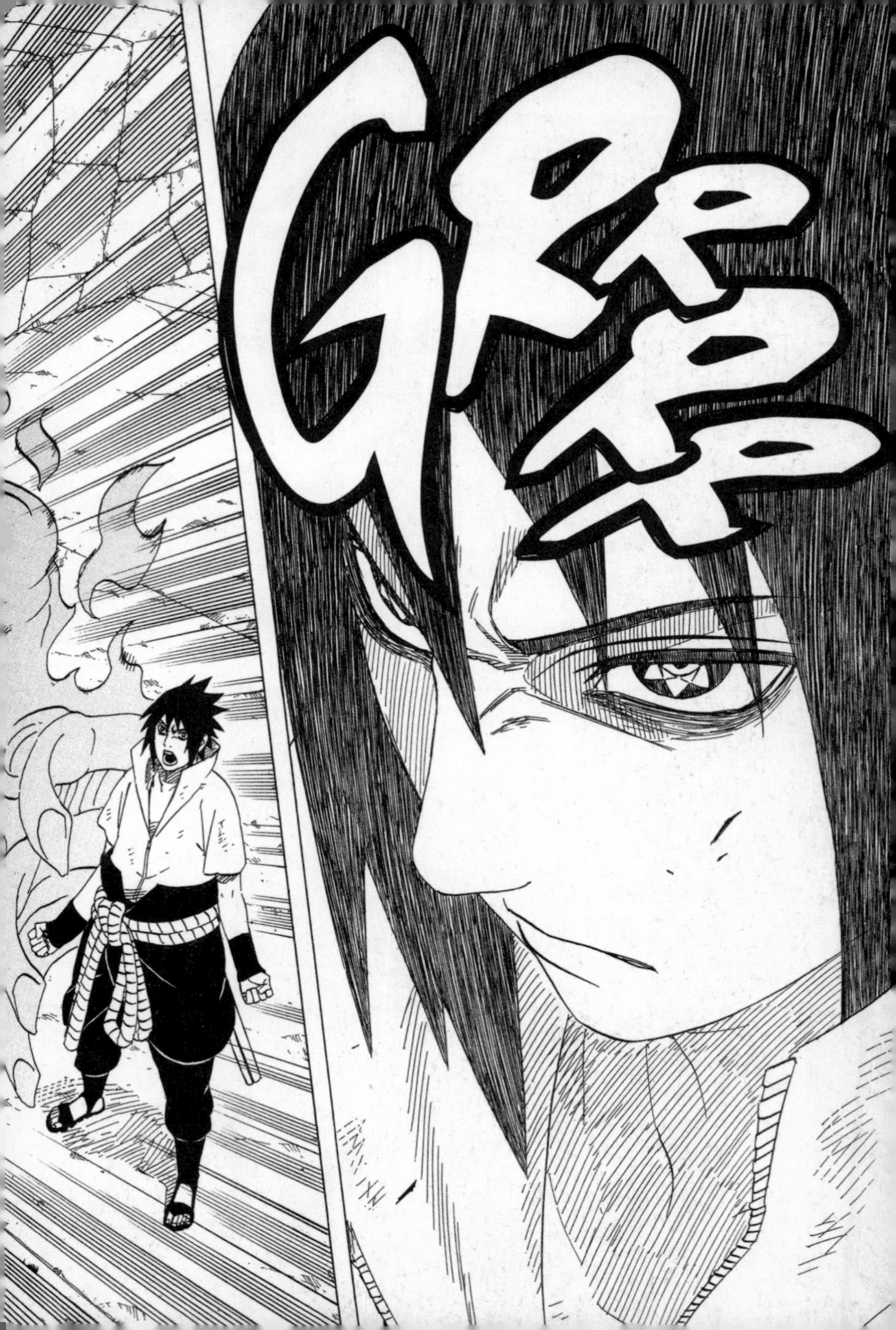

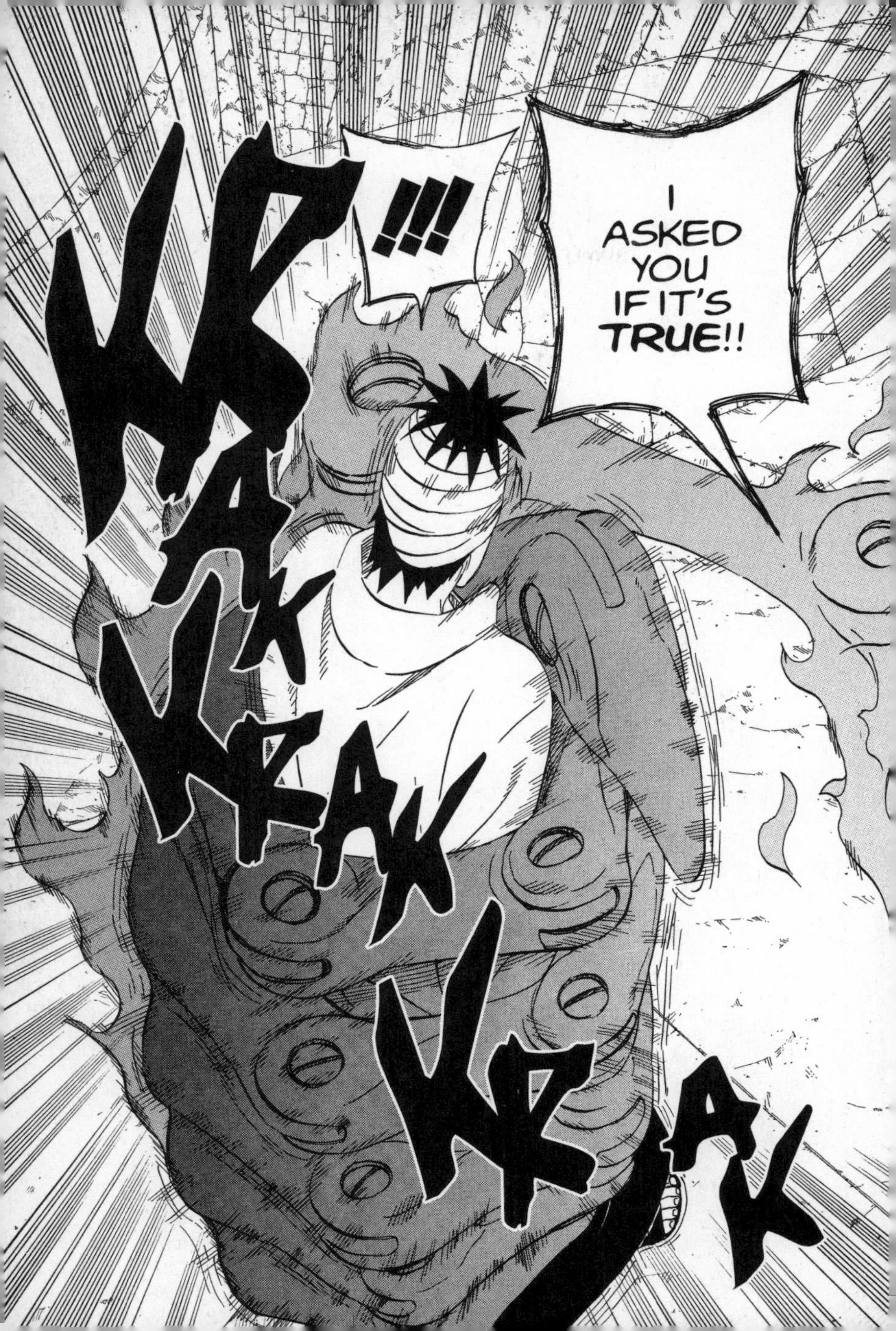
I ASKED YOU IF IT'S TRUE!!
!!!
KRAK KRAK KRAK

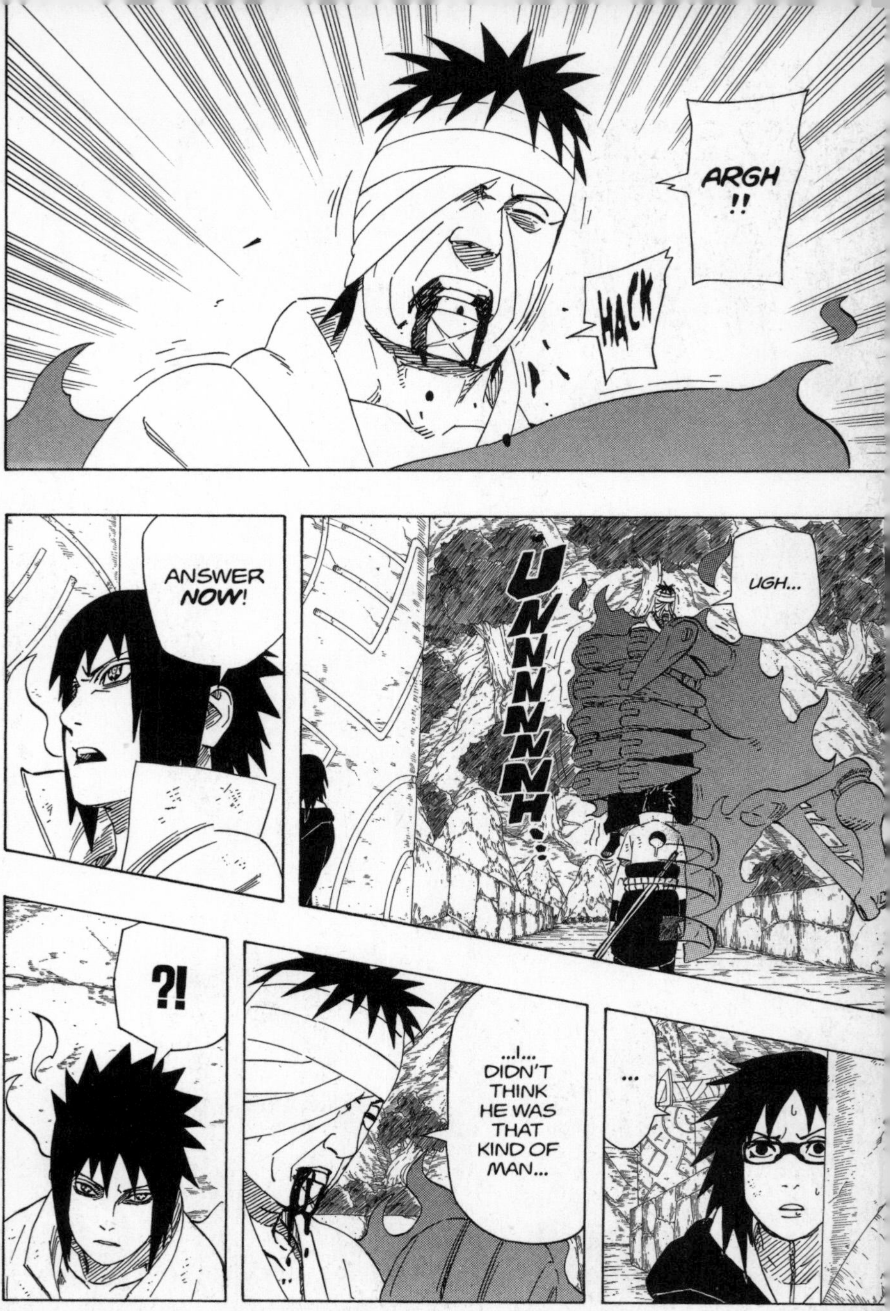
ARGH !!
HACK
UGH...
UNNNNNH...
ANSWER NOW!
...
...I... DIDN'T THINK HE WAS THAT KIND OF MAN...
?!

READ THIS WAY

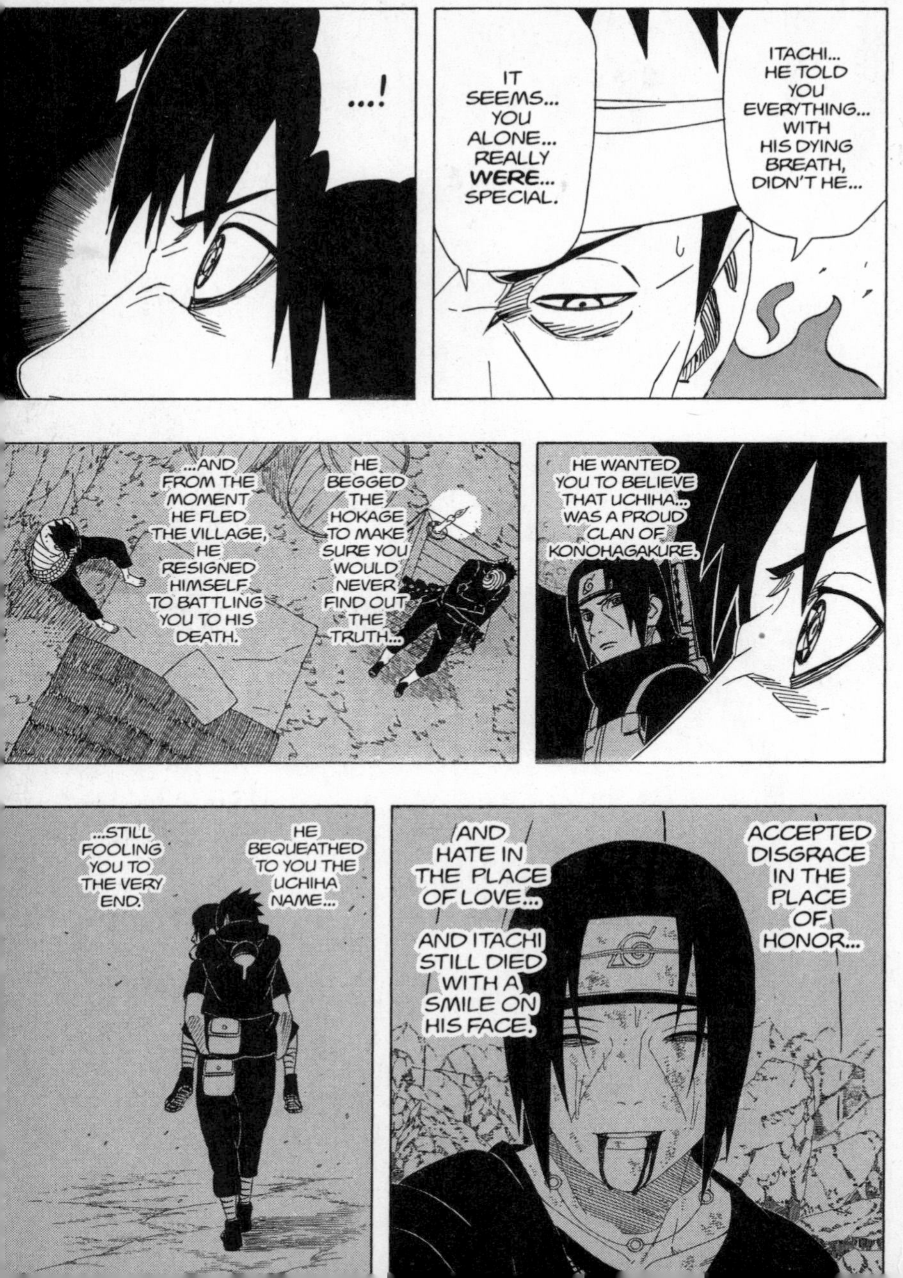

ITACHI... HE TOLD YOU EVERYTHING... WITH HIS DYING BREATH, DIDN'T HE...
IT SEEMS... YOU ALONE... REALLY **WERE**... SPECIAL.
...!
HE WANTED YOU TO BELIEVE THAT UCHIHA... WAS A PROUD CLAN OF KONOHAGAKURE.
HE BEGGED THE HOKAGE TO MAKE SURE YOU WOULD NEVER FIND OUT THE TRUTH...
...AND FROM THE MOMENT HE FLED THE VILLAGE, HE RESIGNED HIMSELF TO BATTLING YOU TO HIS DEATH.
ACCEPTED DISGRACE IN THE PLACE OF HONOR...
AND HATE IN THE PLACE OF LOVE...
AND ITACHI STILL DIED WITH A SMILE ON HIS FACE.
HE BEQUEATHED TO YOU THE UCHIHA NAME...
...STILL FOOLING YOU TO THE VERY END.

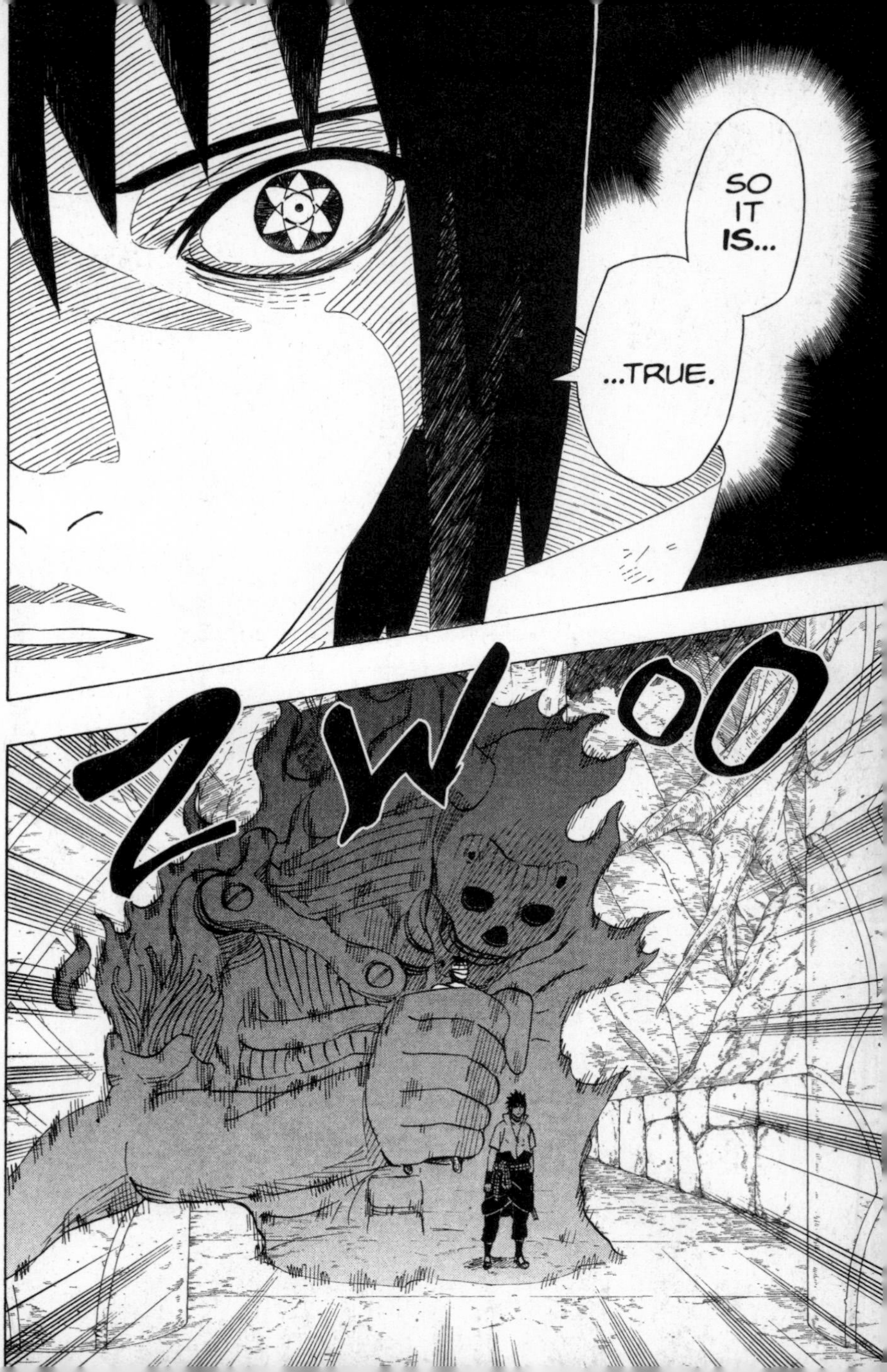
SO IT IS...
...TRUE.
ZWOO

READ THIS WAY

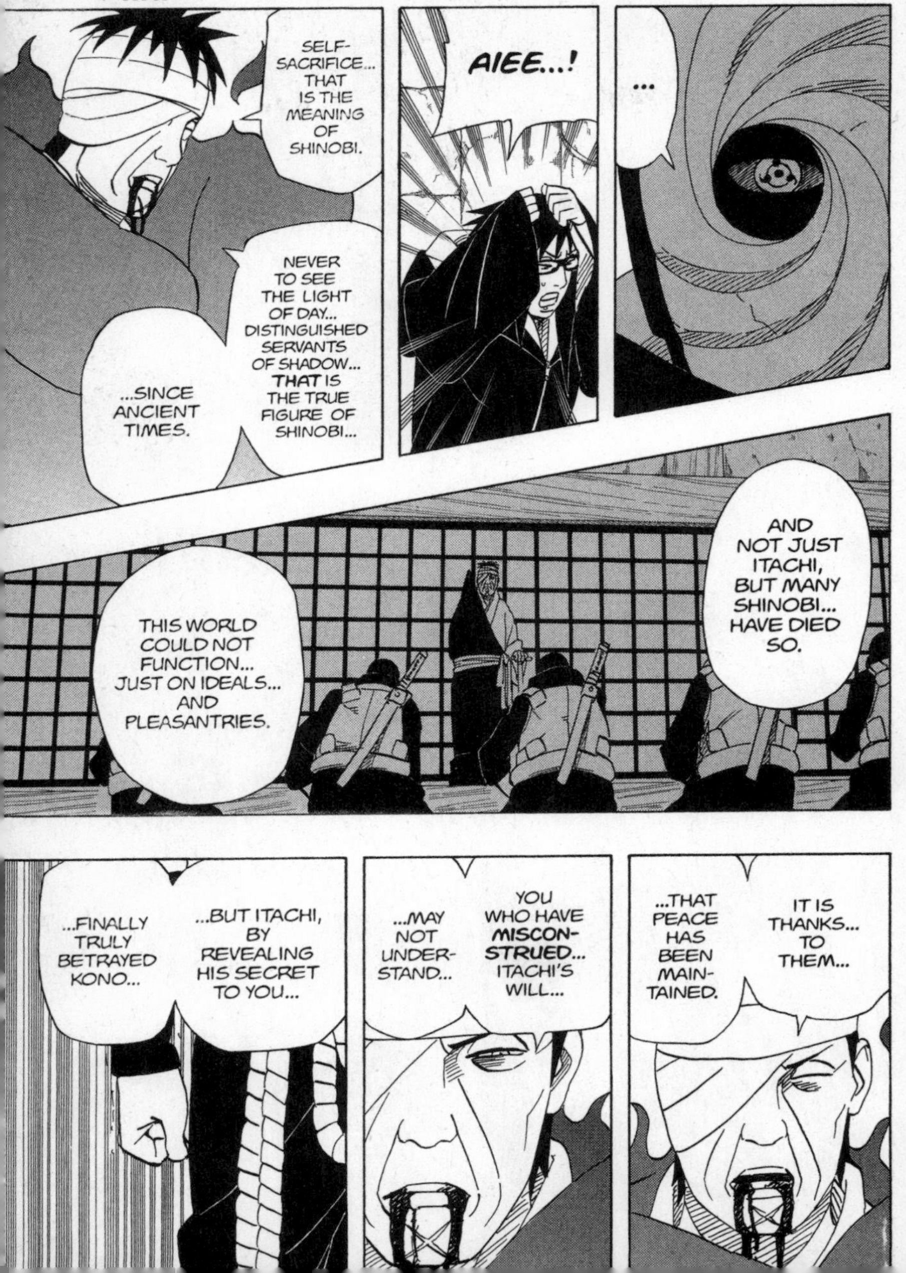
...
AIEE...!
SELF-SACRIFICE... THAT IS THE MEANING OF SHINOBI.
NEVER TO SEE THE LIGHT OF DAY... DISTINGUISHED SERVANTS OF SHADOW... **THAT** IS THE TRUE FIGURE OF SHINOBI...
...SINCE ANCIENT TIMES.
AND NOT JUST ITACHI, BUT MANY SHINOBI... HAVE DIED SO.
THIS WORLD COULD NOT FUNCTION... JUST ON IDEALS... AND PLEASANTRIES.
IT IS THANKS... TO THEM...
...THAT PEACE HAS BEEN MAIN-TAINED.
YOU WHO HAVE **MISCON-STRUED**... ITACHI'S WILL...
...MAY NOT UNDER-STAND...
...BUT ITACHI, BY REVEALING HIS SECRET TO YOU...
...FINALLY TRULY BETRAYED KONO...

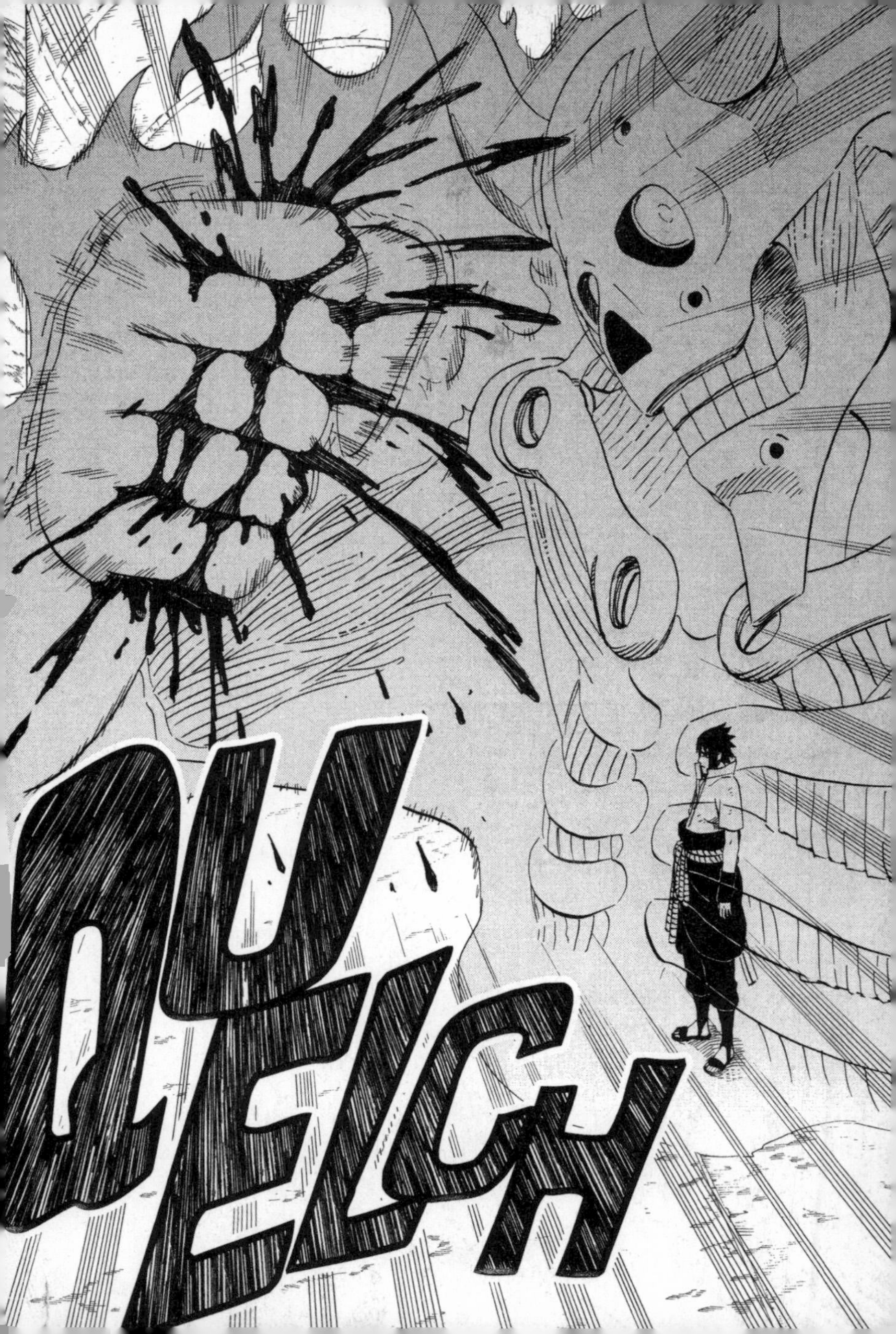
SQUELCH

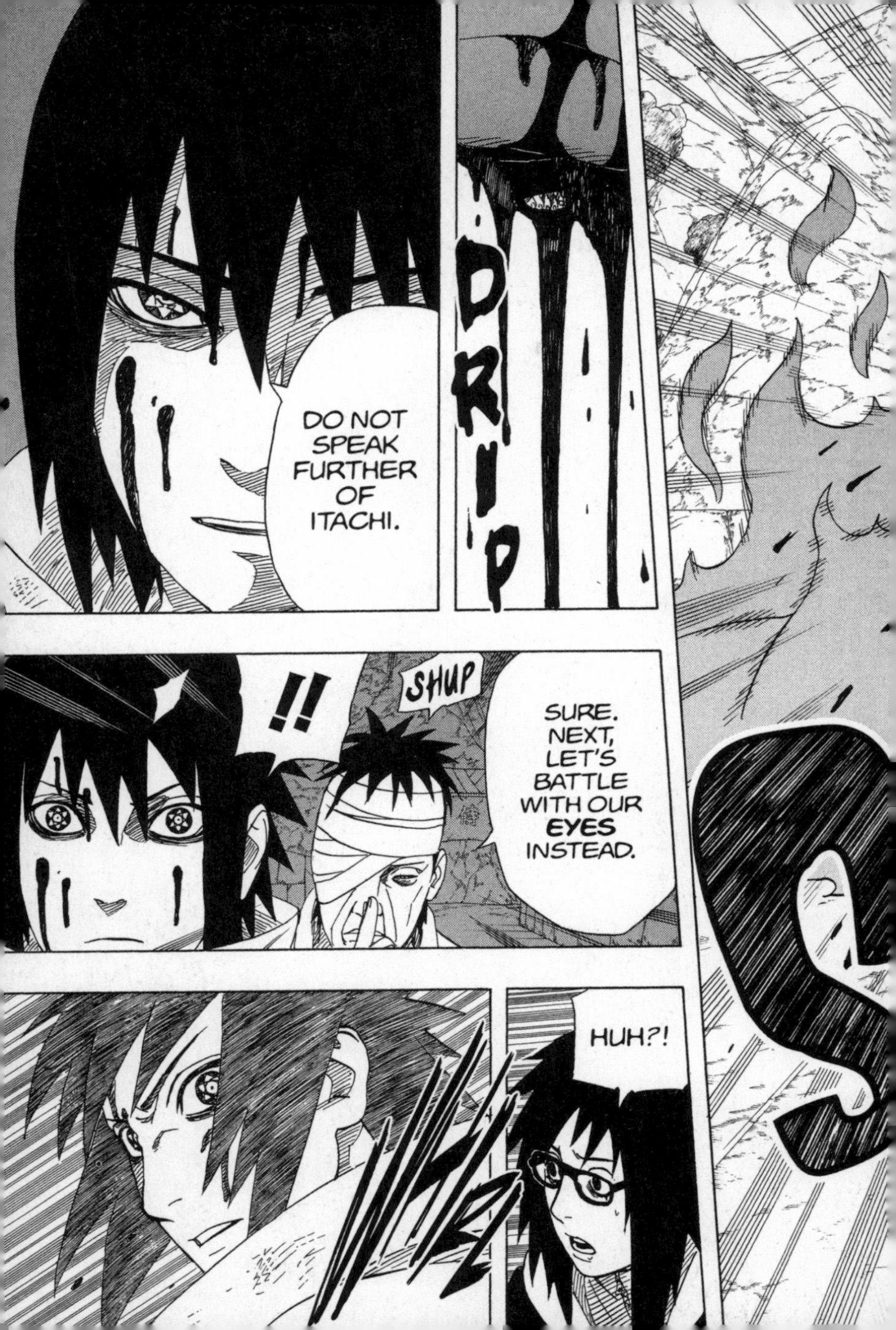
DRIP
DO NOT SPEAK FURTHER OF ITACHI.
SURE. NEXT, LET'S BATTLE WITH OUR EYES INSTEAD.
SHUP
!!
HUH?!

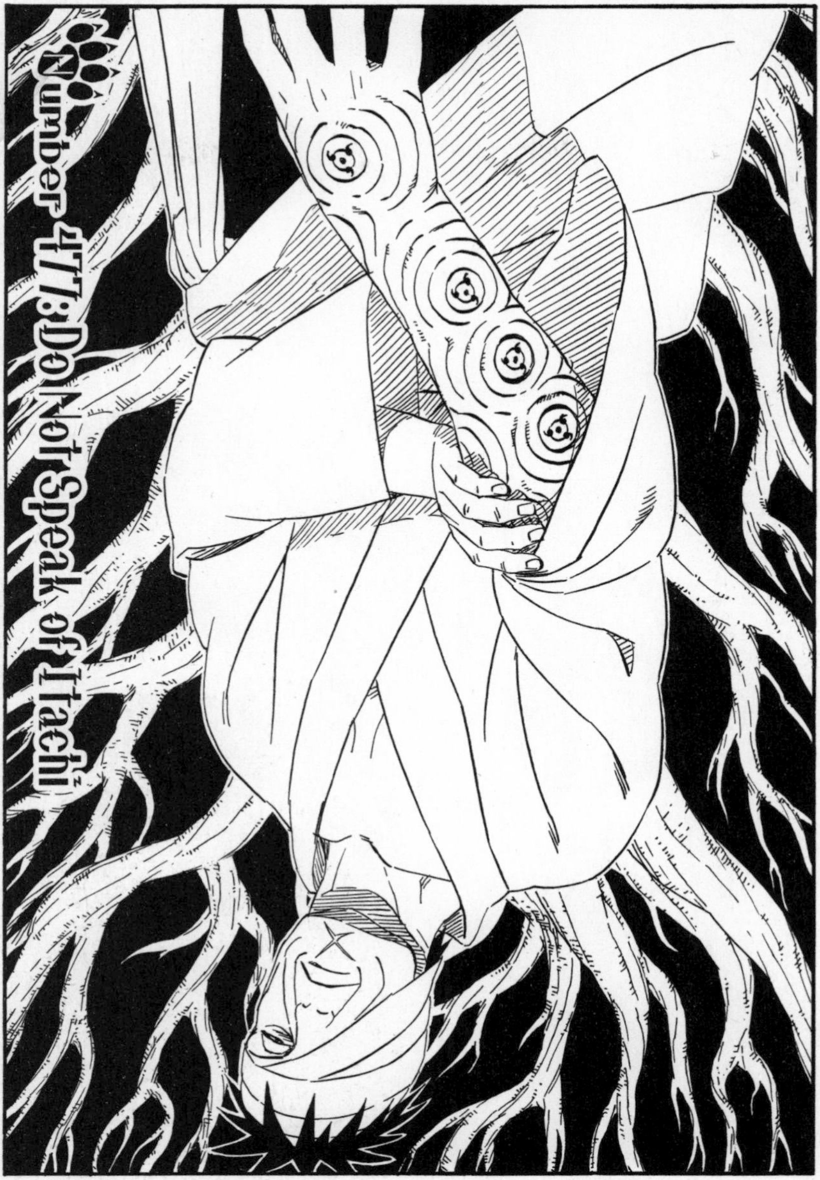
Number 477: Do Not Speak of Itachi

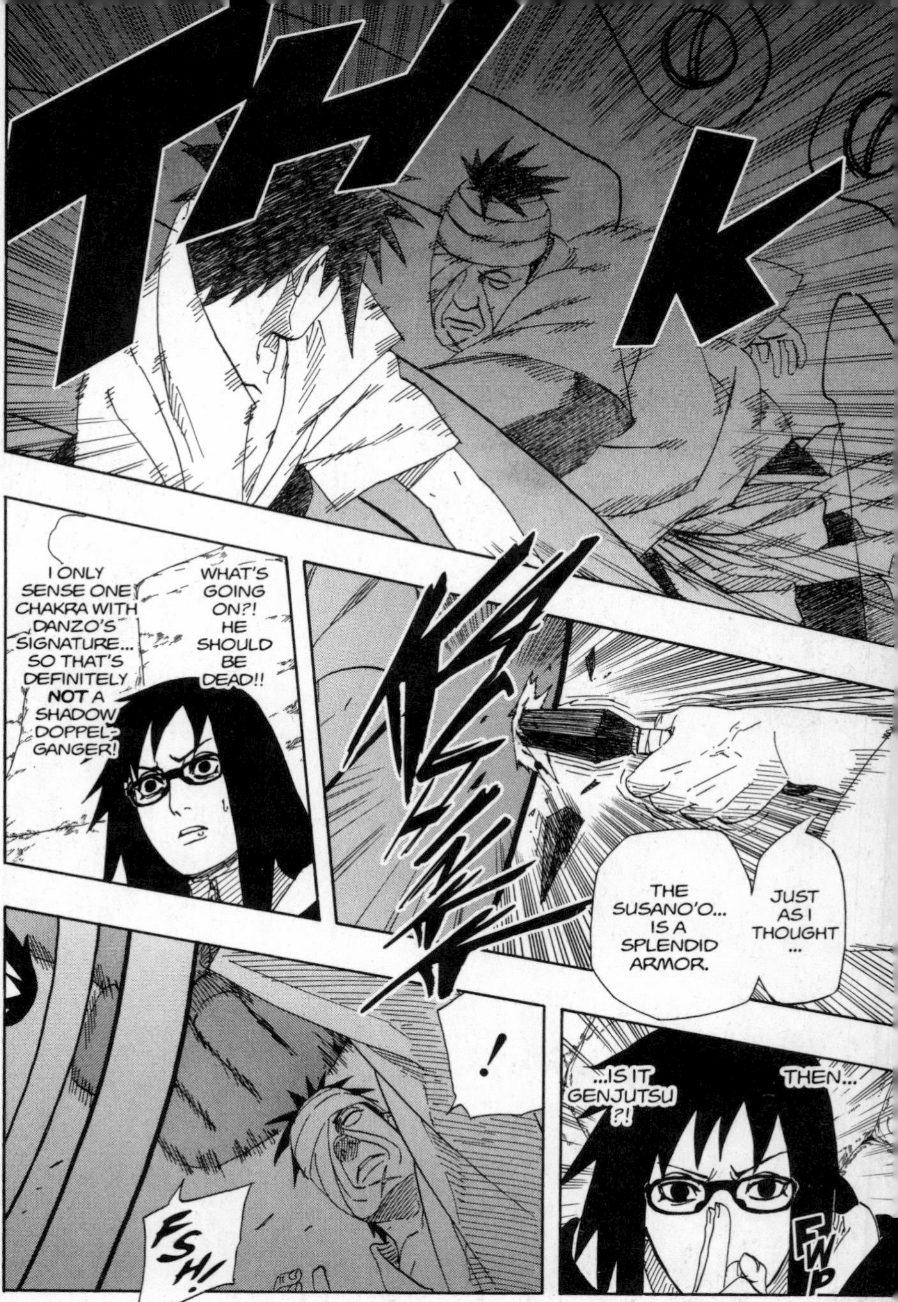
JUST AS I THOUGHT...
THE SUSANO'O... IS A SPLENDID ARMOR.
WHAT'S GOING ON?! HE SHOULD BE DEAD!!
I ONLY SENSE ONE CHAKRA WITH DANZO'S SIGNATURE... SO THAT'S DEFINITELY NOT A SHADOW DOPPELGANGER!
THEN...
...IS IT GENJUTSU?!
FWP
!
FSH!

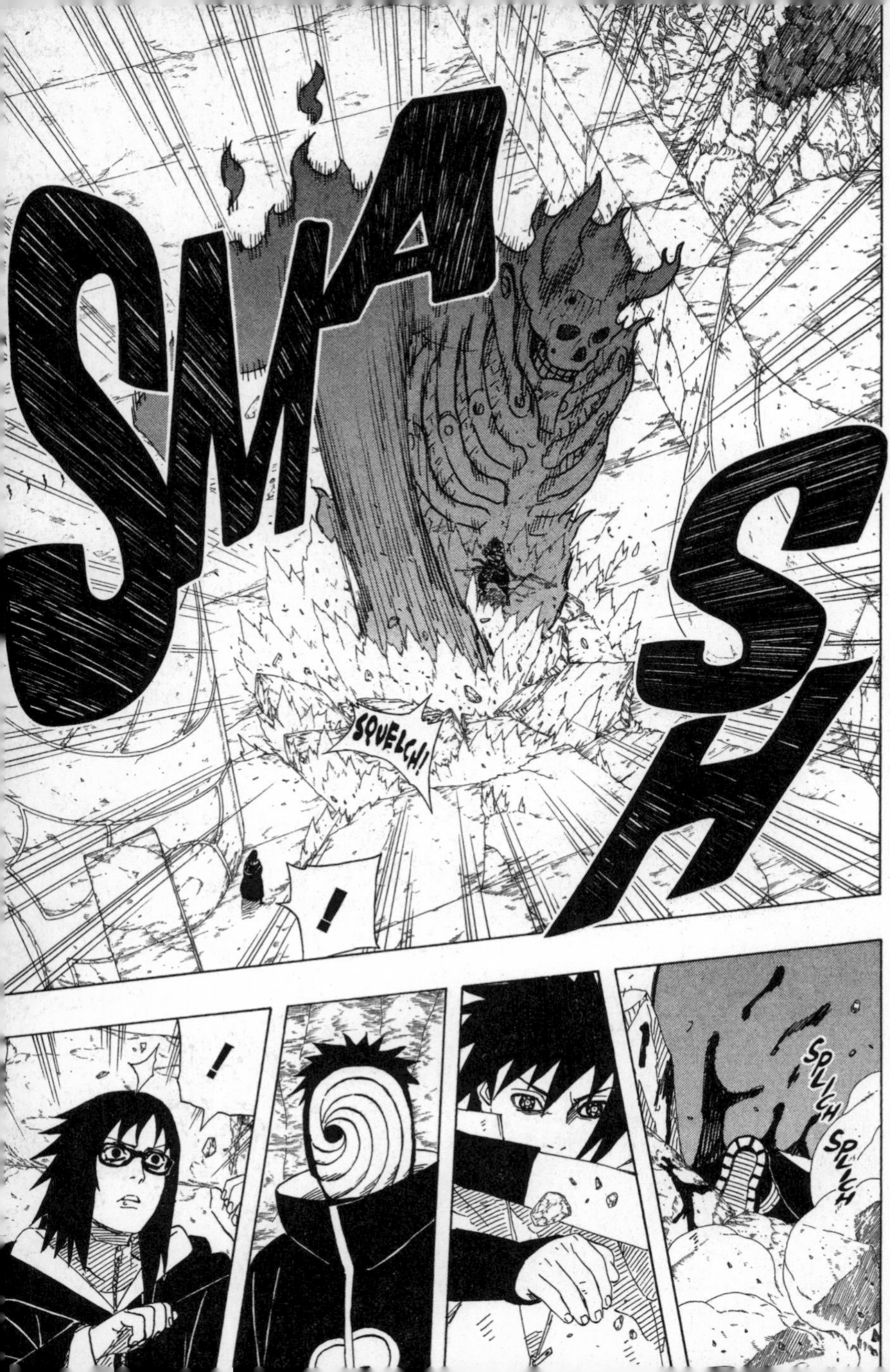
SWASH
SQUELCH!
!
!
SPLCH
SPLCH

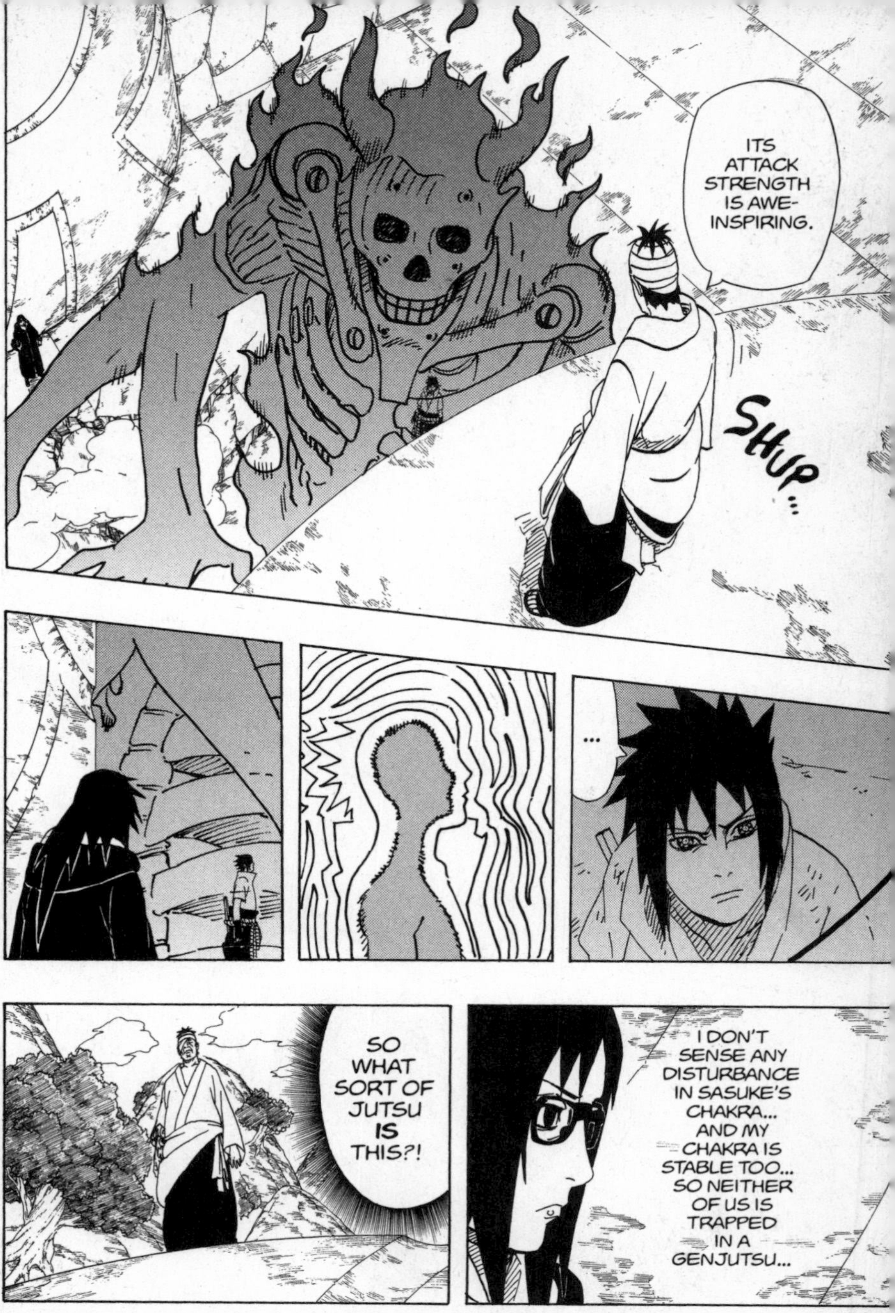
ITS ATTACK STRENGTH IS AWE-INSPIRING.
SHUP...
...
I DON'T SENSE ANY DISTURBANCE IN SASUKE'S CHAKRA... AND MY CHAKRA IS STABLE TOO... SO NEITHER OF US IS TRAPPED IN A GENJUTSU...
SO WHAT SORT OF JUTSU IS THIS?!

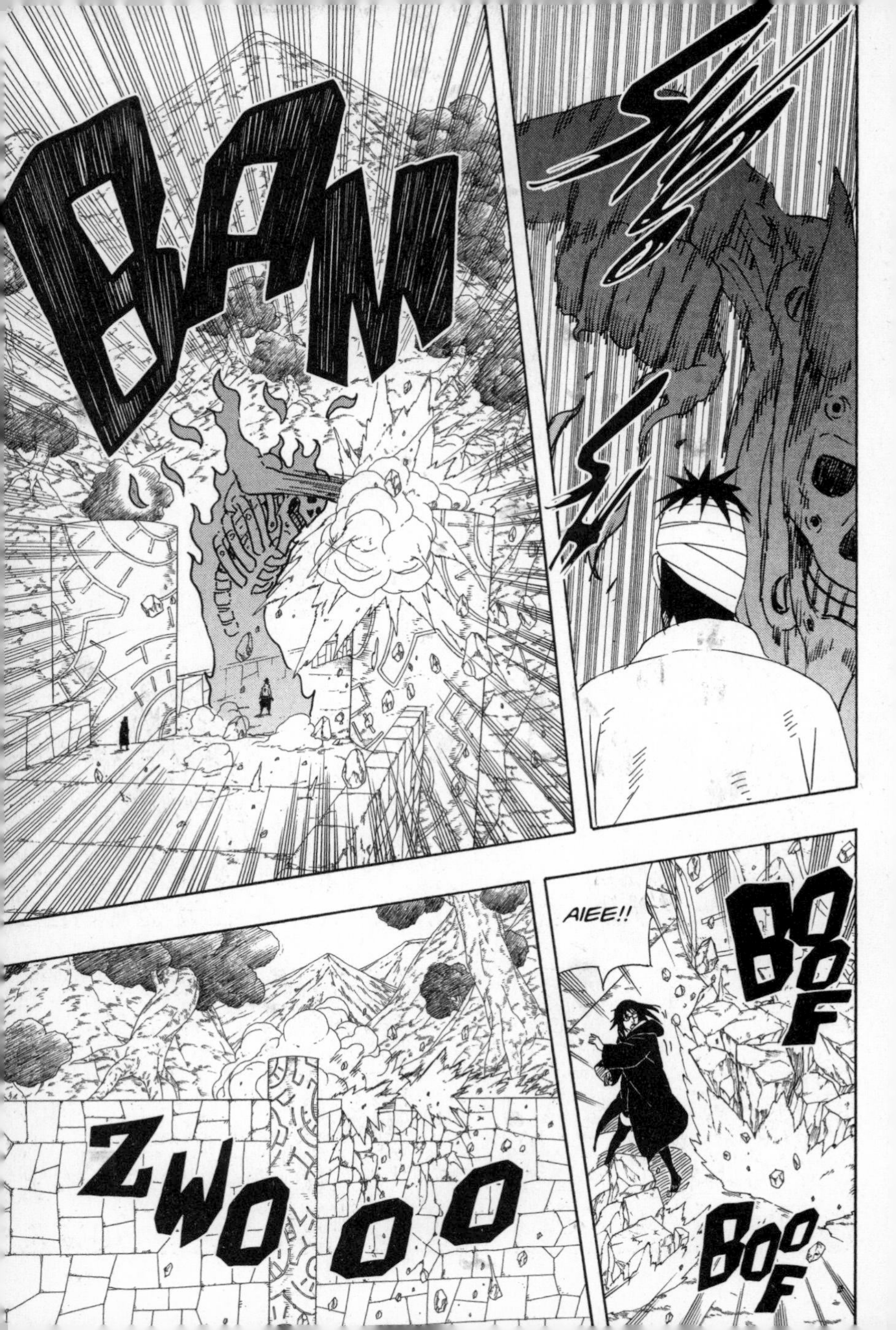
BAM
AIEE!!
BOOF
BOOF
ZWOOOO

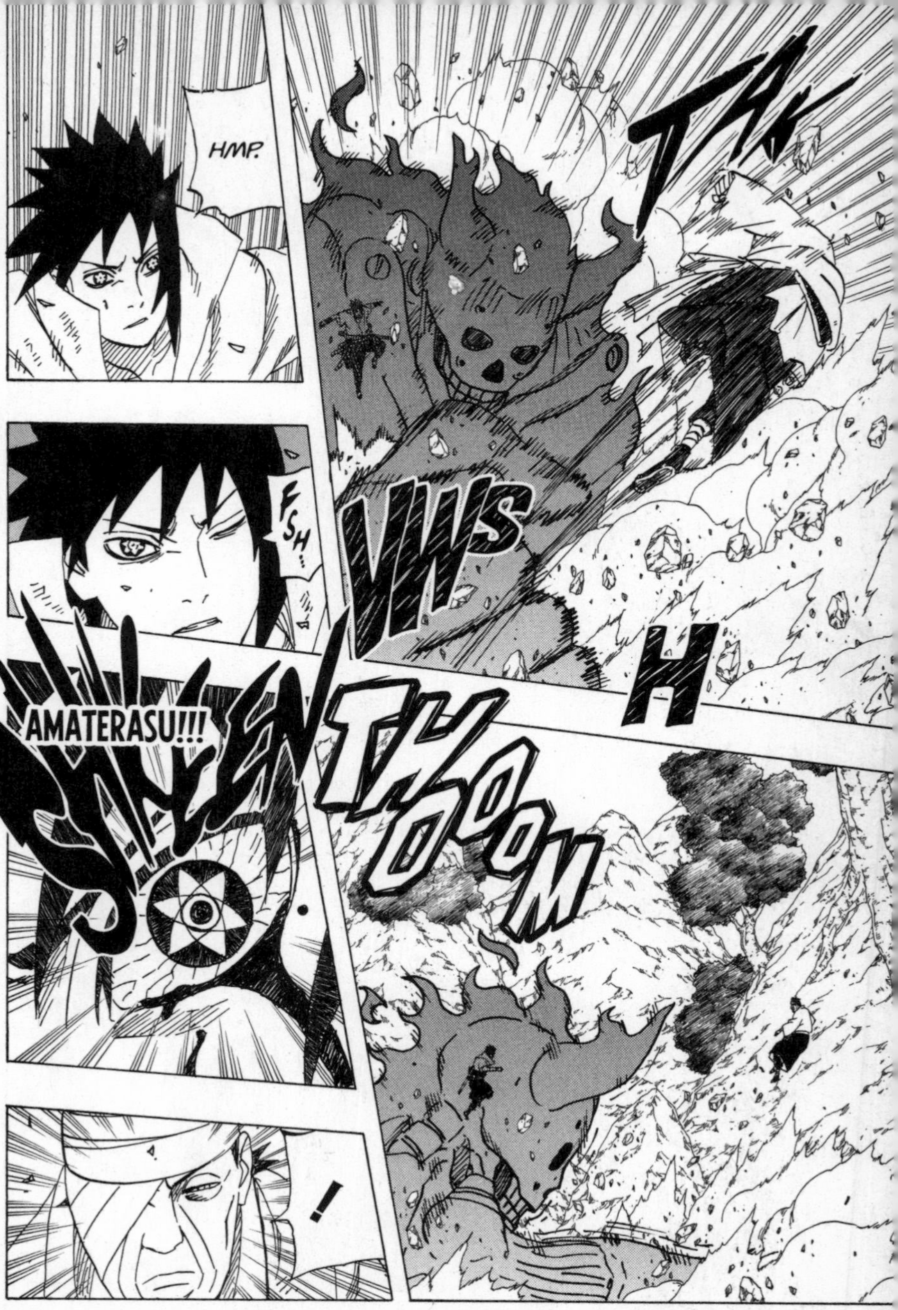
TAK
HMP.
VWSH
FSH...
AMATERASU!!!
THOOOM
!

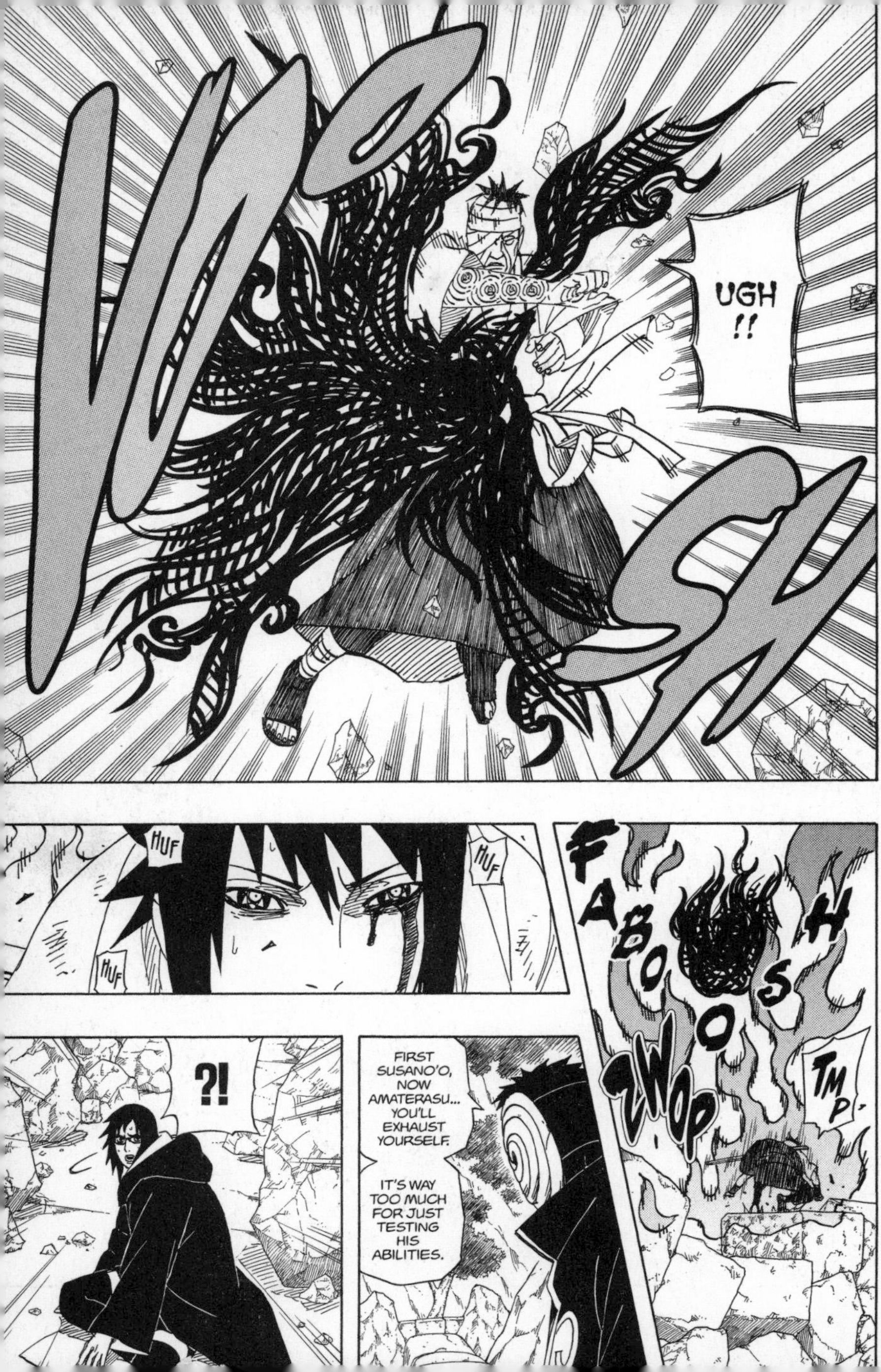
UGH !!
ZWOP
TMP
HUF
HUF
HUF
FIRST SUSANO'O, NOW AMATERASU... YOU'LL EXHAUST YOURSELF.
IT'S WAY TOO MUCH FOR JUST TESTING HIS ABILITIES.
?!

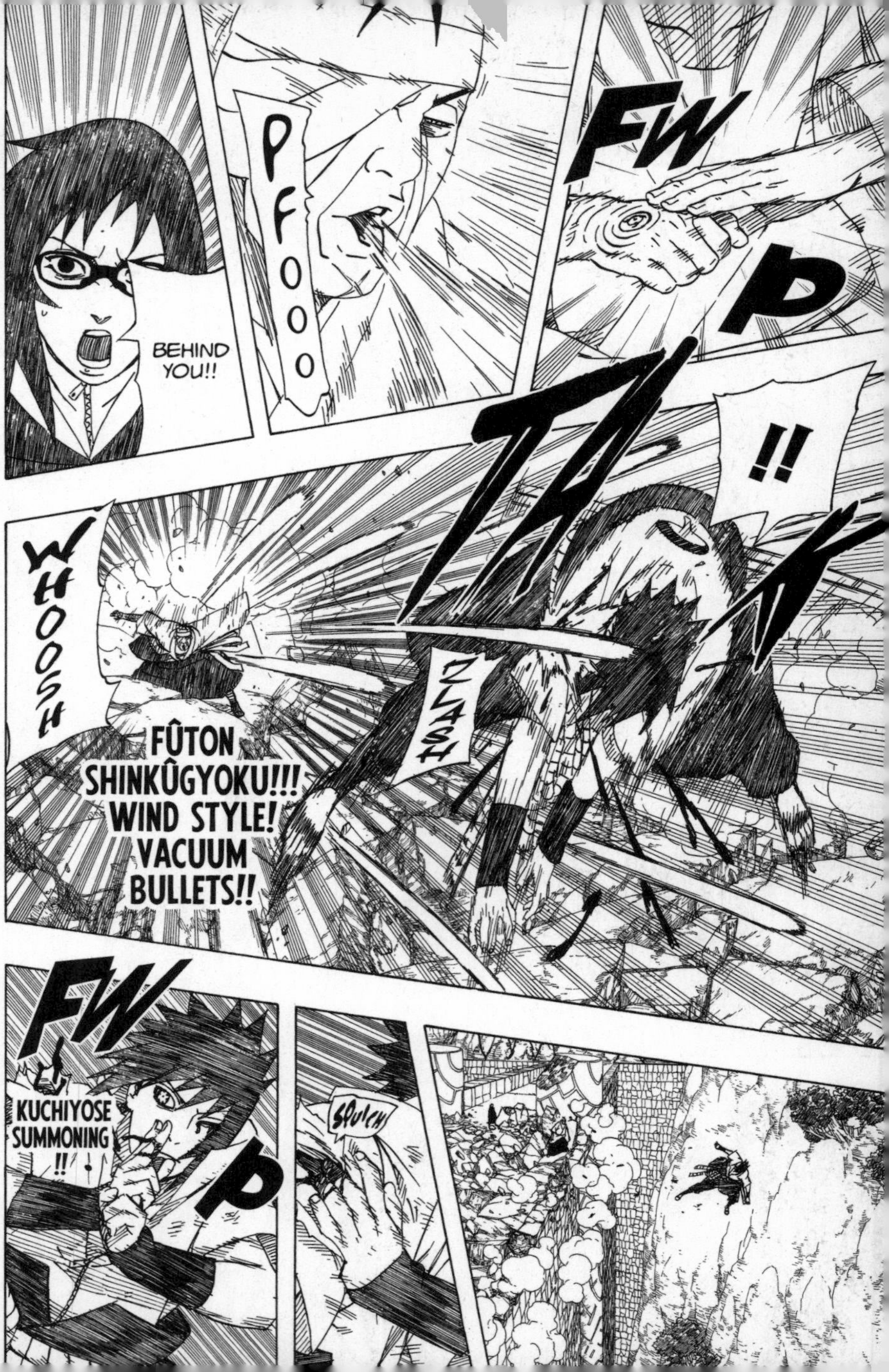
FWP
PFOOOO
BEHIND YOU!!
!!
THAK
WHOOOSH
ZLASH
FÛTON SHINKÛGYOKU!!!
WIND STYLE! VACUUM BULLETS!!
SPLUCH
FWP
KUCHIYOSE SUMMONING !!

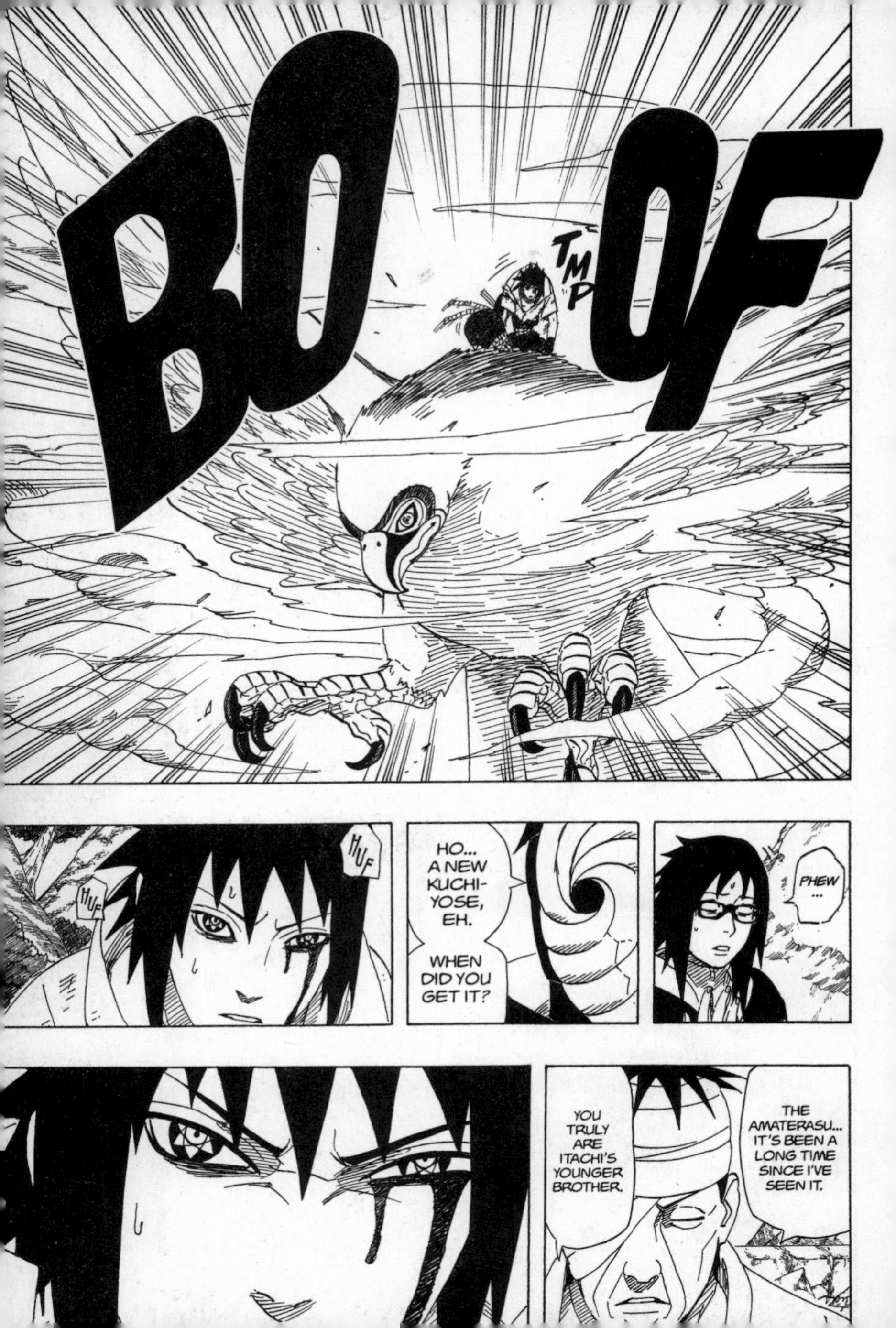
BOOF
TMP
PHEW...
HO... A NEW KUCHI-YOSE, EH.
WHEN DID YOU GET IT?
HUF
HUF
THE AMATERASU... IT'S BEEN A LONG TIME SINCE I'VE SEEN IT.
YOU TRULY ARE ITACHI'S YOUNGER BROTHER.

....!

FLAP

FLAP

....!

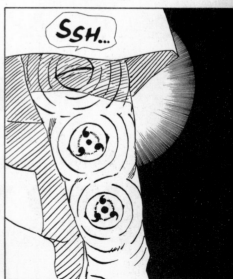

SSH...

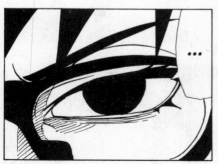

....

READ THIS WAY

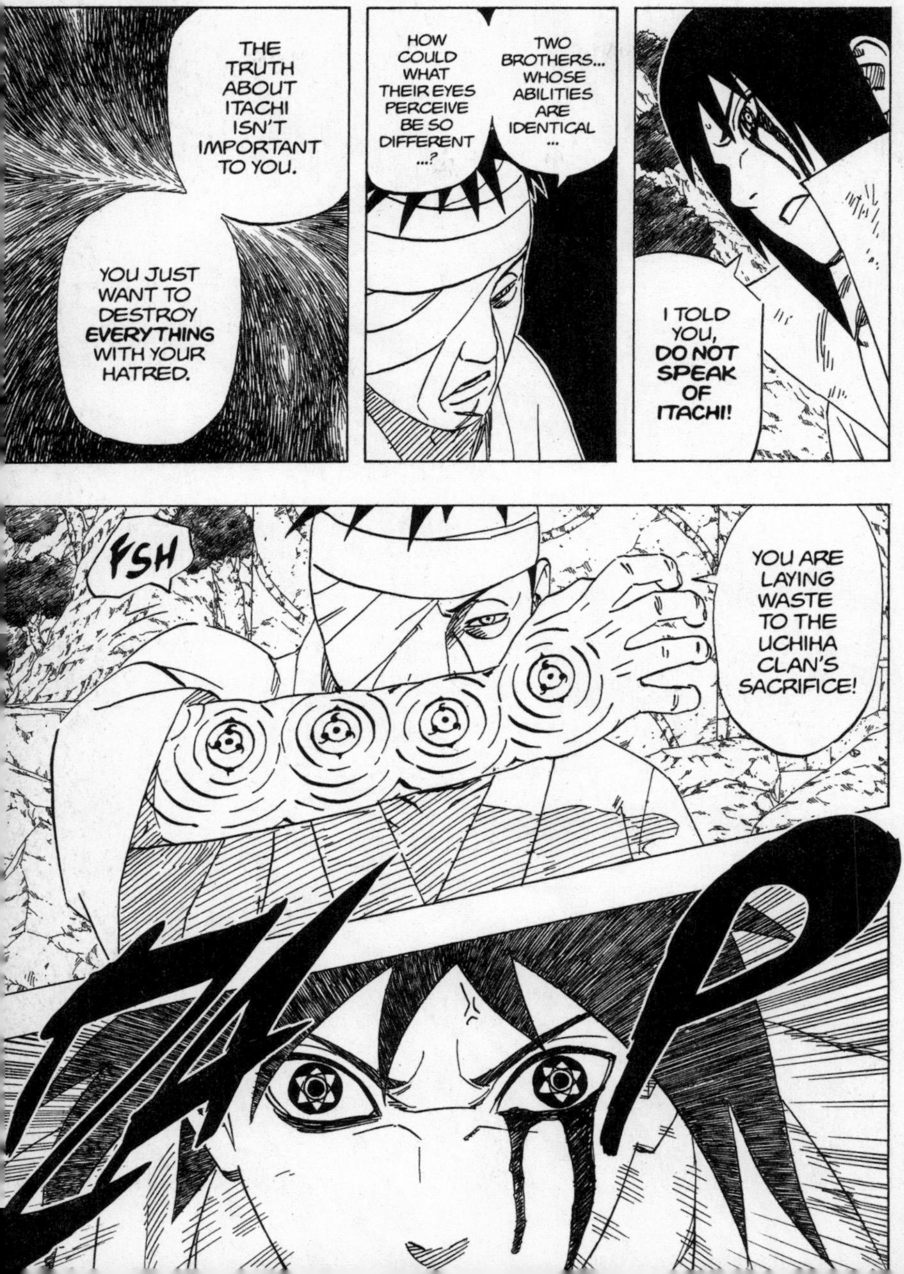
I TOLD YOU, DO NOT SPEAK OF ITACHI!
TWO BROTHERS... WHOSE ABILITIES ARE IDENTICAL ...
HOW COULD WHAT THEIR EYES PERCEIVE BE SO DIFFERENT ...?
THE TRUTH ABOUT ITACHI ISN'T IMPORTANT TO YOU.
YOU JUST WANT TO DESTROY EVERYTHING WITH YOUR HATRED.
YOU ARE LAYING WASTE TO THE UCHIHA CLAN'S SACRIFICE!
FSH

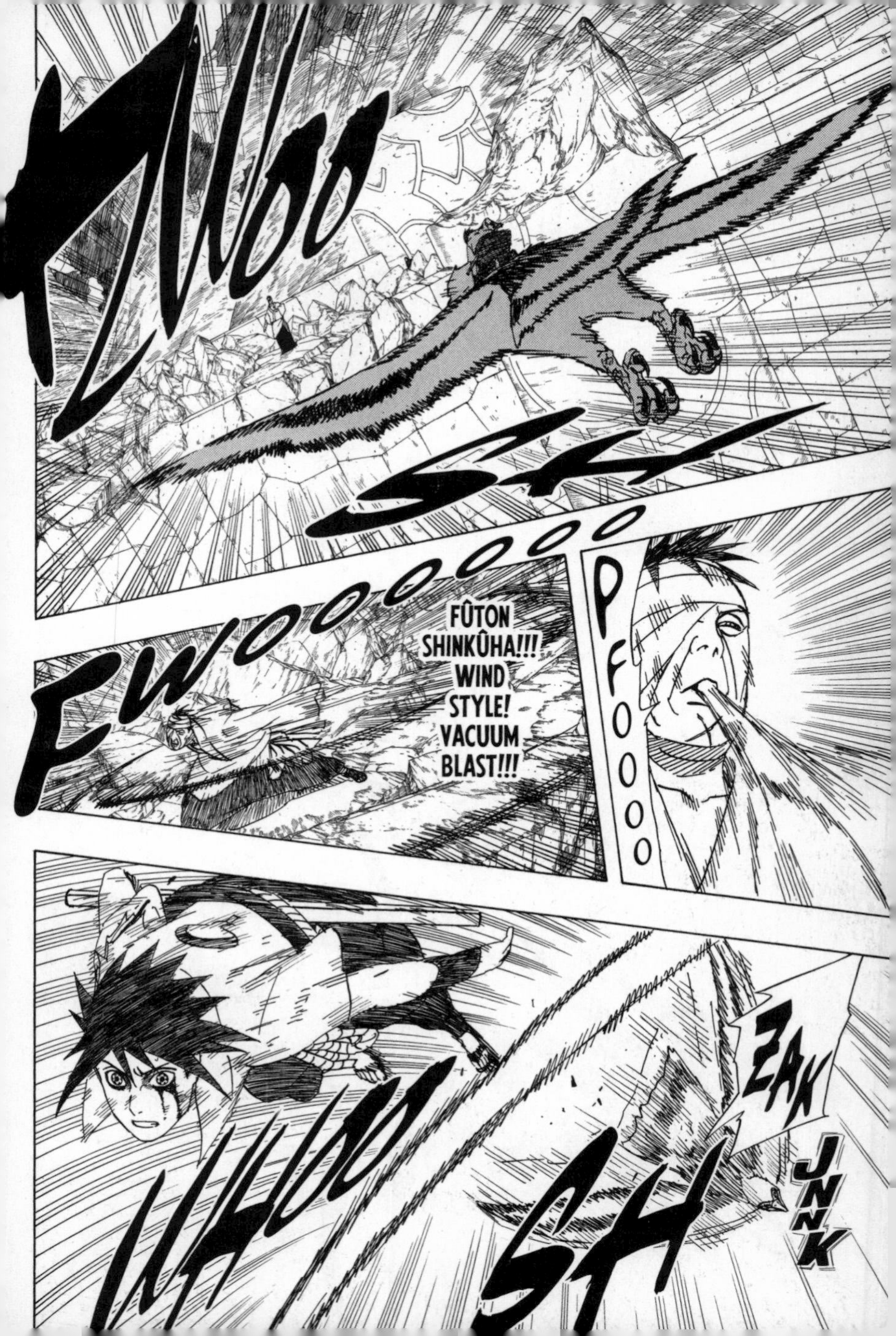
ZWOO
SH
FWOOOOOOO
PFOOOO
FÛTON SHINKÛHA!!! WIND STYLE! VACUUM BLAST!!!
ZAK
JNNK
WHOOSH

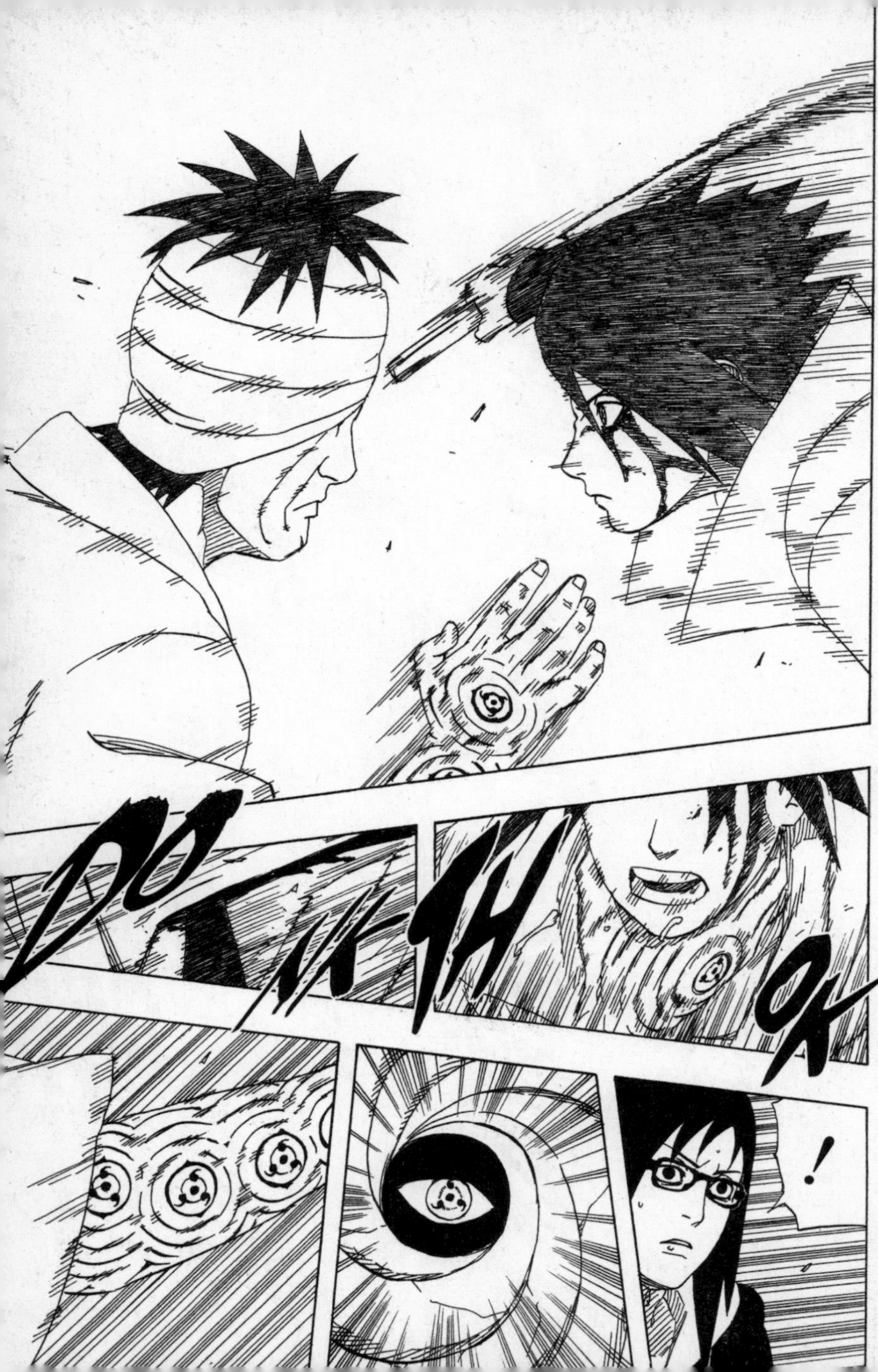

!

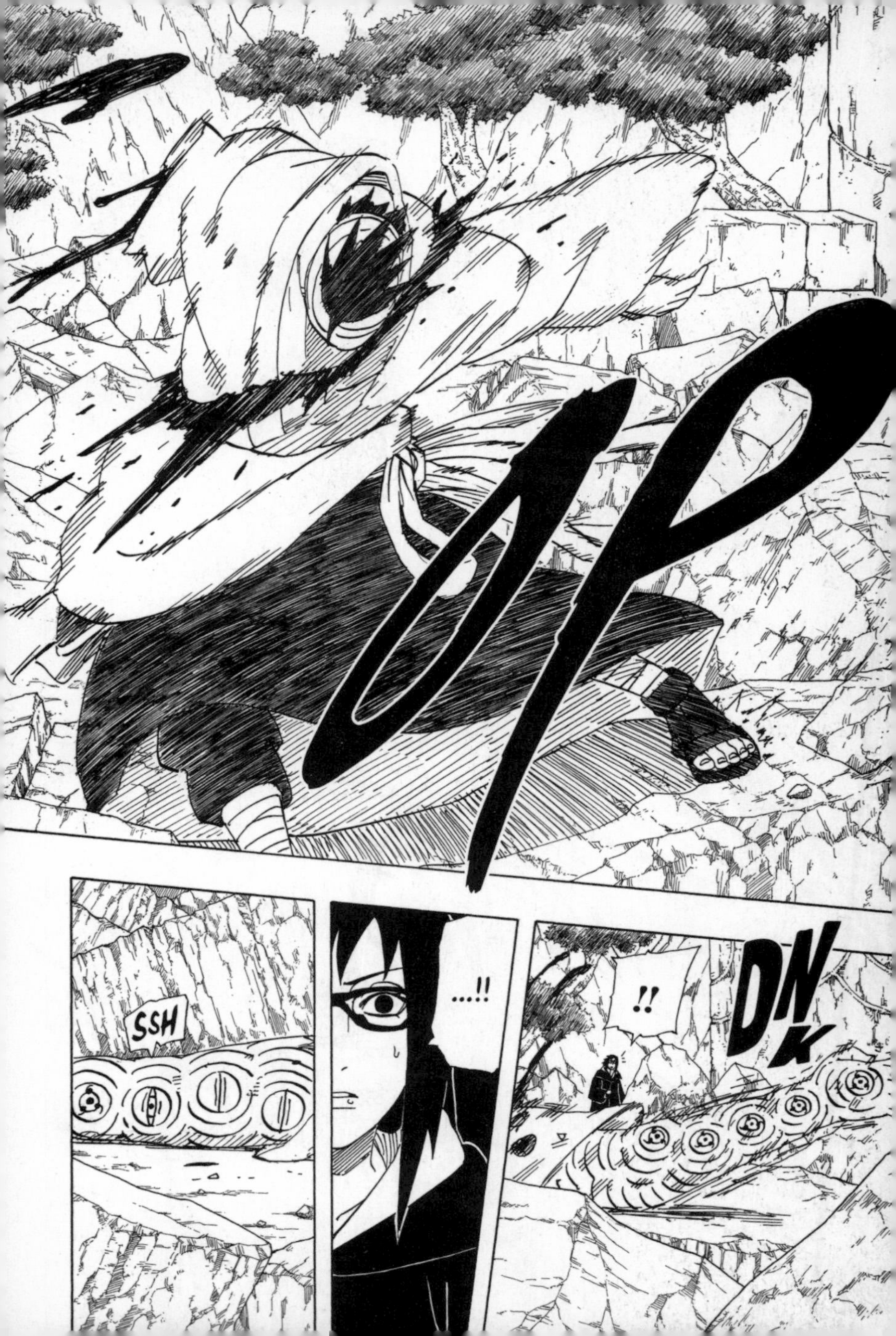

DNK
!!
...!!
SSH

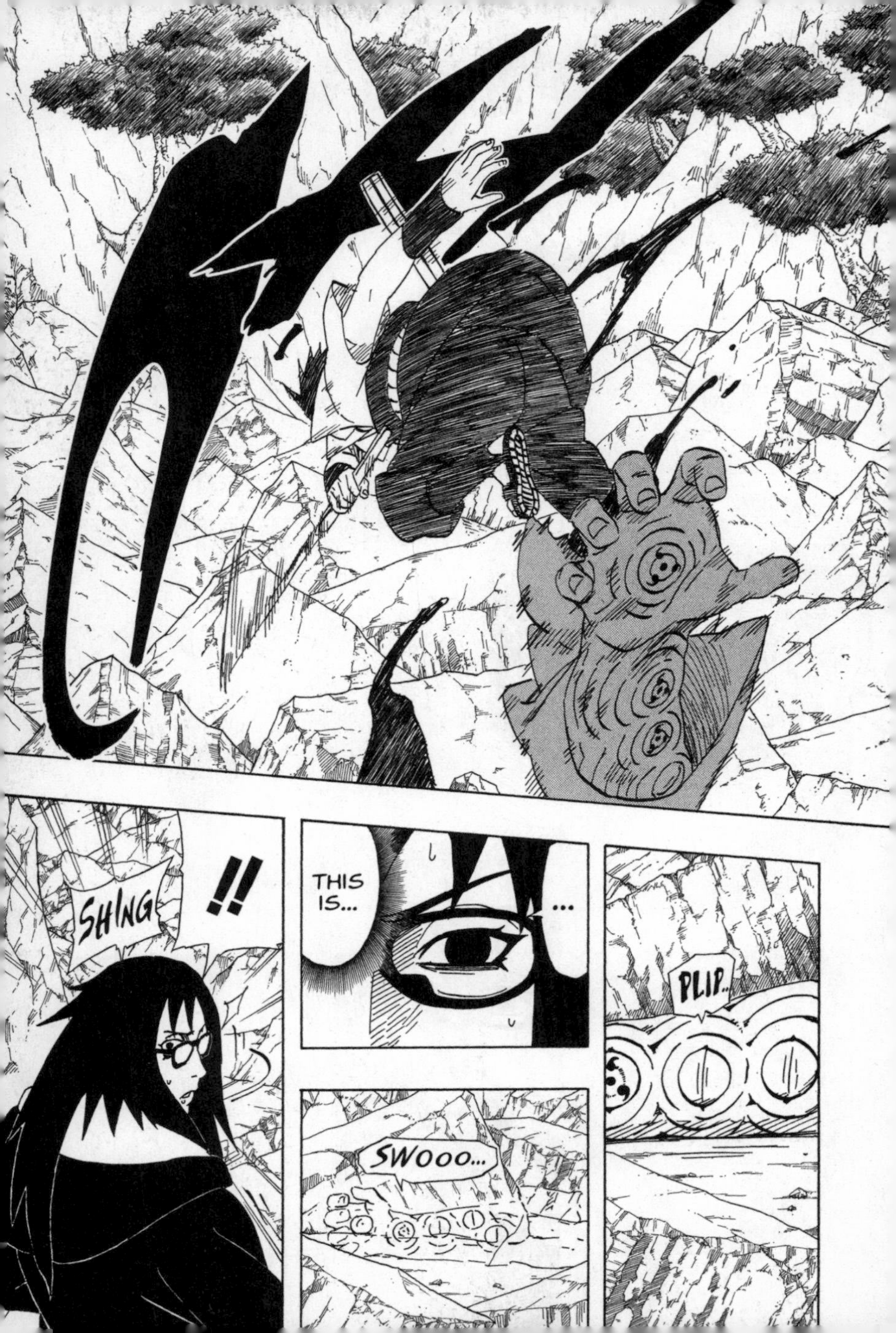
PLIP..
THIS IS...
...
SWOOO...
SHING!!

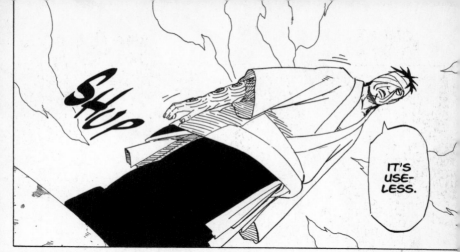

SHUP

IT'S USE-LESS.

GRRR

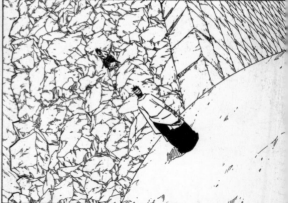

FLAP

FLAP

FLAP

FLAP

?!

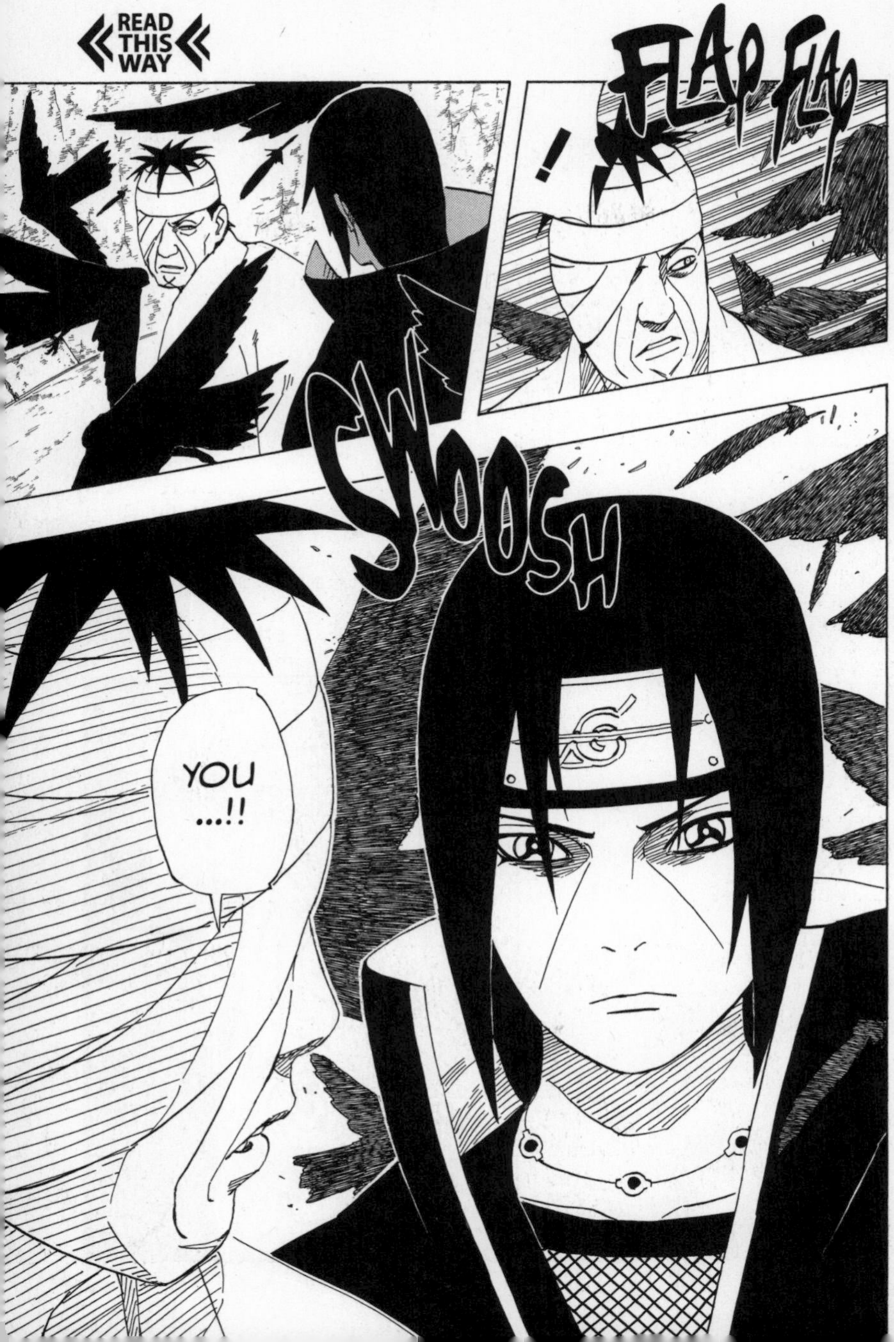
READ THIS WAY
FLAP FLAP
!
SWOOSH
YOU ...!!

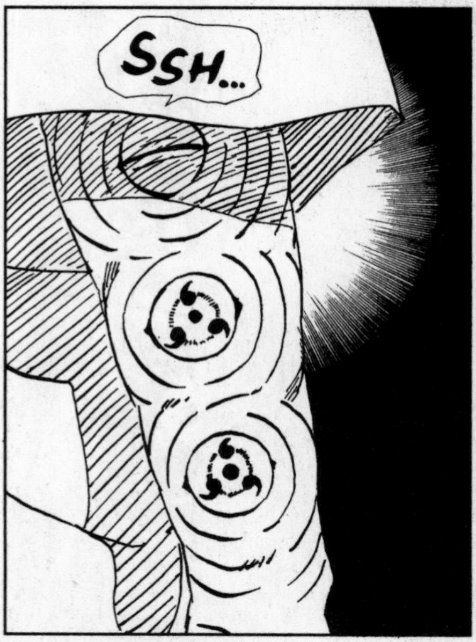
SSH...

Number 478:

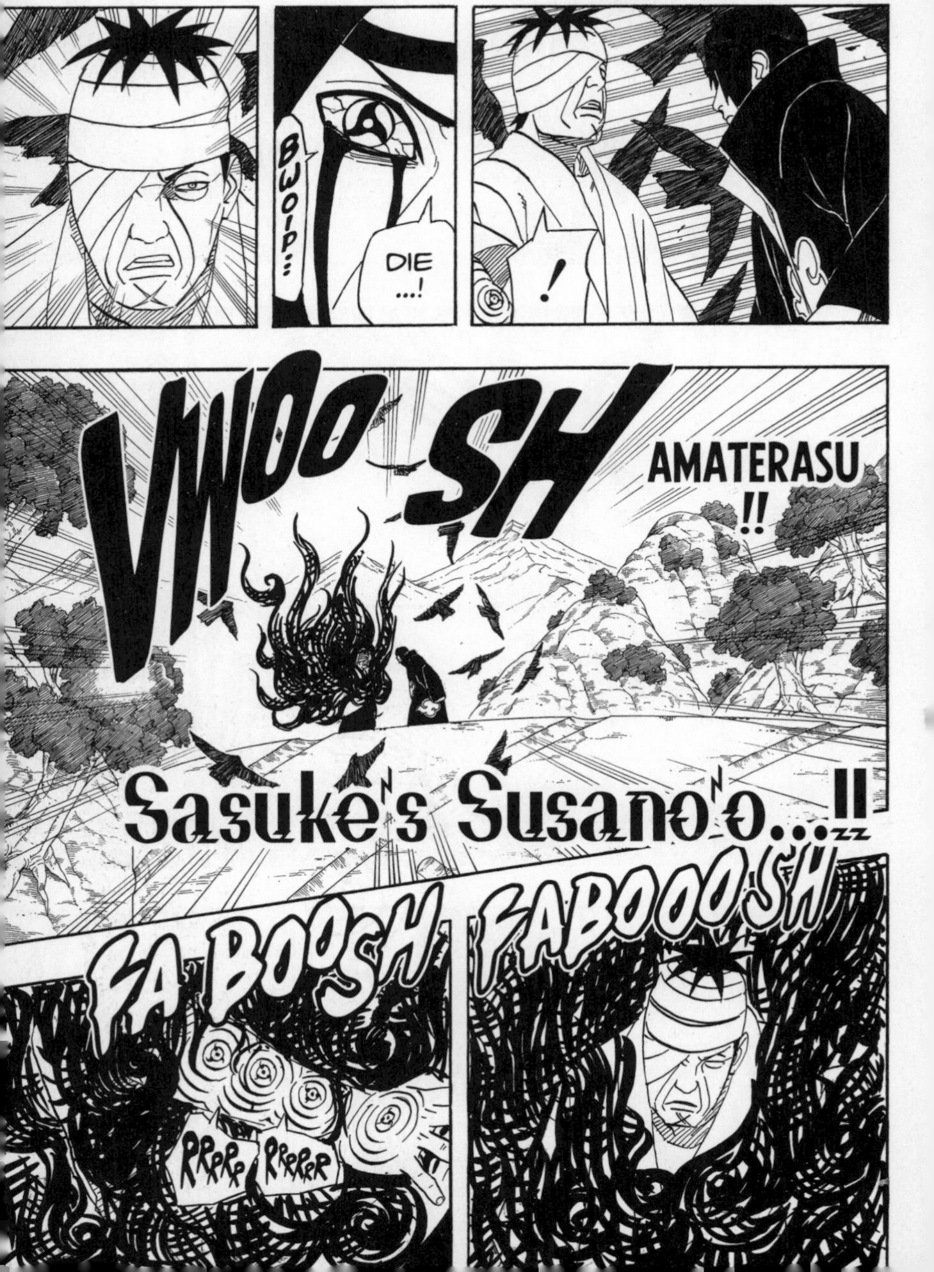
!
BWOIP...
DIE ...!
VWOOSH
AMATERASU!!
Sasuke's Susano'o...!!
FABOOOSH
FA BOOSH
RRRRR
RRRRRR

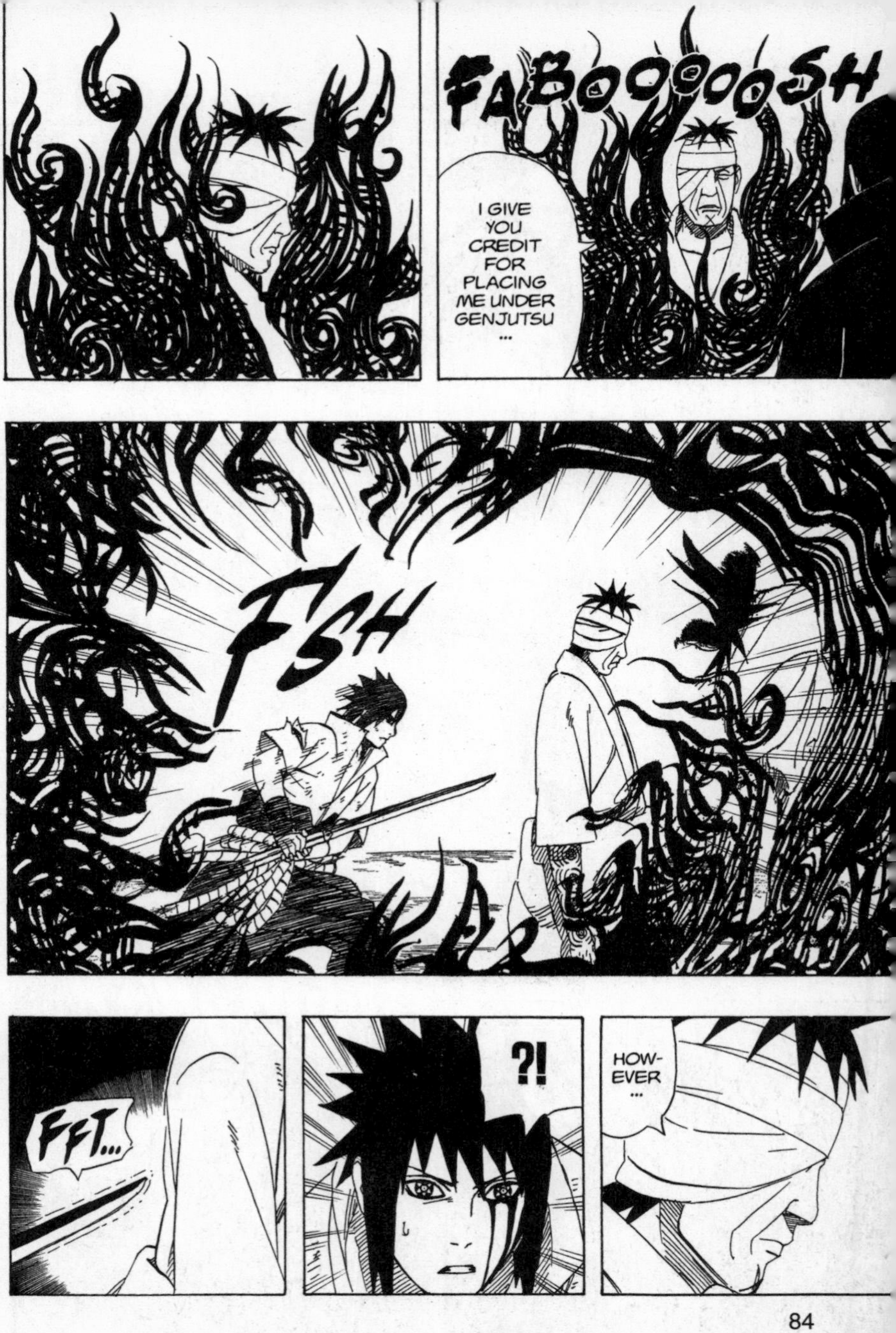
FABOOOOOSH
I GIVE YOU CREDIT FOR PLACING ME UNDER GENJUTSU ...
FSH
HOW-EVER ...
?!
FFT...

READ THIS WAY

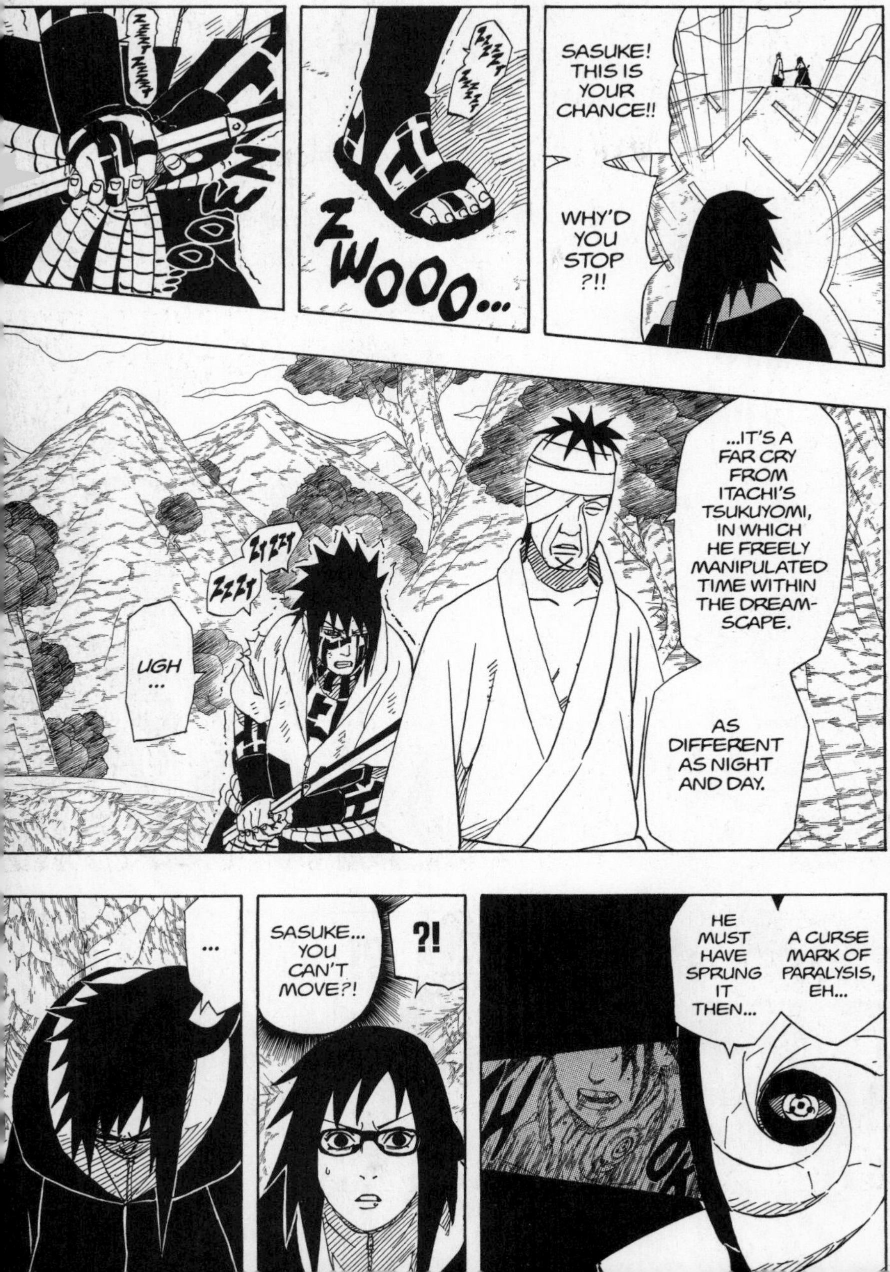
SASUKE! THIS IS YOUR CHANCE!!
WHY'D YOU STOP ?!!
ZWOOO...
...IT'S A FAR CRY FROM ITACHI'S TSUKUYOMI, IN WHICH HE FREELY MANIPULATED TIME WITHIN THE DREAM-SCAPE.
AS DIFFERENT AS NIGHT AND DAY.
UGH ...
A CURSE MARK OF PARALYSIS, EH...
HE MUST HAVE SPRUNG IT THEN...
?!
SASUKE... YOU CAN'T MOVE?!
...

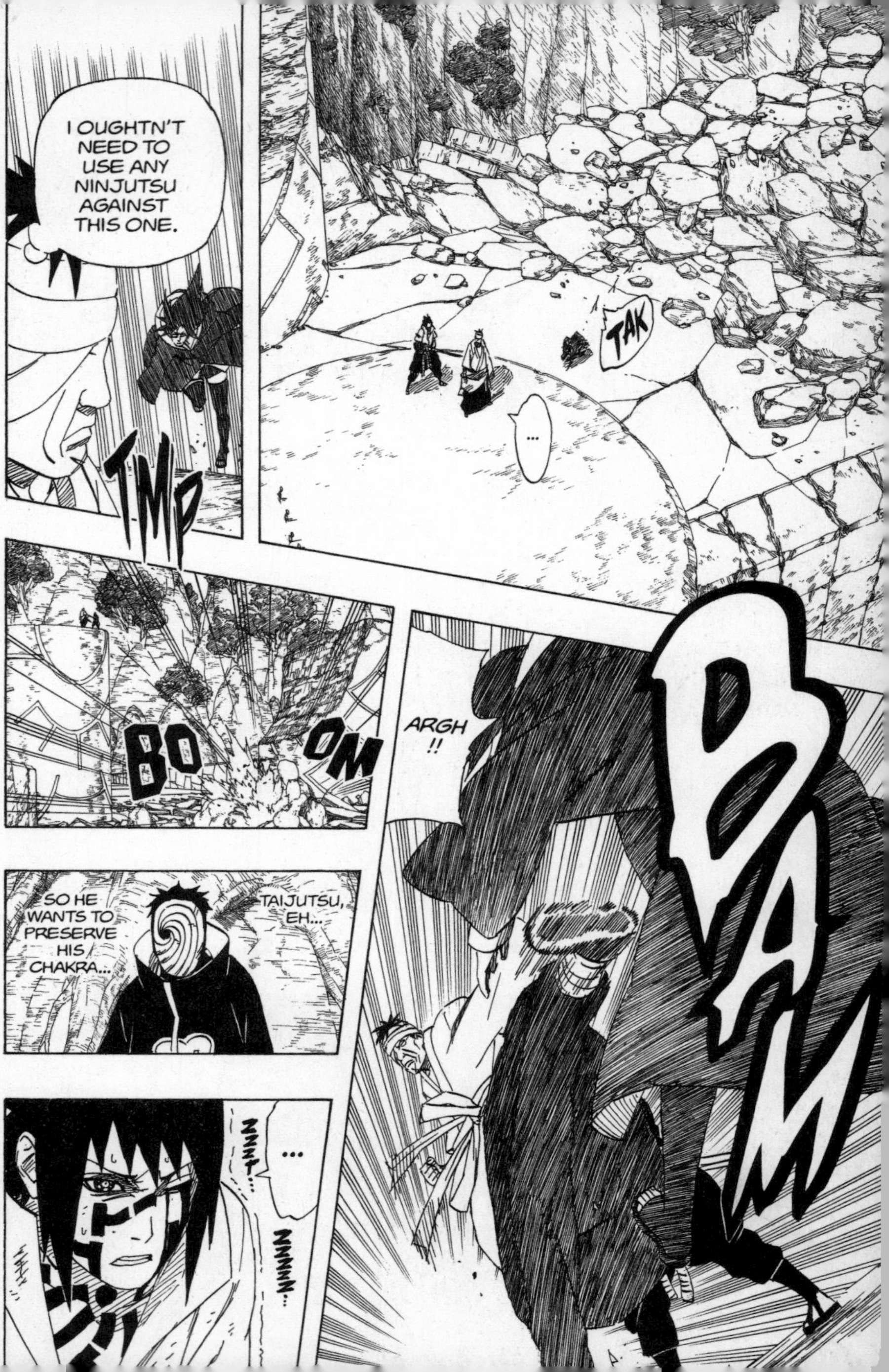
TAK
...
I OUGHTN'T NEED TO USE ANY NINJUTSU AGAINST THIS ONE.
TMP
DAM
ARGH !!
BOOM
TAIJUTSU, EH...
SO HE WANTS TO PRESERVE HIS CHAKRA...
...
ZZZZT...
ZZZZZ...

READ THIS WAY

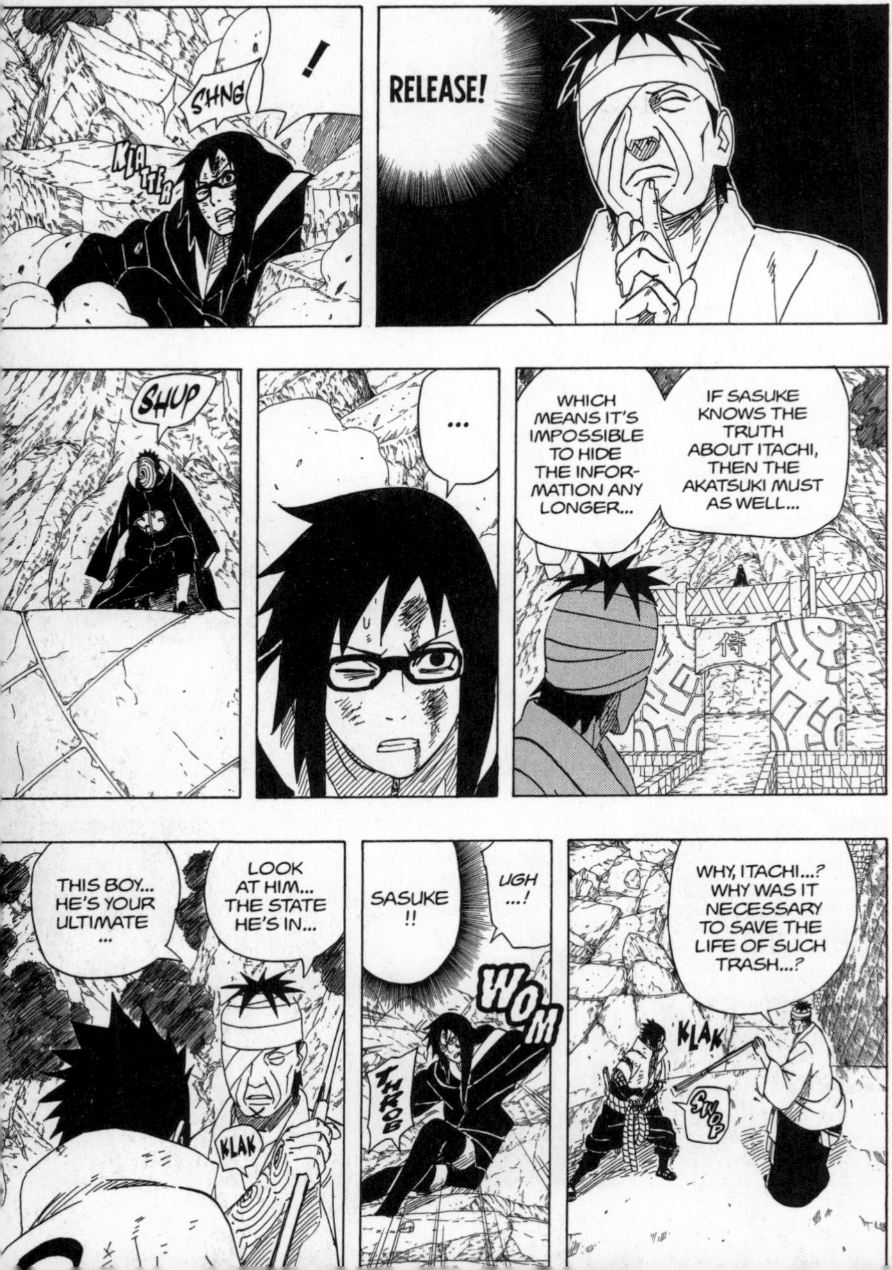
RELEASE!
!
SHNG
KLATTER
IF SASUKE KNOWS THE TRUTH ABOUT ITACHI, THEN THE AKATSUKI MUST AS WELL...
WHICH MEANS IT'S IMPOSSIBLE TO HIDE THE INFORMATION ANY LONGER...
...
SHUP
WHY, ITACHI...? WHY WAS IT NECESSARY TO SAVE THE LIFE OF SUCH TRASH...?
KLAK
SNOP
UGH ...!
SASUKE !!
WOM
THROB
LOOK AT HIM... THE STATE HE'S IN...
THIS BOY... HE'S YOUR ULTIMATE ...
KLAK

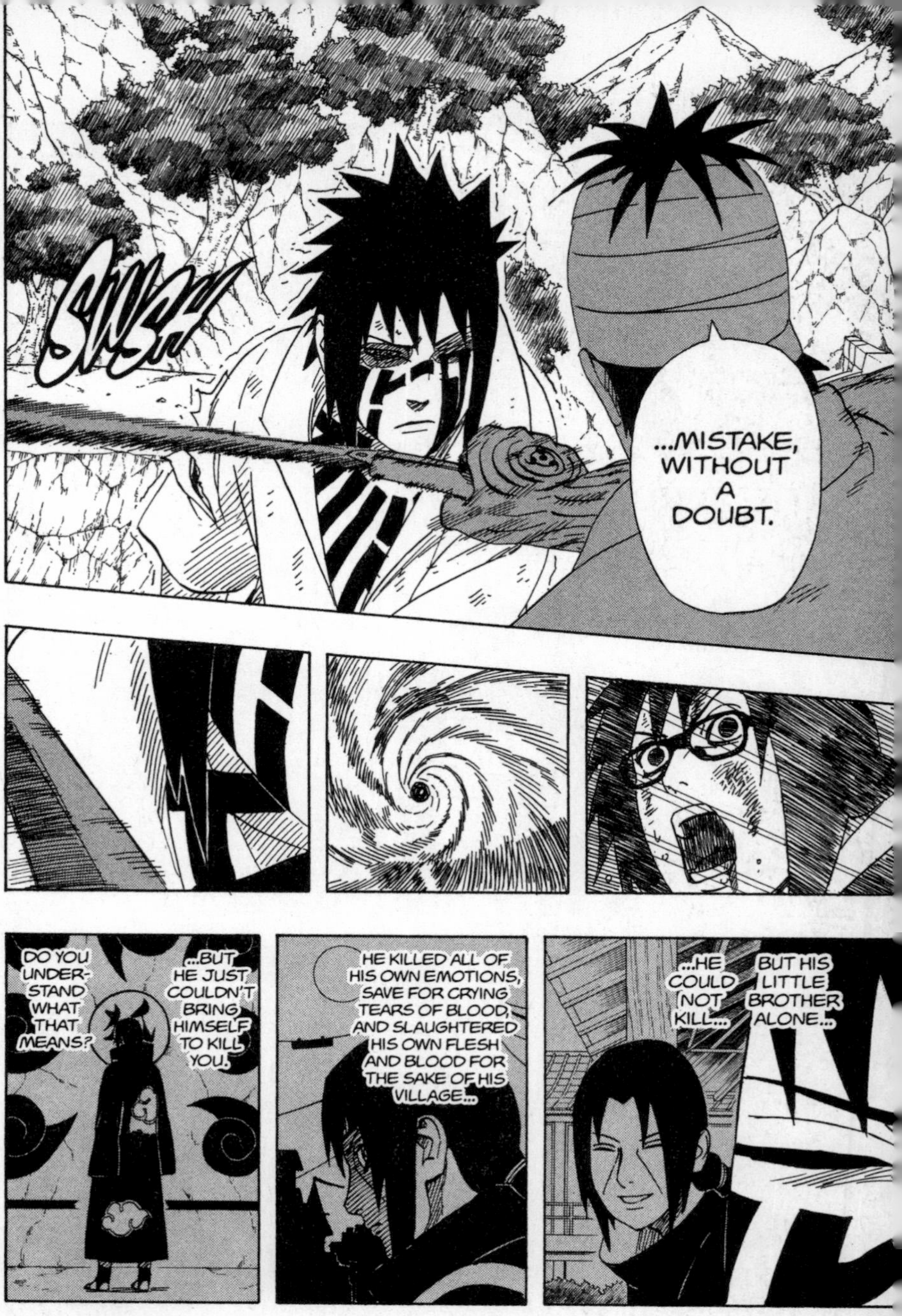
...MISTAKE, WITHOUT A DOUBT.
HE KILLED ALL OF HIS OWN EMOTIONS, SAVE FOR CRYING TEARS OF BLOOD, AND SLAUGHTERED HIS OWN FLESH AND BLOOD FOR THE SAKE OF HIS VILLAGE...
BUT HIS LITTLE BROTHER ALONE...
...HE COULD NOT KILL...
...BUT HE JUST COULDN'T BRING HIMSELF TO KILL YOU.
DO YOU UNDER-STAND WHAT THAT MEANS?

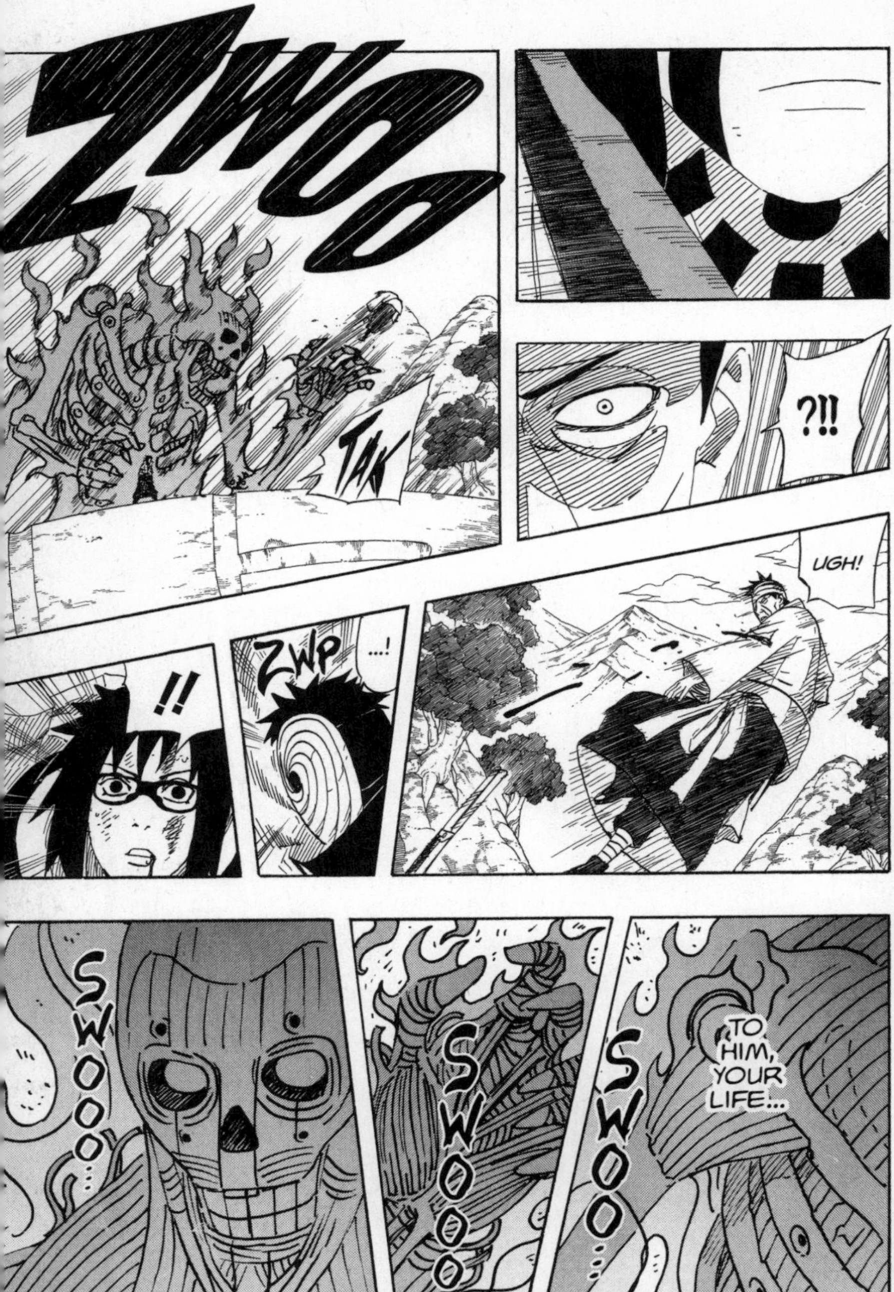
ZWOO
?!!
TAK
UGH!
...!
ZWP
!!
TO HIM, YOUR LIFE...
SWOO...
SWOOO
SWOOO...

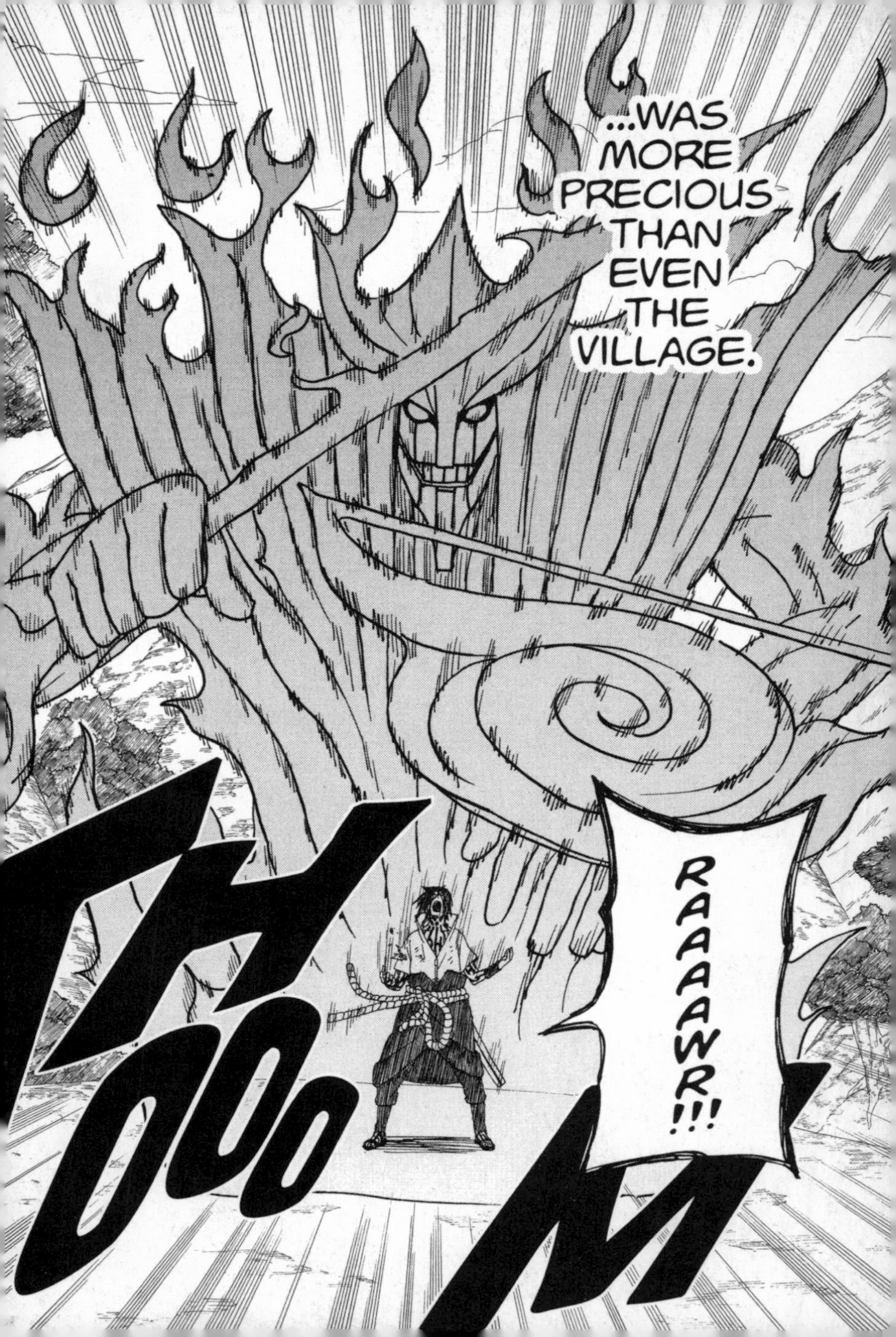
...WAS MORE PRECIOUS THAN EVEN THE VILLAGE.
RAAAAAWR!!!
VOOOM

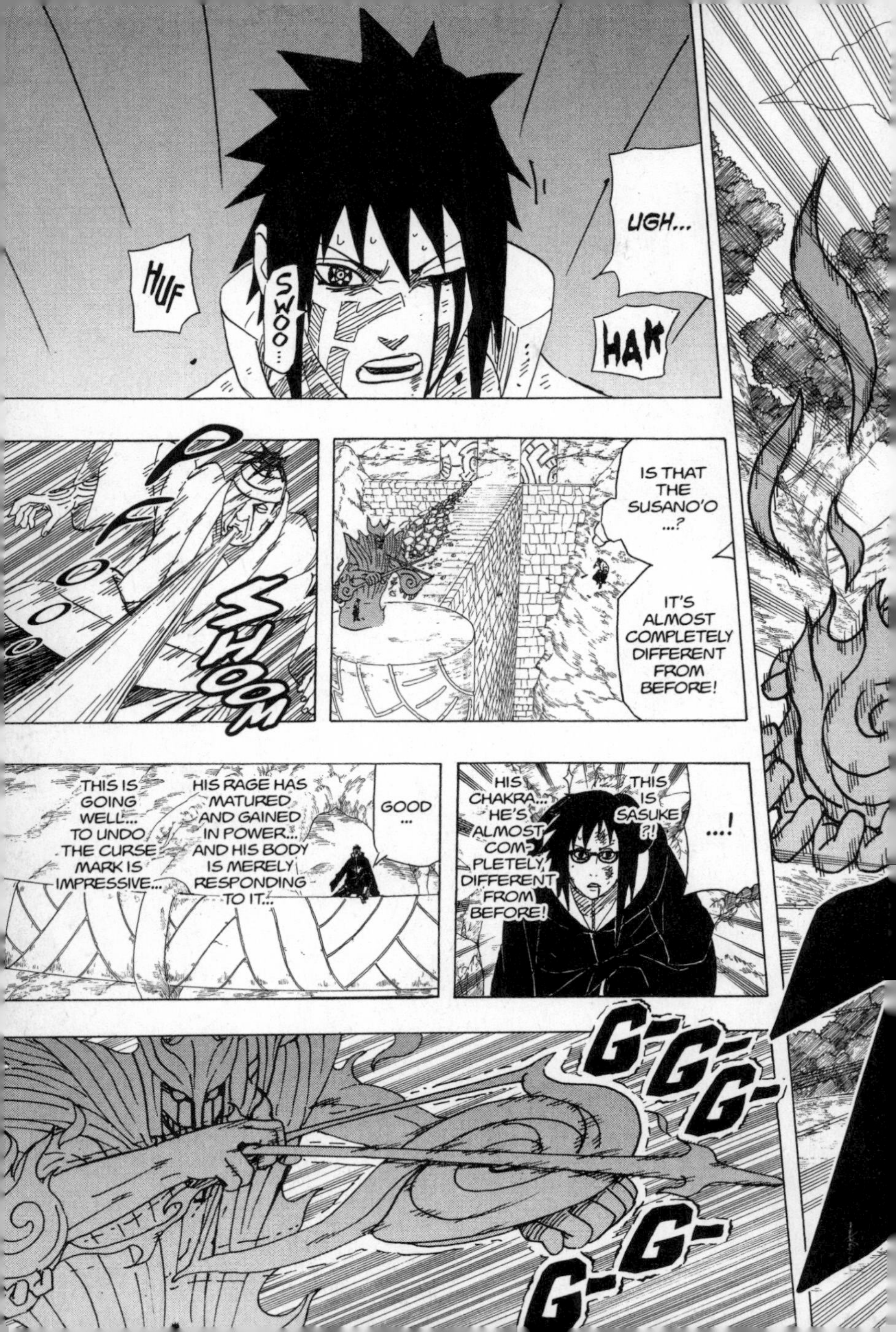

UGH...
HAK
HUF
SWOO...
IS THAT THE SUSANO'O ...?
IT'S ALMOST COMPLETELY DIFFERENT FROM BEFORE!
PFOOOO
WHOOM
...!
THIS IS SASUKE?!
HIS CHAKRA... HE'S ALMOST COMPLETELY DIFFERENT FROM BEFORE!
GOOD...
HIS RAGE HAS MATURED AND GAINED IN POWER... AND HIS BODY IS MERELY RESPONDING TO IT...
THIS IS GOING WELL... TO UNDO THE CURSE MARK IS IMPRESSIVE...
G-G-G-
G-G-

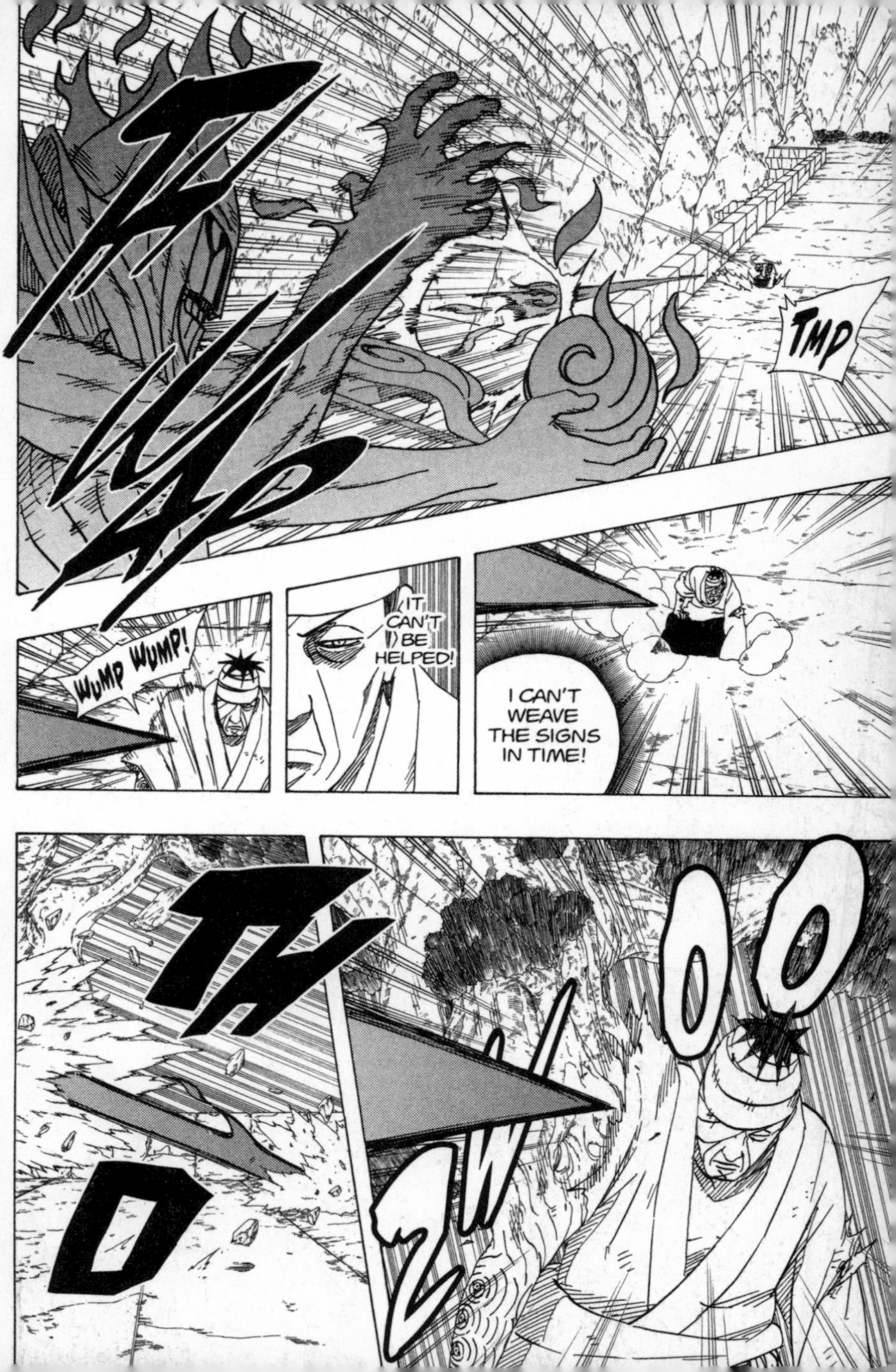

FWUMP
TMP
I CAN'T WEAVE THE SIGNS IN TIME!
IT CAN'T BE HELPED!
WUMP WUMP!
FOOO
THWD

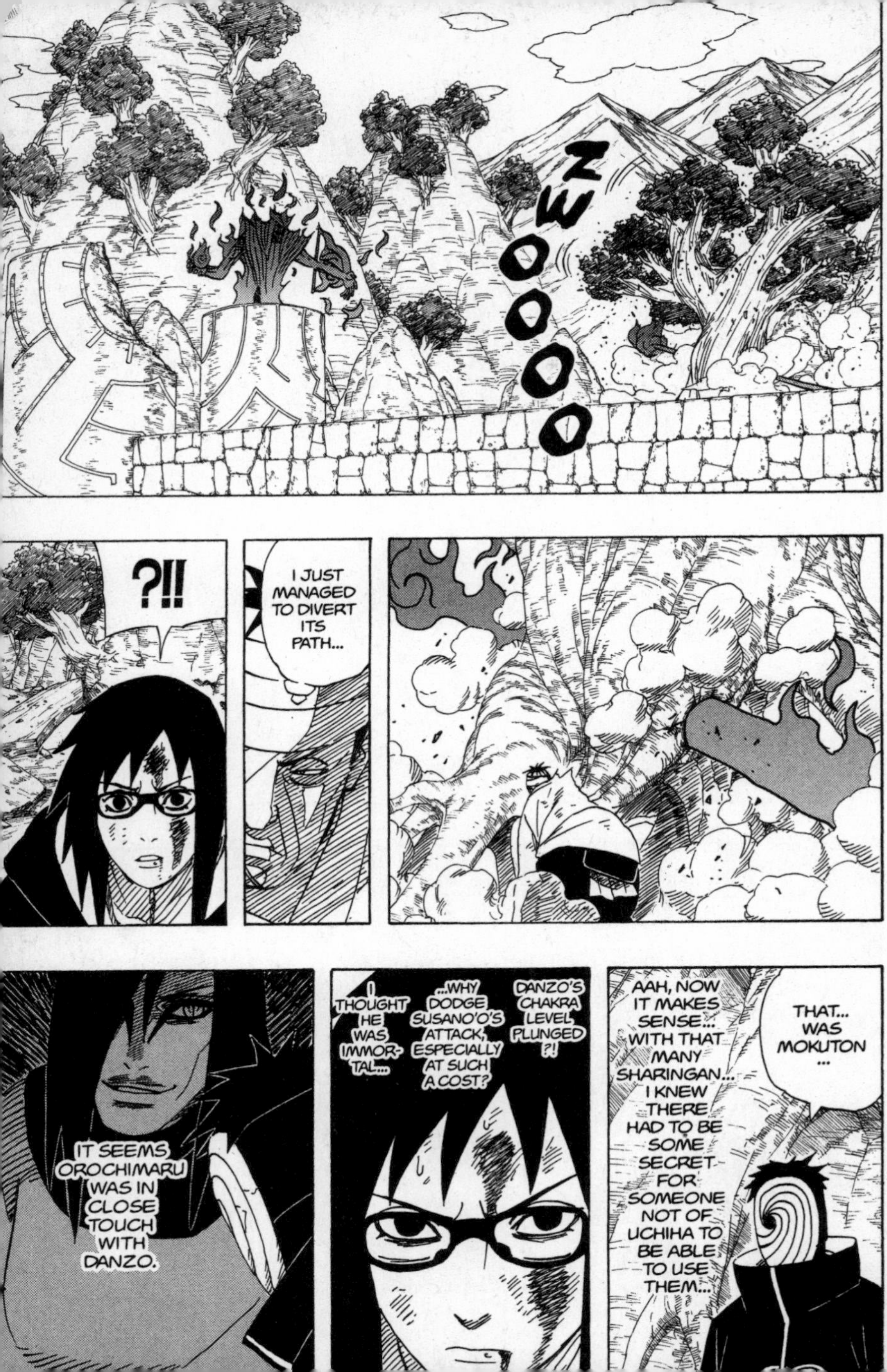
ZWOOOOO
I JUST MANAGED TO DIVERT ITS PATH...
?!!
THAT... WAS MOKUTON ...
AAH, NOW IT MAKES SENSE... WITH THAT MANY SHARINGAN... I KNEW THERE HAD TO BE SOME SECRET FOR SOMEONE NOT OF UCHIHA TO BE ABLE TO USE THEM...
DANZO'S CHAKRA LEVEL PLUNGED?!
...WHY DODGE SUSANO'O'S ATTACK, ESPECIALLY AT SUCH A COST?
I THOUGHT HE WAS IMMORTAL...
IT SEEMS OROCHIMARU WAS IN CLOSE TOUCH WITH DANZO.

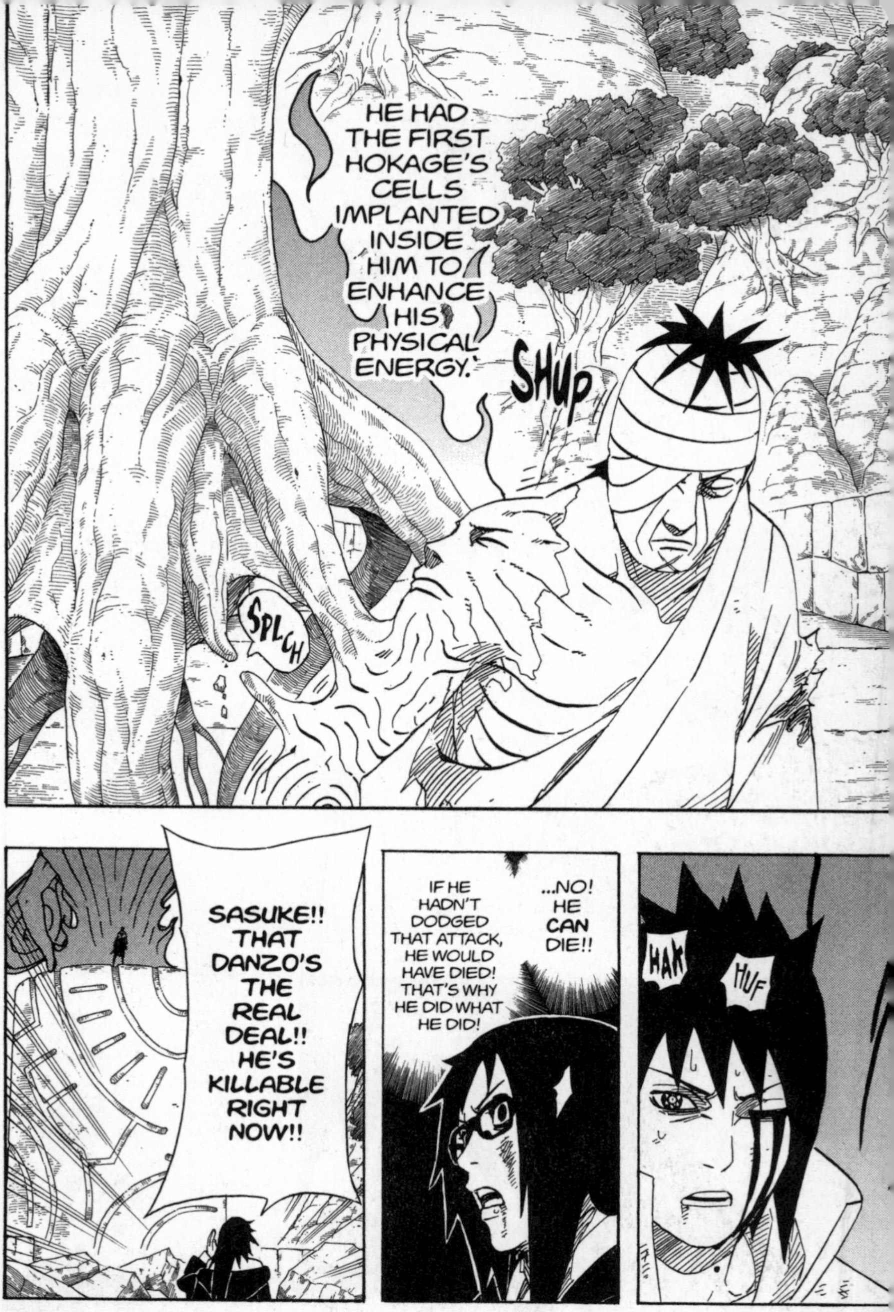
HE HAD THE FIRST HOKAGE'S CELLS IMPLANTED INSIDE HIM TO ENHANCE HIS PHYSICAL ENERGY.
SHUP
SPLCH
HAK
HUF
...NO! HE CAN DIE!!
IF HE HADN'T DODGED THAT ATTACK, HE WOULD HAVE DIED! THAT'S WHY HE DID WHAT HE DID!
SASUKE!! THAT DANZO'S THE REAL DEAL!! HE'S KILLABLE RIGHT NOW!!

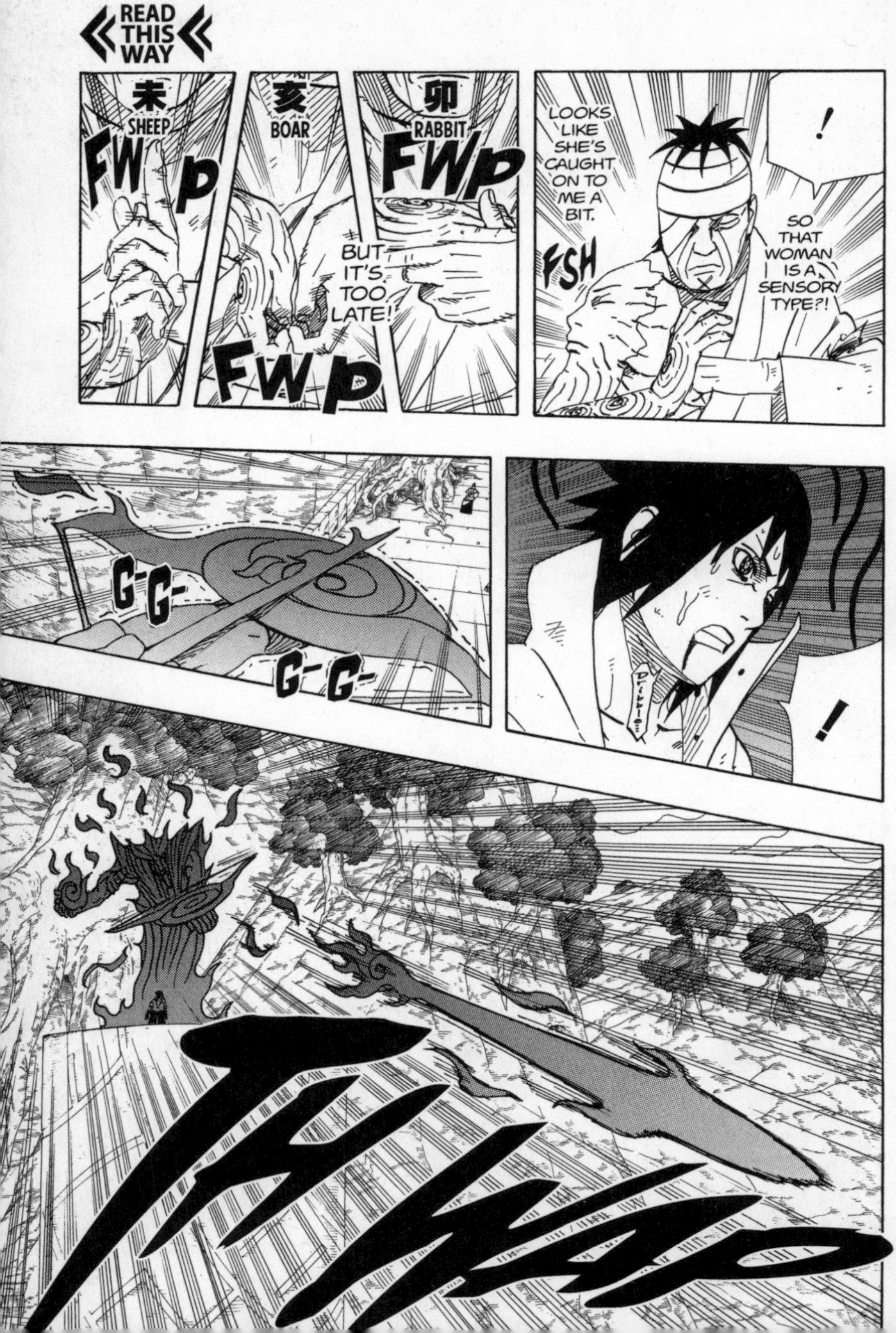
READ THIS WAY
!
SO THAT WOMAN IS A SENSORY TYPE?!
LOOKS LIKE SHE'S CAUGHT ON TO ME A BIT.
FSH
卯
RABBIT
FWP
BUT IT'S TOO LATE!
亥
BOAR
FWP
未
SHEEP
FWP
!
Dribble
G-G-
G-G-
THWAP

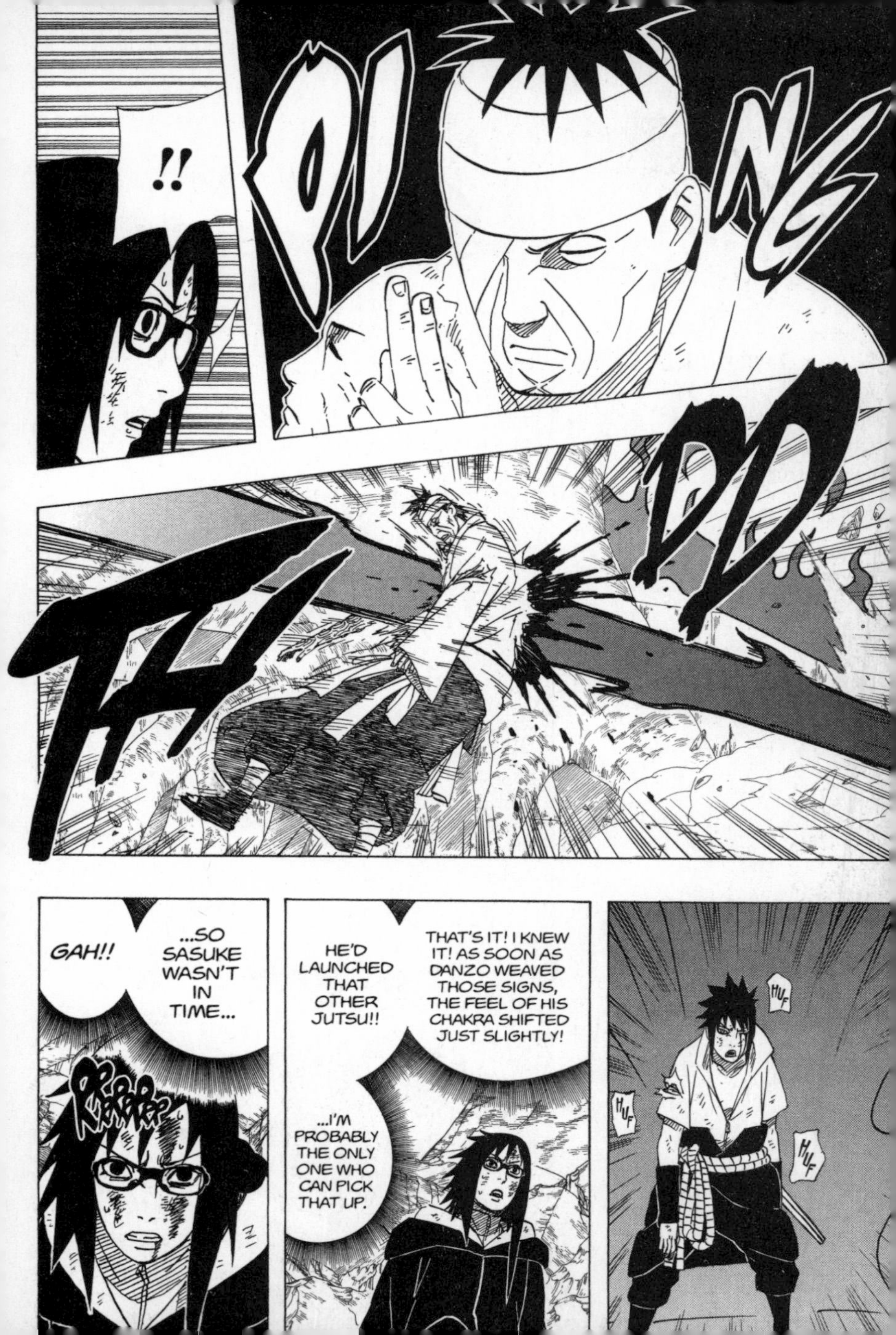
!!
POING
THUDD
...SO SASUKE WASN'T IN TIME...
GAH!!
THAT'S IT! I KNEW IT! AS SOON AS DANZO WEAVED THOSE SIGNS, THE FEEL OF HIS CHAKRA SHIFTED JUST SLIGHTLY!
HE'D LAUNCHED THAT OTHER JUTSU!!
...I'M PROBABLY THE ONLY ONE WHO CAN PICK THAT UP.
HUF
HUF
HUF

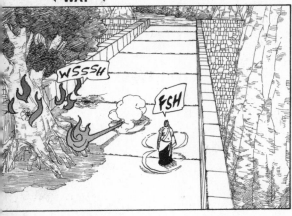

READ THIS WAY

SWOOO...
WSSSH
FSH
UNH...
PFOOOO...
HUF
HUF
!
SO HE RECAST THAT JUTSU AND RETURNED TO THE PREVIOUS DANZO...
...BUT THOSE THREE EYES STAYED SHUT...
AS FAR AS I CAN TELL, THERE ARE TEN SHARINGAN ON THAT ARM...
...PLUS THE FIRST HOKAGE'S CELLS...

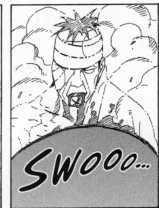

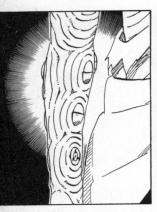

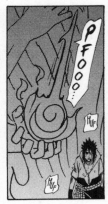

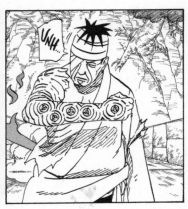

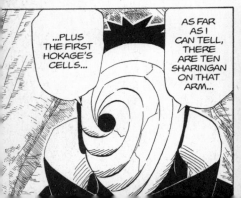

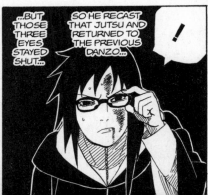

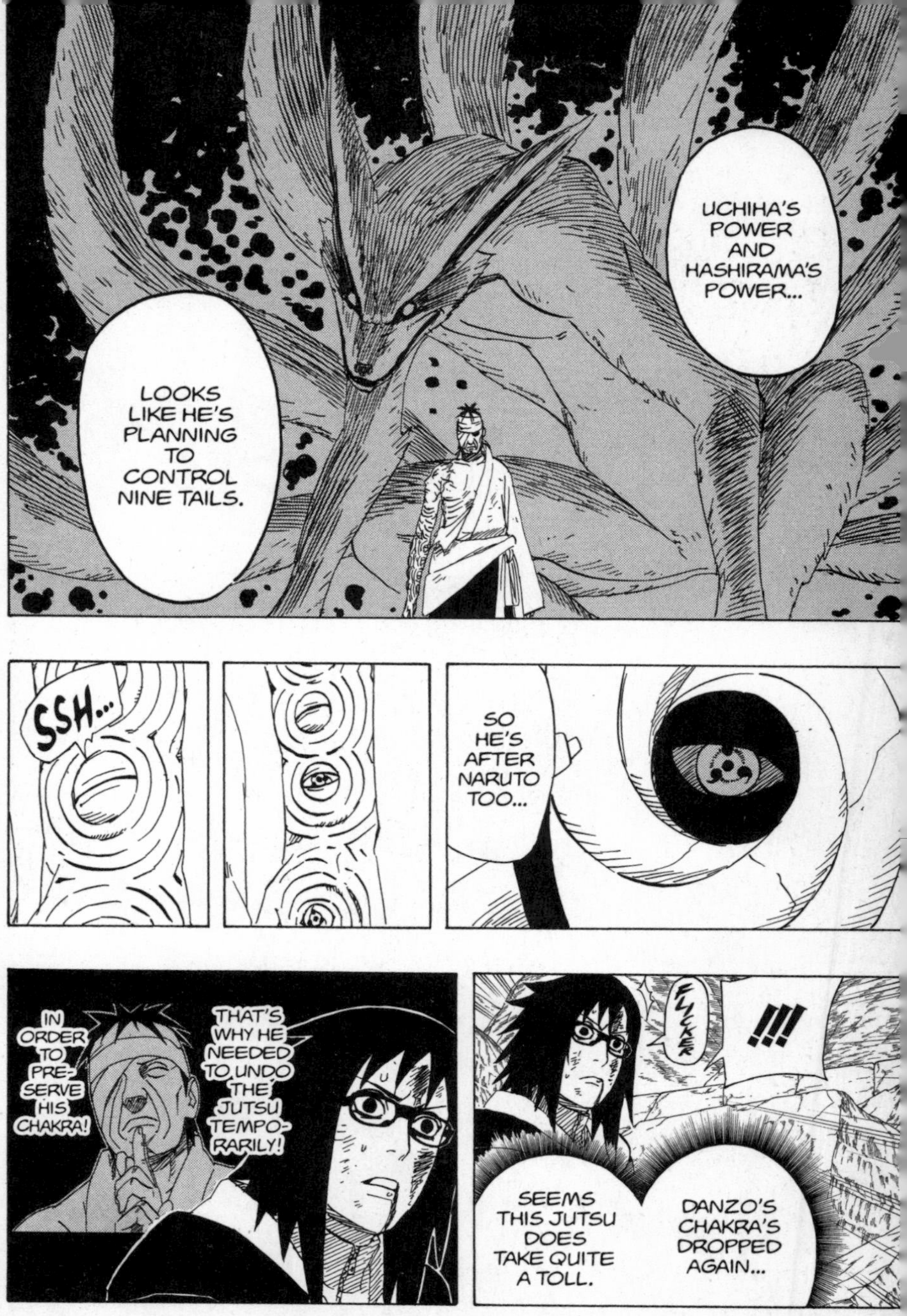
UCHIHA'S POWER AND HASHIRAMA'S POWER...
LOOKS LIKE HE'S PLANNING TO CONTROL NINE TAILS.
SO HE'S AFTER NARUTO TOO...
SSH...
FLICKER
!!!
DANZO'S CHAKRA'S DROPPED AGAIN...
SEEMS THIS JUTSU DOES TAKE QUITE A TOLL.
THAT'S WHY HE NEEDED TO UNDO THE JUTSU TEMPO-RARILY!
IN ORDER TO PRE-SERVE HIS CHAKRA!

READ THIS WAY

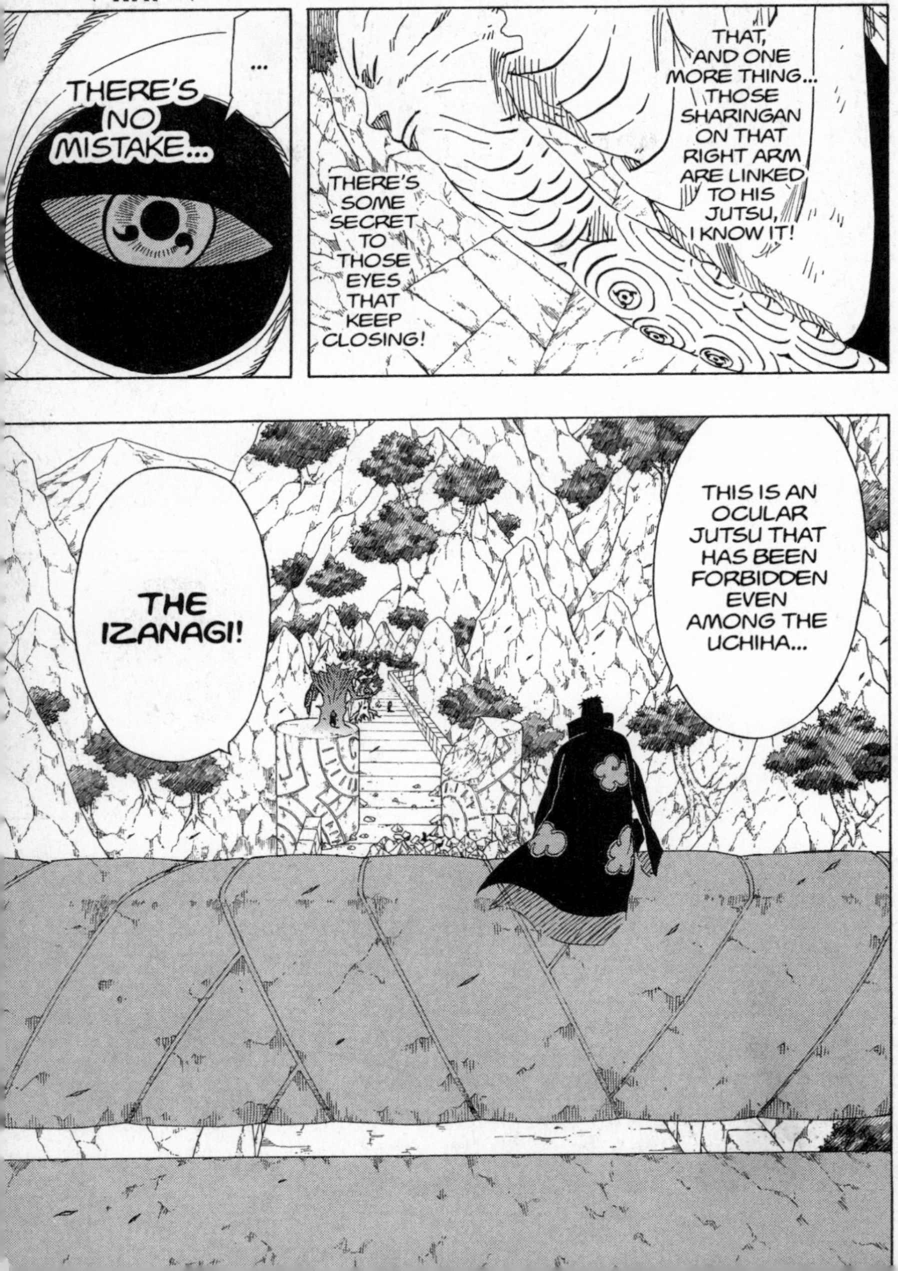

THAT, AND ONE MORE THING... THOSE SHARINGAN ON THAT RIGHT ARM ARE LINKED TO HIS JUTSU, I KNOW IT!
THERE'S SOME SECRET TO THOSE EYES THAT KEEP CLOSING!
...
THERE'S NO MISTAKE...
THIS IS AN OCULAR JUTSU THAT HAS BEEN FORBIDDEN EVEN AMONG THE UCHIHA...
THE IZANAGI!

NARUTO

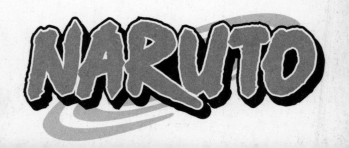

Number 479: The Izanagi

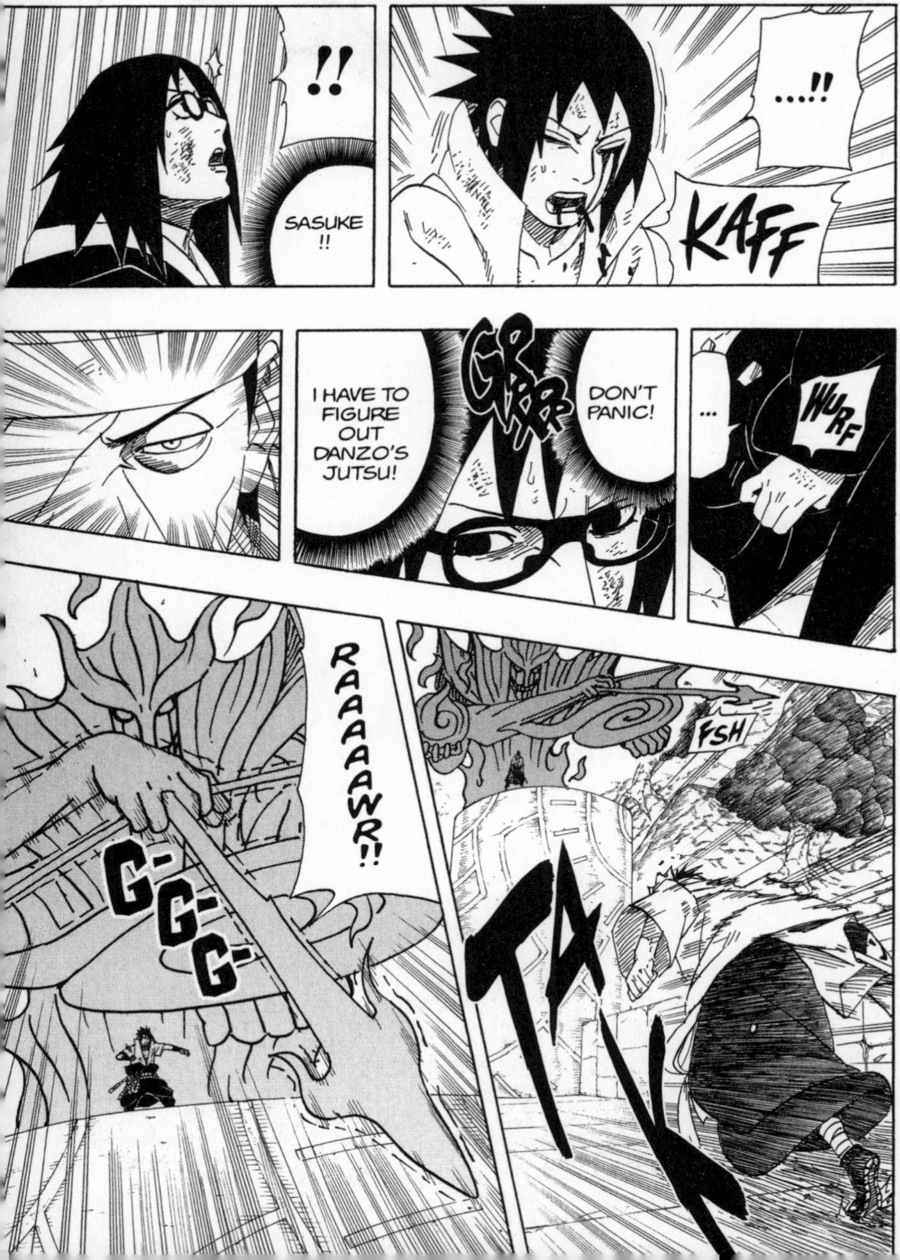

....!!
KAFF
!!
SASUKE !!
...
WURF
DON'T PANIC!
I HAVE TO FIGURE OUT DANZO'S JUTSU!
FSH
TAK
RAAAAAAWR!!
G-G-G-

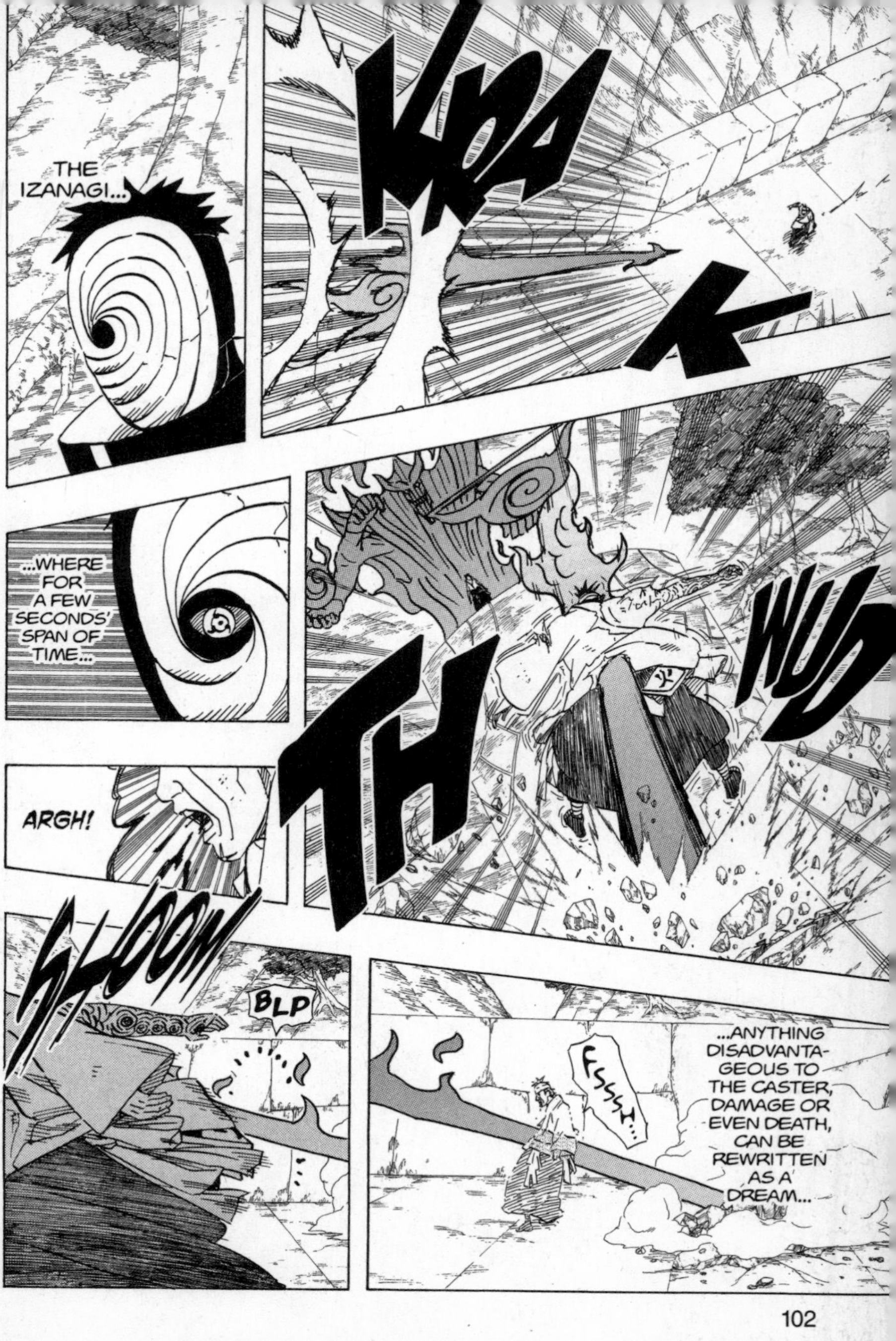
THE IZANAGI...
KRAKK
...WHERE FOR A FEW SECONDS' SPAN OF TIME...
WUD
TH
ARGH!
SHLOOM
BLP
FSSSH...
...ANYTHING DISADVANTAGEOUS TO THE CASTER, DAMAGE OR EVEN DEATH, CAN BE REWRITTEN AS A DREAM...

READ THIS WAY

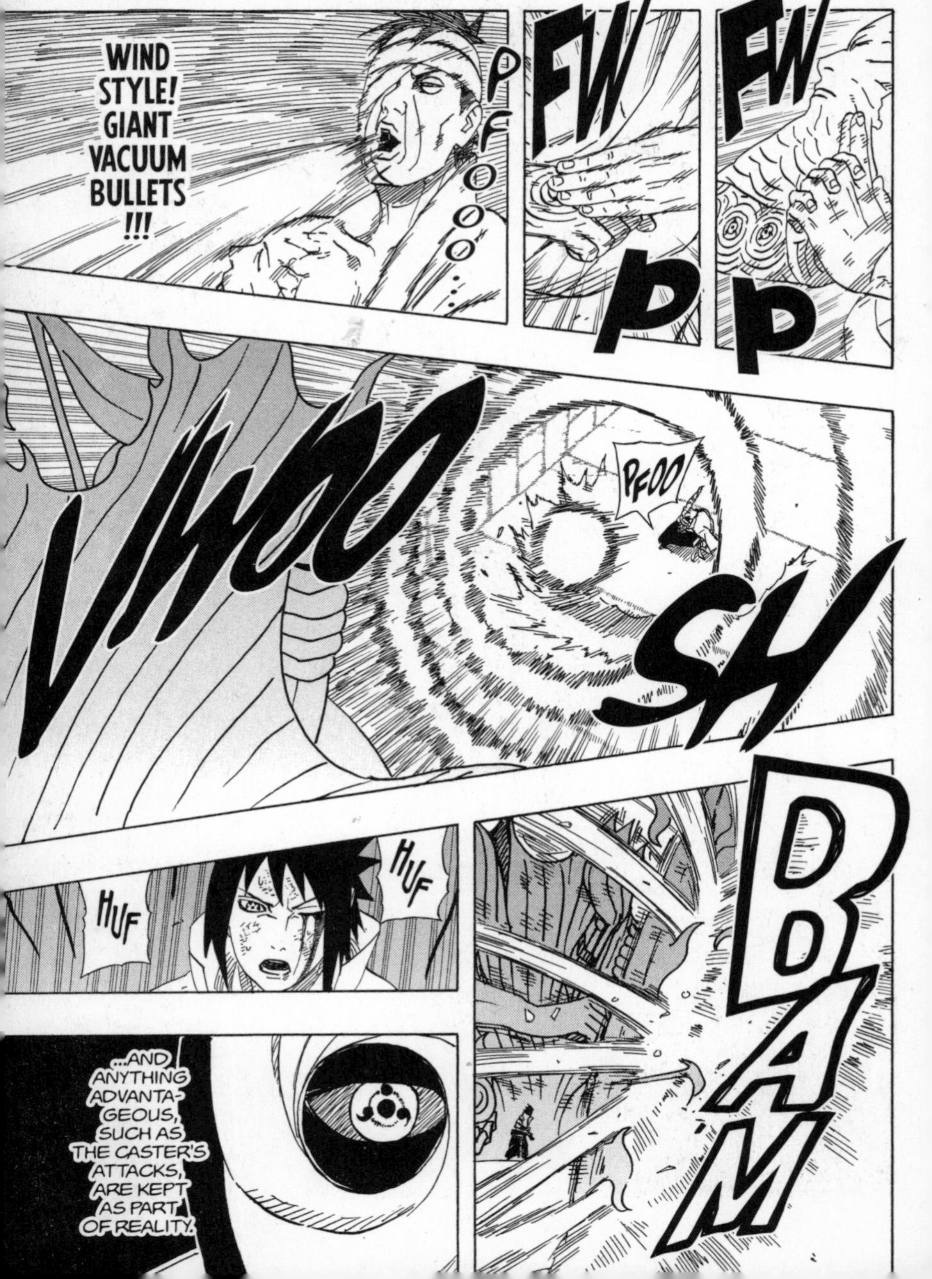

FW
P
FW
P
WIND STYLE! GIANT VACUUM BULLETS !!!
PFOOOOO...
PFOO
VWOO
SH
DBAM
HUF
HUF
...AND ANYTHING ADVANTA-GEOUS, SUCH AS THE CASTER'S ATTACKS, ARE KEPT AS PART OF REALITY.

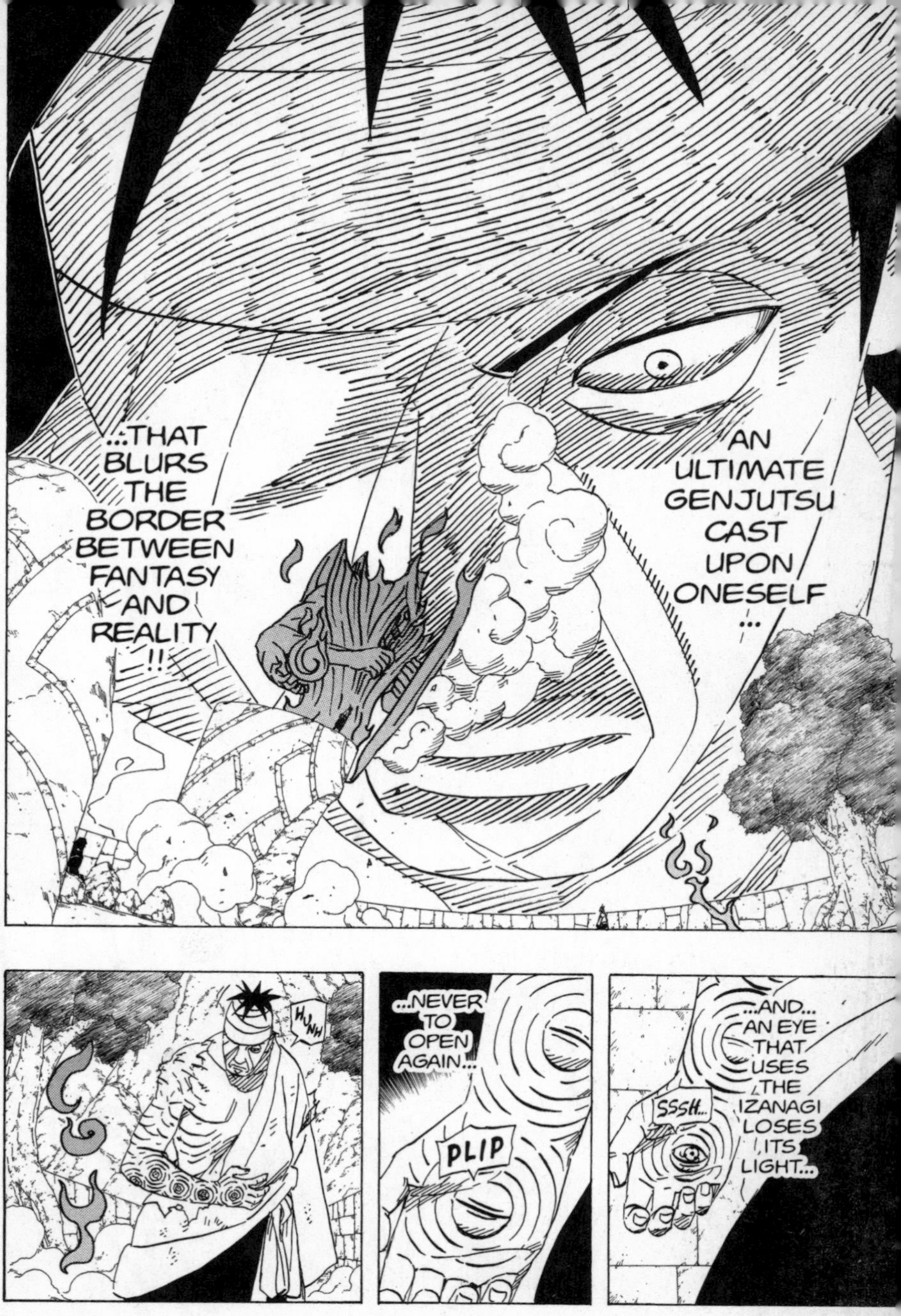
AN ULTIMATE GENJUTSU CAST UPON ONESELF...
...THAT BLURS THE BORDER BETWEEN FANTASY AND REALITY!!
...AND... AN EYE THAT USES THE IZANAGI LOSES ITS LIGHT...
SSSH...
...NEVER TO OPEN AGAIN...
PLIP
HUNH

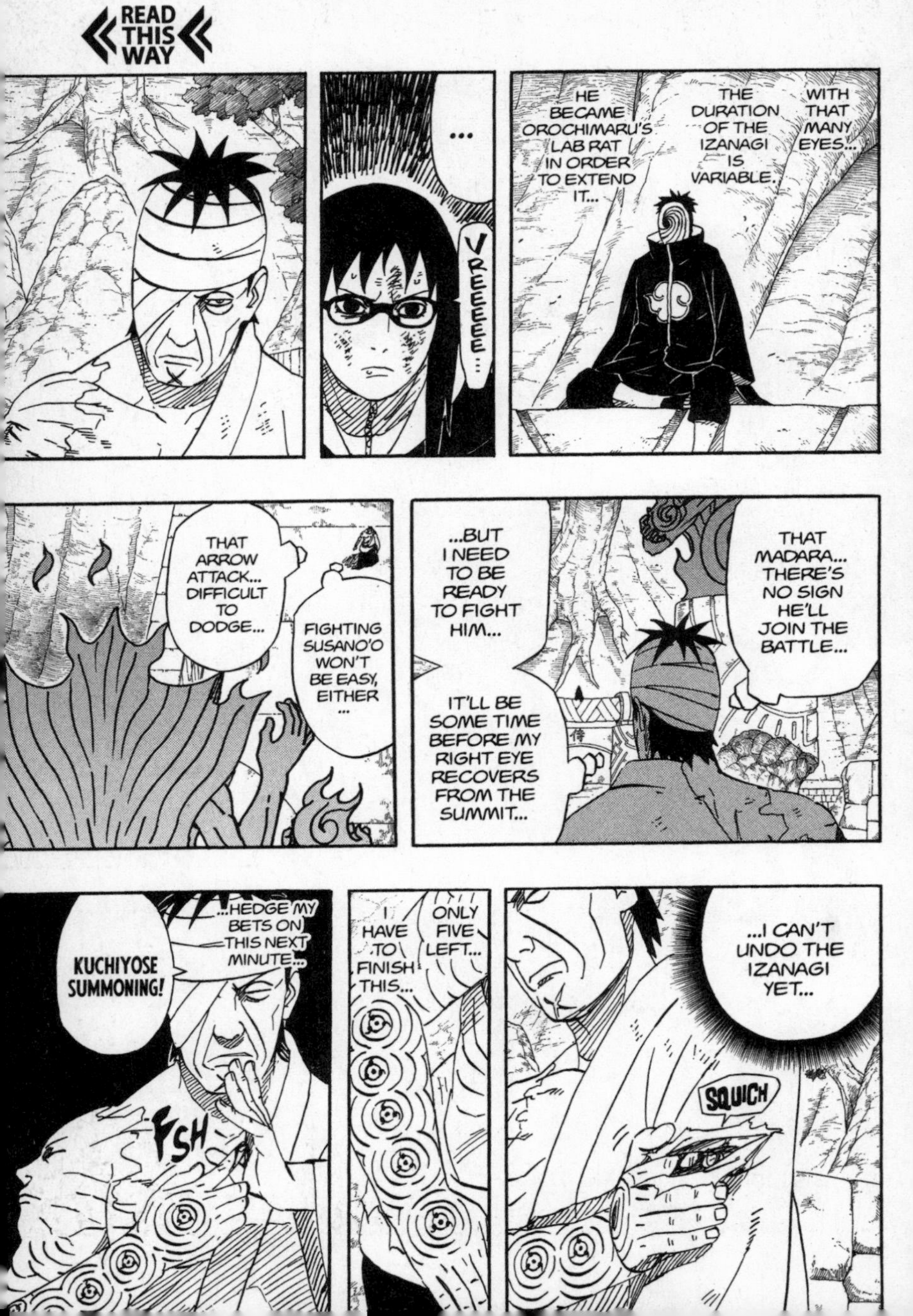
READ THIS WAY
WITH THAT MANY EYES...
THE DURATION OF THE IZANAGI IS VARIABLE.
HE BECAME OROCHIMARU'S LAB RAT IN ORDER TO EXTEND IT...
VREEEEEE...
...
THAT MADARA... THERE'S NO SIGN HE'LL JOIN THE BATTLE...
...BUT I NEED TO BE READY TO FIGHT HIM...
IT'LL BE SOME TIME BEFORE MY RIGHT EYE RECOVERS FROM THE SUMMIT...
THAT ARROW ATTACK... DIFFICULT TO DODGE...
FIGHTING SUSANO'O WON'T BE EASY, EITHER...
...I CAN'T UNDO THE IZANAGI YET...
SQUICH
ONLY FIVE LEFT...
I HAVE TO FINISH THIS...
...HEDGE MY BETS ON THIS NEXT MINUTE...
KUCHIYOSE SUMMONING!
FSH

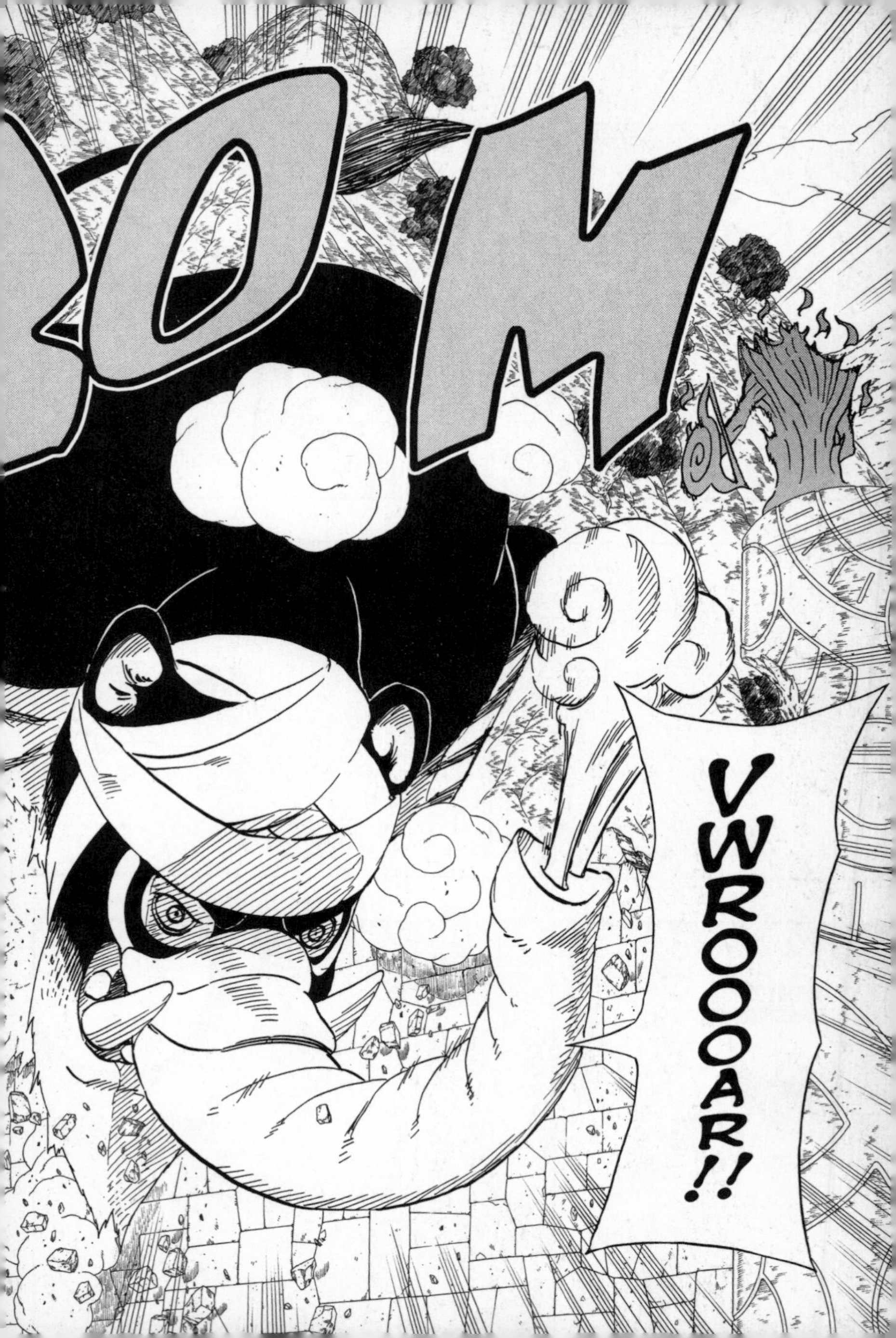
OM
VWROOOAR!!

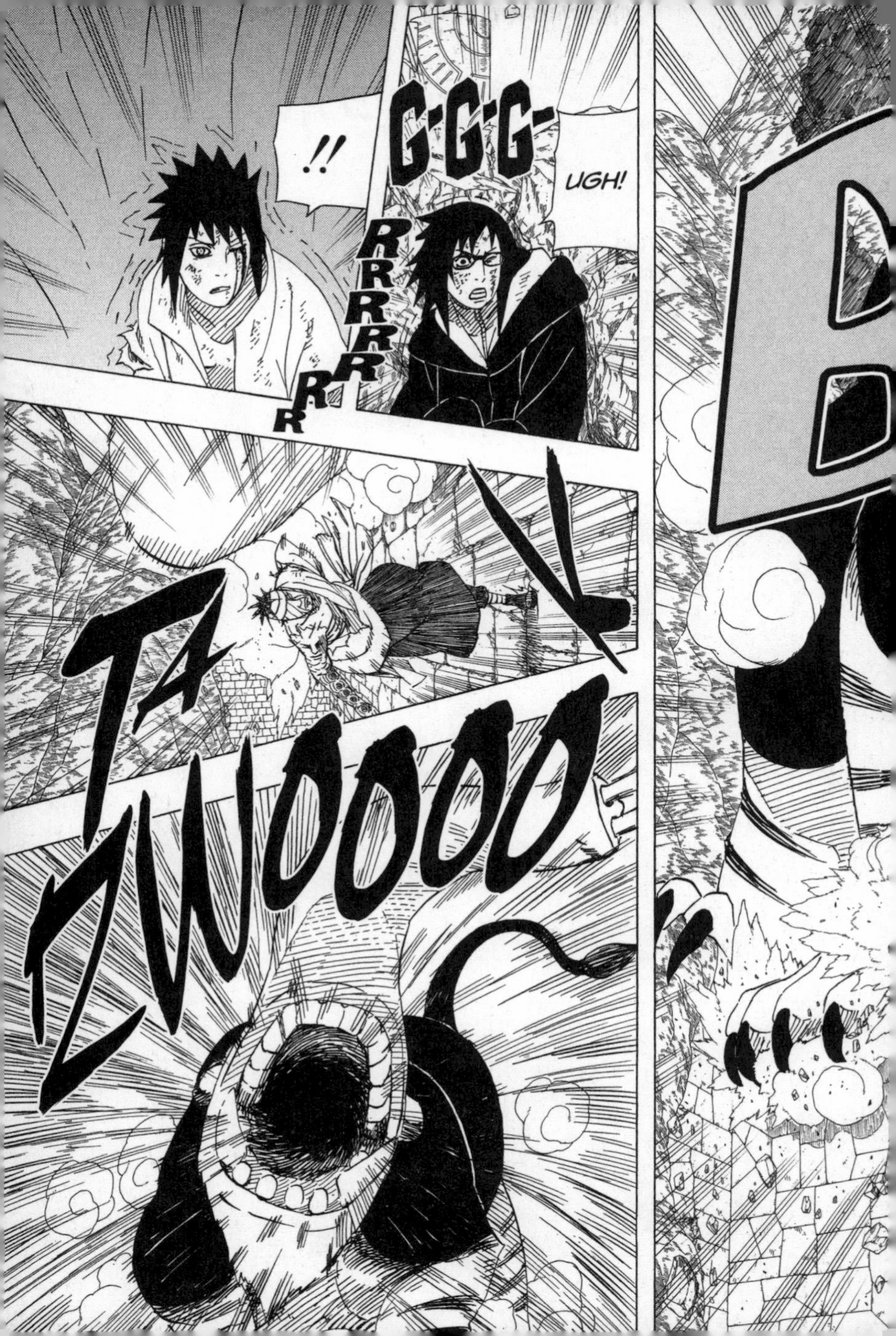
G-G-G-
UGH!
!!
RRRRRRR
TA
ZWOOOOO
B

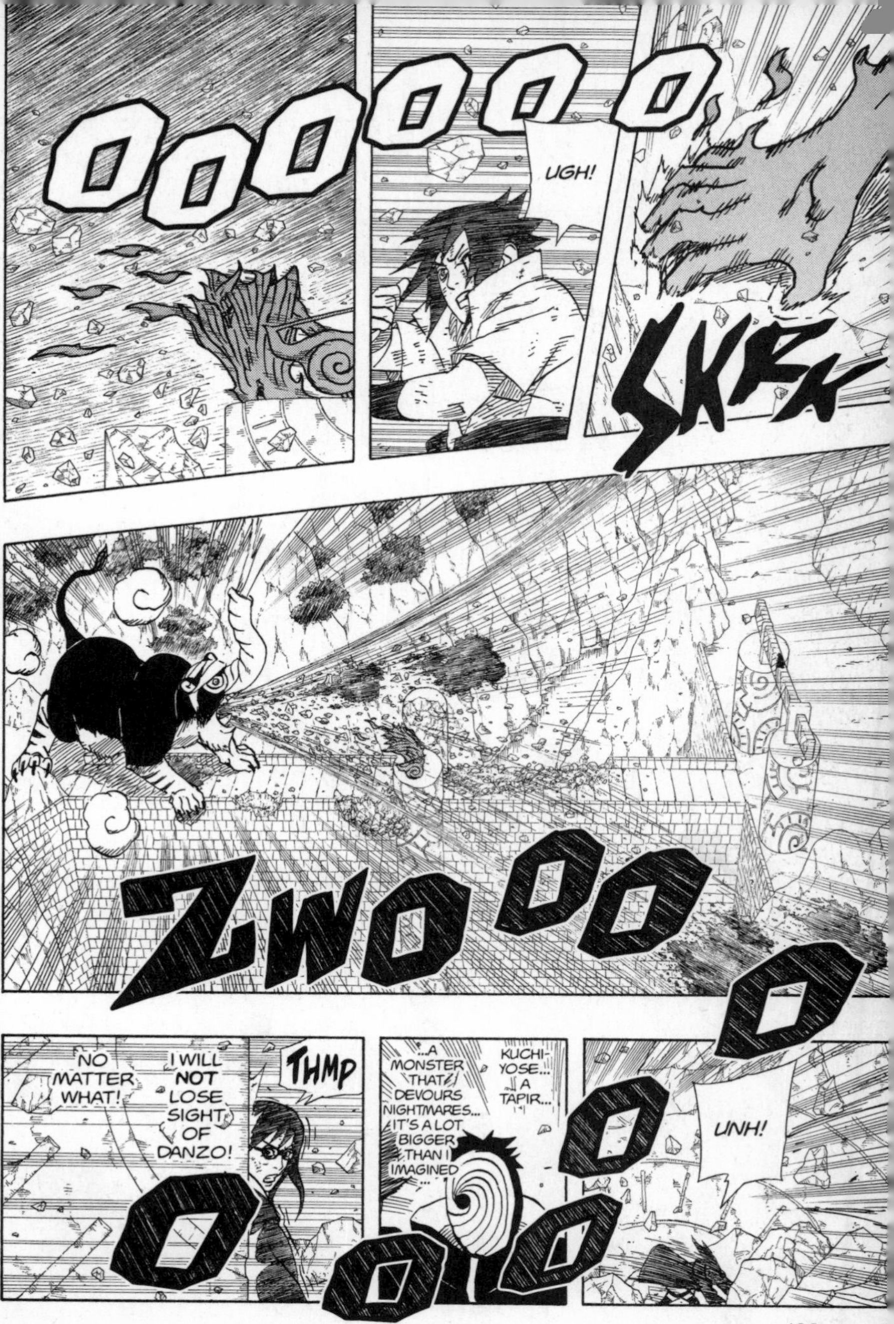
SKRK
UGH!
OOOOOOOO
ZWOOOOOOOOOO
UNH!
KUCHI-YOSE... A TAPIR...
...A MONSTER THAT DEVOURS NIGHTMARES... IT'S A LOT BIGGER THAN I IMAGINED...
THMP
I WILL NOT LOSE SIGHT OF DANZO!
NO MATTER WHAT!

READ THIS WAY

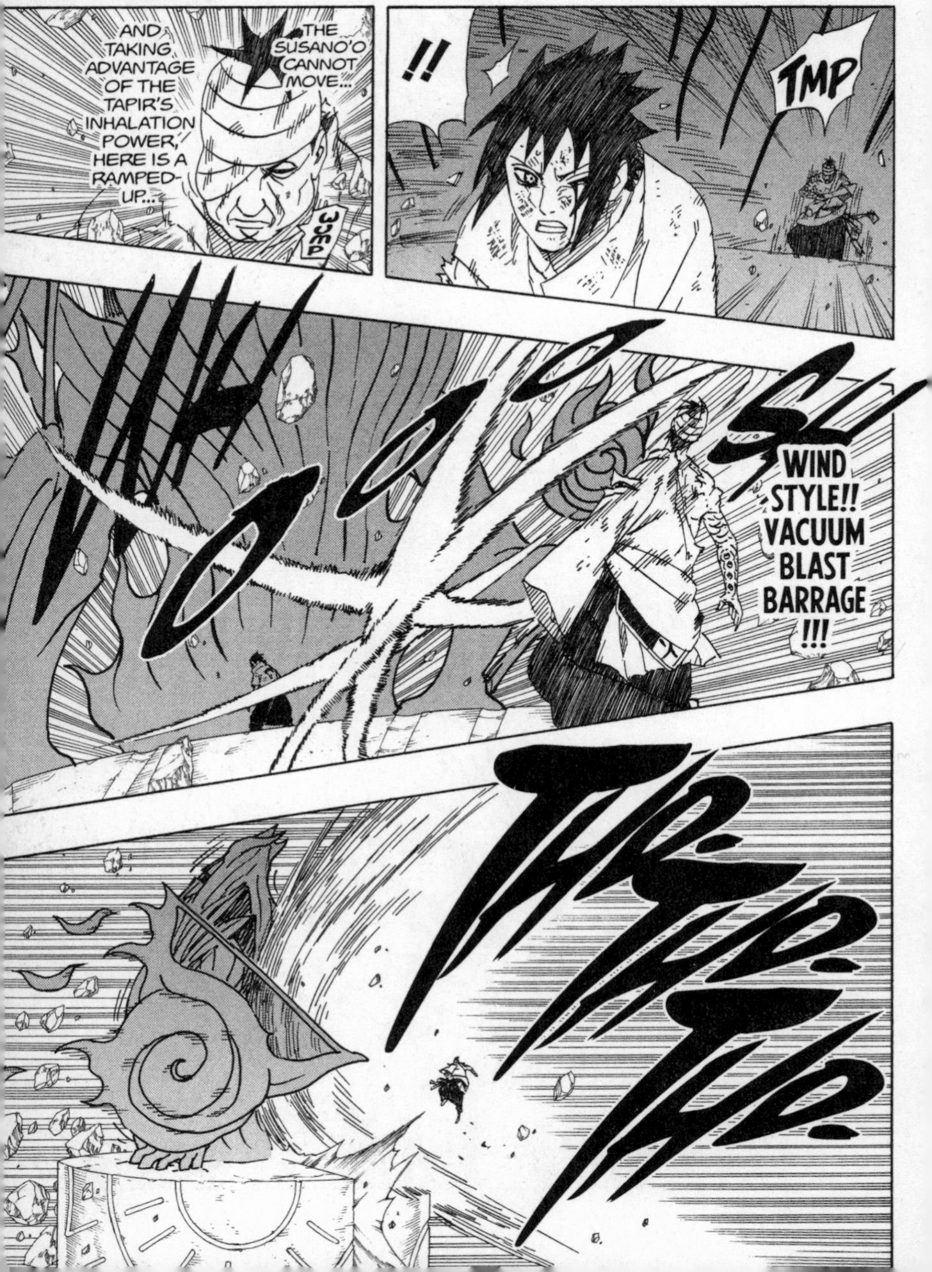

!!
TMP
THE SUSANO'O CANNOT MOVE...
AND TAKING ADVANTAGE OF THE TAPIR'S INHALATION POWER, HERE IS A RAMPED-UP...
JUMP
WIND STYLE!! VACUUM BLAST BARRAGE!!!

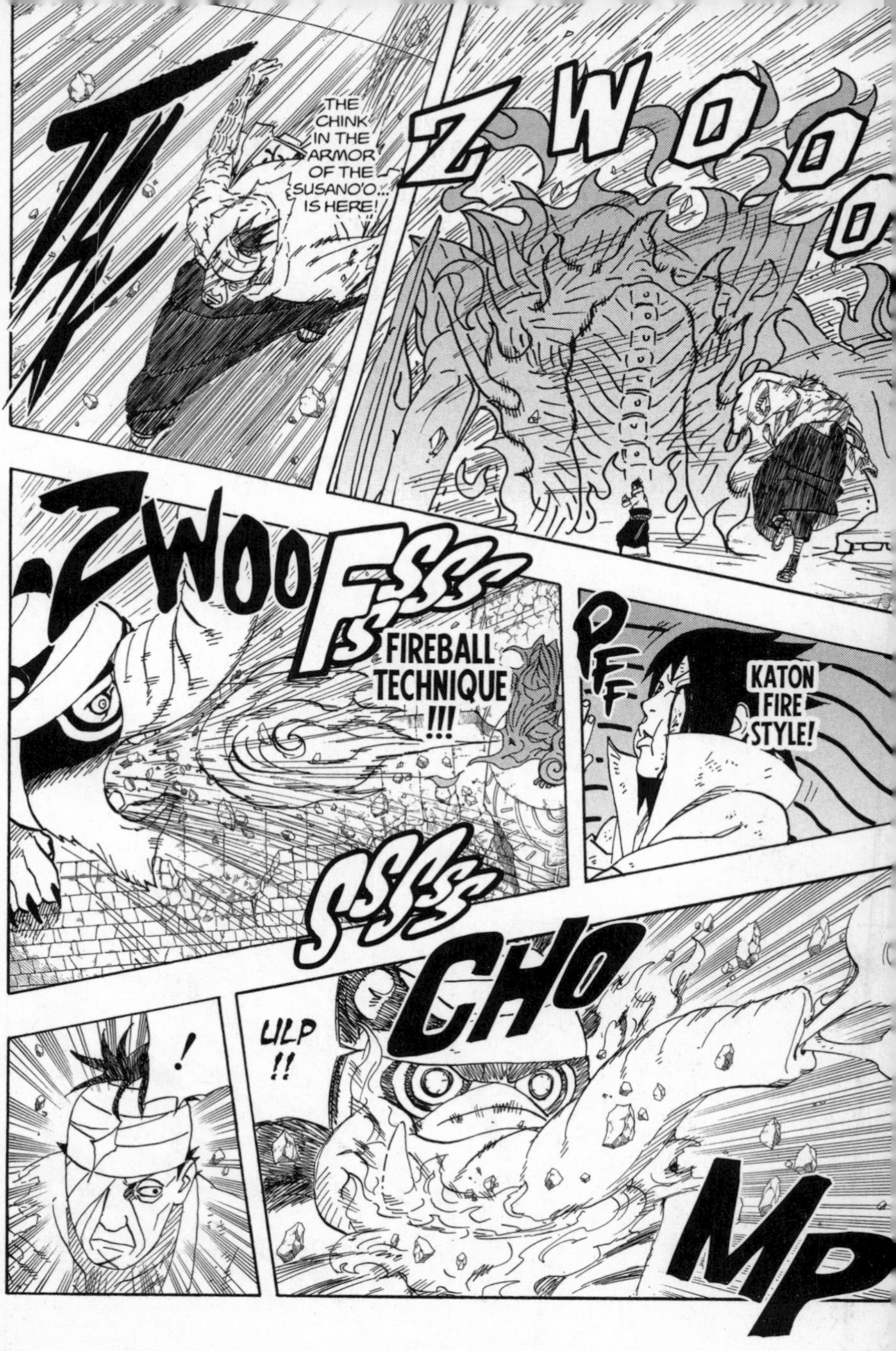
ZWOOOO
ZZ
THE CHINK IN THE ARMOR OF THE SUSANO'O... IS HERE!
PFF
KATON FIRE STYLE!
FIREBALL TECHNIQUE!!!
ZWOOF
FSSS
SSSS
CHOMP
ULP!!
!

...CLEVER, TO USE THE TAPIR'S INHALATION... SASUKE.

KATON, EH...

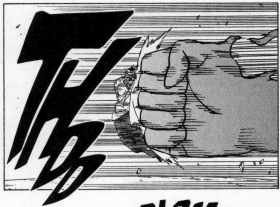

THOO

59...

58...

57... 56...

SLAM

THD

BOOF

YAWWR ...

60.

SSH

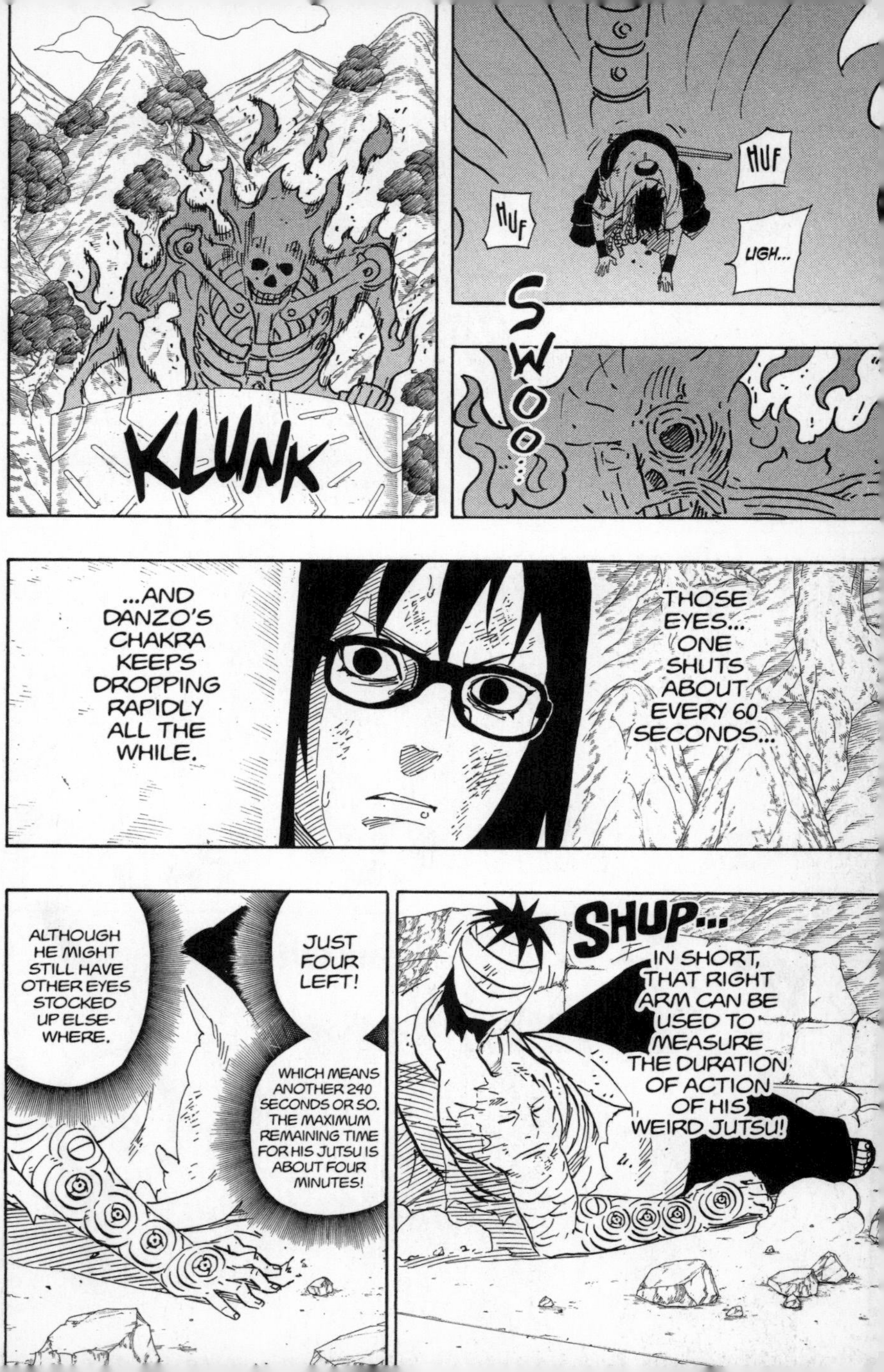

HUF
HUF
UGH...
SWOO...
KLUNK
THOSE EYES... ONE SHUTS ABOUT EVERY 60 SECONDS...
...AND DANZO'S CHAKRA KEEPS DROPPING RAPIDLY ALL THE WHILE.
SHUP...
IN SHORT, THAT RIGHT ARM CAN BE USED TO MEASURE THE DURATION OF ACTION OF HIS WEIRD JUTSU!
JUST FOUR LEFT!
ALTHOUGH HE MIGHT STILL HAVE OTHER EYES STOCKED UP ELSE-WHERE.
WHICH MEANS ANOTHER 240 SECONDS OR SO. THE MAXIMUM REMAINING TIME FOR HIS JUTSU IS ABOUT FOUR MINUTES!

READ THIS WAY

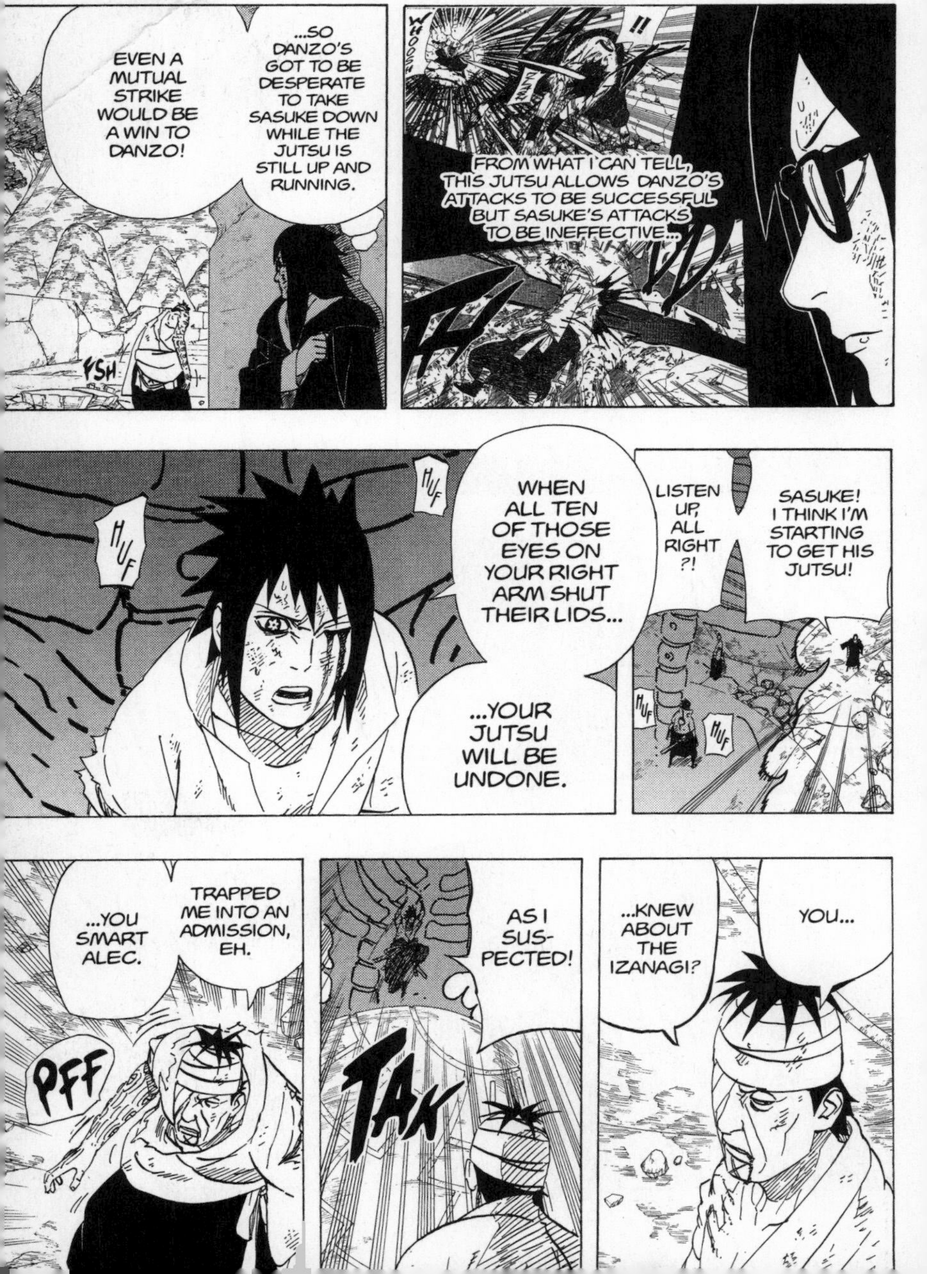

WHOOSH
!!
FROM WHAT I CAN TELL, THIS JUTSU ALLOWS DANZO'S ATTACKS TO BE SUCCESSFUL BUT SASUKE'S ATTACKS TO BE INEFFECTIVE...
...SO DANZO'S GOT TO BE DESPERATE TO TAKE SASUKE DOWN WHILE THE JUTSU IS STILL UP AND RUNNING.
EVEN A MUTUAL STRIKE WOULD BE A WIN TO DANZO!
YSH
SASUKE! I THINK I'M STARTING TO GET HIS JUTSU!
LISTEN UP, ALL RIGHT?!
HUF
HUF
WHEN ALL TEN OF THOSE EYES ON YOUR RIGHT ARM SHUT THEIR LIDS...
...YOUR JUTSU WILL BE UNDONE.
HUF
HUF
YOU...
...KNEW ABOUT THE IZANAGI?
AS I SUS-PECTED!
TAK
TRAPPED ME INTO AN ADMISSION, EH.
...YOU SMART ALEC.
PFF

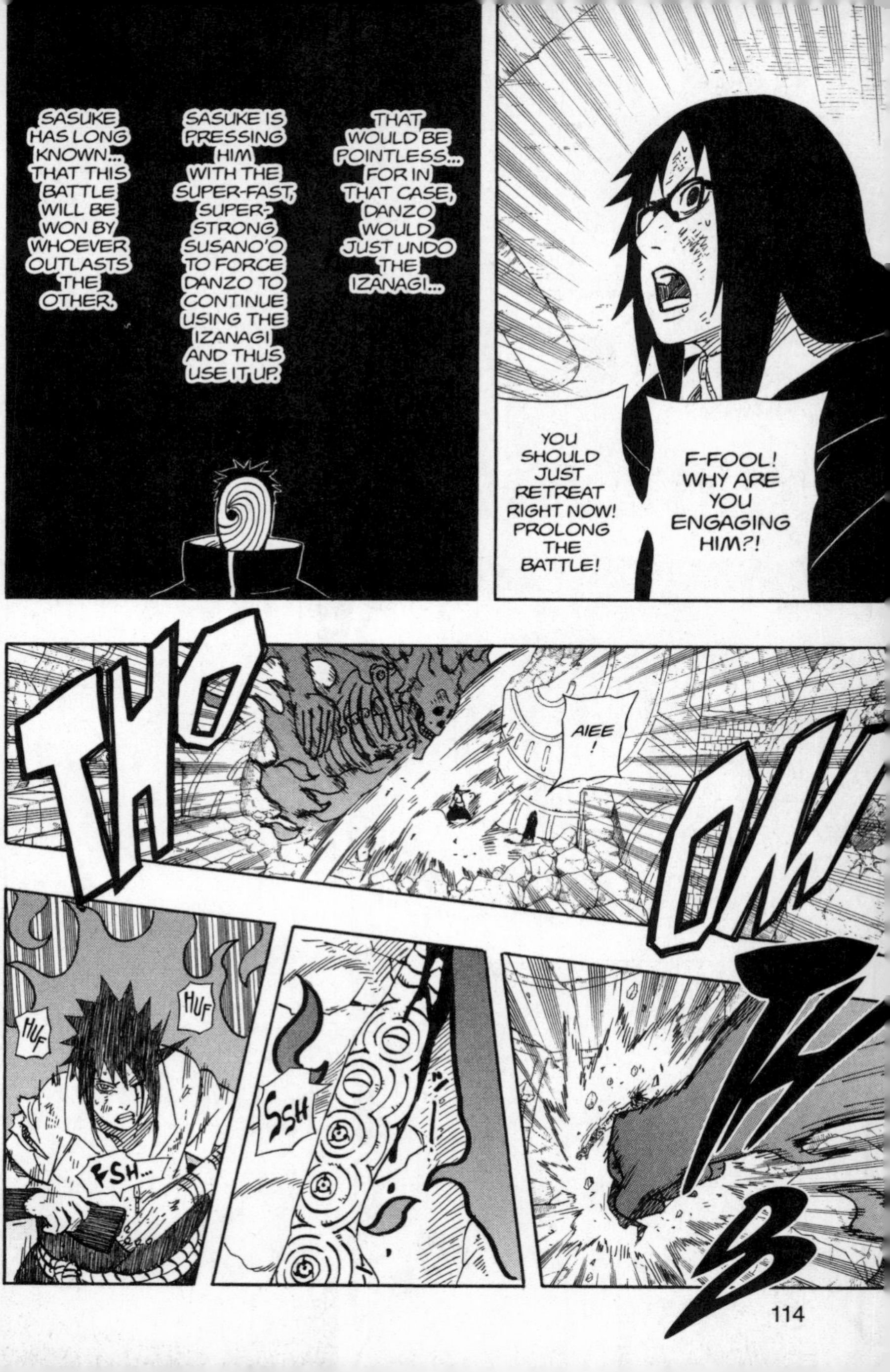
F-FOOL! WHY ARE YOU ENGAGING HIM?!
YOU SHOULD JUST RETREAT RIGHT NOW! PROLONG THE BATTLE!
THAT WOULD BE POINTLESS... FOR IN THAT CASE, DANZO WOULD JUST UNDO THE IZANAGI...
SASUKE IS PRESSING HIM WITH THE SUPER-FAST, SUPER-STRONG SUSANO'O TO FORCE DANZO TO CONTINUE USING THE IZANAGI AND THUS USE IT UP.
SASUKE HAS LONG KNOWN... THAT THIS BATTLE WILL BE WON BY WHOEVER OUTLASTS THE OTHER.
THOOM
AIEE!
SSH
HUF
HUF
FSH...

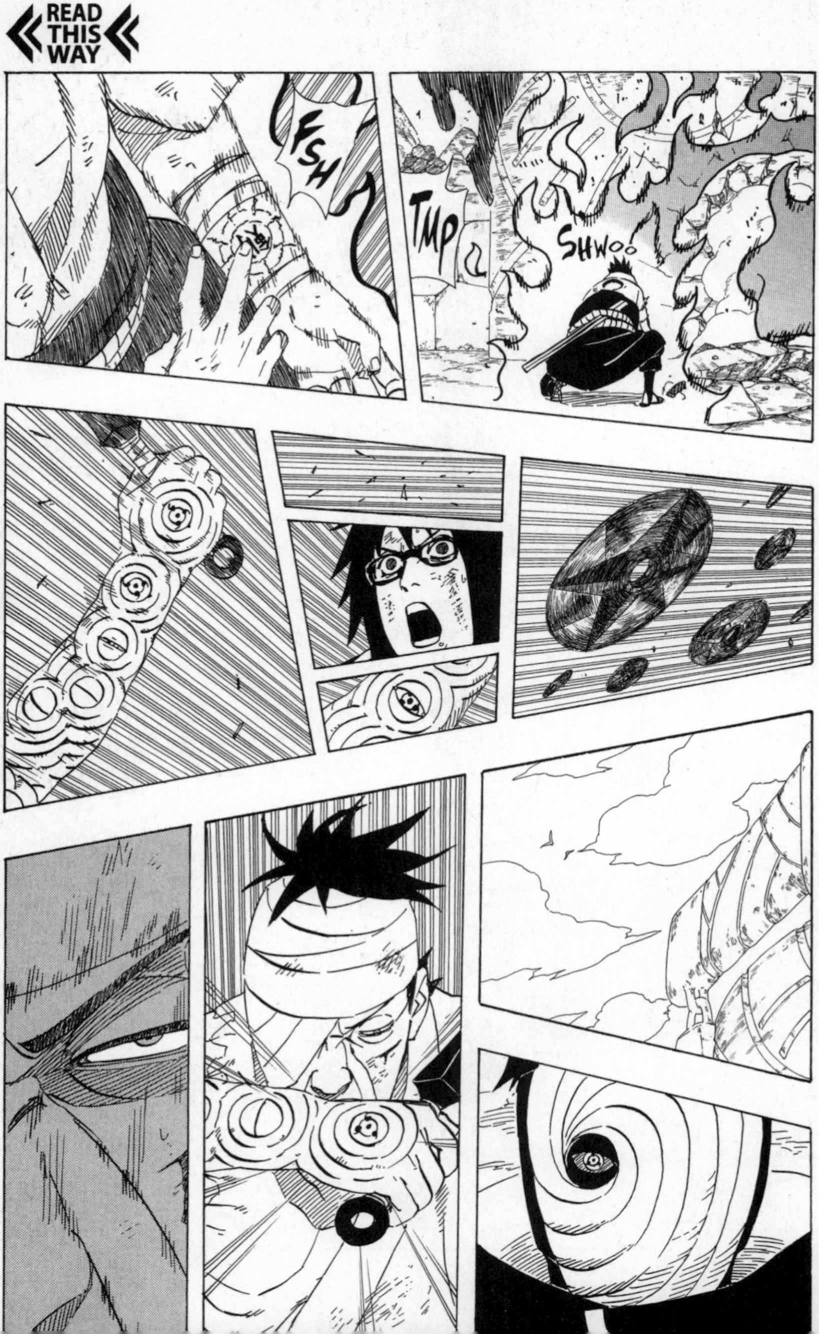
READ THIS WAY
FSH
TMP
SHWOO

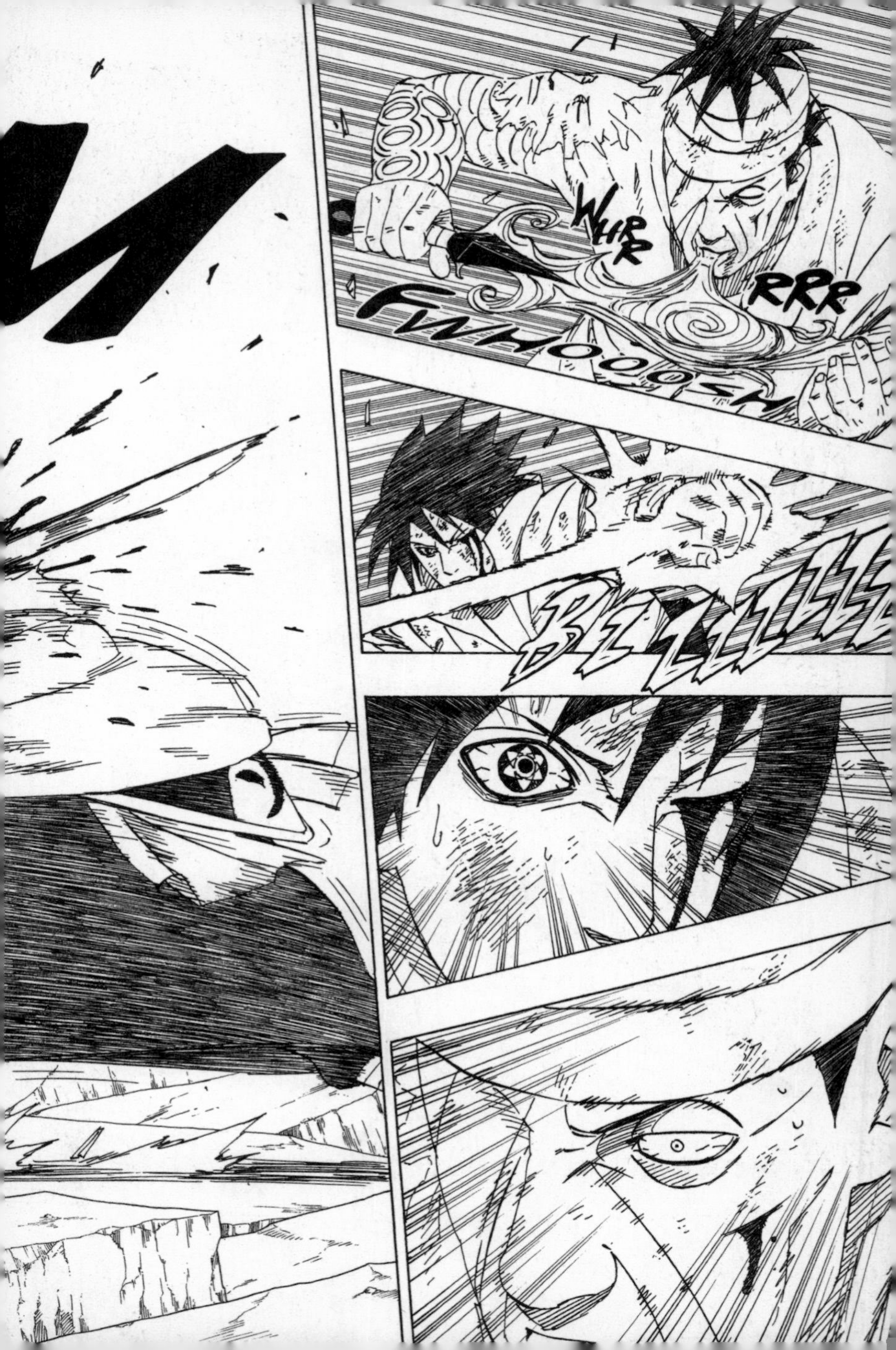
WHRR
RRR
FWHOOOSH
BZZZZZ

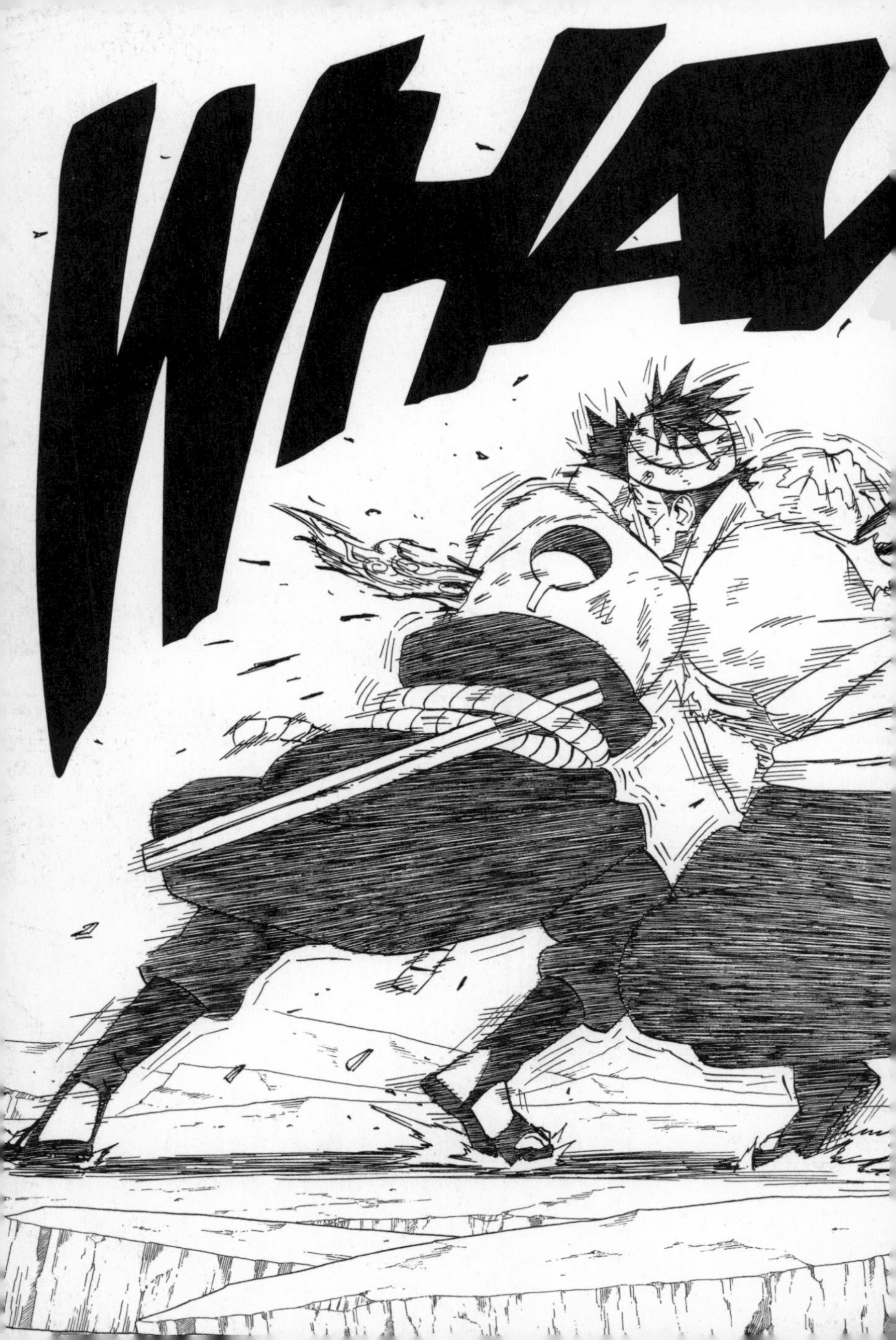
WHA

NARUTO

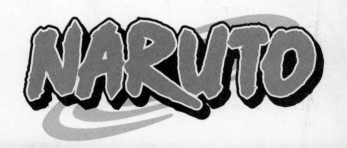

Number 480: Sacrifice

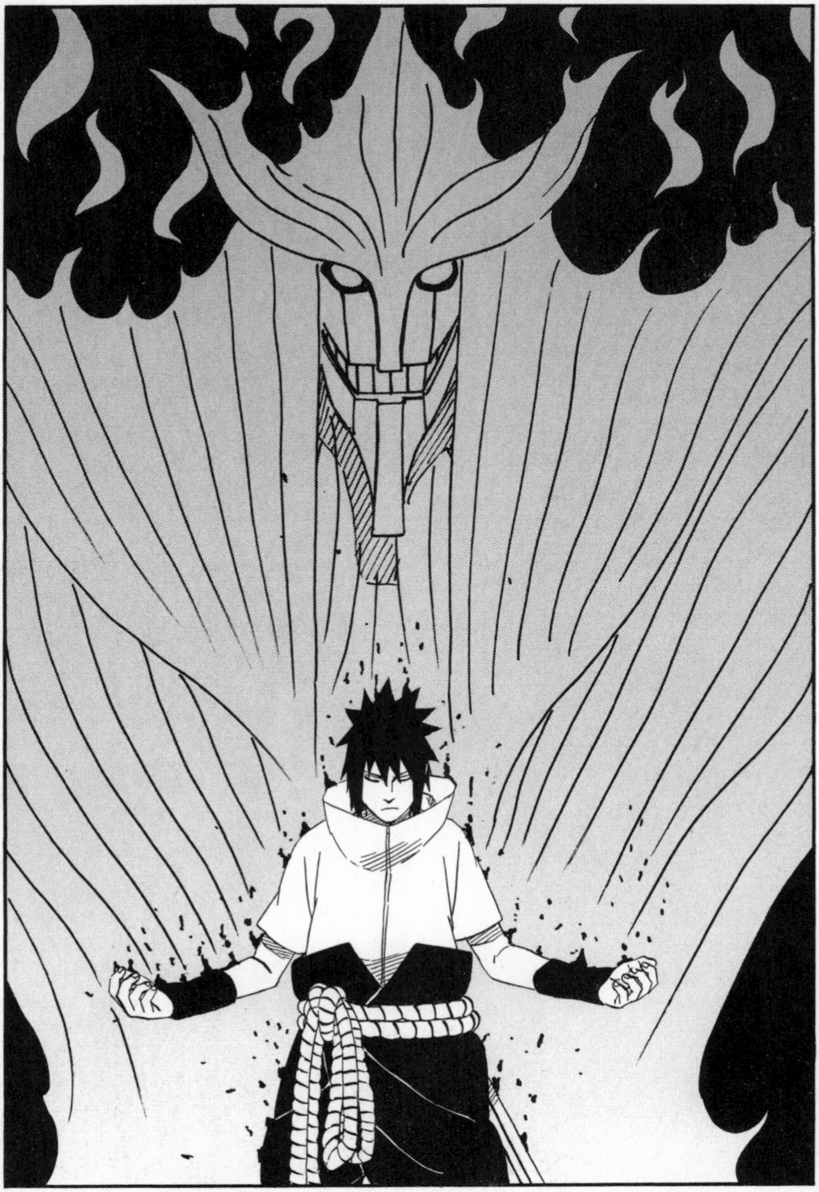

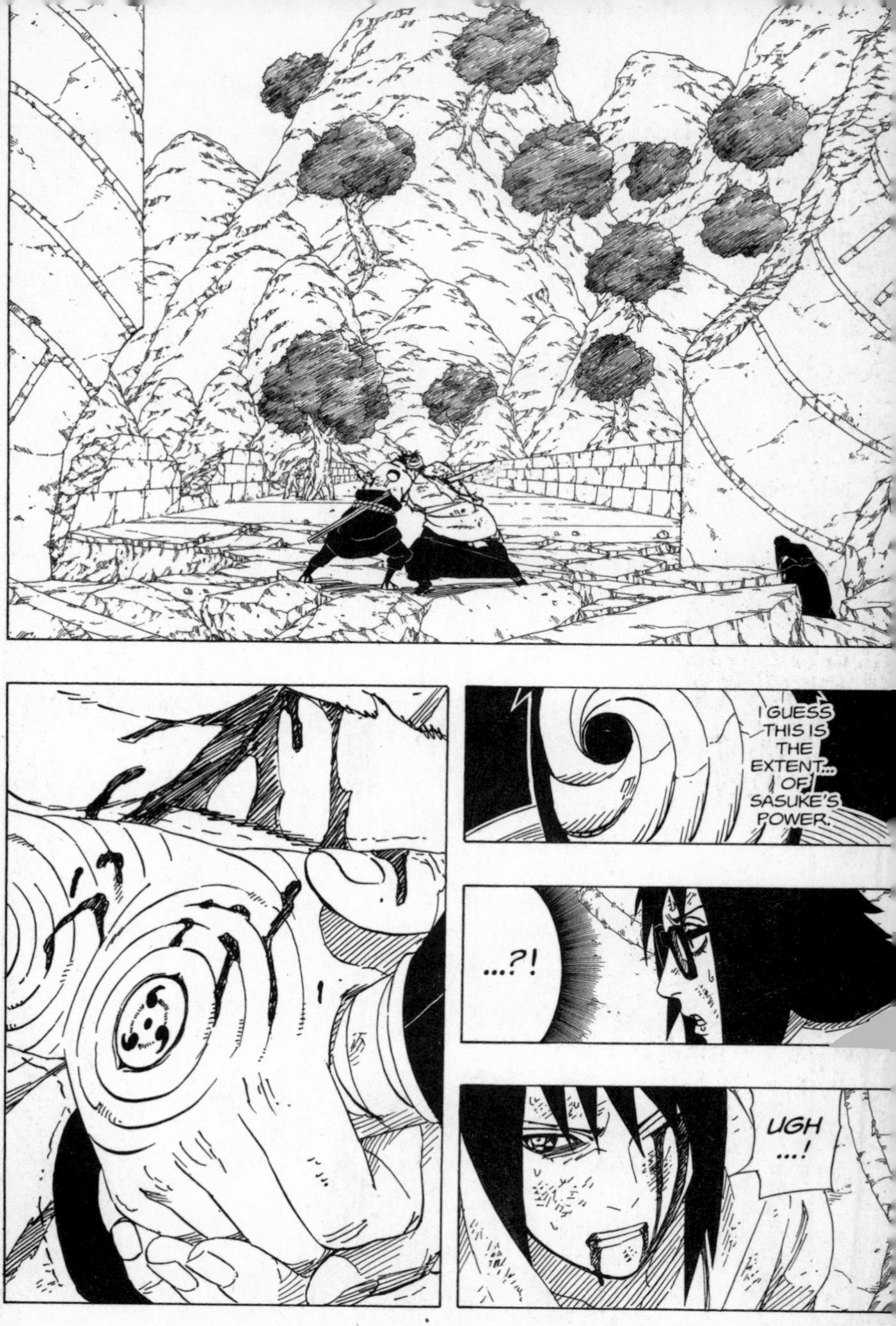
I GUESS THIS IS THE EXTENT... OF SASUKE'S POWER.
...?!
UGH ...!

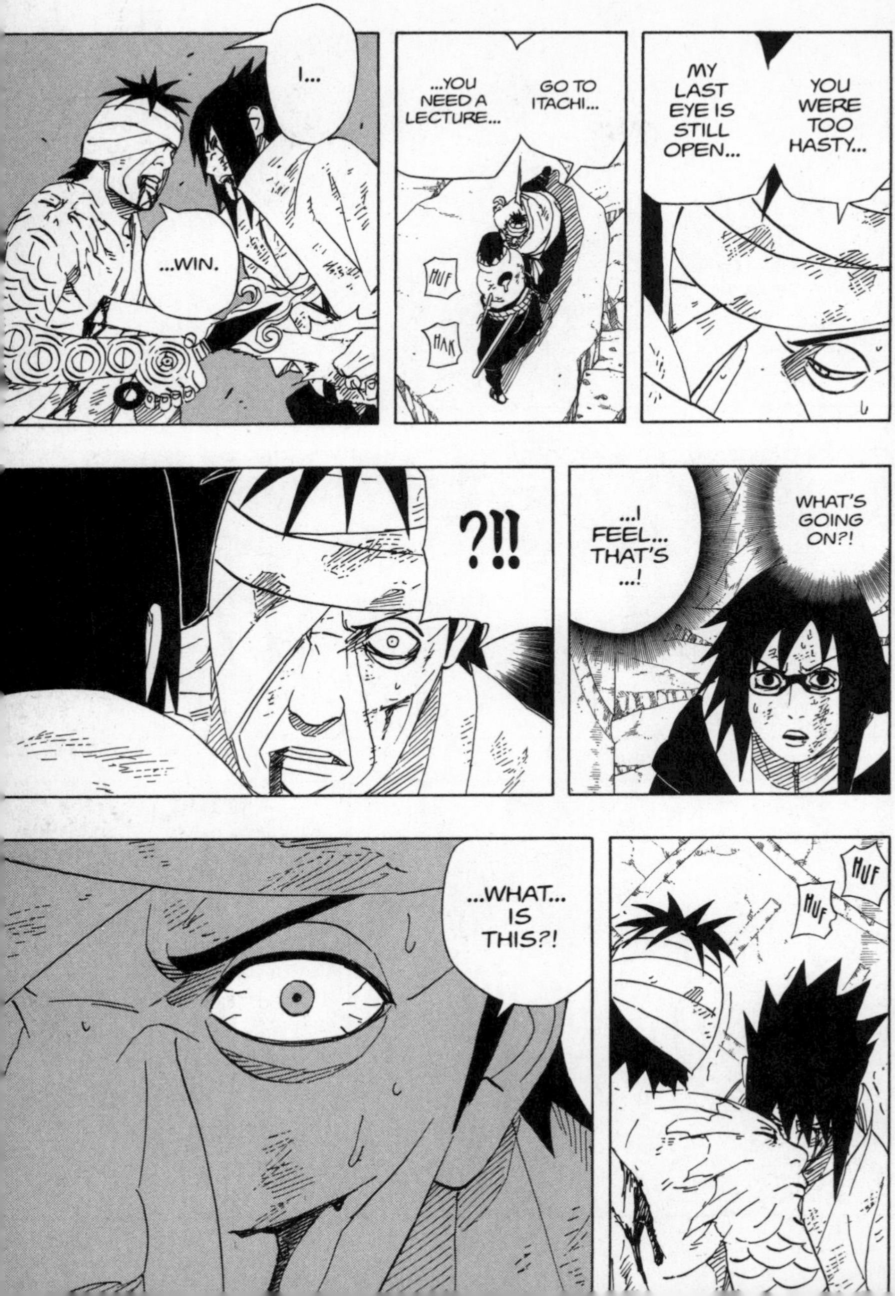
YOU WERE TOO HASTY...
MY LAST EYE IS STILL OPEN...
GO TO ITACHI...
...YOU NEED A LECTURE...
HUF
HAK
I...
...WIN.
WHAT'S GOING ON?!
...I FEEL... THAT'S ...!
?!!
MUF
MUF
...WHAT... IS THIS?!

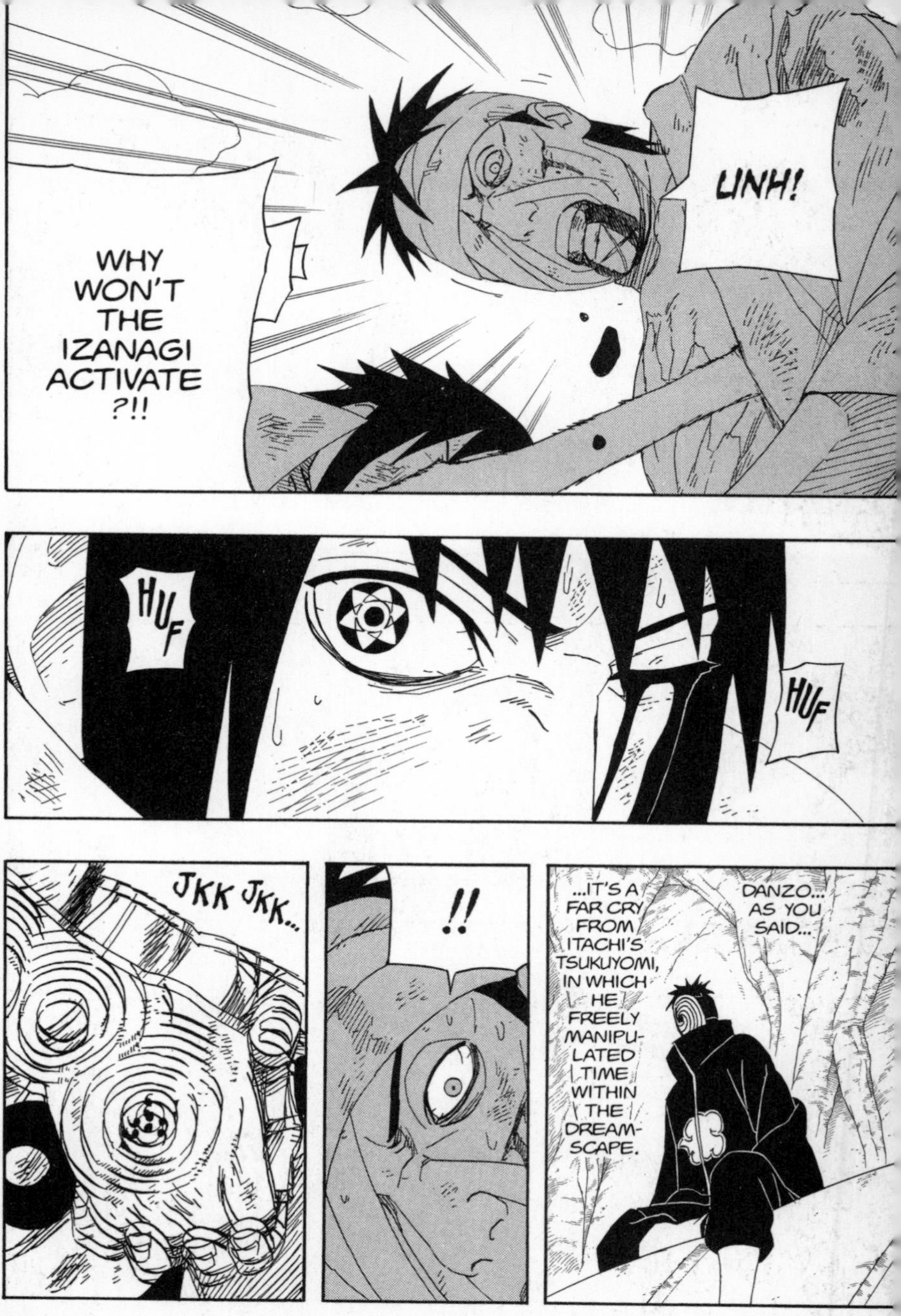
UNH!
WHY WON'T THE IZANAGI ACTIVATE ?!!
HUF
HUF
DANZO... AS YOU SAID...
...IT'S A FAR CRY FROM ITACHI'S TSUKUYOMI, IN WHICH HE FREELY MANIPULATED TIME WITHIN THE DREAMSCAPE.
!!
JKK JKK...

READ THIS WAY

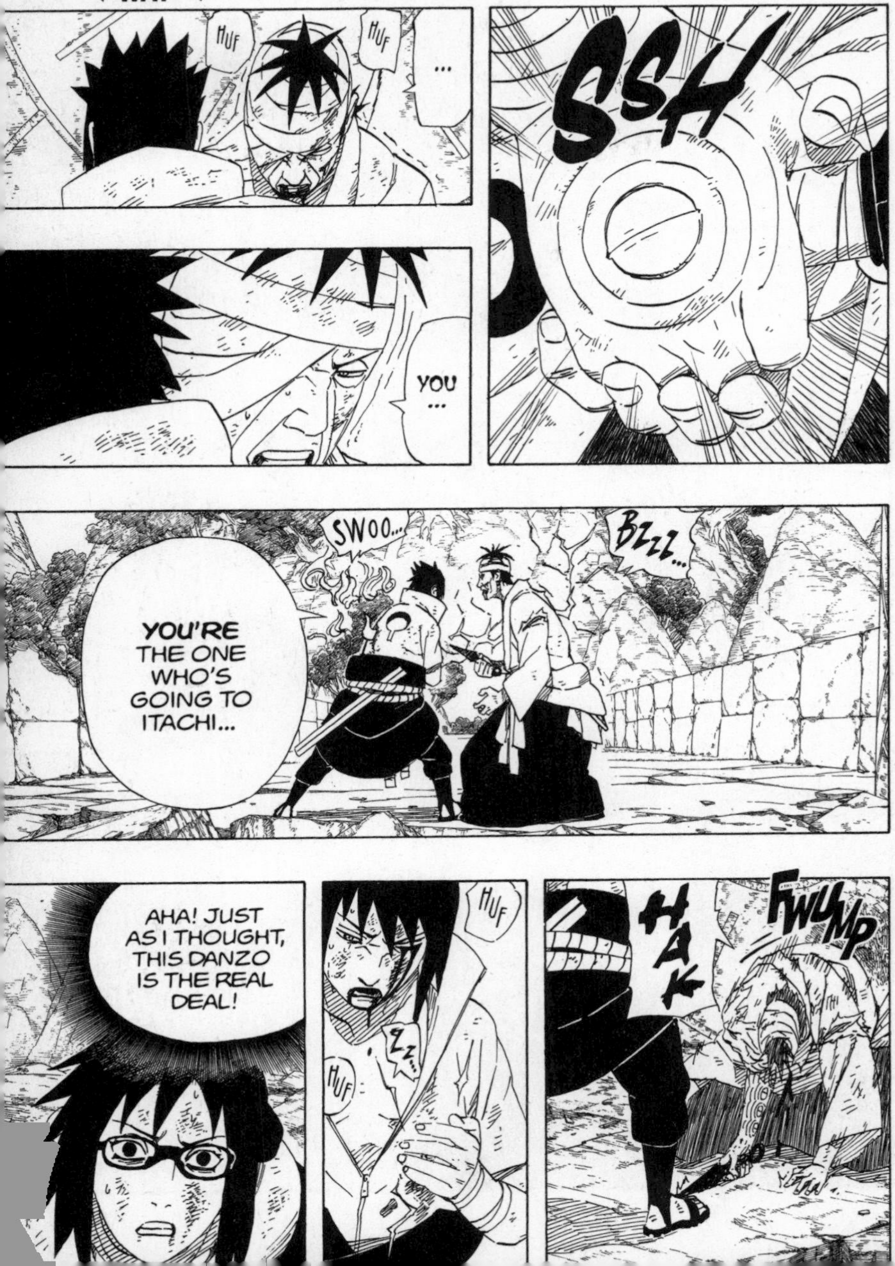

SSH
HUF
HUF
...
YOU ...
BZZZ...
SWOO...
YOU'RE THE ONE WHO'S GOING TO ITACHI...
FWUMP
HAK
HUF
ZZ...
HUF
AHA! JUST AS I THOUGHT, THIS DANZO IS THE REAL DEAL!

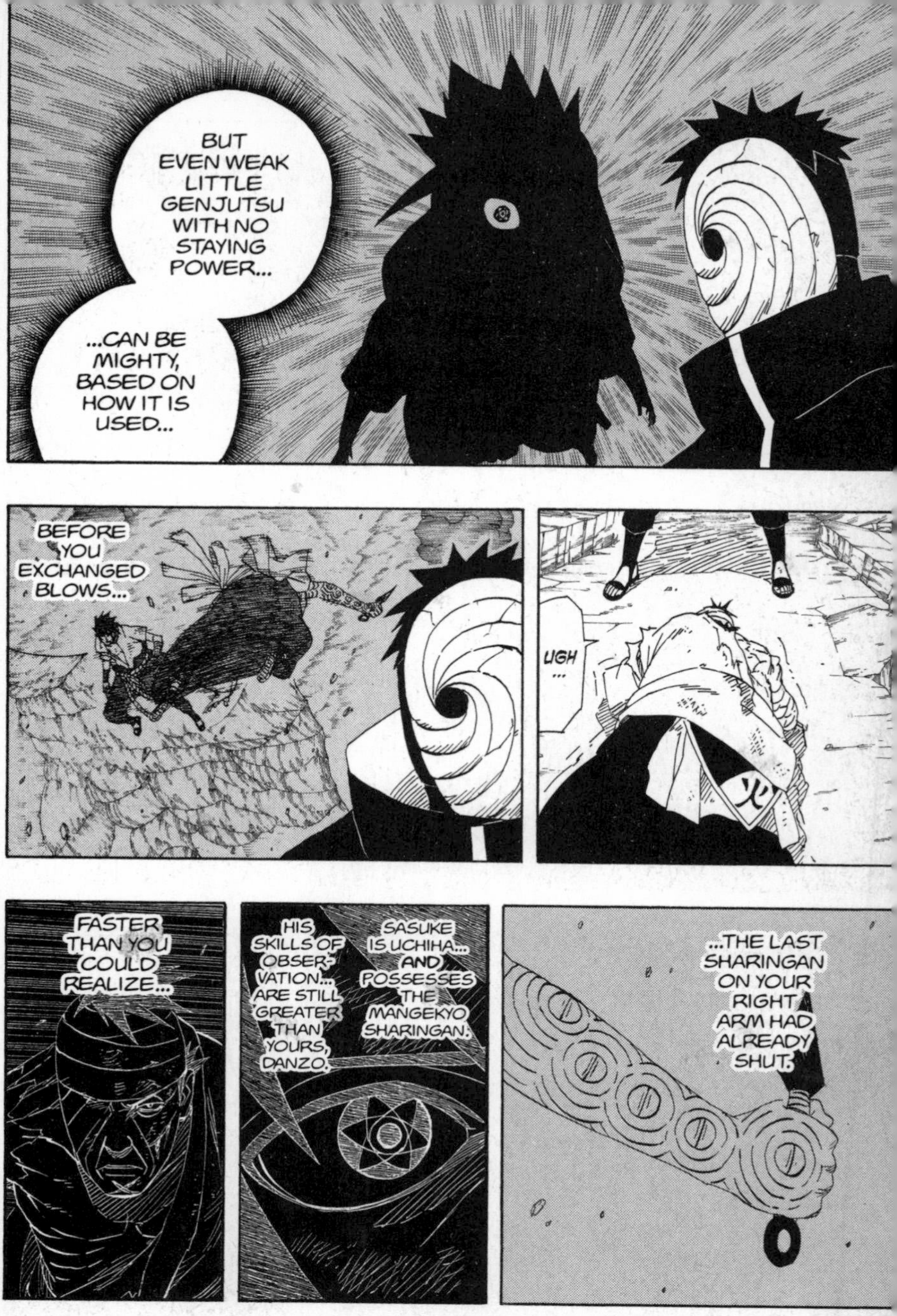

BUT EVEN WEAK LITTLE GENJUTSU WITH NO STAYING POWER...
...CAN BE MIGHTY, BASED ON HOW IT IS USED...
UGH ...
BEFORE YOU EXCHANGED BLOWS...
...THE LAST SHARINGAN ON YOUR RIGHT ARM HAD ALREADY SHUT.
SASUKE IS UCHIHA... AND POSSESSES THE MANGEKYO SHARINGAN.
HIS SKILLS OF OBSERVATION... ARE STILL GREATER THAN YOURS, DANZO.
FASTER THAN YOU COULD REALIZE...

READ THIS WAY

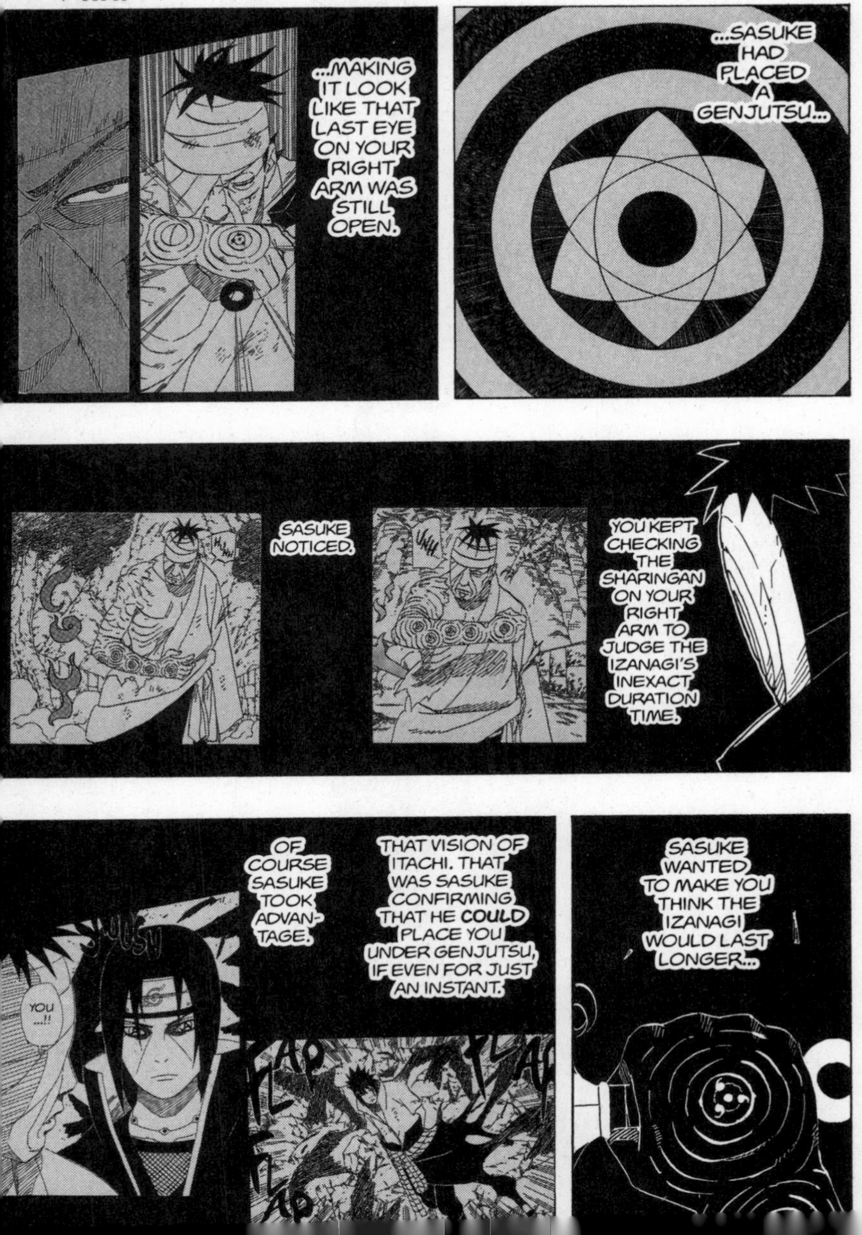
...SASUKE HAD PLACED A GENJUTSU...
...MAKING IT LOOK LIKE THAT LAST EYE ON YOUR RIGHT ARM WAS STILL OPEN.
YOU KEPT CHECKING THE SHARINGAN ON YOUR RIGHT ARM TO JUDGE THE IZANAGI'S INEXACT DURATION TIME.
UNH
SASUKE NOTICED.
SASUKE WANTED TO MAKE YOU THINK THE IZANAGI WOULD LAST LONGER...
THAT VISION OF ITACHI. THAT WAS SASUKE CONFIRMING THAT HE **COULD** PLACE YOU UNDER GENJUTSU, IF EVEN FOR JUST AN INSTANT.
FLAP FLAP
FLAP
OF COURSE SASUKE TOOK ADVANTAGE.
YOU ...!!

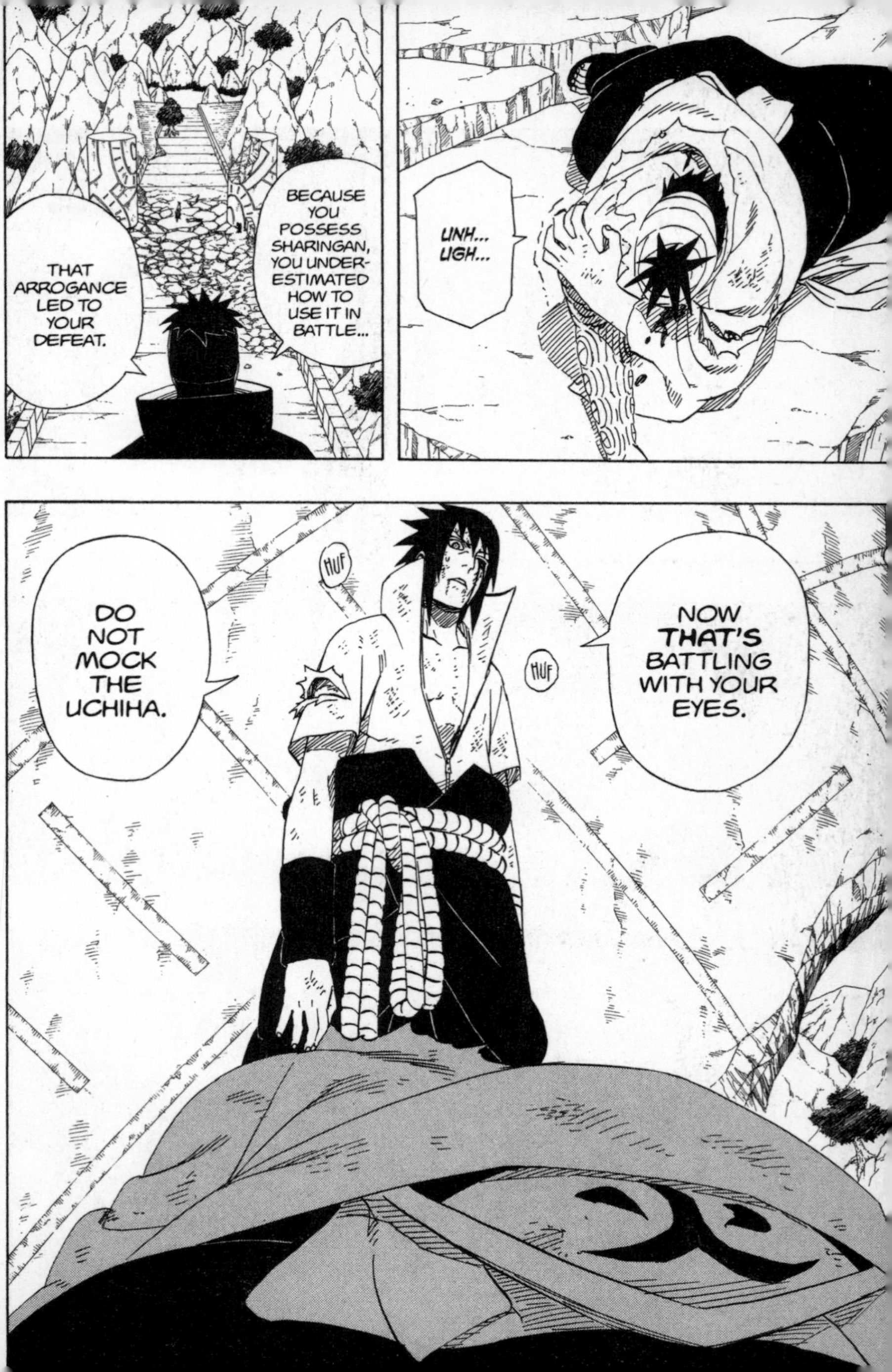
UNH... UGH...
BECAUSE YOU POSSESS SHARINGAN, YOU UNDER-ESTIMATED HOW TO USE IT IN BATTLE...
THAT ARROGANCE LED TO YOUR DEFEAT.
NOW THAT'S BATTLING WITH YOUR EYES.
HUF
HUF
DO NOT MOCK THE UCHIHA.

READ THIS WAY

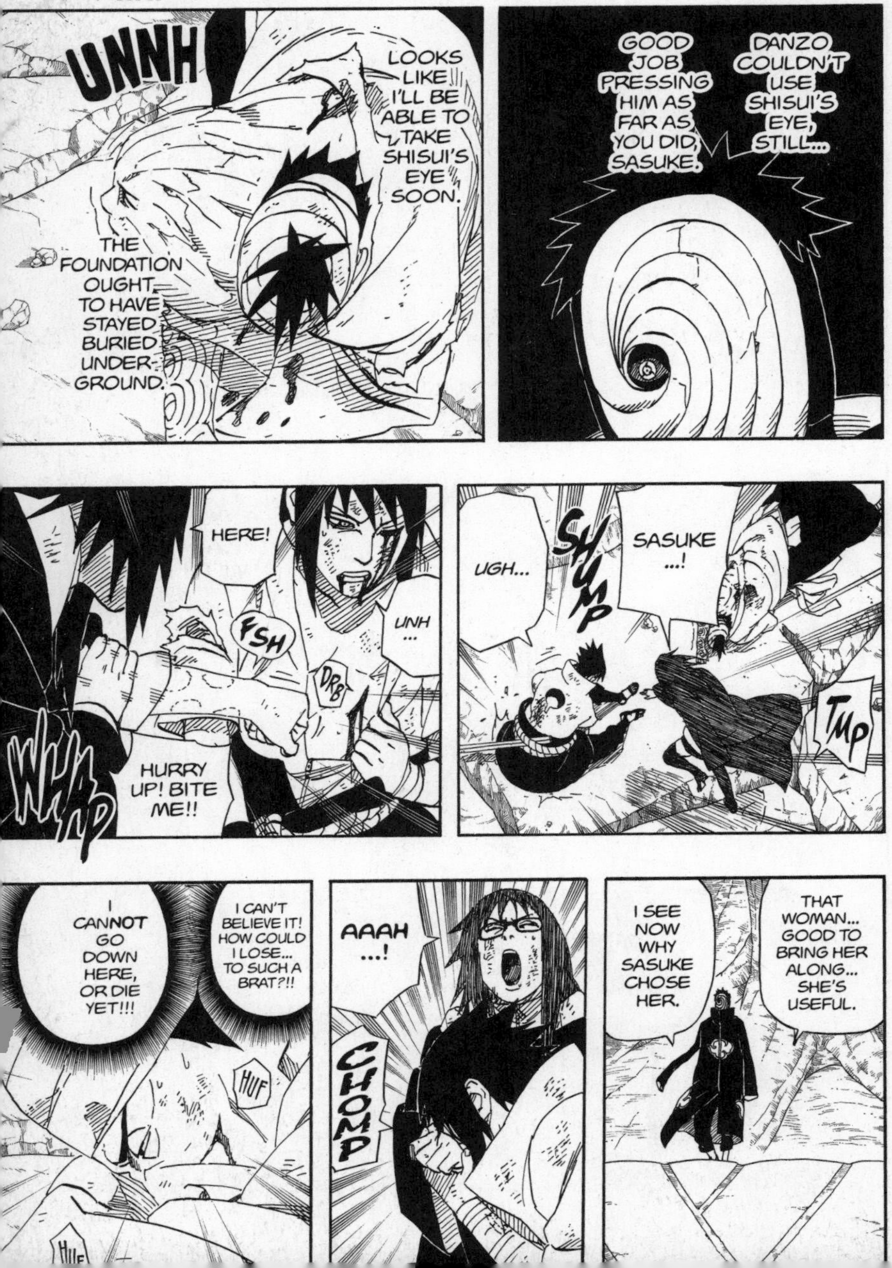
DANZO COULDN'T USE SHISUI'S EYE, STILL...
GOOD JOB PRESSING HIM AS FAR AS YOU DID, SASUKE.
UNNH
LOOKS LIKE I'LL BE ABLE TO TAKE SHISUI'S EYE SOON.
THE FOUNDATION OUGHT TO HAVE STAYED BURIED UNDERGROUND.
SASUKE ...!
SHUMP
UGH...
TMP
HERE!
UNH ...
FSH
DRB
HURRY UP! BITE ME!!
WHAP
THAT WOMAN... GOOD TO BRING HER ALONG... SHE'S USEFUL.
I SEE NOW WHY SASUKE CHOSE HER.
AAAH ...!
CHOMP
I CAN'T BELIEVE IT! HOW COULD I LOSE... TO SUCH A BRAT?!!
I CANNOT GO DOWN HERE, OR DIE YET!!!
HUF
HUF

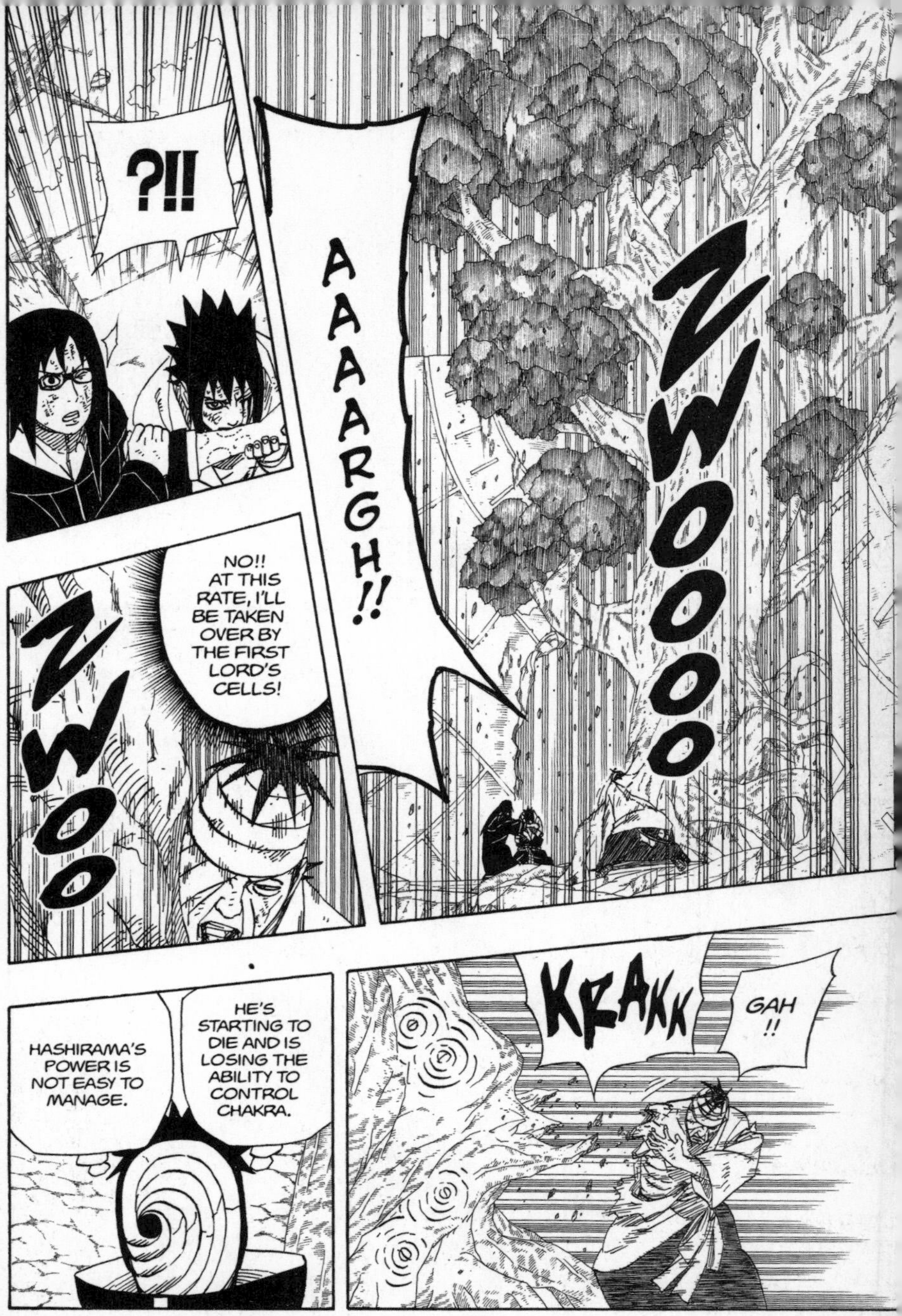
ZWOOOO
AAAARGH!!
?!!
NO!! AT THIS RATE, I'LL BE TAKEN OVER BY THE FIRST LORD'S CELLS!
ZWOO
KRAKK
GAH!!
HE'S STARTING TO DIE AND IS LOSING THE ABILITY TO CONTROL CHAKRA.
HASHIRAMA'S POWER IS NOT EASY TO MANAGE.

READ THIS WAY

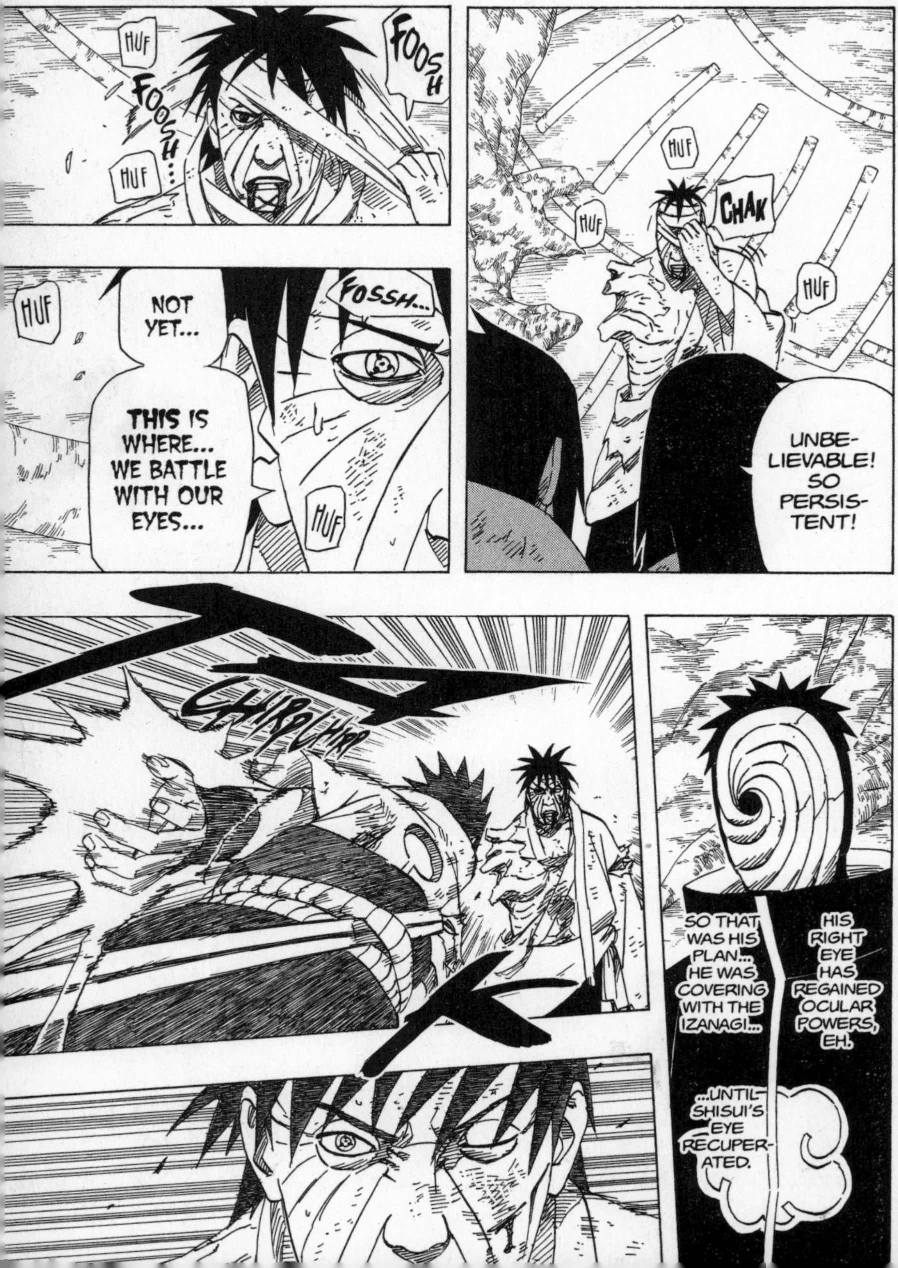
HUF
HUF
CHAK
HUF
HUF
UNBELIEVABLE! SO PERSISTENT!
FOOSH
HUF
FOOSH...
HUF
YOSSH...
NOT YET...
THIS IS WHERE... WE BATTLE WITH OUR EYES...
HUF
HUF
HIS RIGHT EYE HAS REGAINED OCULAR POWERS, EH.
SO THAT WAS HIS PLAN... HE WAS COVERING WITH THE IZANAGI...
...UNTIL SHISUI'S EYE RECUPERATED.
CHIRP CHIRP

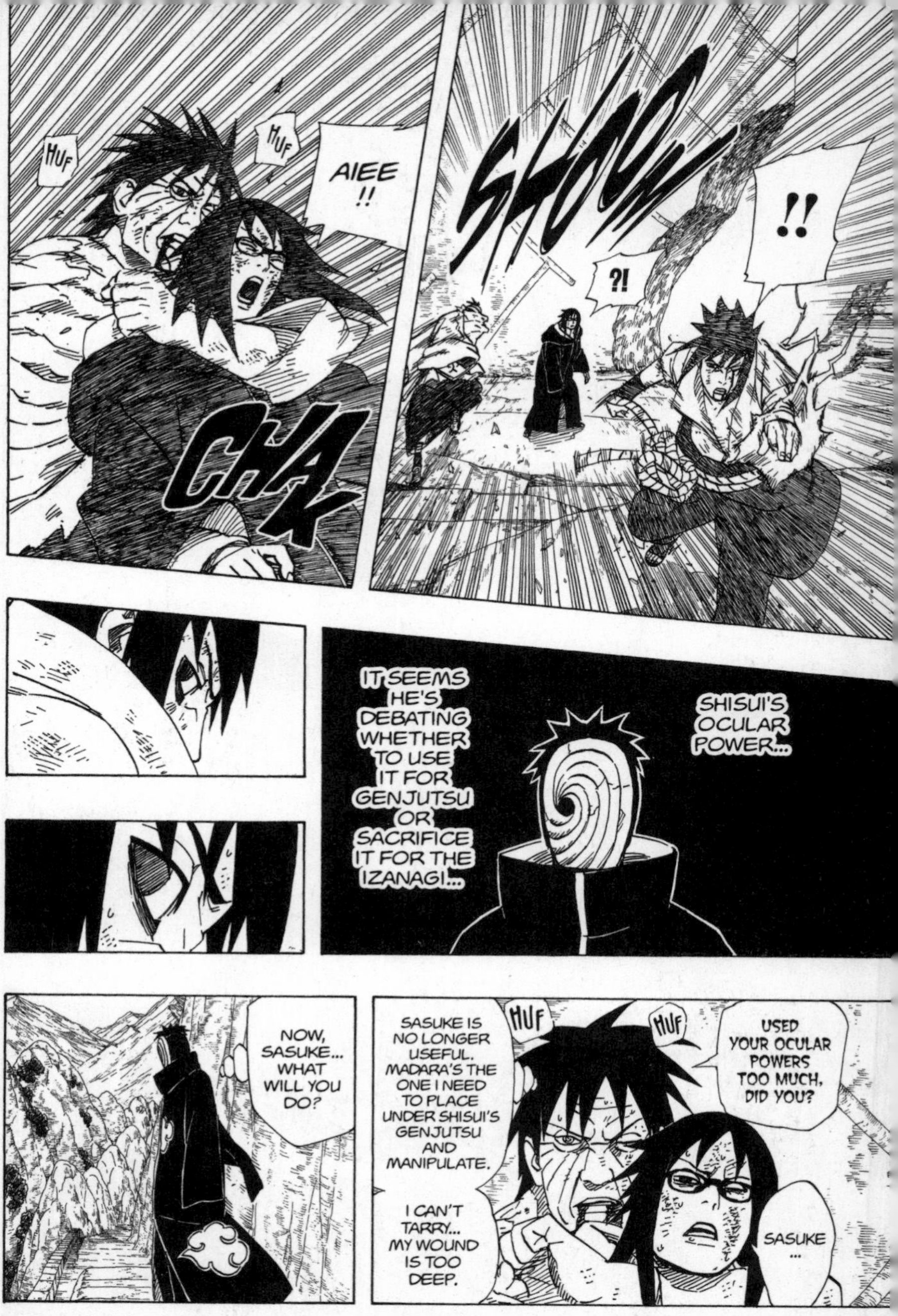
HUF
HUF
AIEE!!
CHAK
SHOOK
?!
!!
IT SEEMS HE'S DEBATING WHETHER TO USE IT FOR GENJUTSU OR SACRIFICE IT FOR THE IZANAGI...
SHISUI'S OCULAR POWER...
NOW, SASUKE... WHAT WILL YOU DO?
HUF
HUF
USED YOUR OCULAR POWERS TOO MUCH, DID YOU?
SASUKE IS NO LONGER USEFUL. MADARA'S THE ONE I NEED TO PLACE UNDER SHISUI'S GENJUTSU AND MANIPULATE.
I CAN'T TARRY... MY WOUND IS TOO DEEP.
SASUKE...

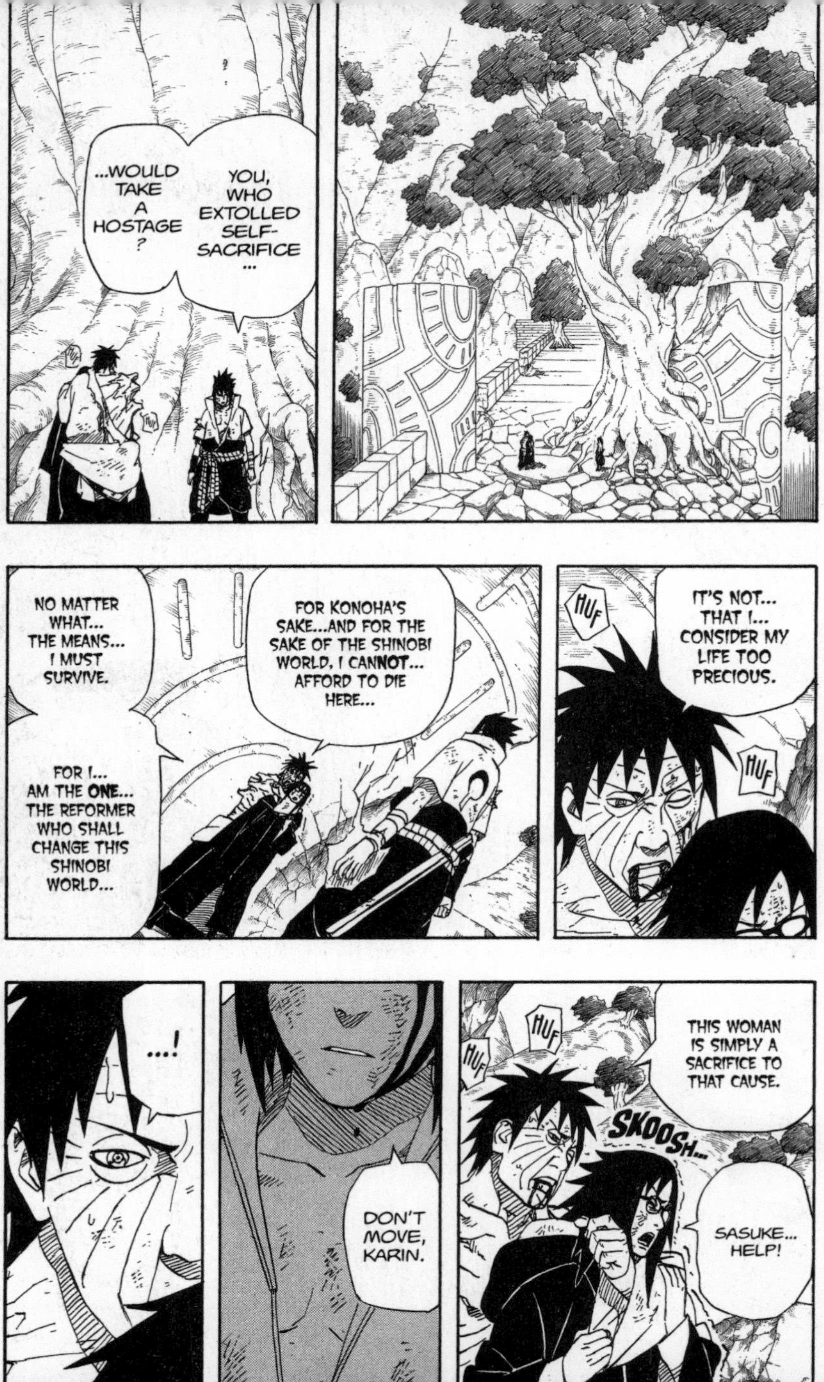

YOU, WHO EXTOLLED SELF-SACRIFICE...
...WOULD TAKE A HOSTAGE?
HUF
IT'S NOT... THAT I... CONSIDER MY LIFE TOO PRECIOUS.
HUF
FOR KONOHA'S SAKE...AND FOR THE SAKE OF THE SHINOBI WORLD, I CANNOT... AFFORD TO DIE HERE...
NO MATTER WHAT... THE MEANS... I MUST SURVIVE.
FOR I... AM THE ONE... THE REFORMER WHO SHALL CHANGE THIS SHINOBI WORLD...
HUF
HUF
THIS WOMAN IS SIMPLY A SACRIFICE TO THAT CAUSE.
SKOOSH...
SASUKE... HELP!
DON'T MOVE, KARIN.
...!

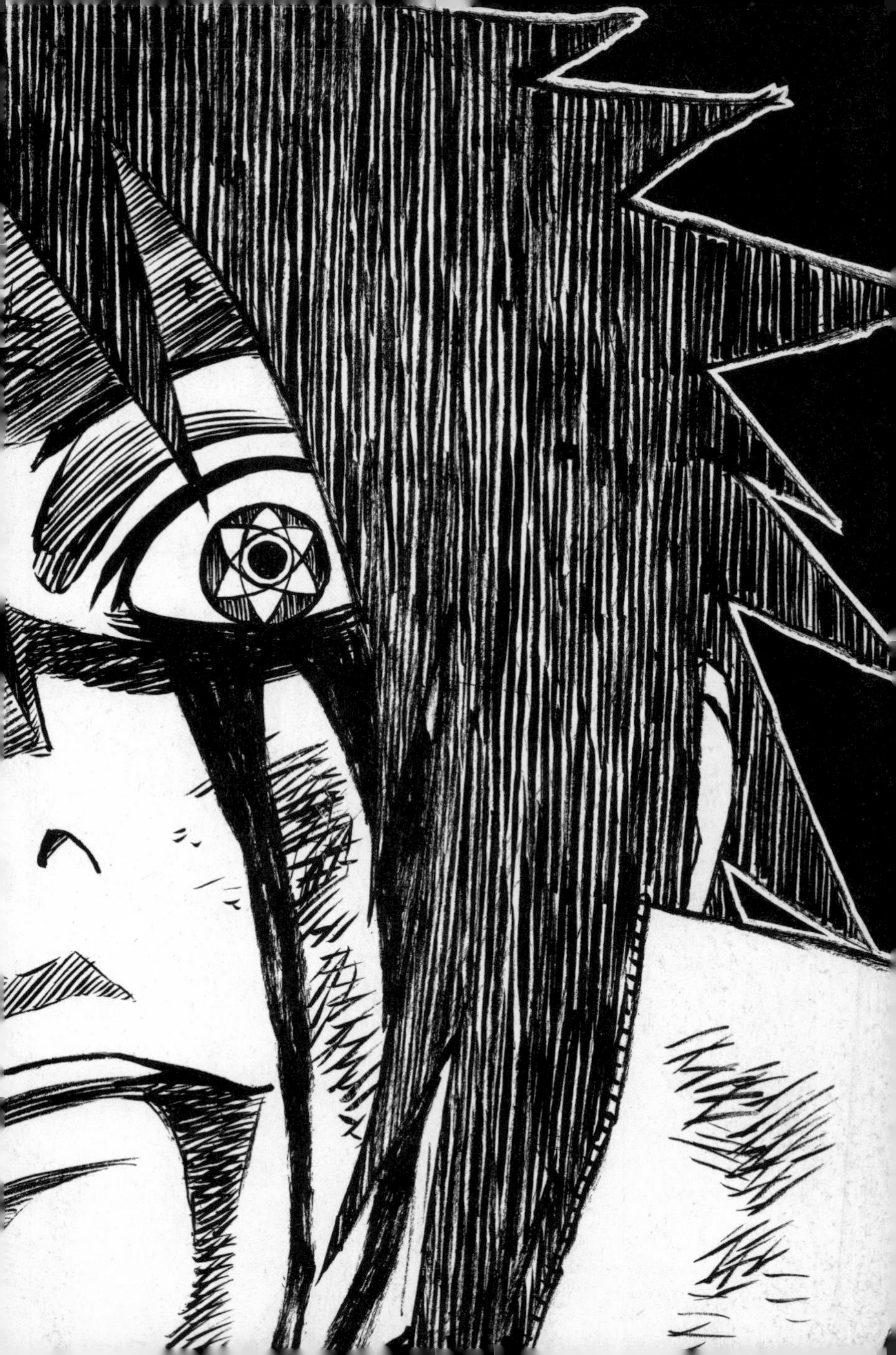

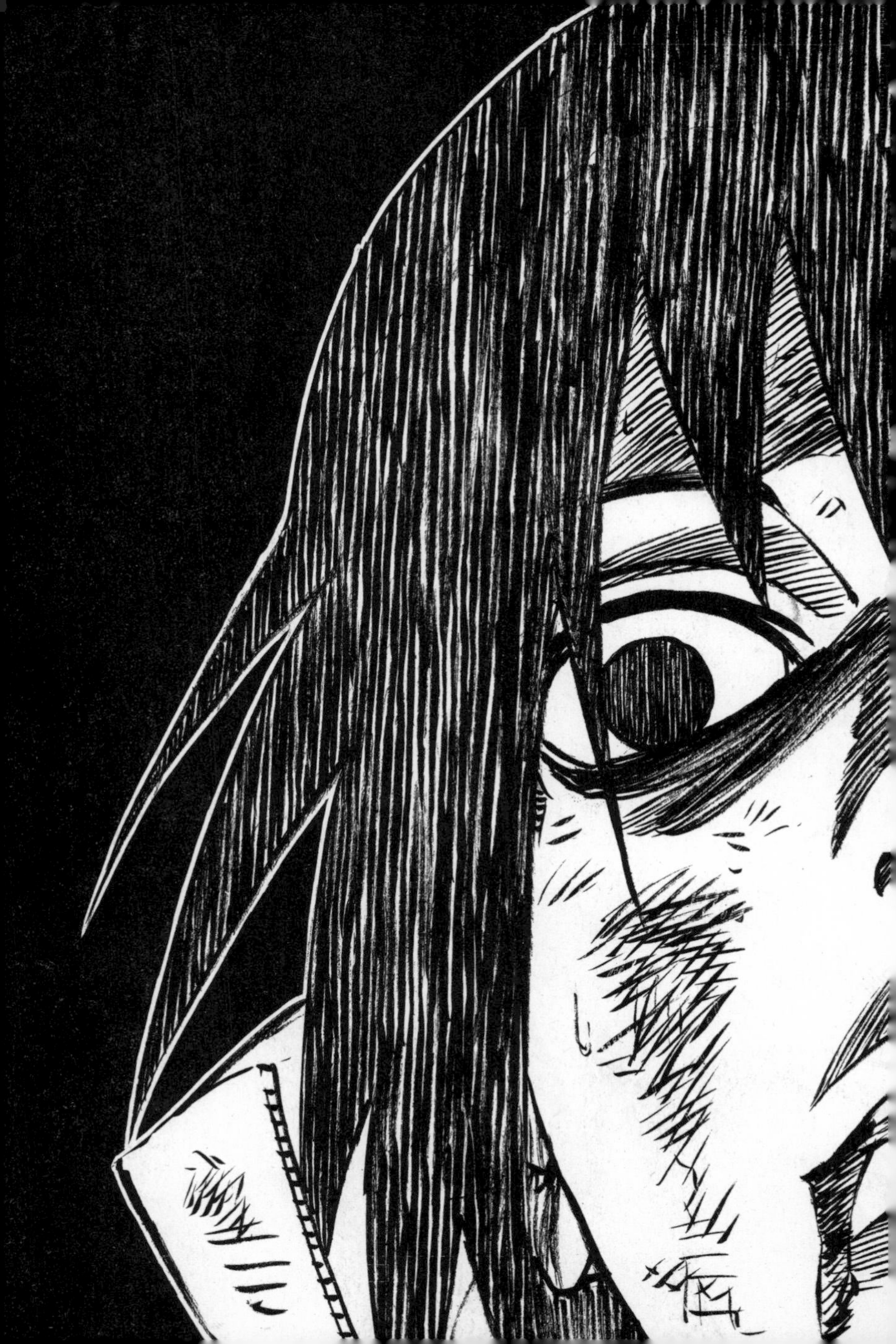

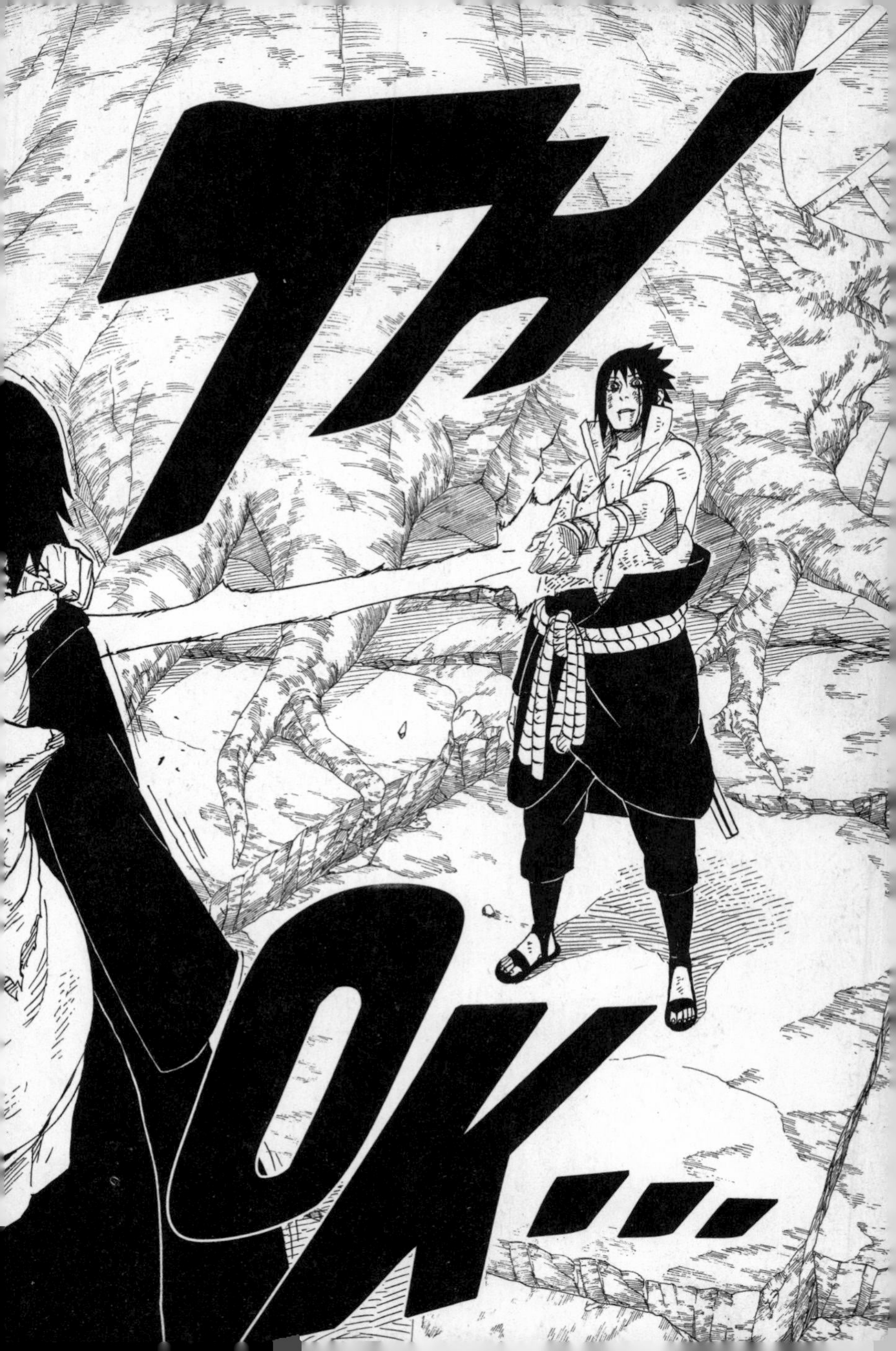

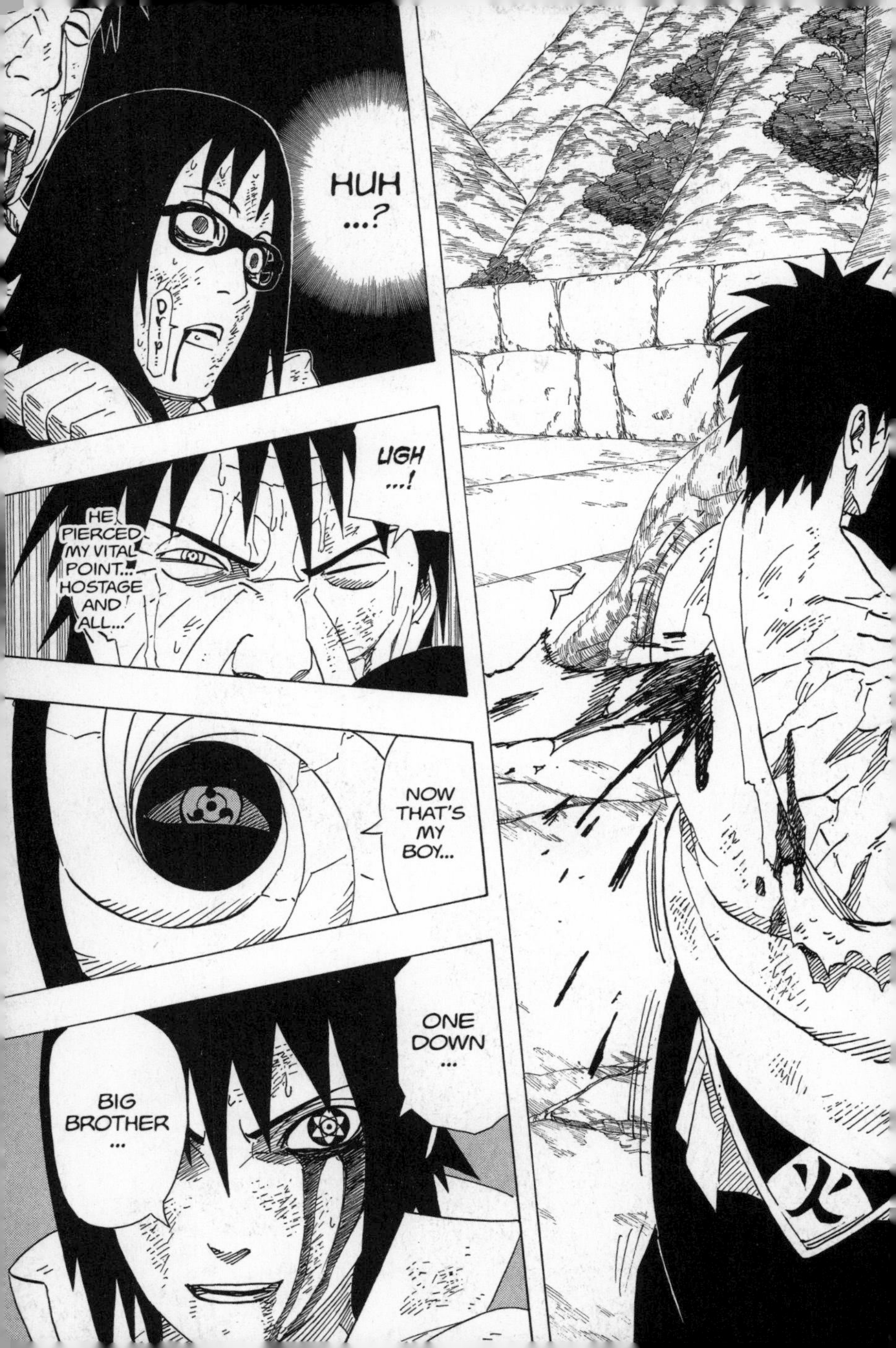
HUH ...?
Drip...
UGH ...!
HE PIERCED MY VITAL POINT... HOSTAGE AND ALL...
NOW THAT'S MY BOY...
ONE DOWN ...
BIG BROTHER ...

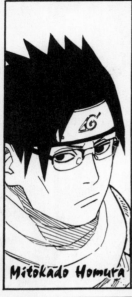

Number 481: The Death of Danzo!!

Mitokado Homura
Sarutobi Hiruzen
Utatane Koharu
Akimichi Torifu
Shimura Danzo
Uchiha Kagami

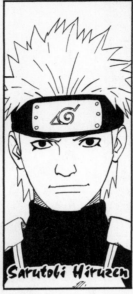

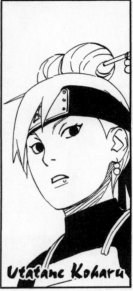

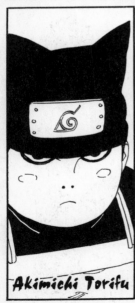

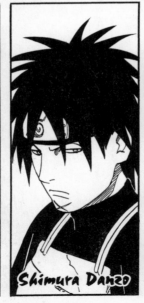

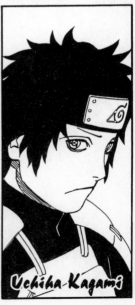

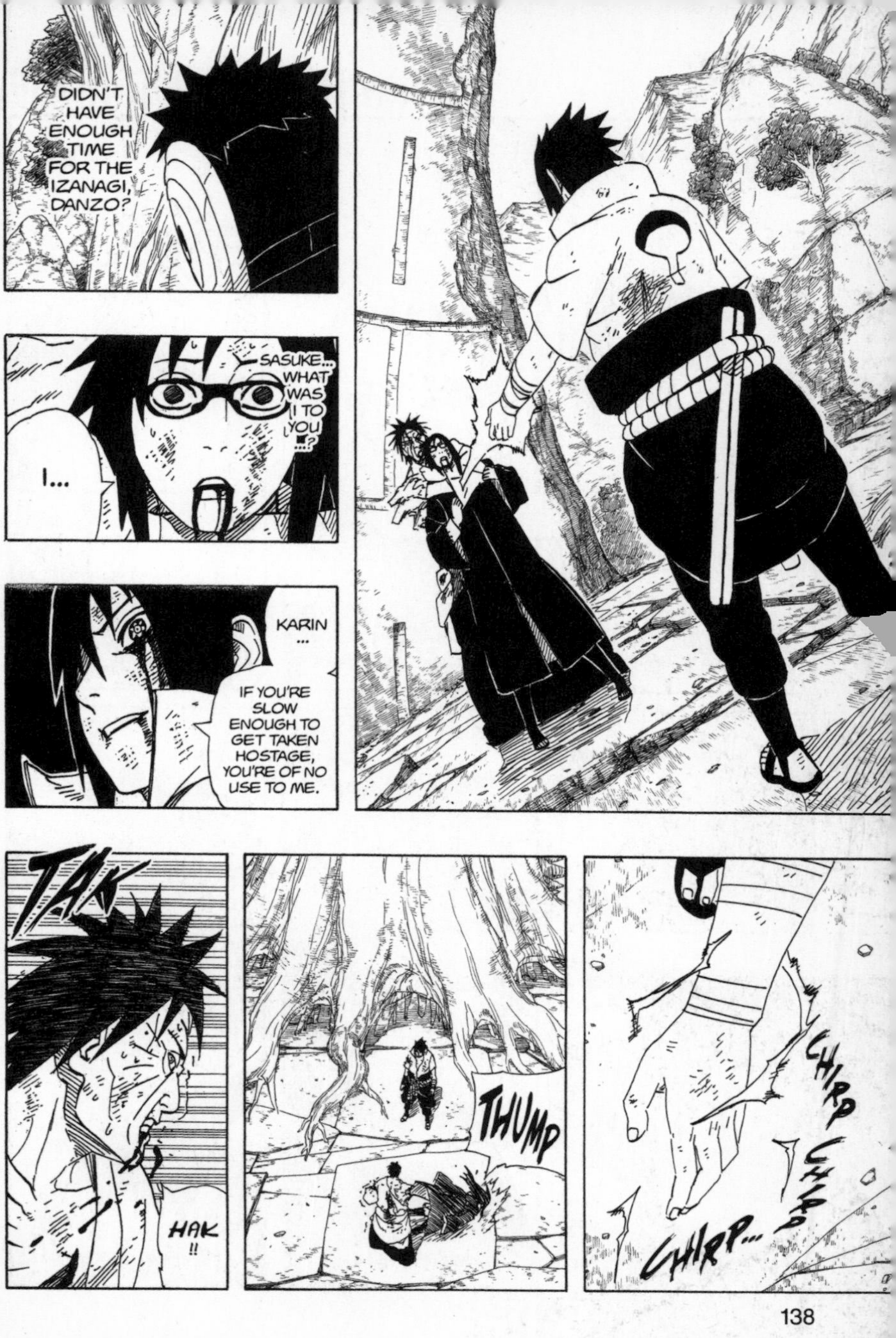
DIDN'T HAVE ENOUGH TIME FOR THE IZANAGI, DANZO?
SASUKE... WHAT WAS I TO YOU ...?
I...
KARIN ...
IF YOU'RE SLOW ENOUGH TO GET TAKEN HOSTAGE, YOU'RE OF NO USE TO ME.
CHIRP CHIRP CHIRP...
THUMP
TAK
HAK !!

READ THIS WAY

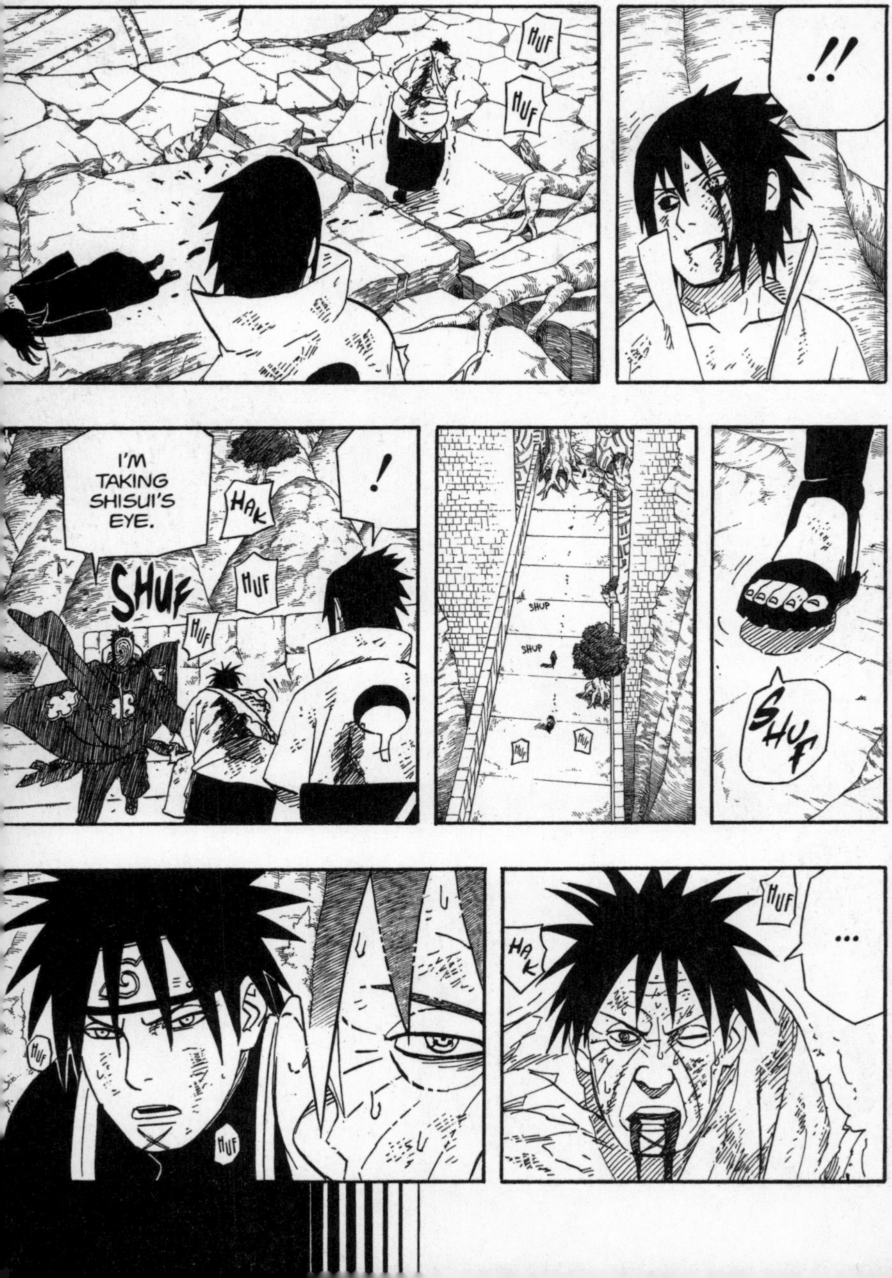
!!
HUF
HUF
SHUF
SHUP
SHUP
HUF
HUF
!
HAK
I'M TAKING SHISUI'S EYE.
SHUF
HUF
HUF
HUF
HAK
...
HUF
HUF

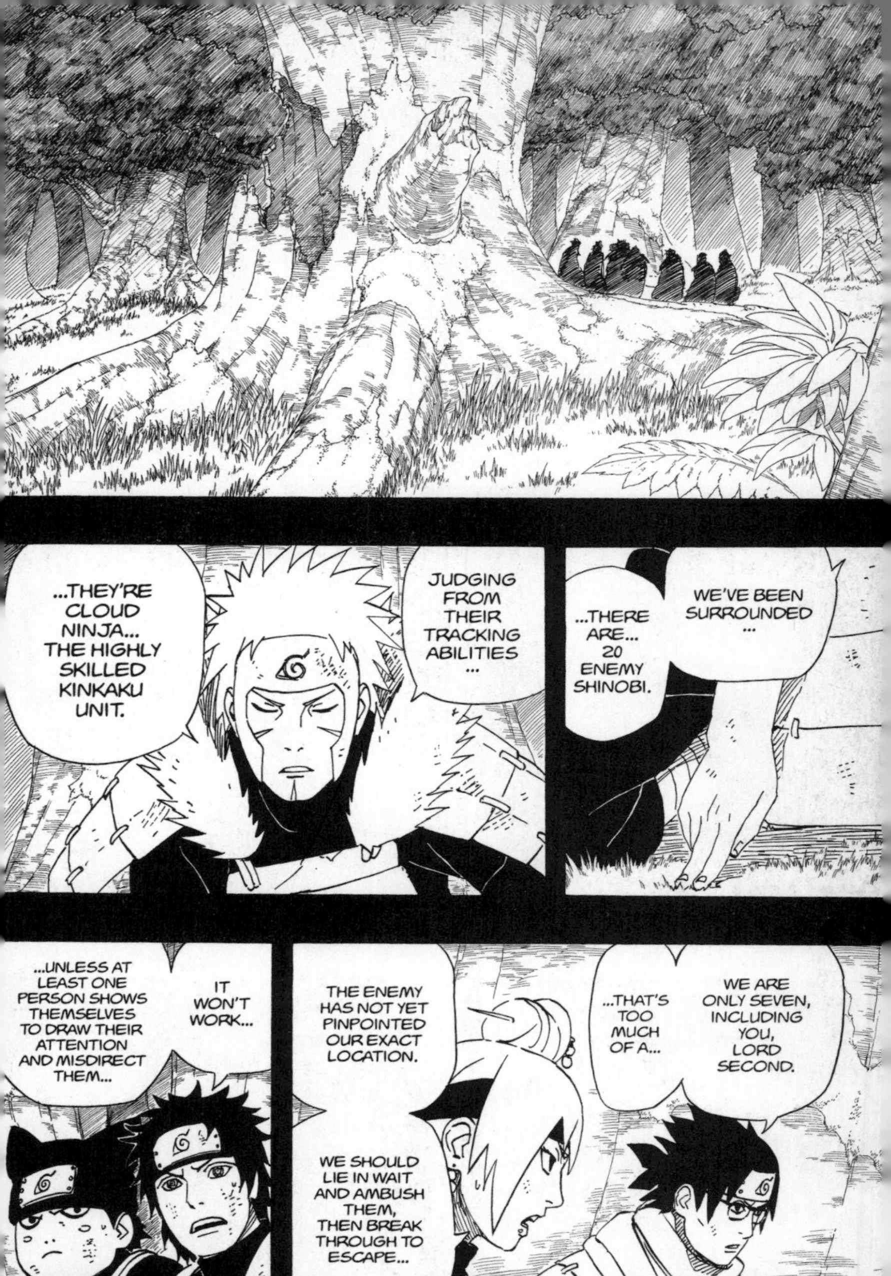
WE'VE BEEN SURROUNDED ...
...THERE ARE... 20 ENEMY SHINOBI.
JUDGING FROM THEIR TRACKING ABILITIES ...
...THEY'RE CLOUD NINJA... THE HIGHLY SKILLED KINKAKU UNIT.
WE ARE ONLY SEVEN, INCLUDING YOU, LORD SECOND.
...THAT'S TOO MUCH OF A...
THE ENEMY HAS NOT YET PINPOINTED OUR EXACT LOCATION.
WE SHOULD LIE IN WAIT AND AMBUSH THEM, THEN BREAK THROUGH TO ESCAPE...
IT WON'T WORK...
...UNLESS AT LEAST ONE PERSON SHOWS THEMSELVES TO DRAW THEIR ATTENTION AND MISDIRECT THEM...

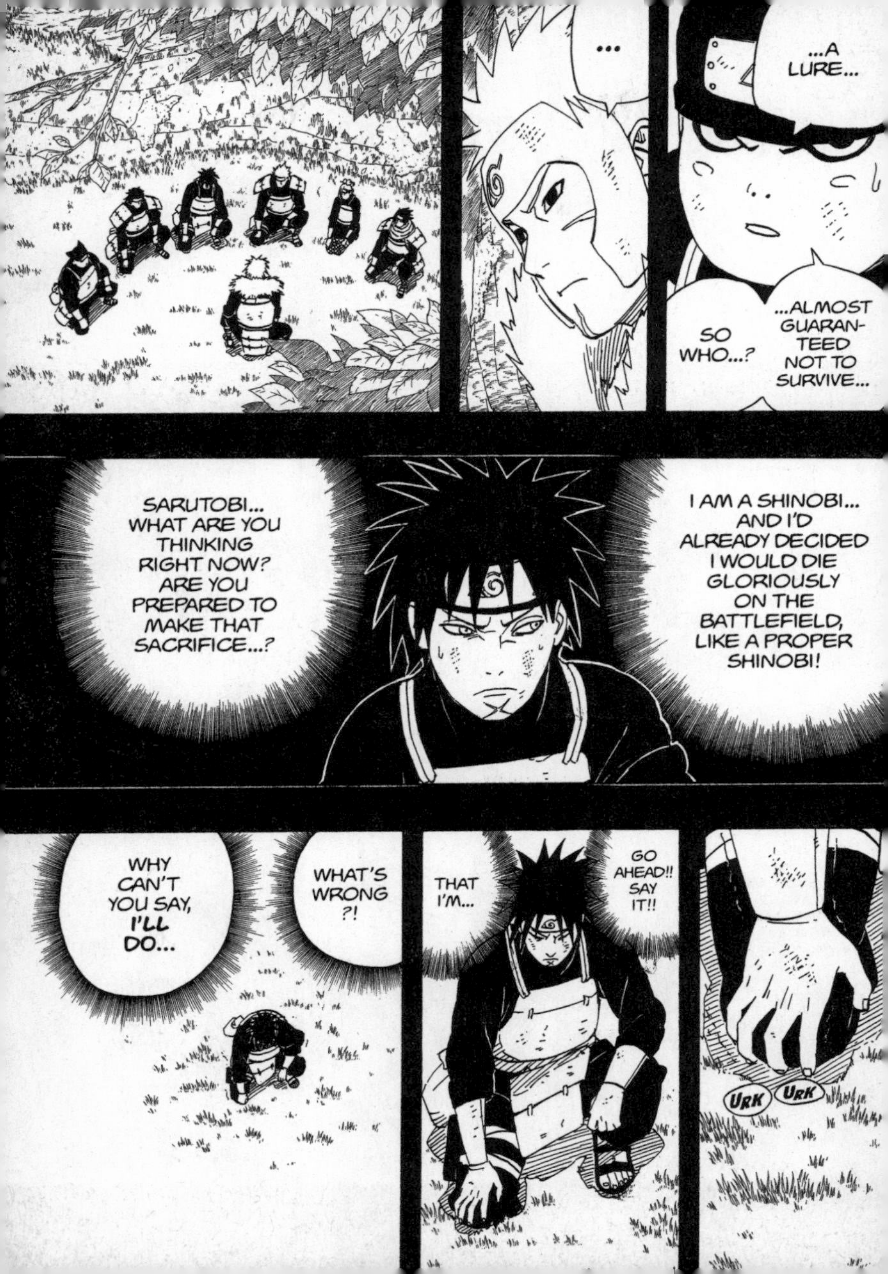

...A LURE...
...ALMOST GUARANTEED NOT TO SURVIVE...
SO WHO...?
...
I AM A SHINOBI... AND I'D ALREADY DECIDED I WOULD DIE GLORIOUSLY ON THE BATTLEFIELD, LIKE A PROPER SHINOBI!
SARUTOBI... WHAT ARE YOU THINKING RIGHT NOW? ARE YOU PREPARED TO MAKE THAT SACRIFICE...?
URK
URK
GO AHEAD!! SAY IT!!
THAT I'M...
WHAT'S WRONG ?!
WHY CAN'T YOU SAY, I'LL DO...

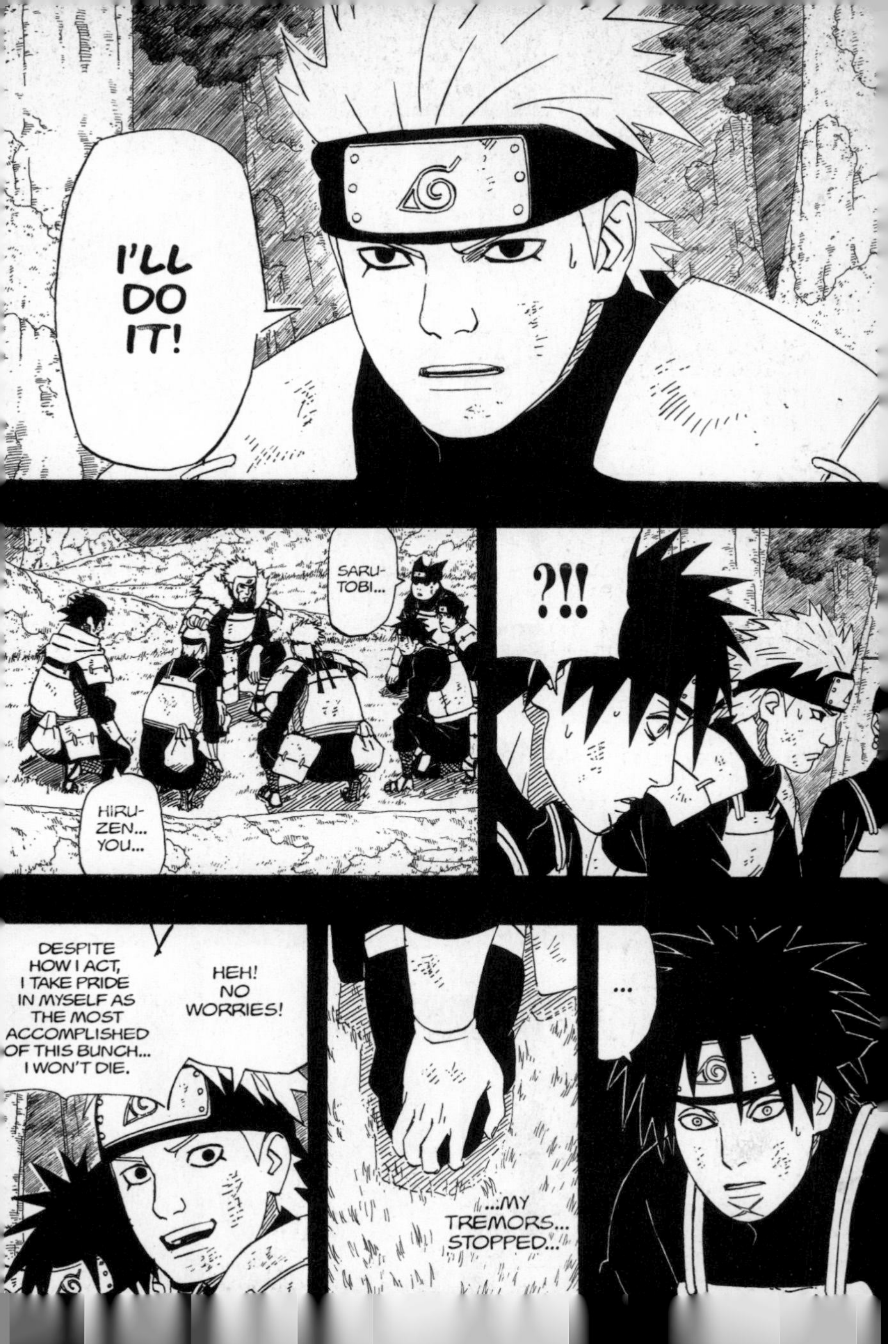
I'LL DO IT!
?!!
SARU-TOBI...
HIRU-ZEN... YOU...
...
...MY TREMORS... STOPPED...
HEH! NO WORRIES!
DESPITE HOW I ACT, I TAKE PRIDE IN MYSELF AS THE MOST ACCOMPLISHED OF THIS BUNCH... I WON'T DIE.

READ THIS WAY

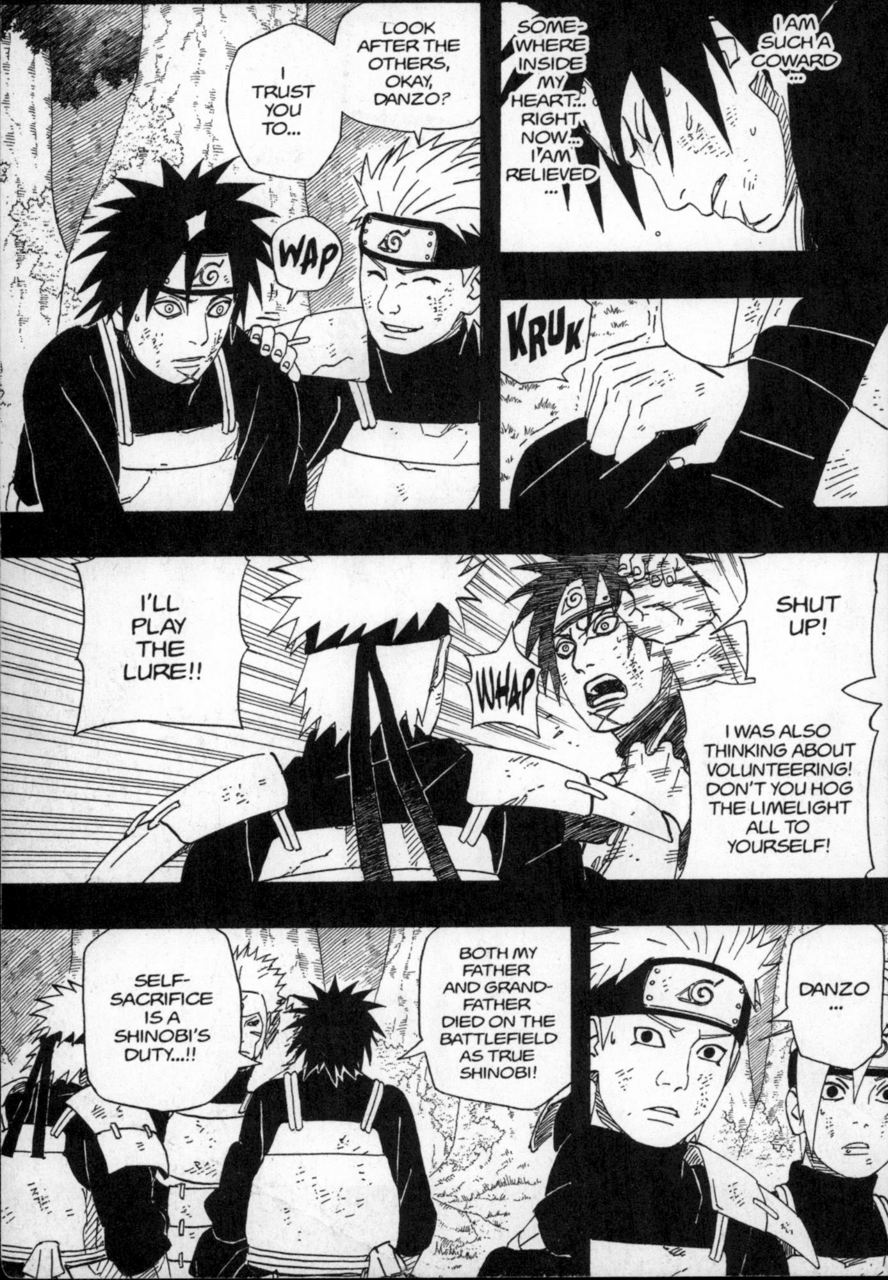
I AM SUCH A COWARD...
SOME-WHERE INSIDE MY HEART... RIGHT NOW... I'AM RELIEVED...
KRUK
LOOK AFTER THE OTHERS, OKAY, DANZO?
I TRUST YOU TO...
WAP
SHUT UP!
I WAS ALSO THINKING ABOUT VOLUNTEERING! DON'T YOU HOG THE LIMELIGHT ALL TO YOURSELF!
WHAP
I'LL PLAY THE LURE!!
DANZO...
BOTH MY FATHER AND GRAND-FATHER DIED ON THE BATTLEFIELD AS TRUE SHINOBI!
SELF-SACRIFICE IS A SHINOBI'S DUTY...!!

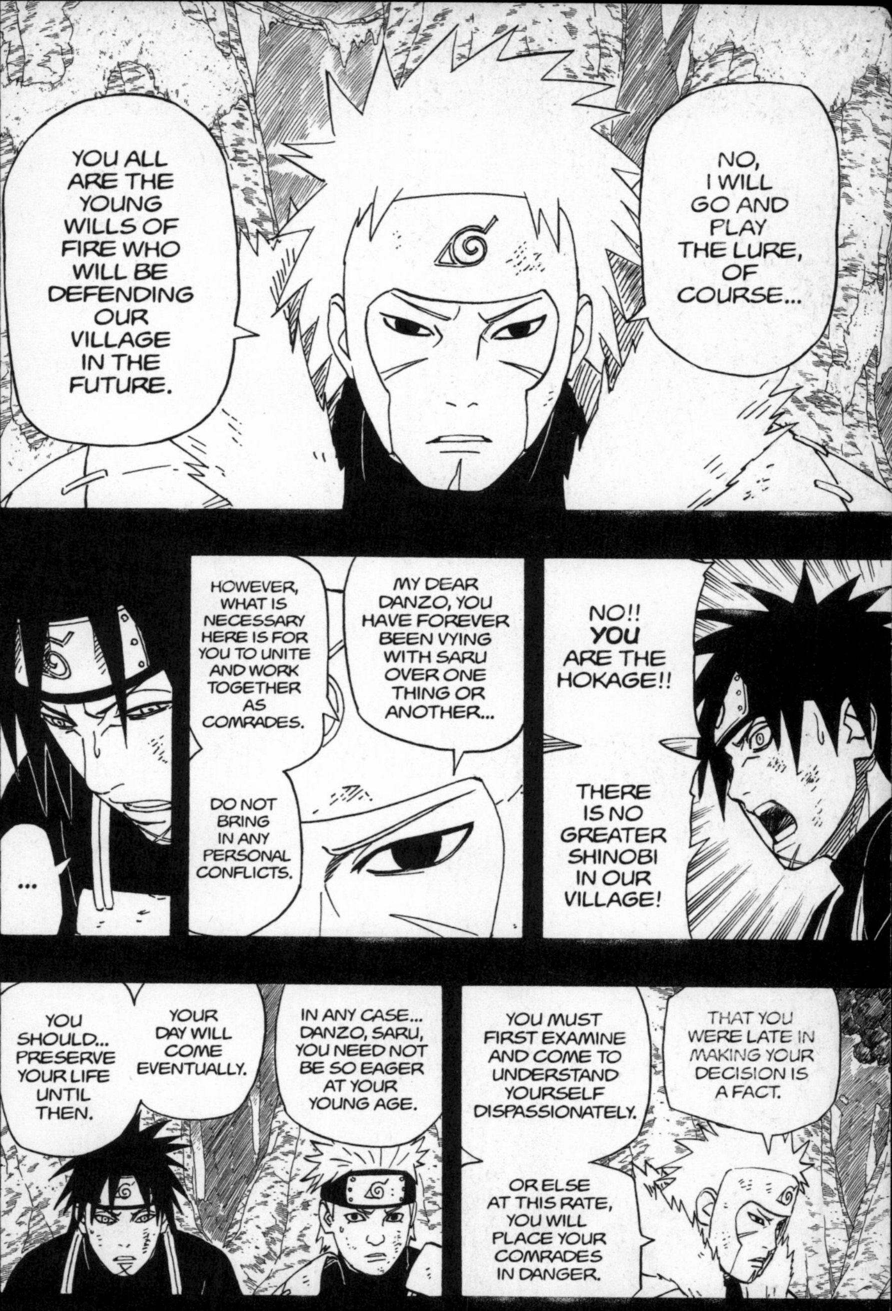
NO, I WILL GO AND PLAY THE LURE, OF COURSE...
YOU ALL ARE THE YOUNG WILLS OF FIRE WHO WILL BE DEFENDING OUR VILLAGE IN THE FUTURE.
NO!! YOU ARE THE HOKAGE!!
THERE IS NO GREATER SHINOBI IN OUR VILLAGE!
MY DEAR DANZO, YOU HAVE FOREVER BEEN VYING WITH SARU OVER ONE THING OR ANOTHER...
HOWEVER, WHAT IS NECESSARY HERE IS FOR YOU TO UNITE AND WORK TOGETHER AS COMRADES.
DO NOT BRING IN ANY PERSONAL CONFLICTS.
...
THAT YOU WERE LATE IN MAKING YOUR DECISION IS A FACT.
YOU MUST FIRST EXAMINE AND COME TO UNDERSTAND YOURSELF DISPASSIONATELY.
OR ELSE AT THIS RATE, YOU WILL PLACE YOUR COMRADES IN DANGER.
IN ANY CASE... DANZO, SARU, YOU NEED NOT BE SO EAGER AT YOUR YOUNG AGE.
YOUR DAY WILL COME EVENTUALLY.
YOU SHOULD... PRESERVE YOUR LIFE UNTIL THEN.

READ THIS WAY

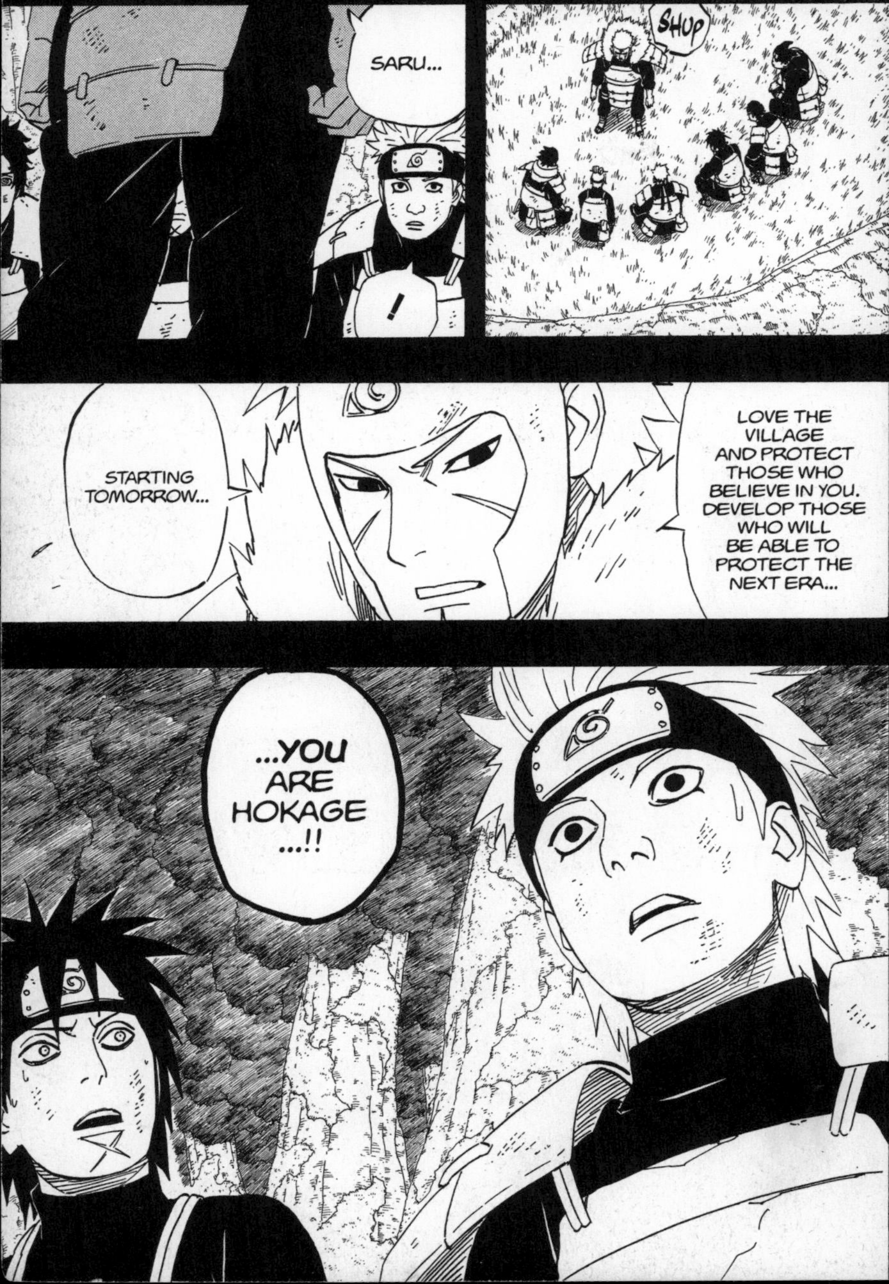
SHUP
SARU...
!
LOVE THE VILLAGE AND PROTECT THOSE WHO BELIEVE IN YOU. DEVELOP THOSE WHO WILL BE ABLE TO PROTECT THE NEXT ERA...
STARTING TOMORROW...
...YOU ARE HOKAGE ...!!

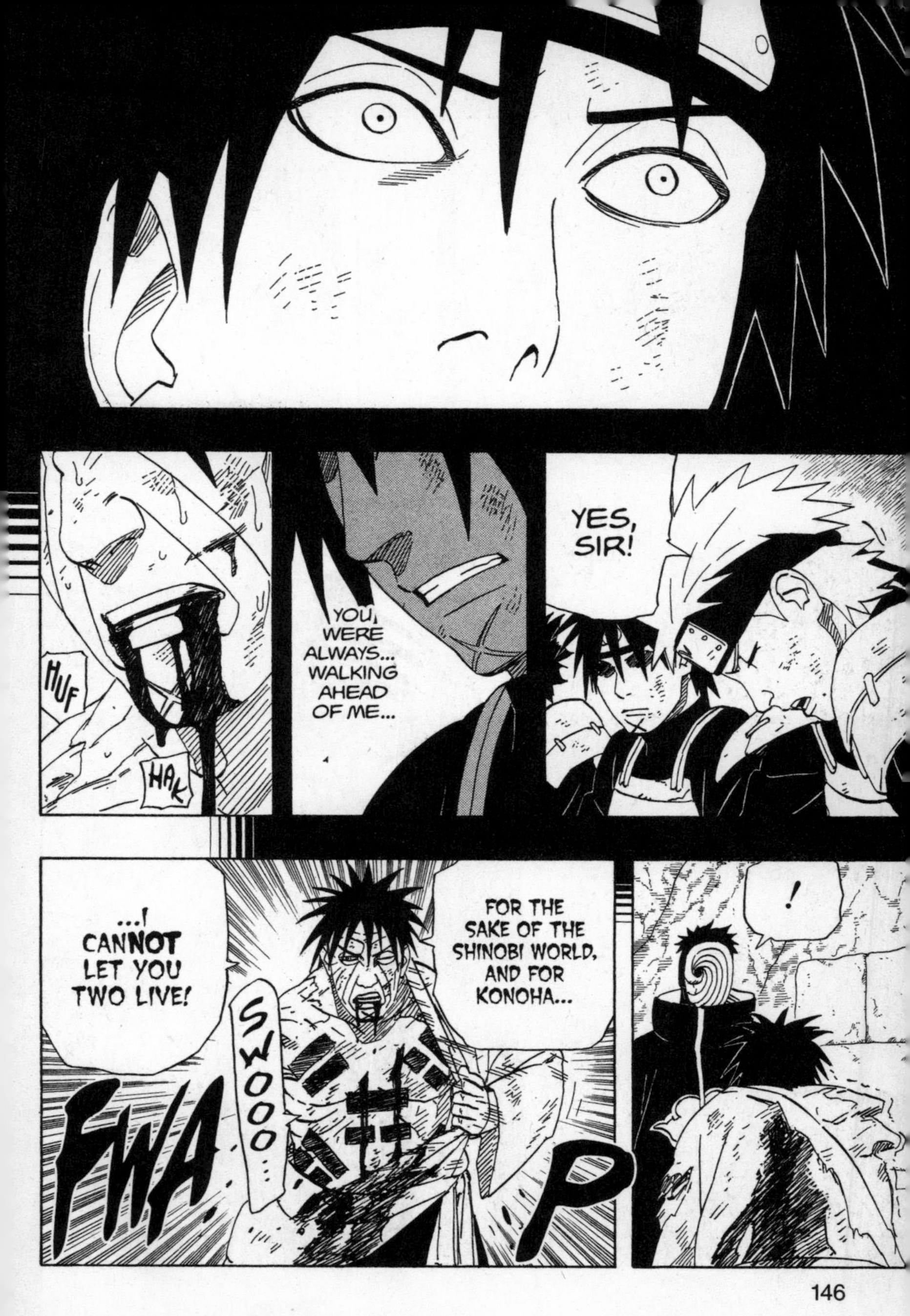
YES, SIR!
YOU WERE ALWAYS... WALKING AHEAD OF ME...
HUF
HAK
!
FOR THE SAKE OF THE SHINOBI WORLD, AND FOR KONOHA...
...I CANNOT LET YOU TWO LIVE!
SWOOO...
FWAP

READ THIS WAY

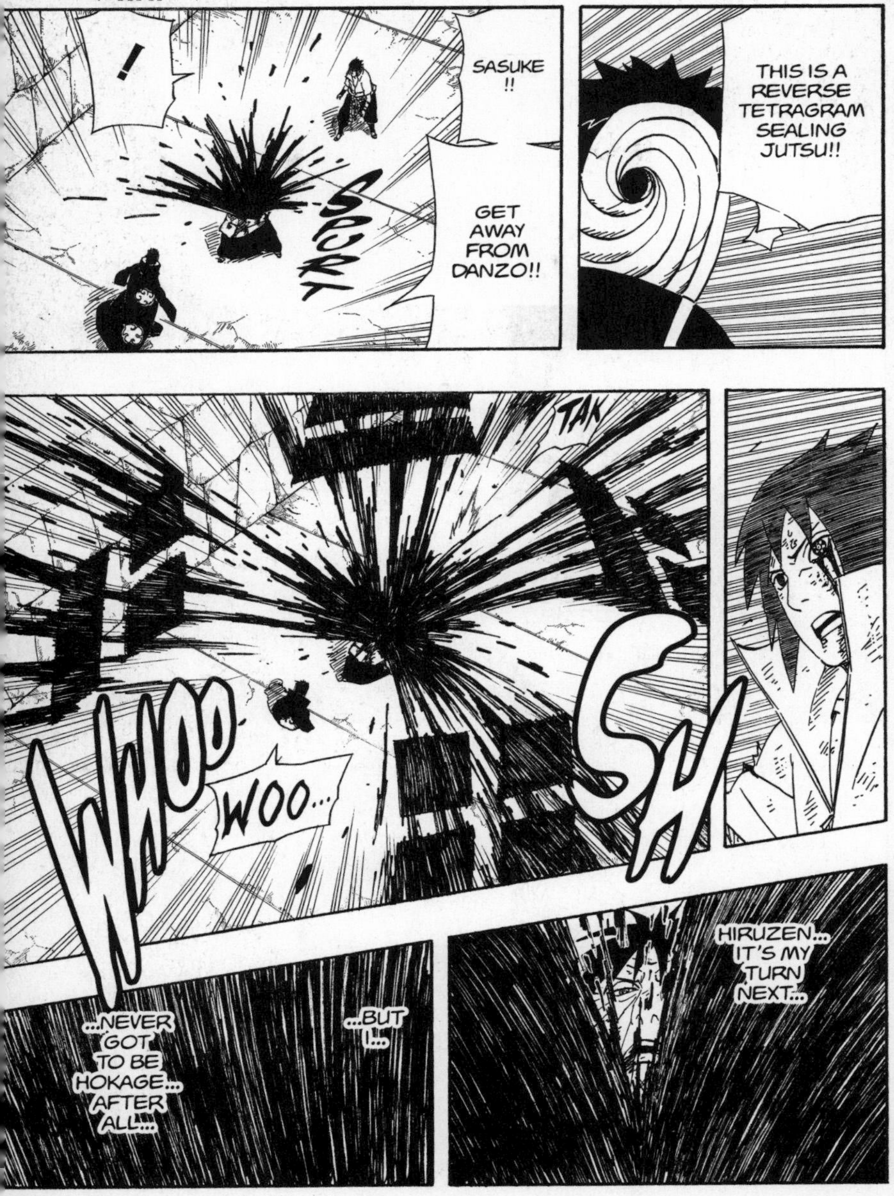
THIS IS A REVERSE TETRAGRAM SEALING JUTSU!!
SASUKE!!
GET AWAY FROM DANZO!!
!
SPURT
SH
TAK
WHOO
WOO...
HIRUZEN... IT'S MY TURN NEXT...
...BUT I...
...NEVER GOT TO BE HOKAGE... AFTER ALL...

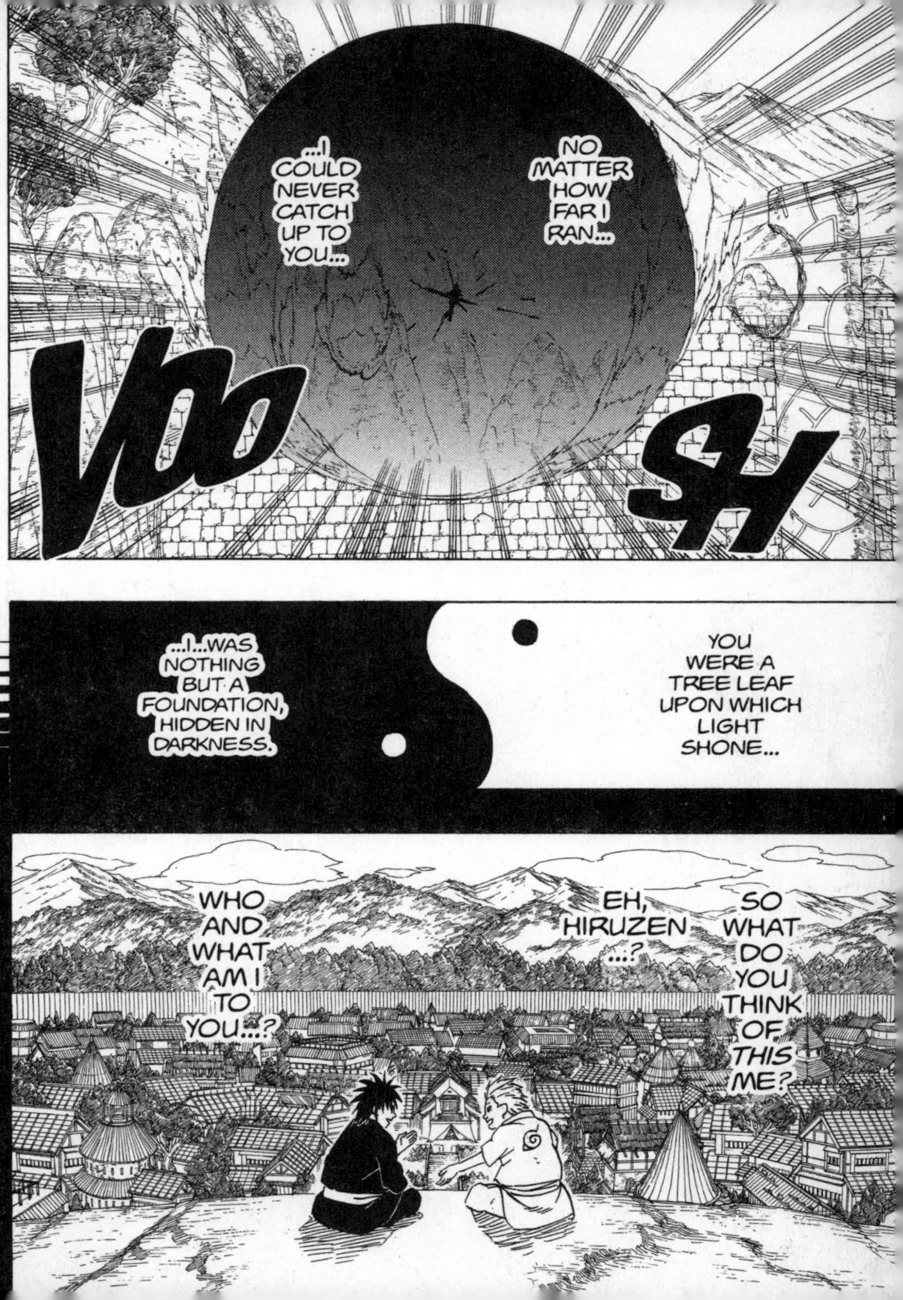
NO MATTER HOW FAR I RAN...
...I COULD NEVER CATCH UP TO YOU...
VOOSH
YOU WERE A TREE LEAF UPON WHICH LIGHT SHONE...
...I...WAS NOTHING BUT A FOUNDATION, HIDDEN IN DARKNESS.
SO WHAT DO YOU THINK OF THIS ME?
EH, HIRUZEN ...?
WHO AND WHAT AM I TO YOU...?

READ THIS WAY

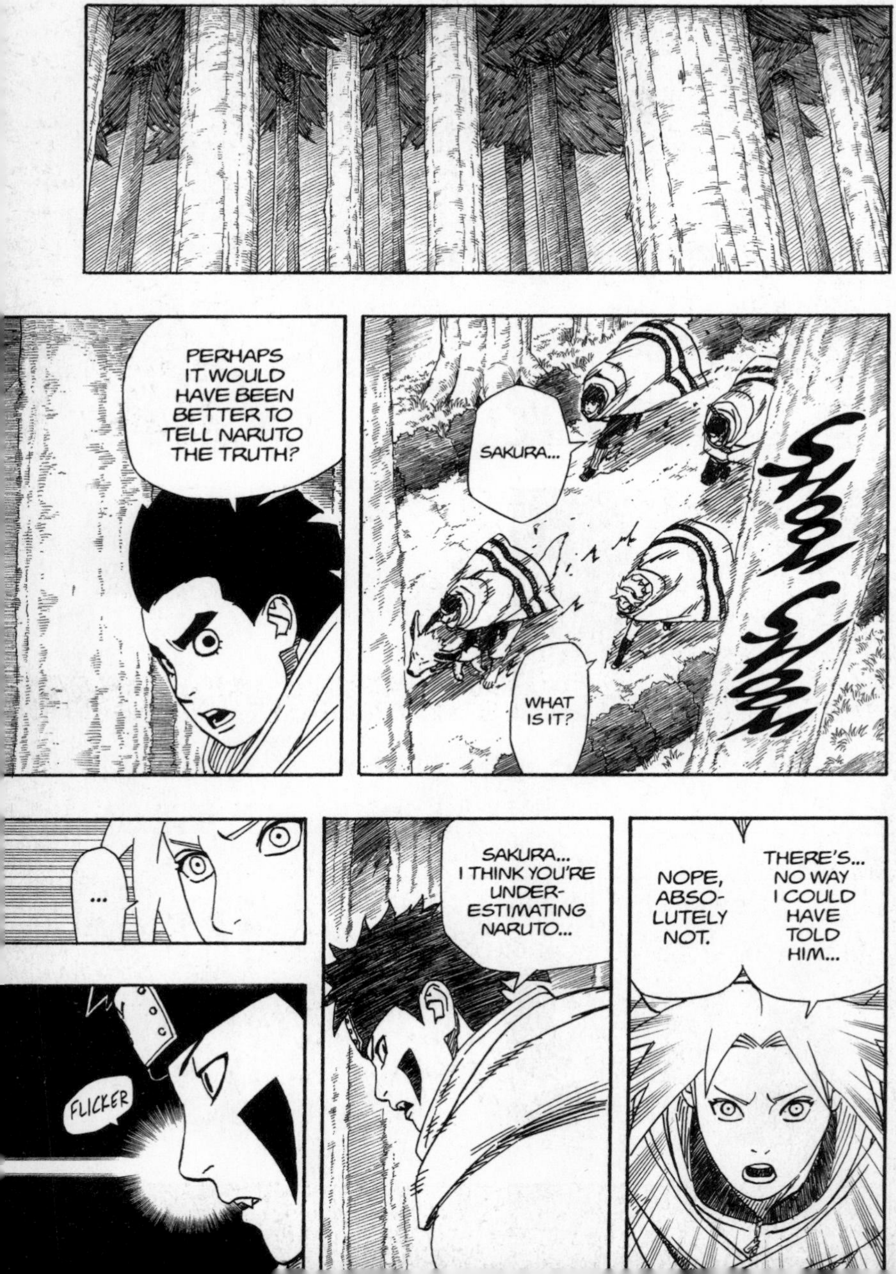
SAKURA...
WHAT IS IT?
SHOOM SHOOM SHOOM
PERHAPS IT WOULD HAVE BEEN BETTER TO TELL NARUTO THE TRUTH?
THERE'S... NO WAY I COULD HAVE TOLD HIM...
NOPE, ABSO-LUTELY NOT.
SAKURA... I THINK YOU'RE UNDER-ESTIMATING NARUTO...
...
FLICKER

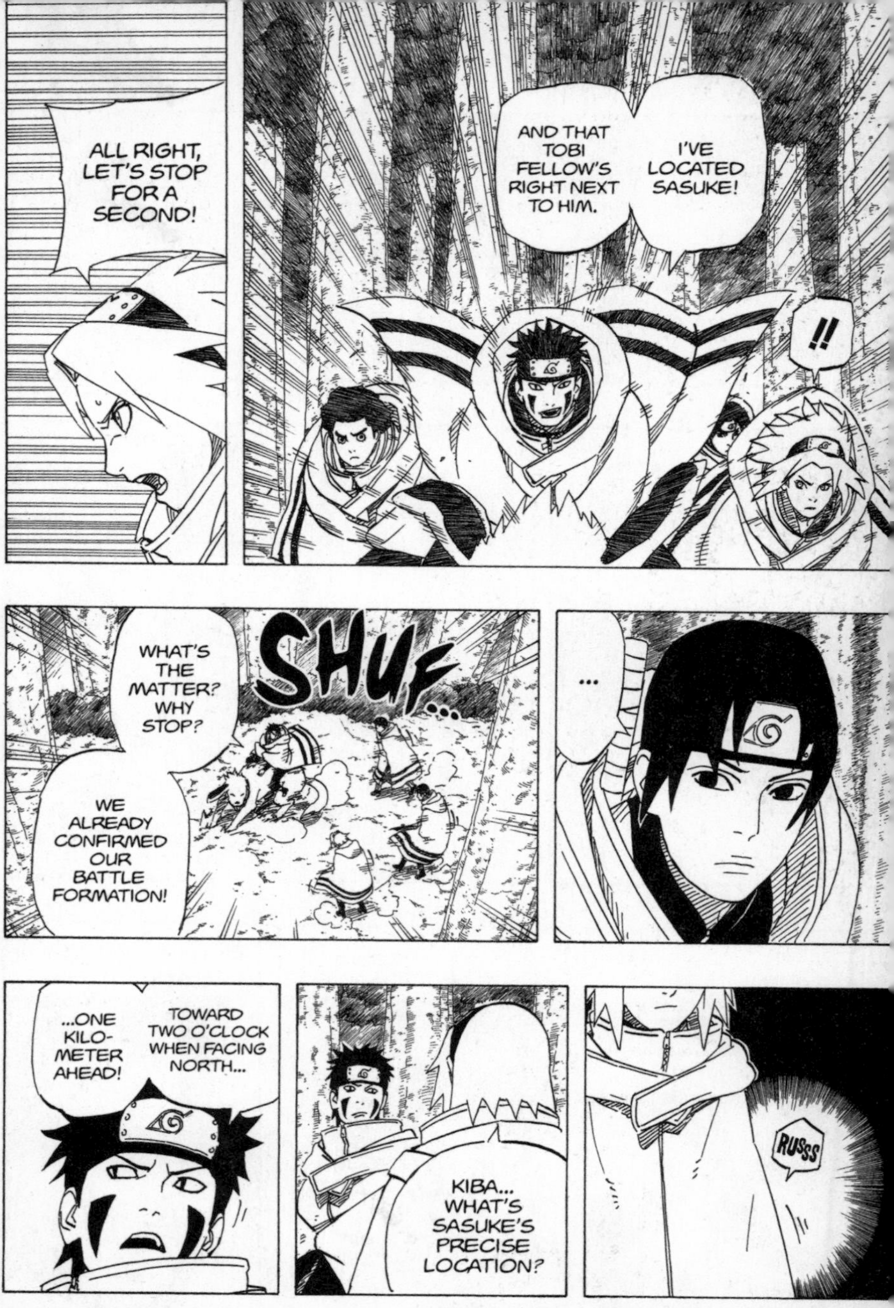
I'VE LOCATED SASUKE!
AND THAT TOBI FELLOW'S RIGHT NEXT TO HIM.
!!
ALL RIGHT, LET'S STOP FOR A SECOND!
...
SHUF...
WHAT'S THE MATTER? WHY STOP?
WE ALREADY CONFIRMED OUR BATTLE FORMATION!
RUSSS
KIBA... WHAT'S SASUKE'S PRECISE LOCATION?
TOWARD TWO O'CLOCK WHEN FACING NORTH...
...ONE KILO-METER AHEAD!

READ THIS WAY

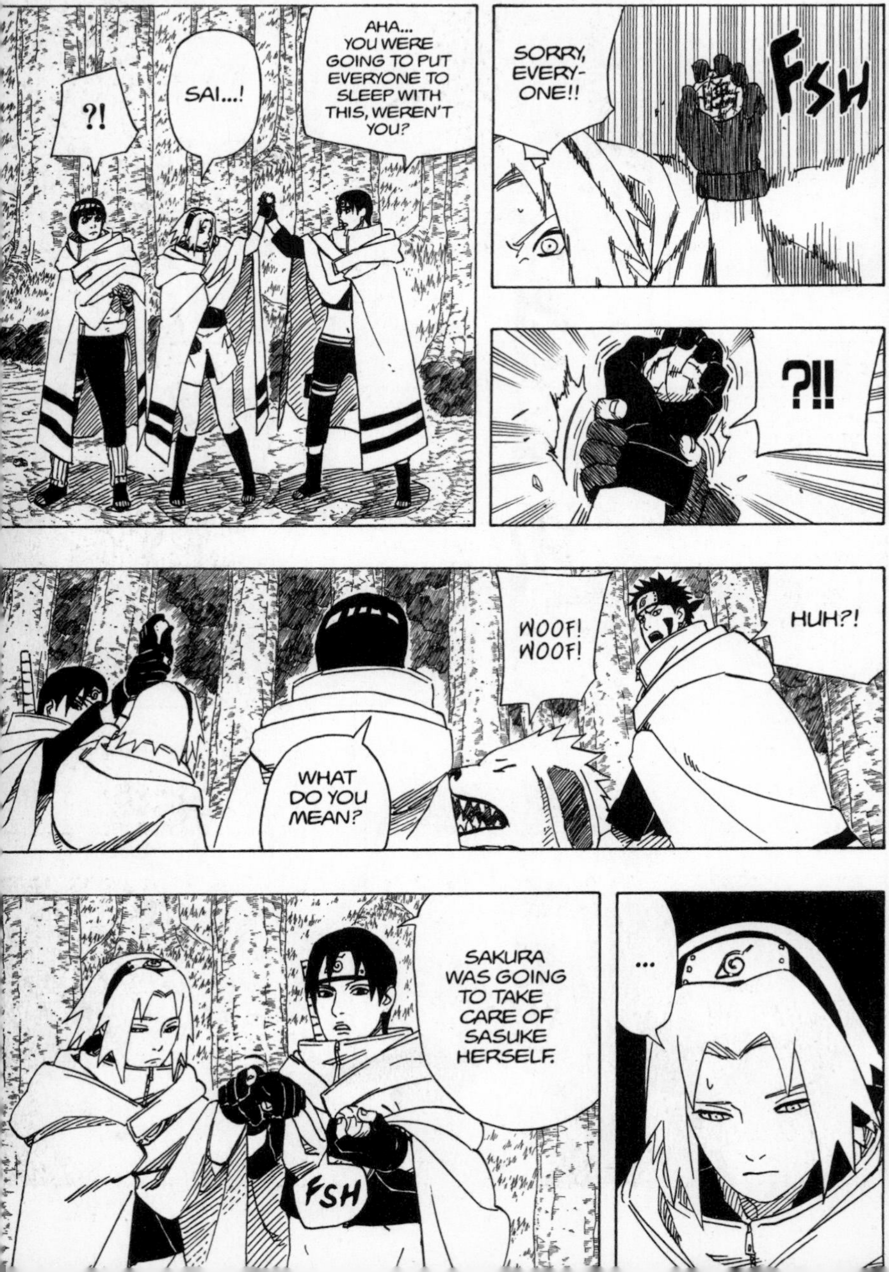
SORRY, EVERY-ONE!!
FSH
?!!
AHA... YOU WERE GOING TO PUT EVERYONE TO SLEEP WITH THIS, WEREN'T YOU?
SAI...!
?!
HUH?!
WOOF! WOOF!
WHAT DO YOU MEAN?
...
SAKURA WAS GOING TO TAKE CARE OF SASUKE HERSELF.
FSH

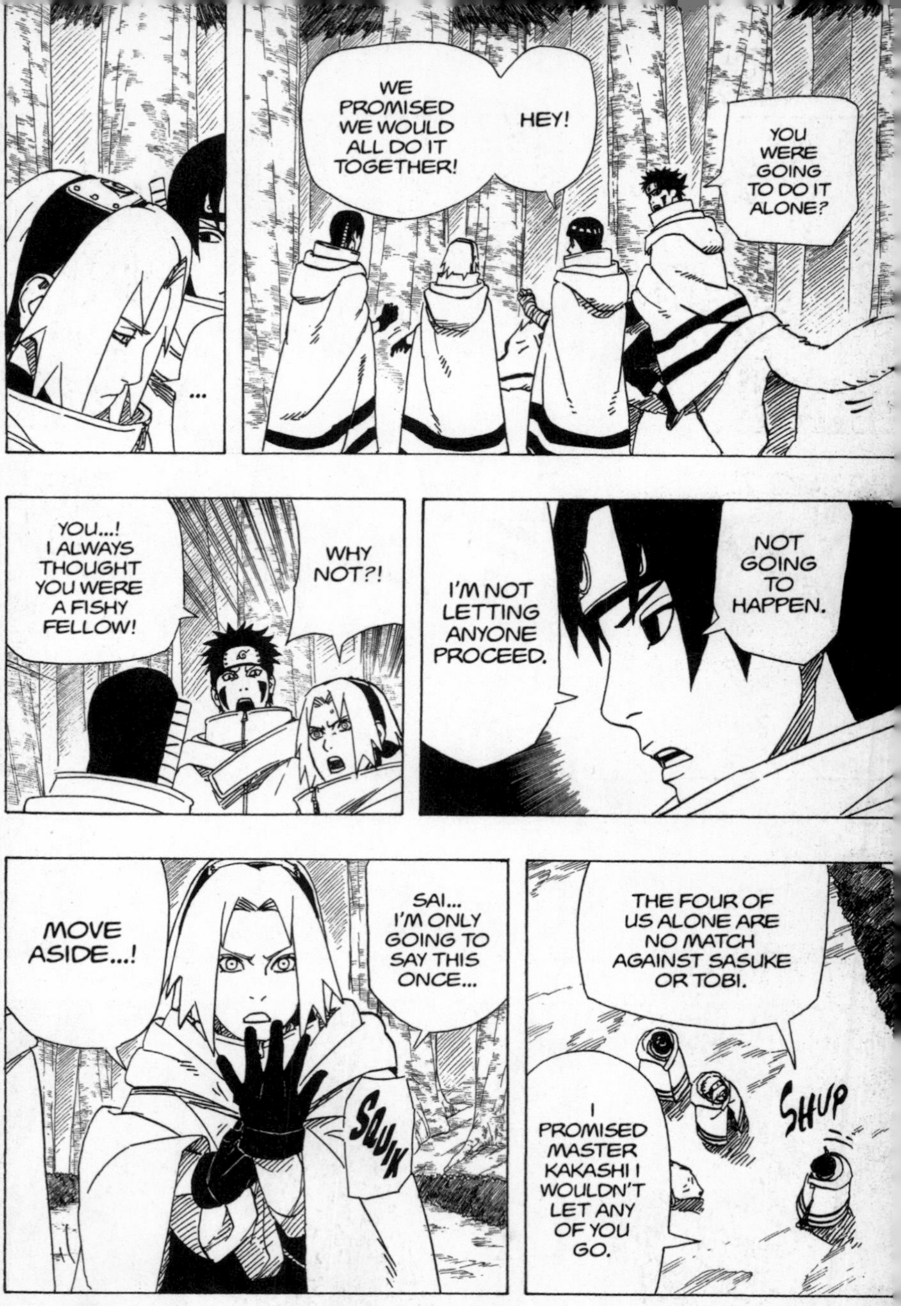
YOU WERE GOING TO DO IT ALONE?
HEY!
WE PROMISED WE WOULD ALL DO IT TOGETHER!
...
NOT GOING TO HAPPEN.
I'M NOT LETTING ANYONE PROCEED.
WHY NOT?!
YOU...! I ALWAYS THOUGHT YOU WERE A FISHY FELLOW!
THE FOUR OF US ALONE ARE NO MATCH AGAINST SASUKE OR TOBI.
I PROMISED MASTER KAKASHI I WOULDN'T LET ANY OF YOU GO.
SHUP
SAI... I'M ONLY GOING TO SAY THIS ONCE...
MOVE ASIDE...!
SQUIK

READ THIS WAY

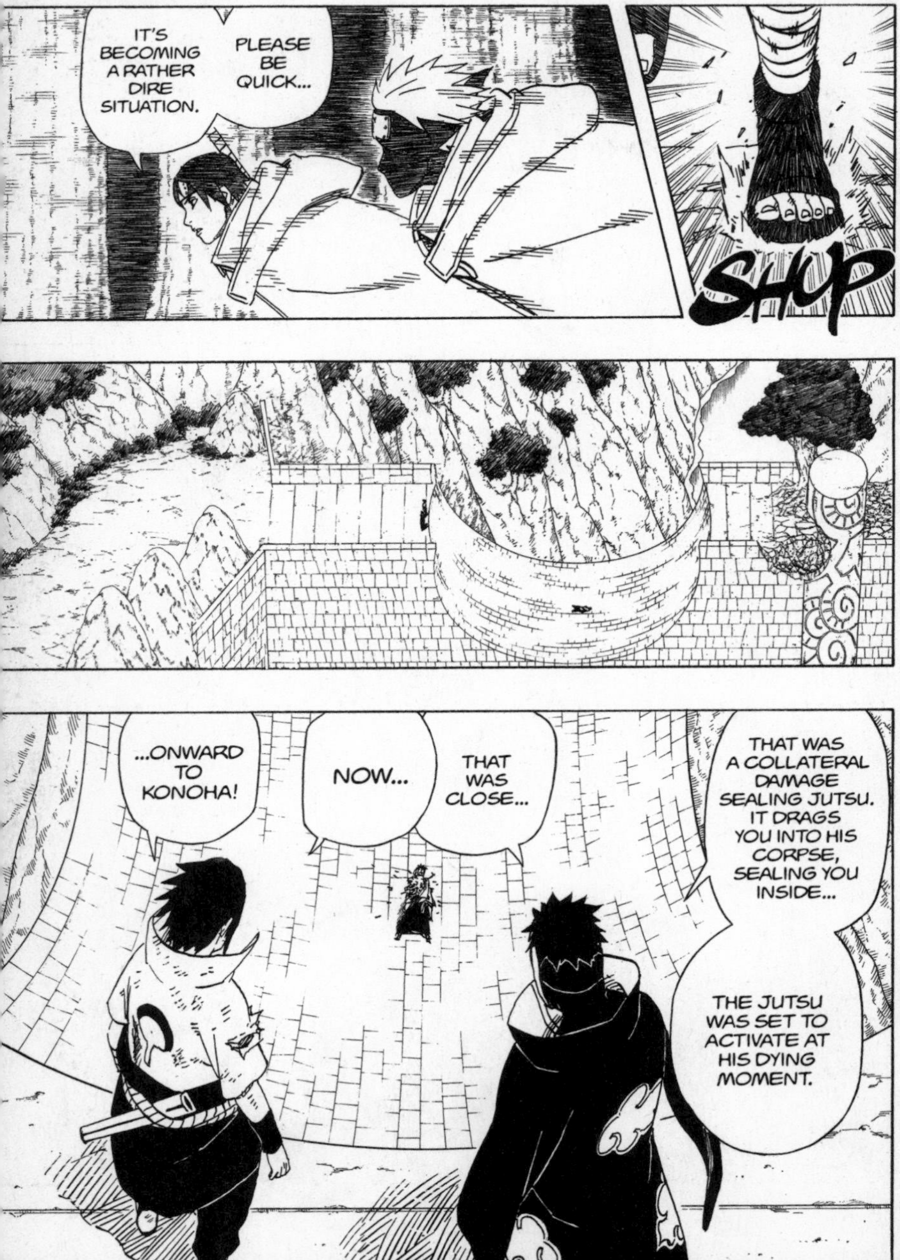
SHUP
PLEASE BE QUICK...
IT'S BECOMING A RATHER DIRE SITUATION.
THAT WAS A COLLATERAL DAMAGE SEALING JUTSU. IT DRAGS YOU INTO HIS CORPSE, SEALING YOU INSIDE...
THE JUTSU WAS SET TO ACTIVATE AT HIS DYING MOMENT.
THAT WAS CLOSE...
NOW...
...ONWARD TO KONOHA!

NARUTO

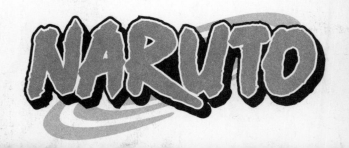

Number 482: Just One More Time...

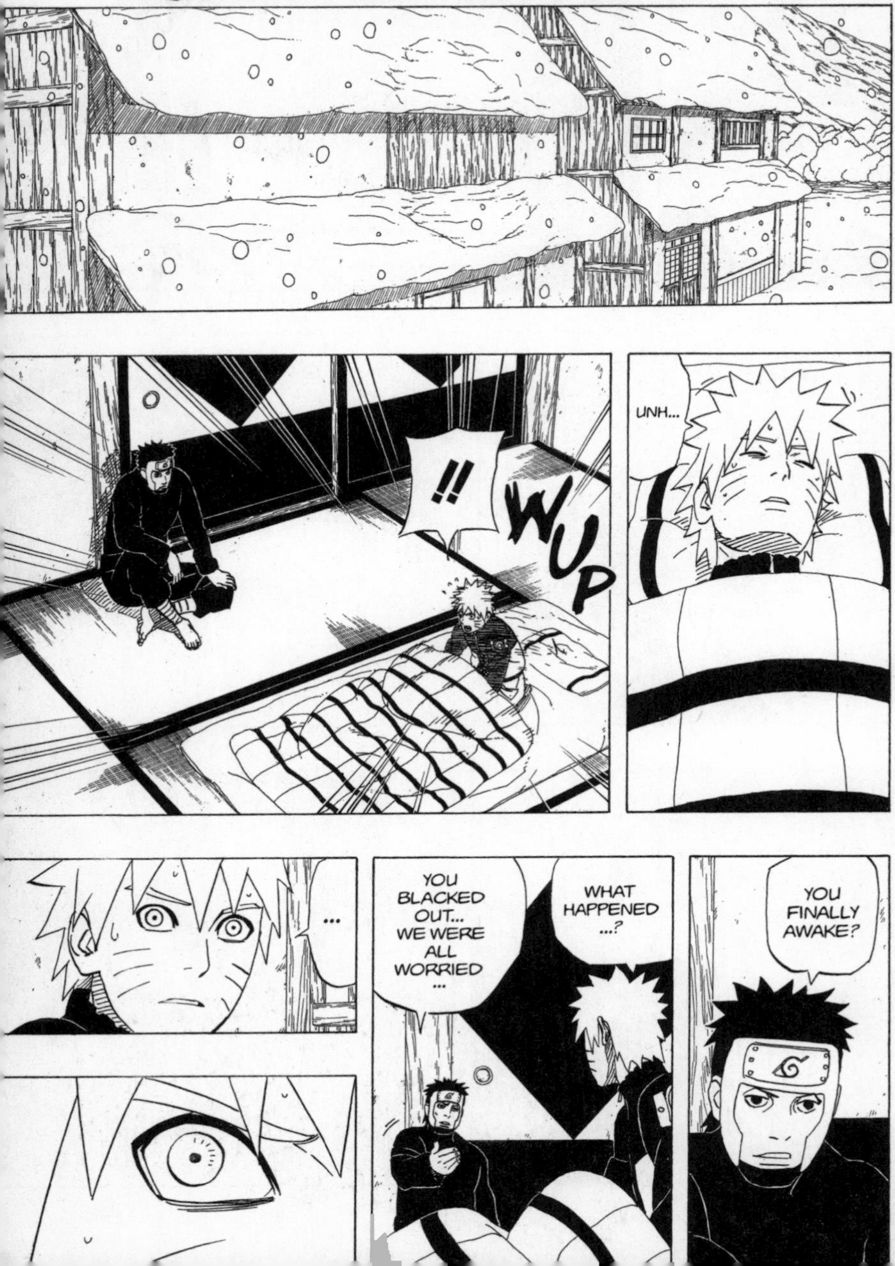
UNH...
!!
WUP
YOU FINALLY AWAKE?
WHAT HAPPENED ...?
YOU BLACKED OUT... WE WERE ALL WORRIED ...
...

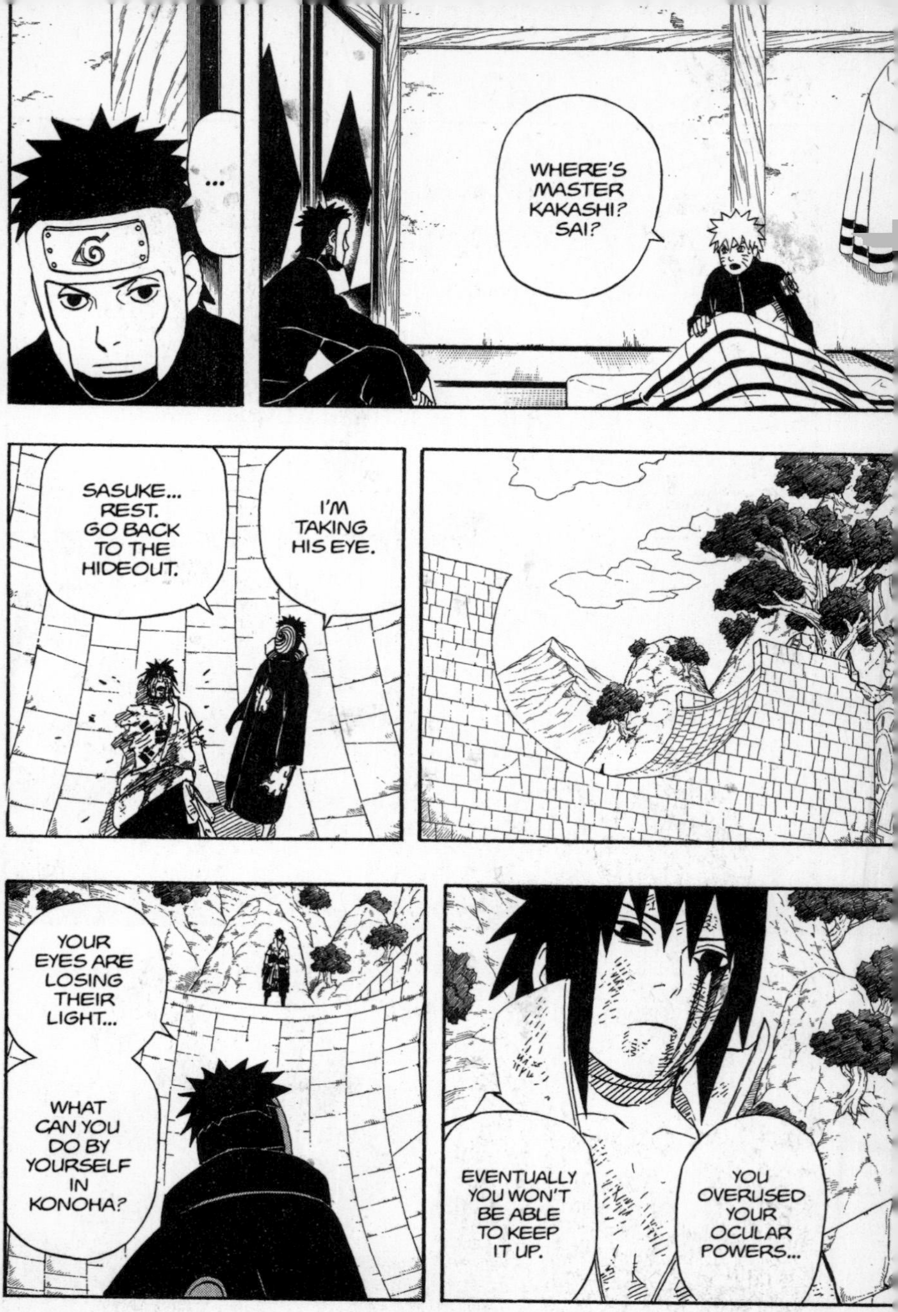
WHERE'S MASTER KAKASHI? SAI?
...
I'M TAKING HIS EYE.
SASUKE... REST. GO BACK TO THE HIDEOUT.
YOU OVERUSED YOUR OCULAR POWERS...
EVENTUALLY YOU WON'T BE ABLE TO KEEP IT UP.
YOUR EYES ARE LOSING THEIR LIGHT...
WHAT CAN YOU DO BY YOURSELF IN KONOHA?

(GUESTHOUSE)

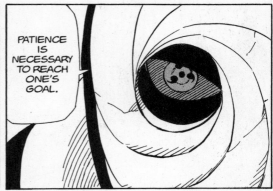

PATIENCE IS NECESSARY TO REACH ONE'S GOAL.

...

YOU'RE COMING WITH ME TO THE VILLAGE.

MASTER KAKASHI'S ORDERS.

SIGH ...

FSH

!

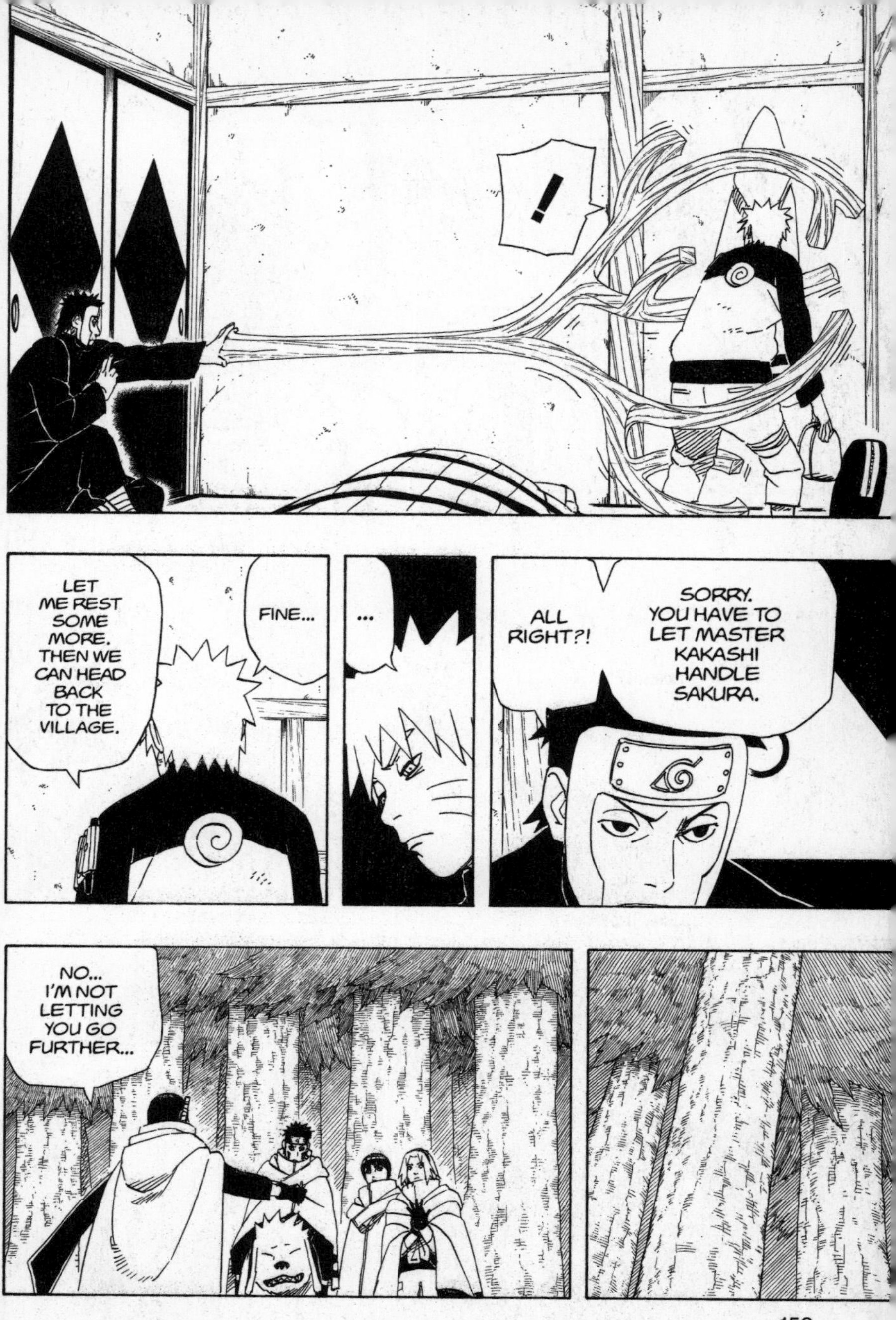
!
SORRY. YOU HAVE TO LET MASTER KAKASHI HANDLE SAKURA.
ALL RIGHT?!
...
FINE...
LET ME REST SOME MORE. THEN WE CAN HEAD BACK TO THE VILLAGE.
NO... I'M NOT LETTING YOU GO FURTHER...

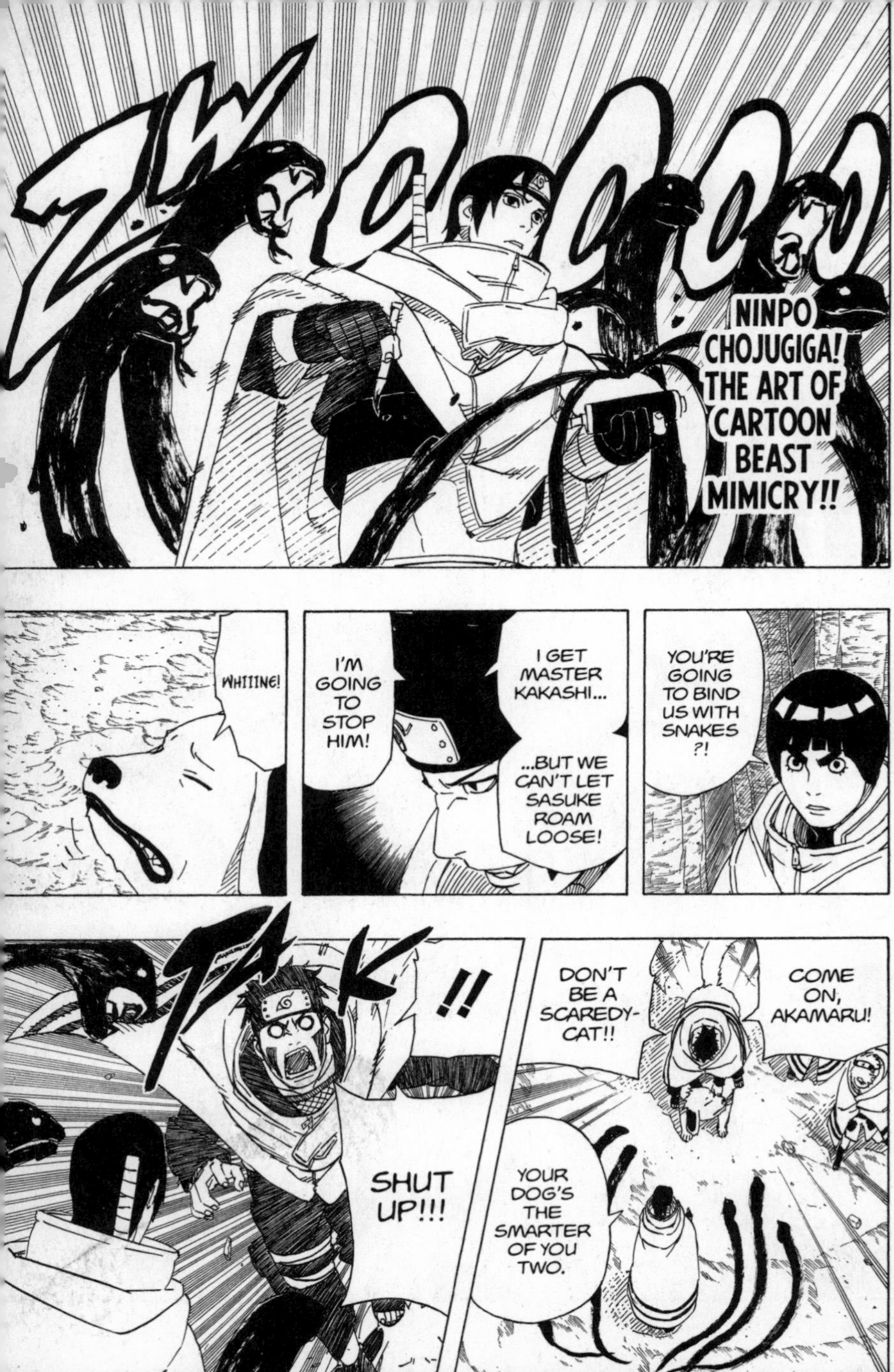

ZWOOOOOO
NINPO CHOJUGIGA! THE ART OF CARTOON BEAST MIMICRY!!
YOU'RE GOING TO BIND US WITH SNAKES?!
I GET MASTER KAKASHI...
...BUT WE CAN'T LET SASUKE ROAM LOOSE!
I'M GOING TO STOP HIM!
WHIIINE!
COME ON, AKAMARU!
DON'T BE A SCAREDY-CAT!!
YOUR DOG'S THE SMARTER OF YOU TWO.
SHUT UP!!!
TAK!!

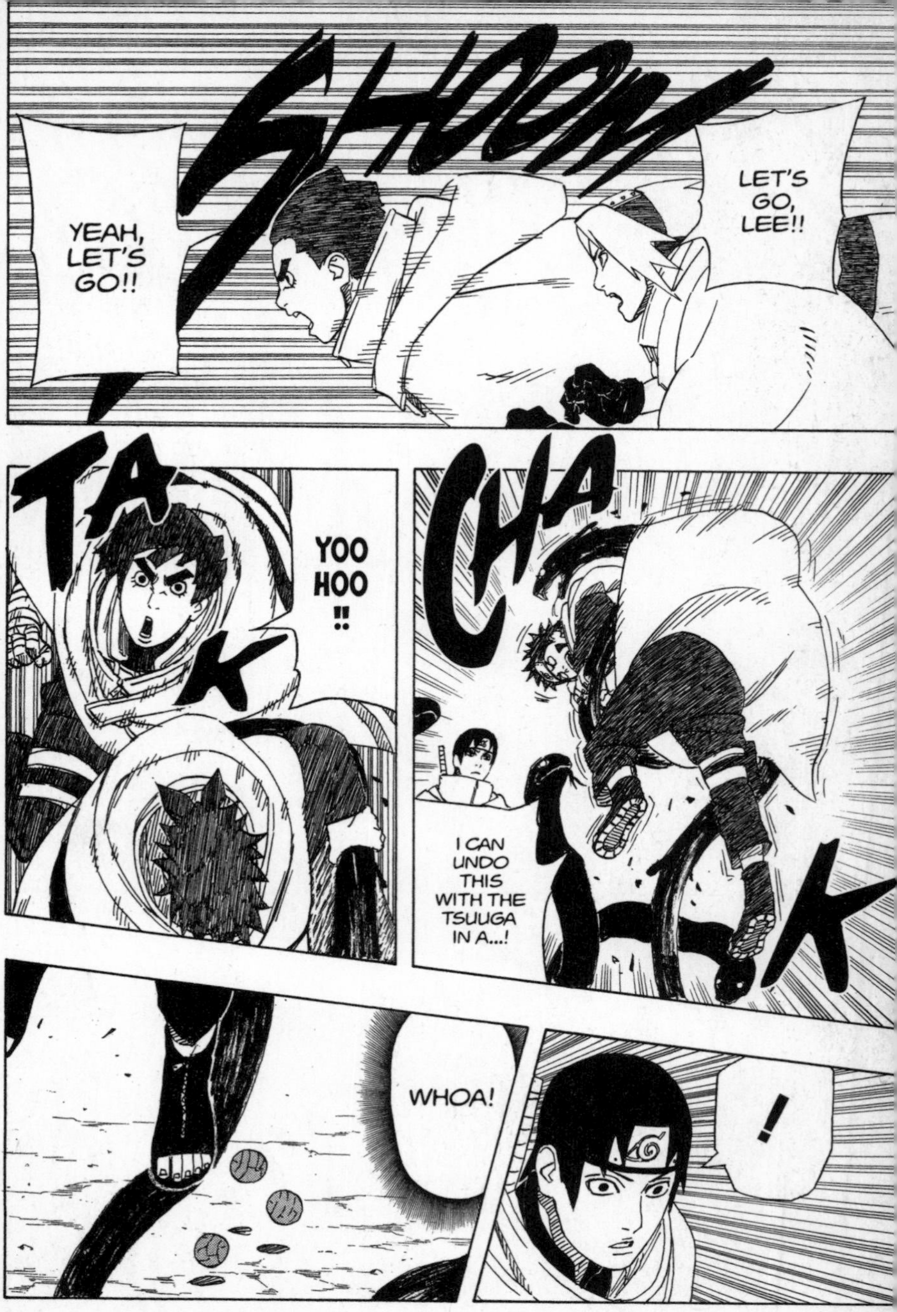
SHOOM
LET'S GO, LEE!!
YEAH, LET'S GO!!
CHAK
I CAN UNDO THIS WITH THE TSUUGA IN A...!
TAK
YOO HOO!!
!
WHOA!

READ THIS WAY

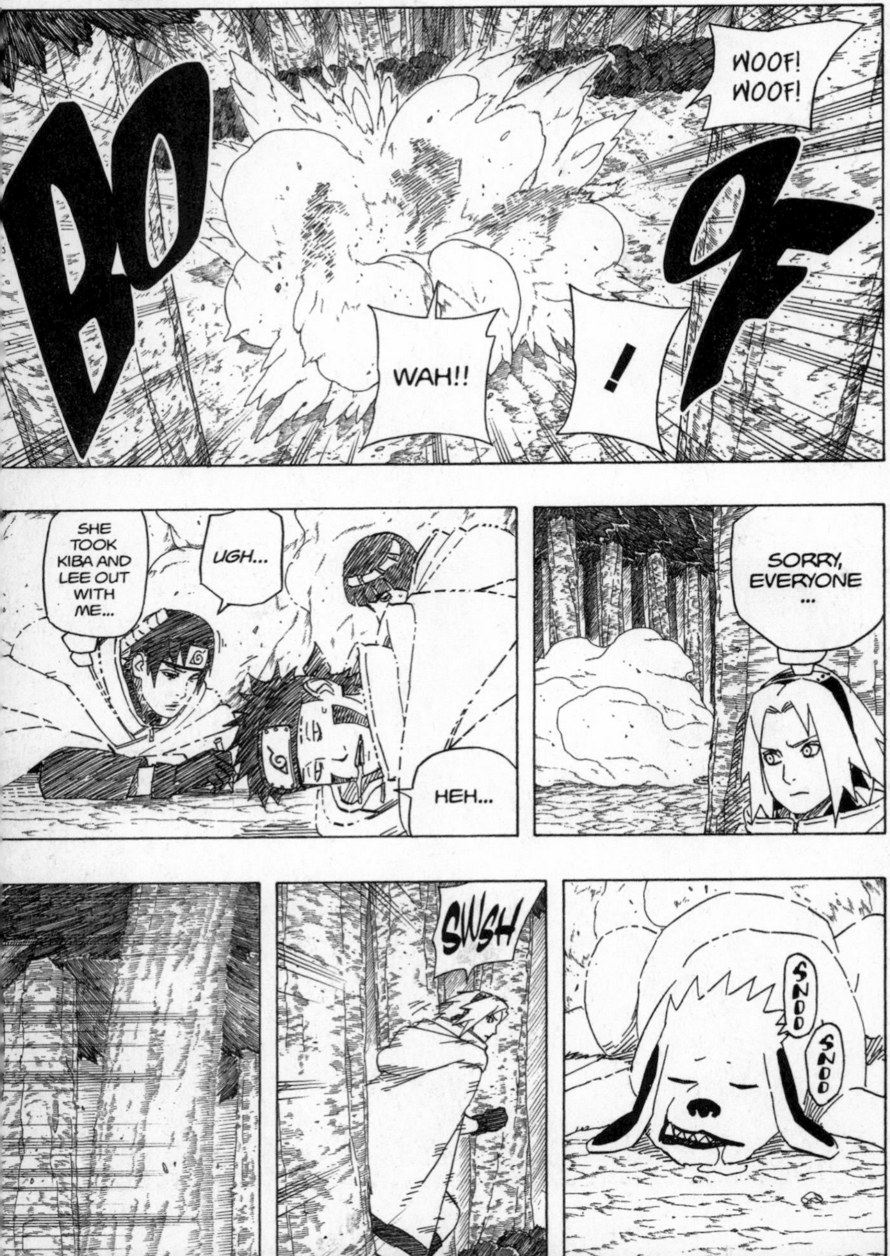
WOOF! WOOF!
BOOF
!
WAH!!
SORRY, EVERYONE ...
UGH...
SHE TOOK KIBA AND LEE OUT WITH ME...
HEH...
SNOO
SNOO
SWSH

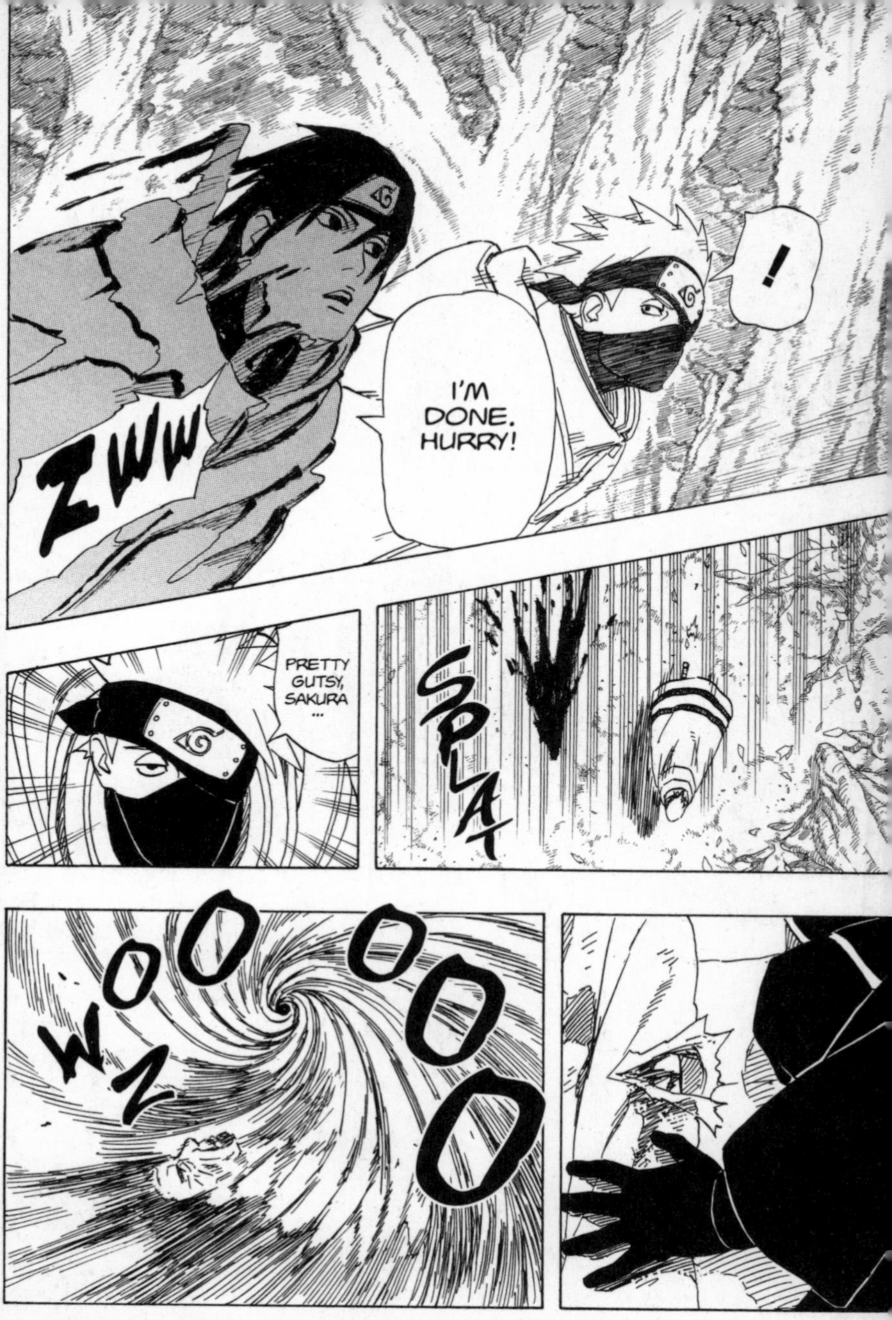
!
I'M DONE. HURRY!
ZWW
SPLAT
PRETTY GUTSY, SAKURA ...
WOOOOOOO

READ THIS WAY

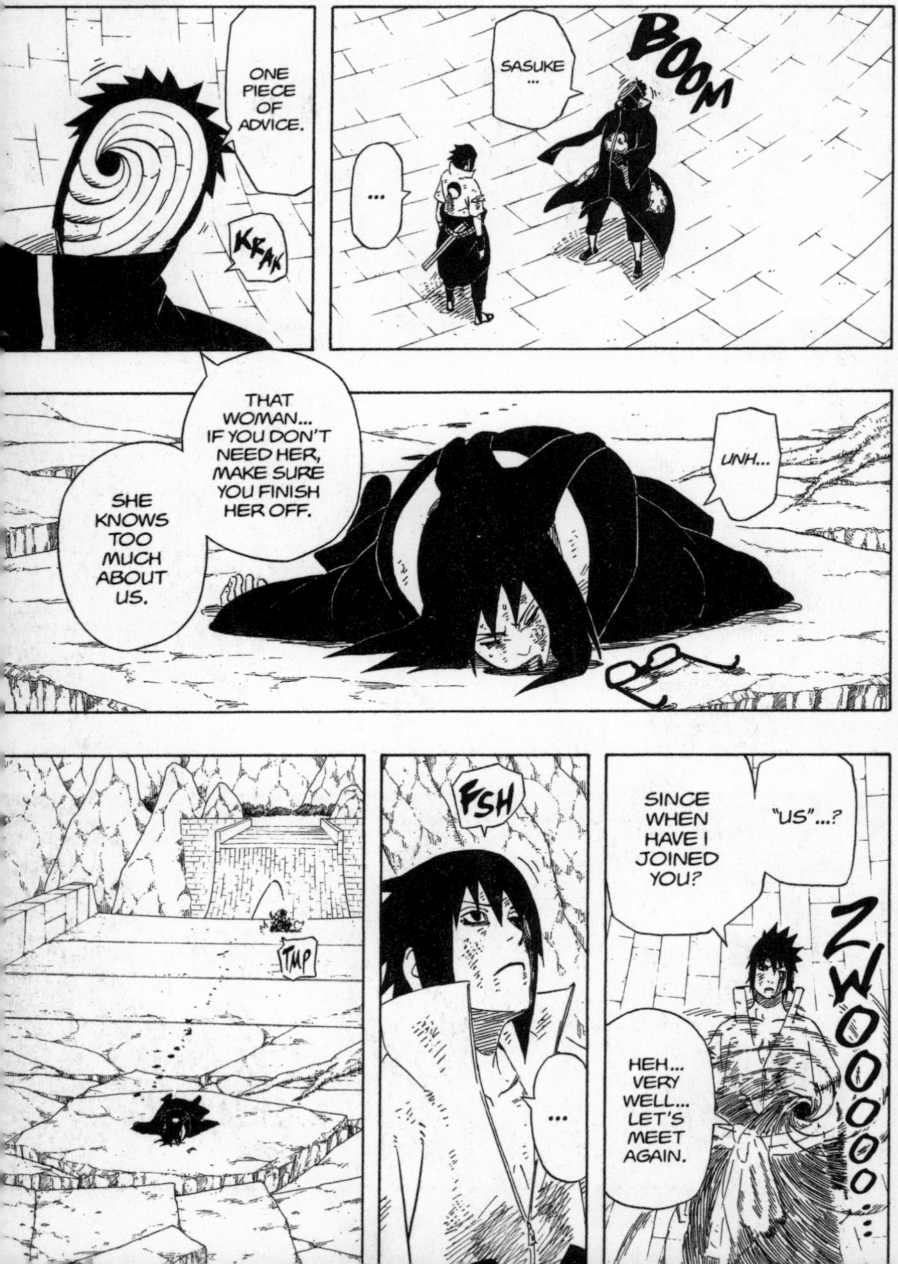
SASUKE ...
BOOM
...
ONE PIECE OF ADVICE.
KRAK
UNH...
THAT WOMAN... IF YOU DON'T NEED HER, MAKE SURE YOU FINISH HER OFF.
SHE KNOWS TOO MUCH ABOUT US.
"US"...?
SINCE WHEN HAVE I JOINED YOU?
ZWOOOO...
HEH... VERY WELL... LET'S MEET AGAIN.
FSH
...
TMP

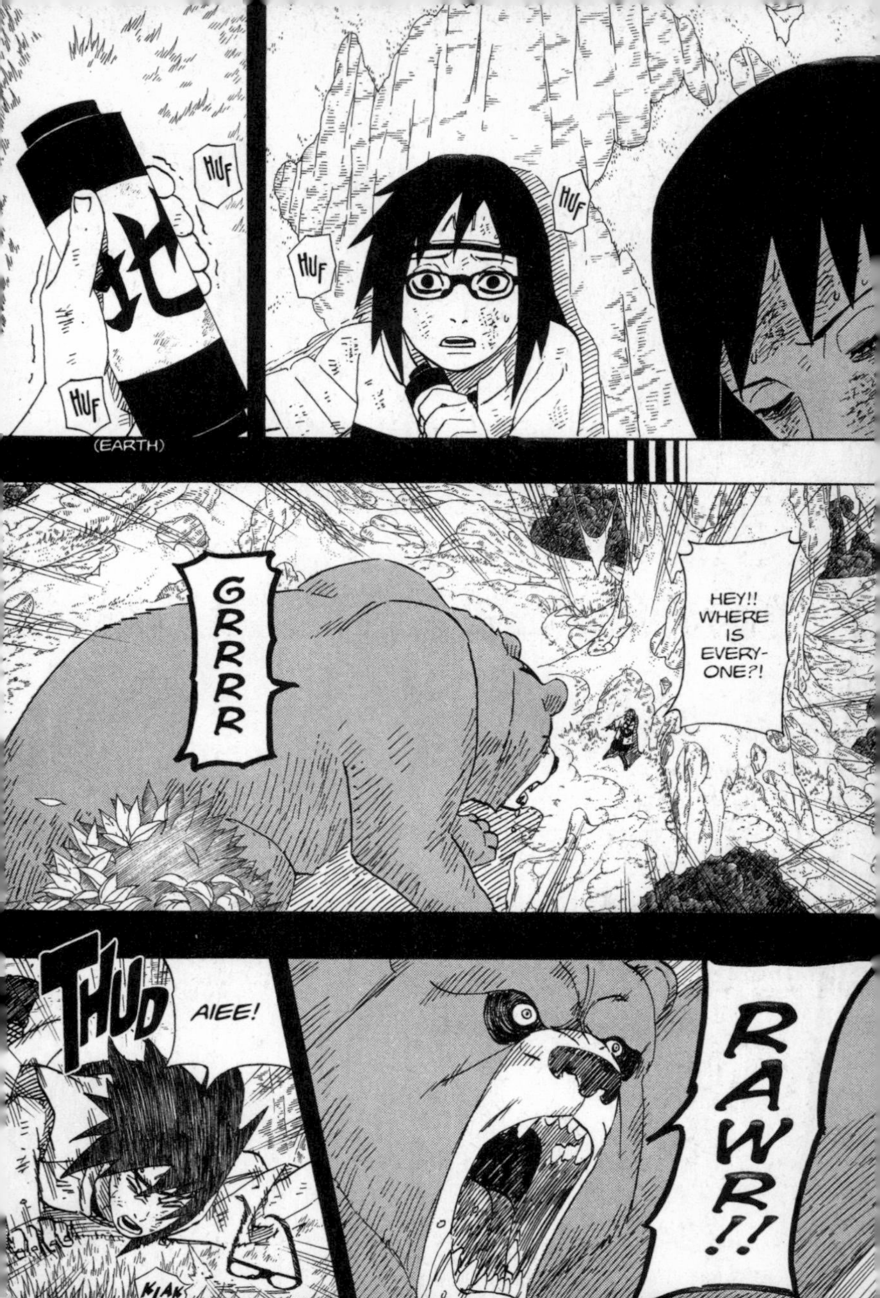

HUF
HUF
HUF
HUF
(EARTH)
HEY!! WHERE IS EVERYONE?!
GRRRR
RAWR?!
AIEE!
THUD
KLAK

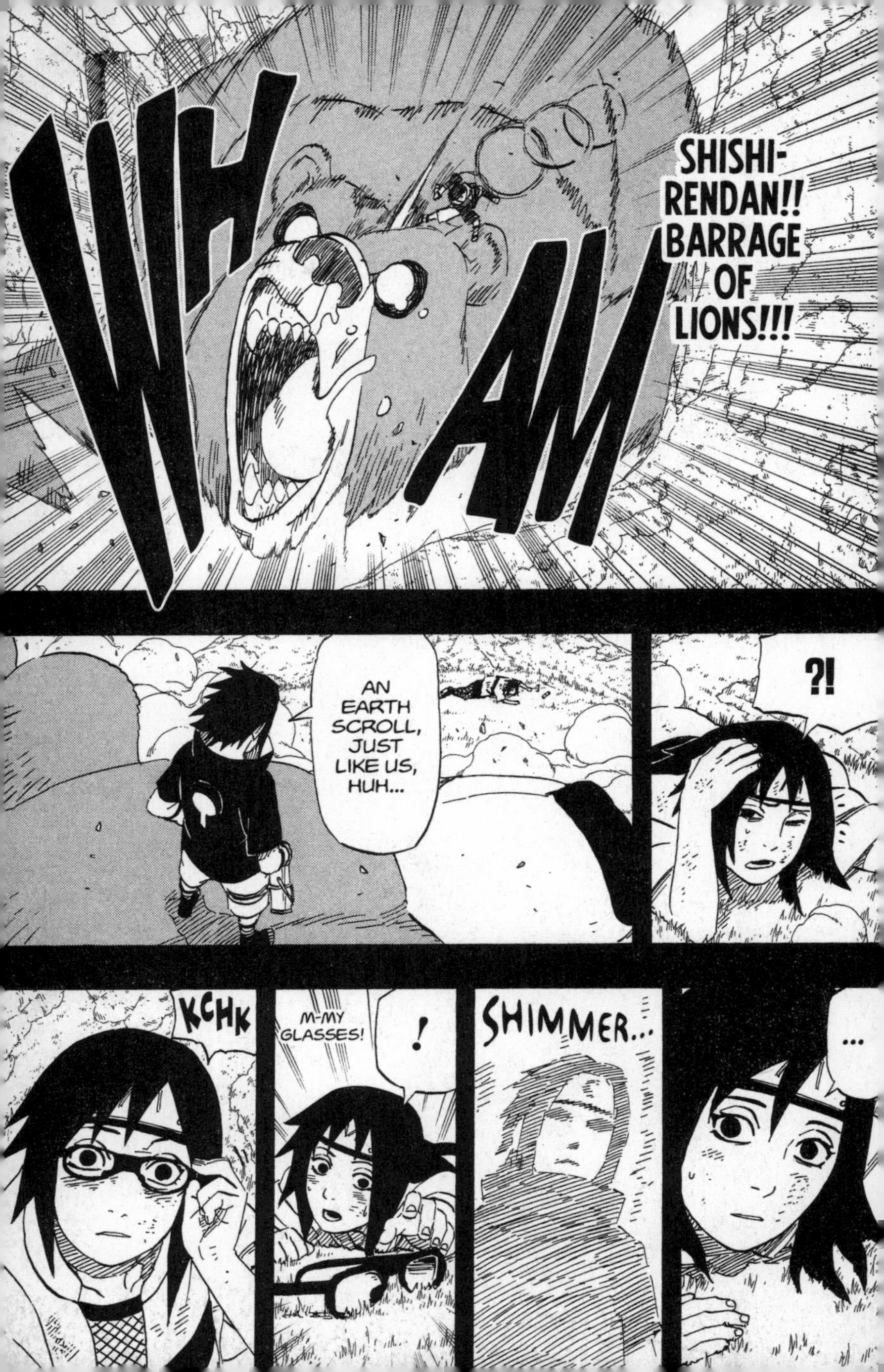
WHAM
SHISHI-RENDAN!! BARRAGE OF LIONS!!!
?!
AN EARTH SCROLL, JUST LIKE US, HUH...
...
SHIMMER...
!
M-MY GLASSES!
KCHK

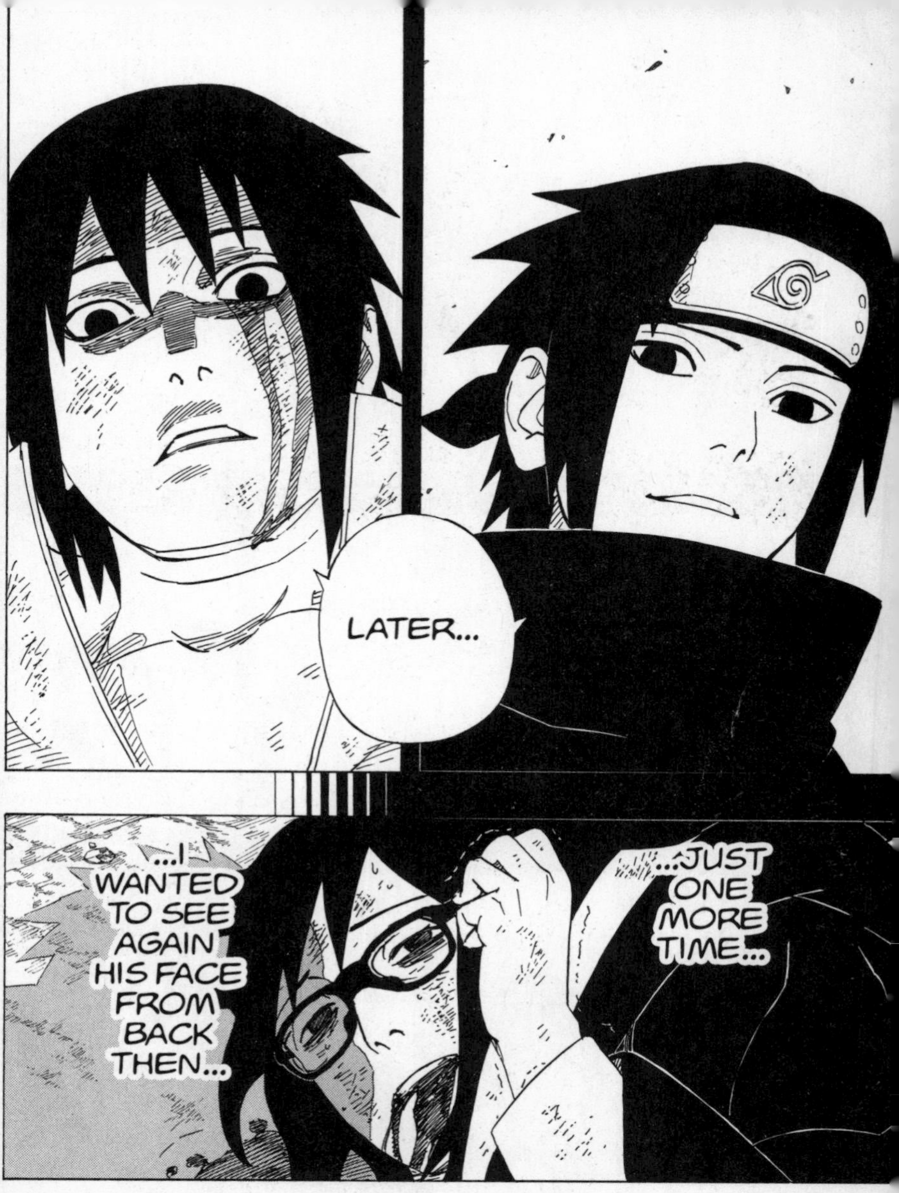
LATER...
...JUST ONE MORE TIME...
...I WANTED TO SEE AGAIN HIS FACE FROM BACK THEN...

READ THIS WAY

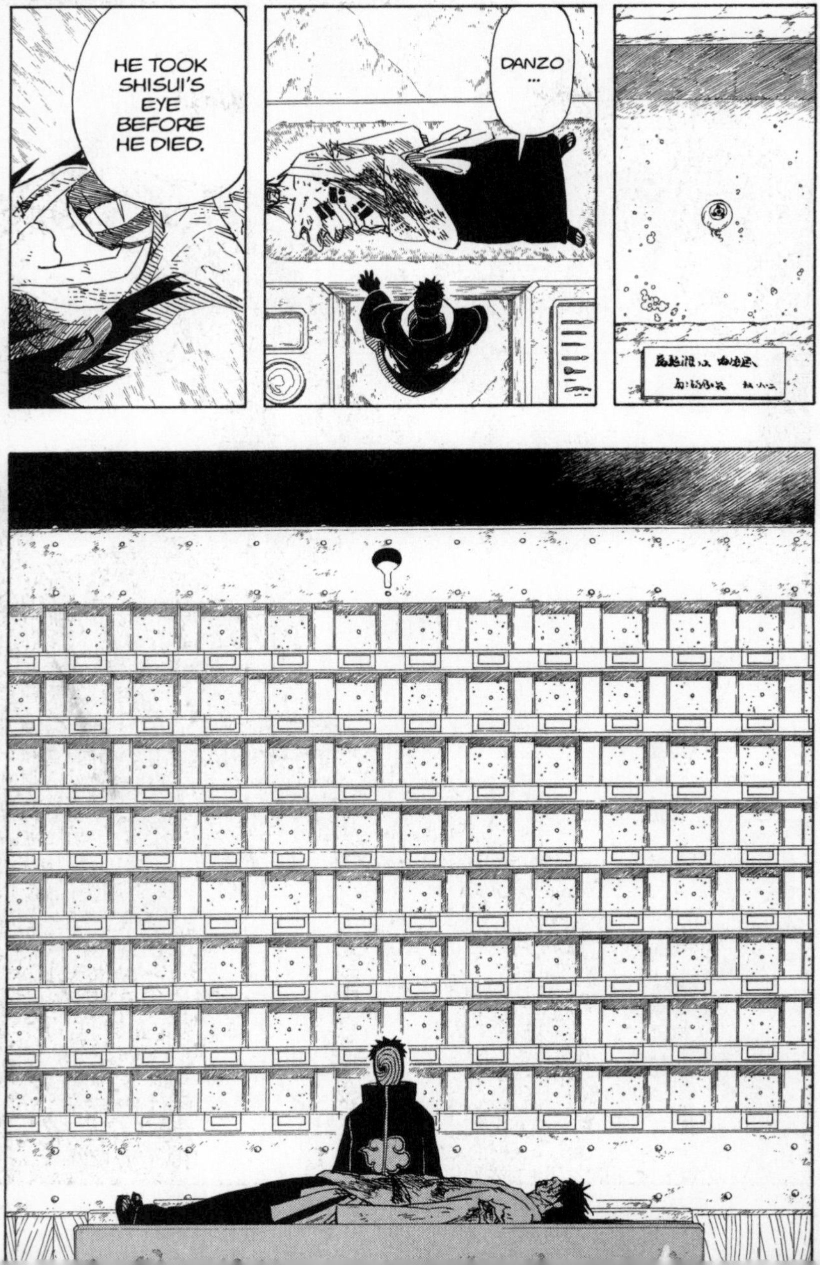
DANZO ...
HE TOOK SHISUI'S EYE BEFORE HE DIED.

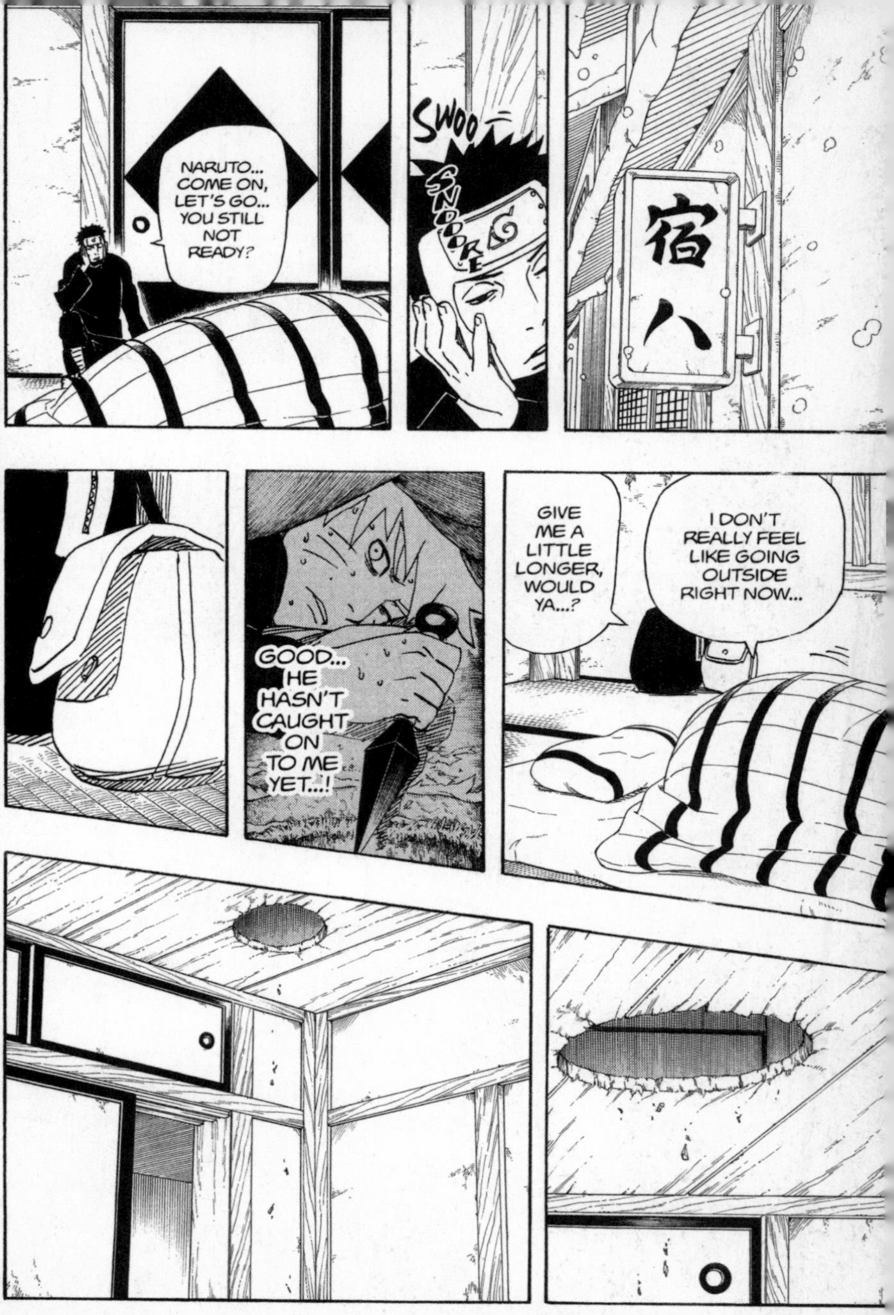

宿八
SWOO
SNOOORE
NARUTO... COME ON, LET'S GO... YOU STILL NOT READY?
I DON'T REALLY FEEL LIKE GOING OUTSIDE RIGHT NOW...
GIVE ME A LITTLE LONGER, WOULD YA...?
GOOD... HE HASN'T CAUGHT ON TO ME YET...!

READ THIS WAY

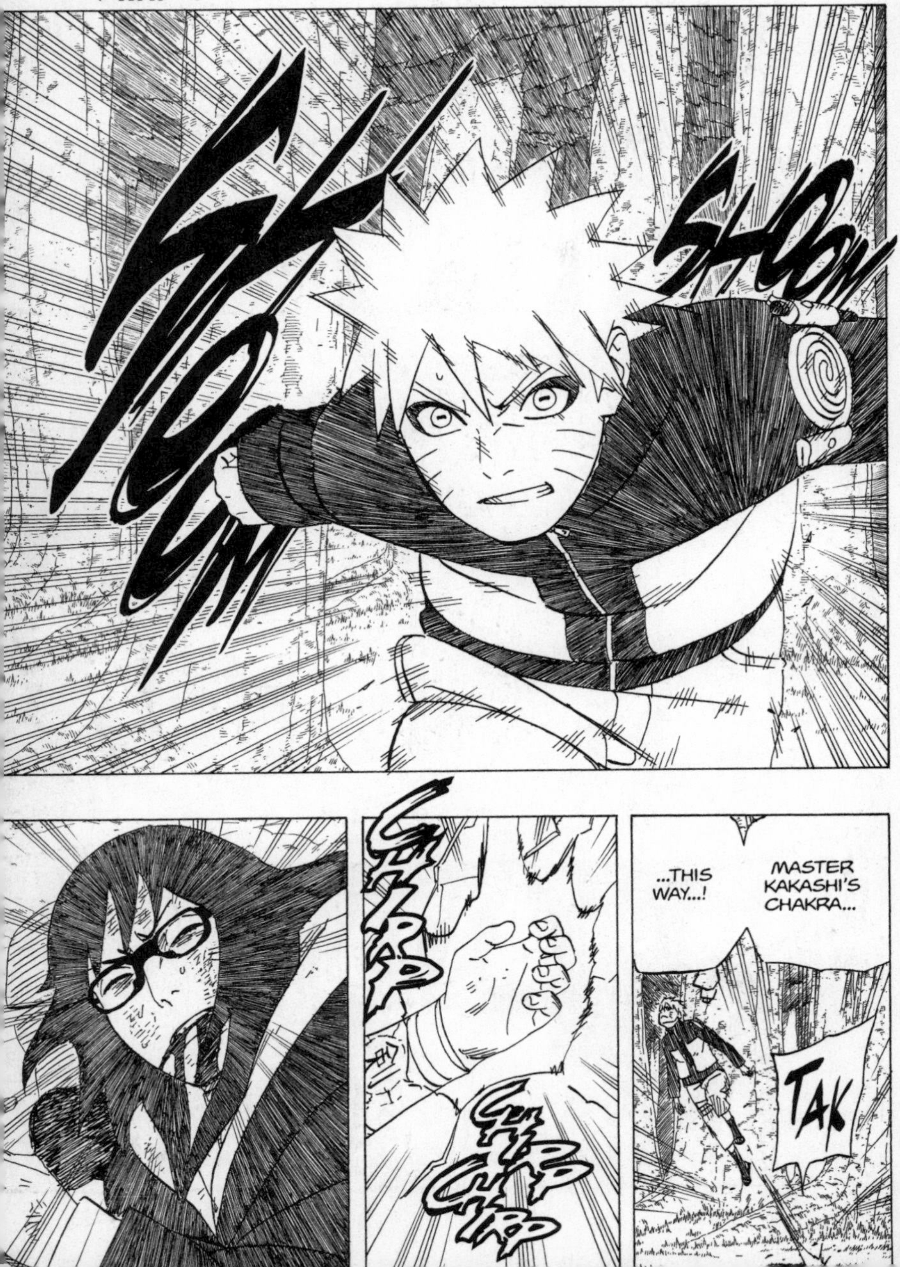

SHOOM
SHOOM
MASTER KAKASHI'S CHAKRA...
...THIS WAY...!
TAK
GRIP
GRIP
GRIP

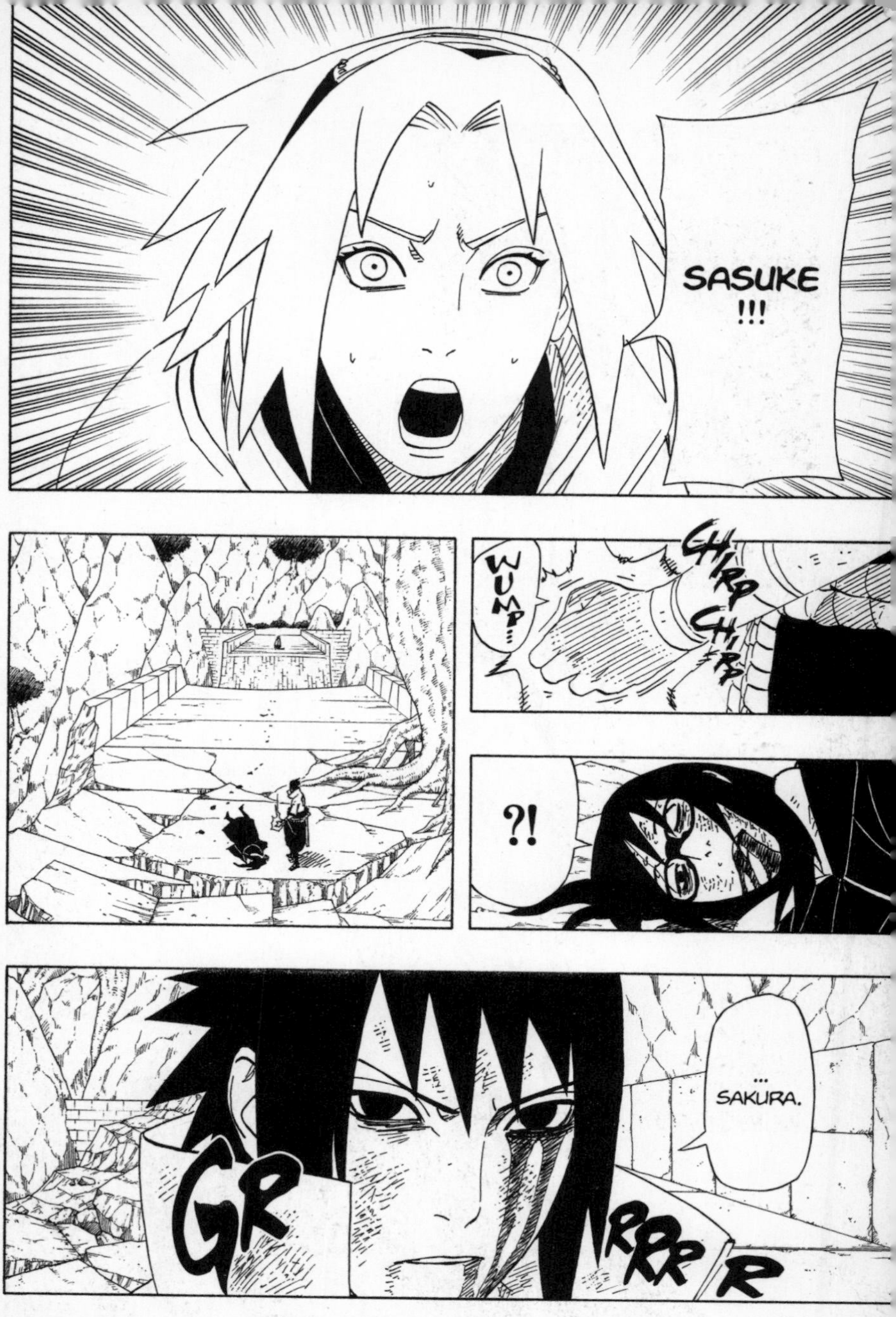
SASUKE !!!
CHIRP CHIRP CHIRP
WUMP...
?!
... SAKURA.
GRRRRR

READ THIS WAY

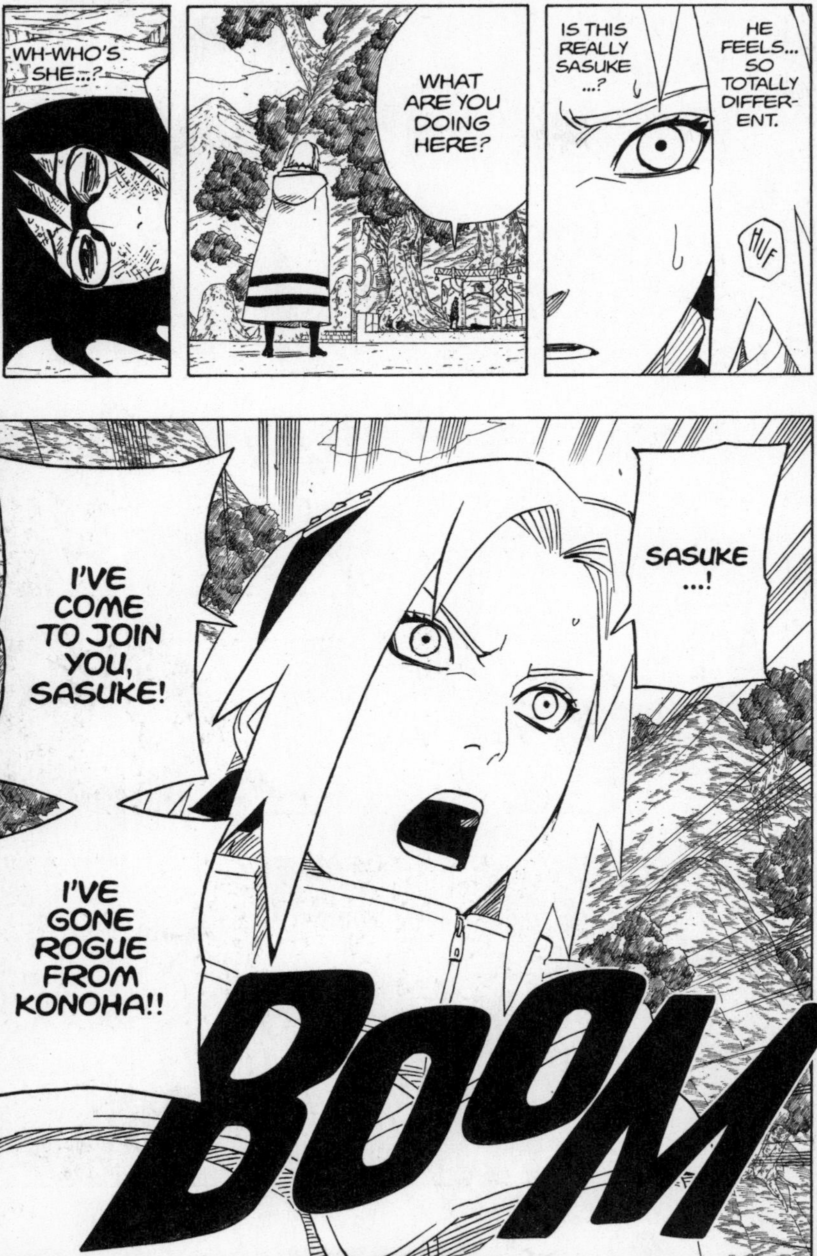
HE FEELS... SO TOTALLY DIFFERENT.
IS THIS REALLY SASUKE ...?
HUF
WHAT ARE YOU DOING HERE?
WH-WHO'S SHE...?
SASUKE ...!
I'VE COME TO JOIN YOU, SASUKE!
I'VE GONE ROGUE FROM KONOHA!!
BOOM

NARUTO

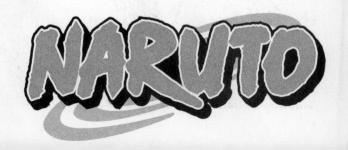

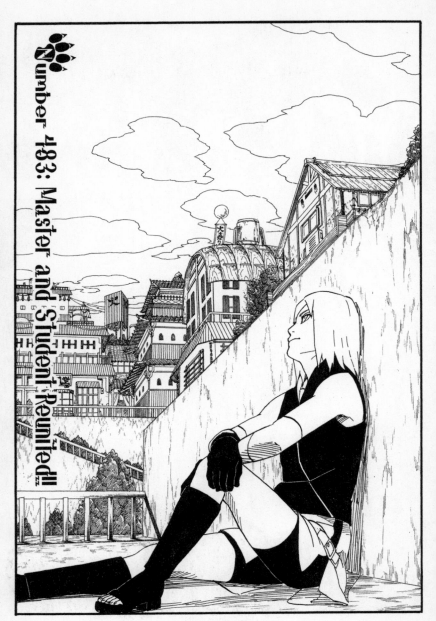

Number 483: Master and Student Reunited!!

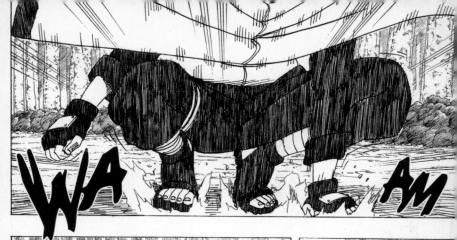

UH-OH...

WHERE'S SAKURA?

UNH... HMM...?

...

WAP

WAP

HEYA!

READ THIS WAY

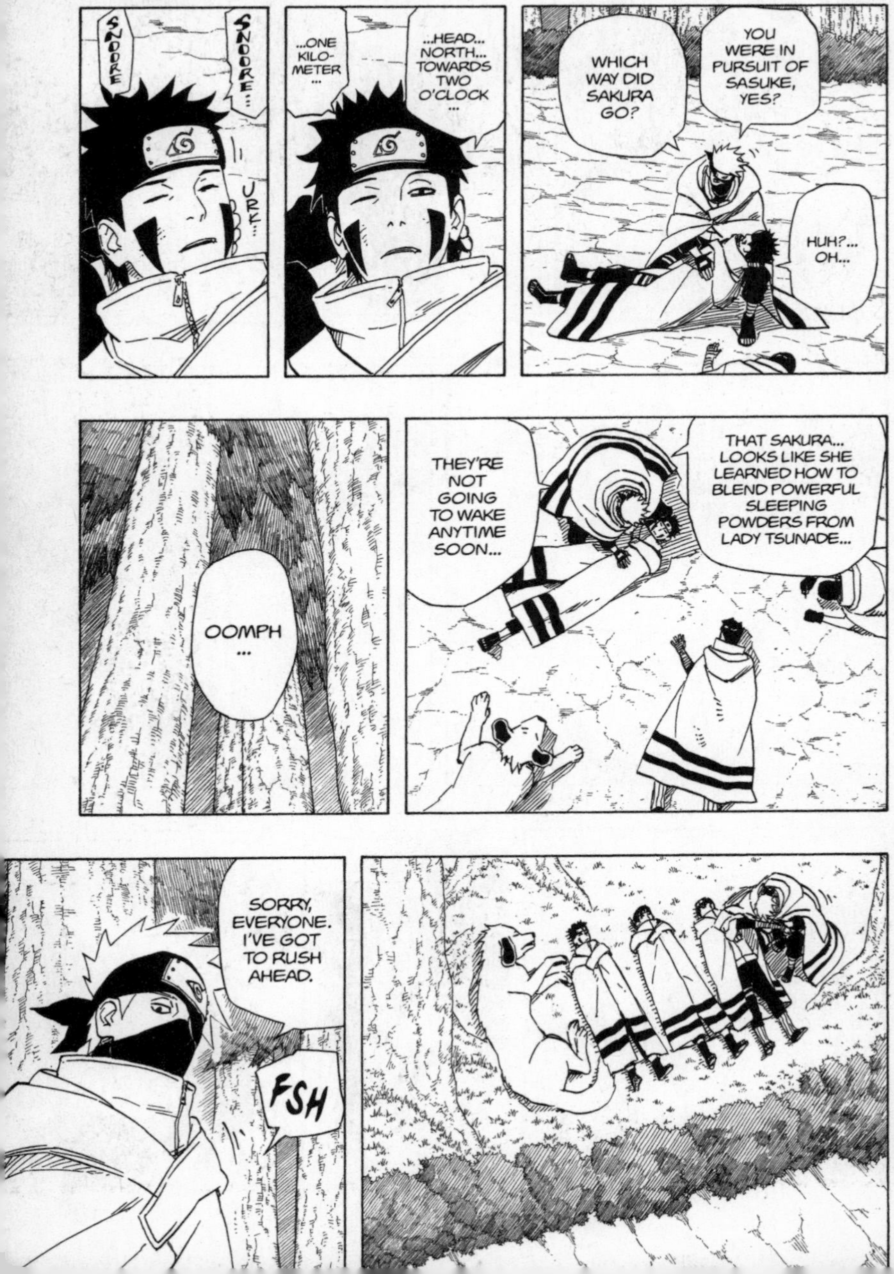
YOU WERE IN PURSUIT OF SASUKE, YES?
WHICH WAY DID SAKURA GO?
HUH?... OH...
...HEAD... NORTH... TOWARDS TWO O'CLOCK ...
...ONE KILO-METER ...
SNOORE...
URK...
SNOORE
THAT SAKURA... LOOKS LIKE SHE LEARNED HOW TO BLEND POWERFUL SLEEPING POWDERS FROM LADY TSUNADE...
THEY'RE NOT GOING TO WAKE ANYTIME SOON...
OOMPH ...
SORRY, EVERYONE. I'VE GOT TO RUSH AHEAD.
FSH

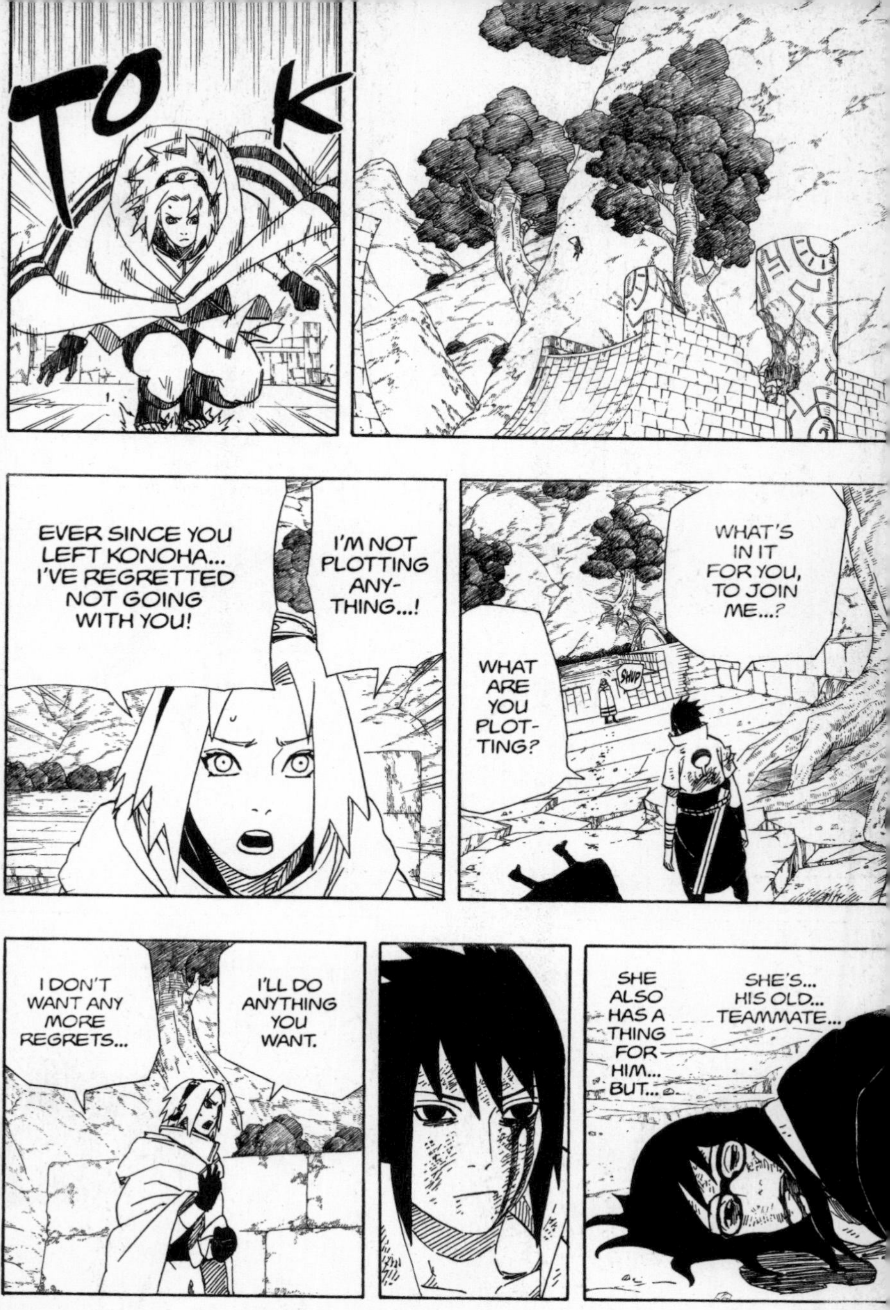
TOK
WHAT'S IN IT FOR YOU, TO JOIN ME...?
WHAT ARE YOU PLOTTING?
SHUP
I'M NOT PLOTTING ANYTHING...!
EVER SINCE YOU LEFT KONOHA... I'VE REGRETTED NOT GOING WITH YOU!
SHE'S... HIS OLD... TEAMMATE...
SHE ALSO HAS A THING FOR HIM... BUT...
I'LL DO ANYTHING YOU WANT.
I DON'T WANT ANY MORE REGRETS...

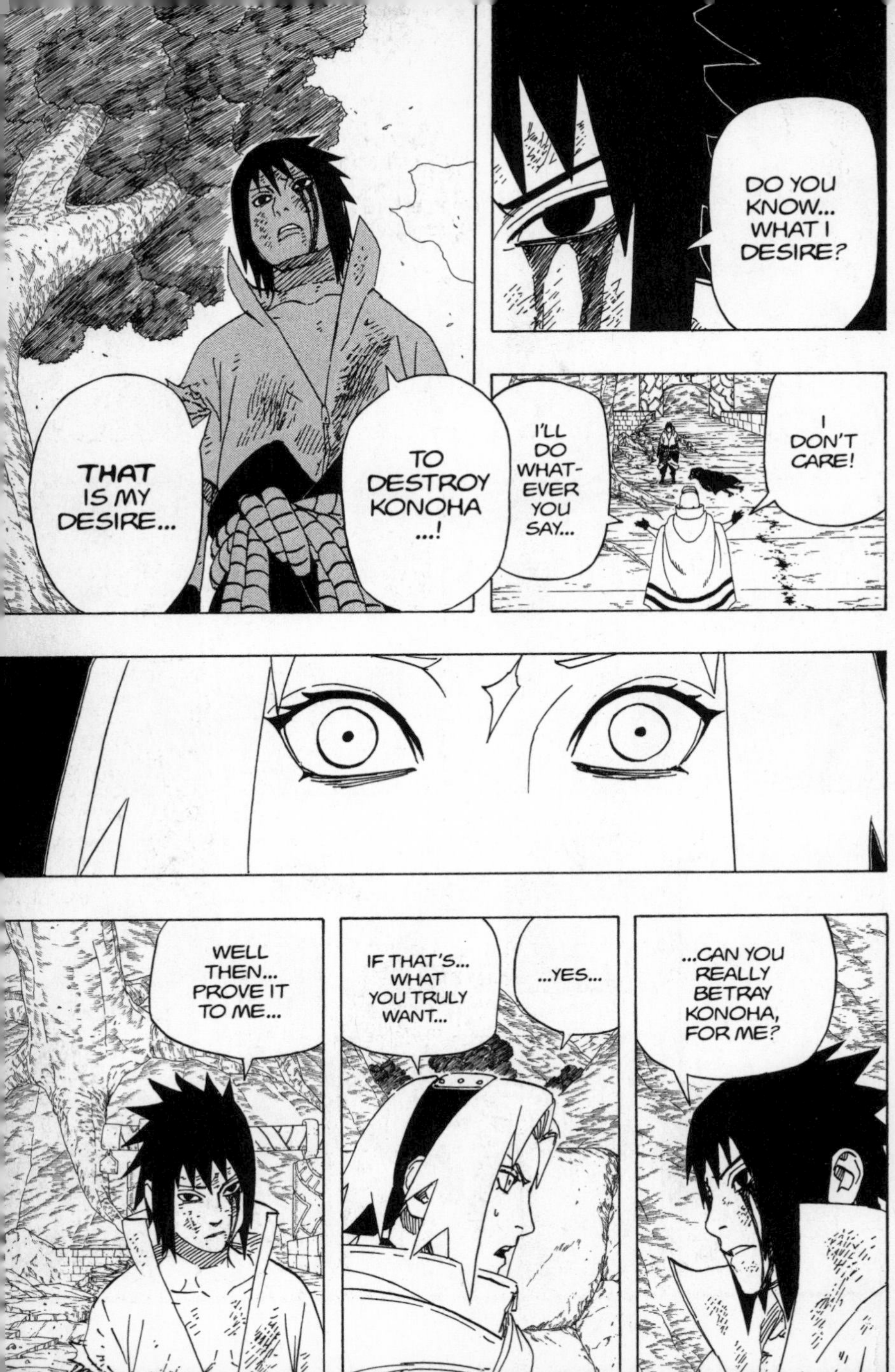
DO YOU KNOW... WHAT I DESIRE?
TO DESTROY KONOHA ...!
THAT IS MY DESIRE...
I DON'T CARE!
I'LL DO WHAT-EVER YOU SAY...
...CAN YOU REALLY BETRAY KONOHA, FOR ME?
...YES...
IF THAT'S... WHAT YOU TRULY WANT...
WELL THEN... PROVE IT TO ME...

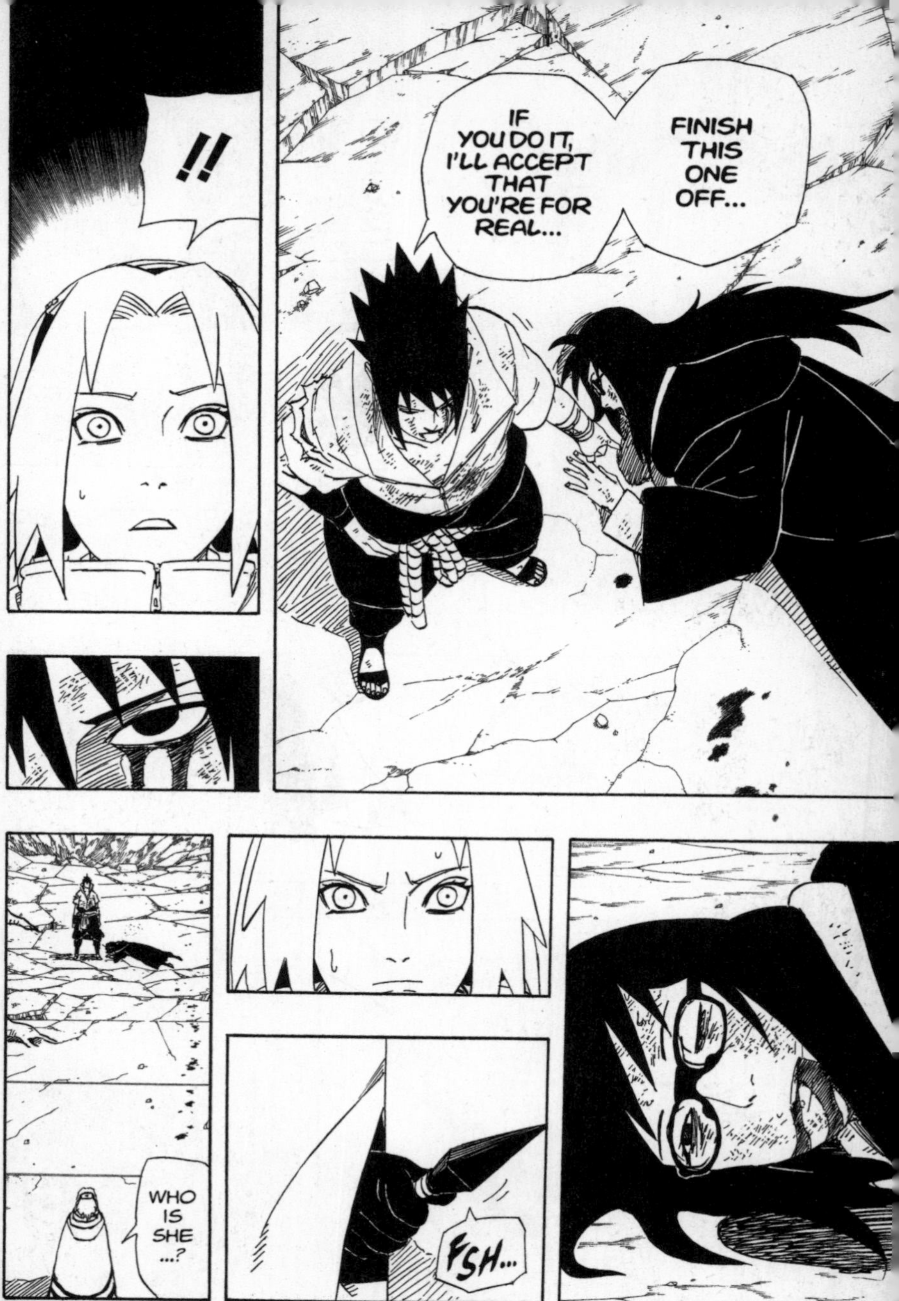
FINISH THIS ONE OFF...
IF YOU DO IT, I'LL ACCEPT THAT YOU'RE FOR REAL...
!!
FSH...
WHO IS SHE ...?

READ THIS WAY

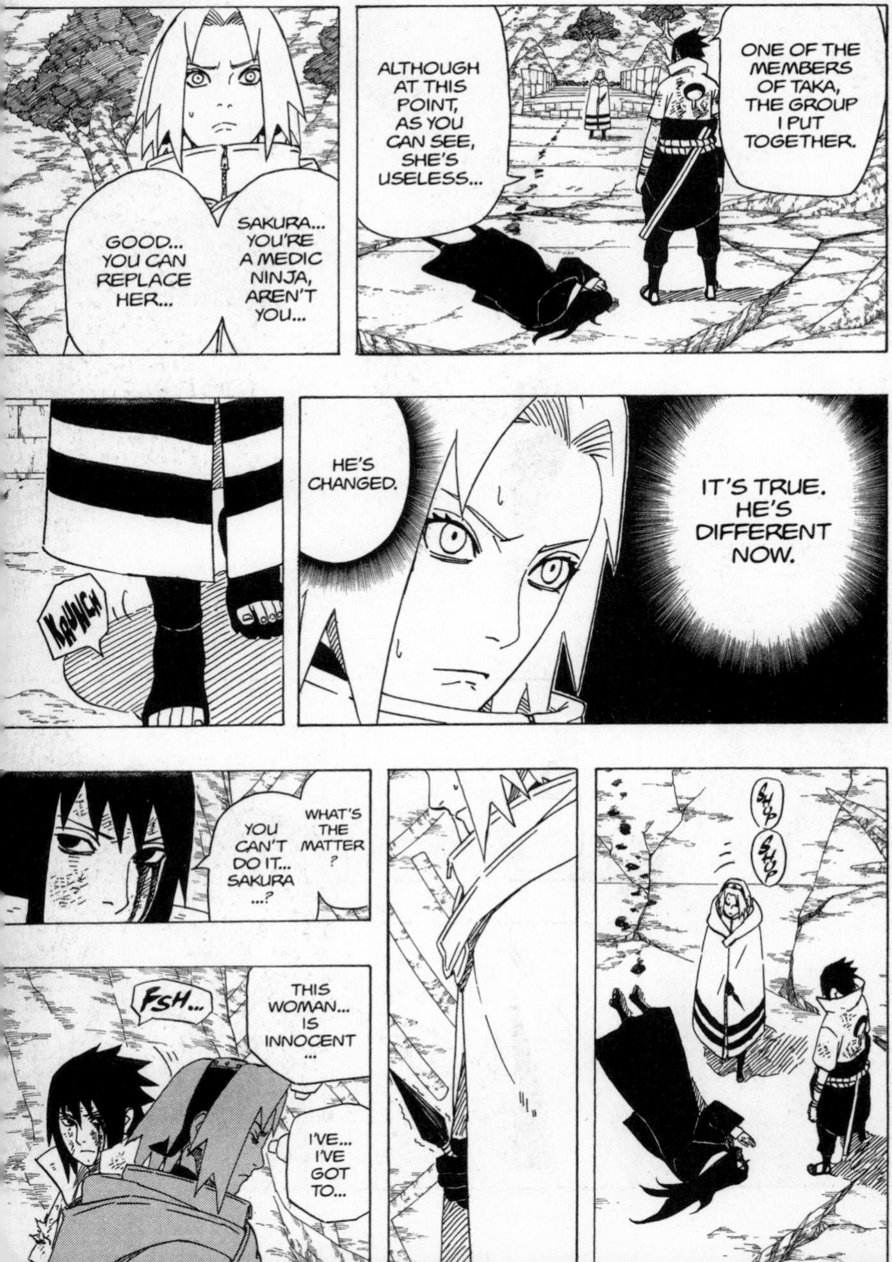

ONE OF THE MEMBERS OF TAKA, THE GROUP I PUT TOGETHER.
ALTHOUGH AT THIS POINT, AS YOU CAN SEE, SHE'S USELESS...
SAKURA... YOU'RE A MEDIC NINJA, AREN'T YOU...
GOOD... YOU CAN REPLACE HER...
IT'S TRUE. HE'S DIFFERENT NOW.
HE'S CHANGED.
KRUNCH
SHOP
SHOP
WHAT'S THE MATTER?
YOU CAN'T DO IT... SAKURA...?
FSH...
THIS WOMAN... IS INNOCENT...
I'VE... I'VE GOT TO...

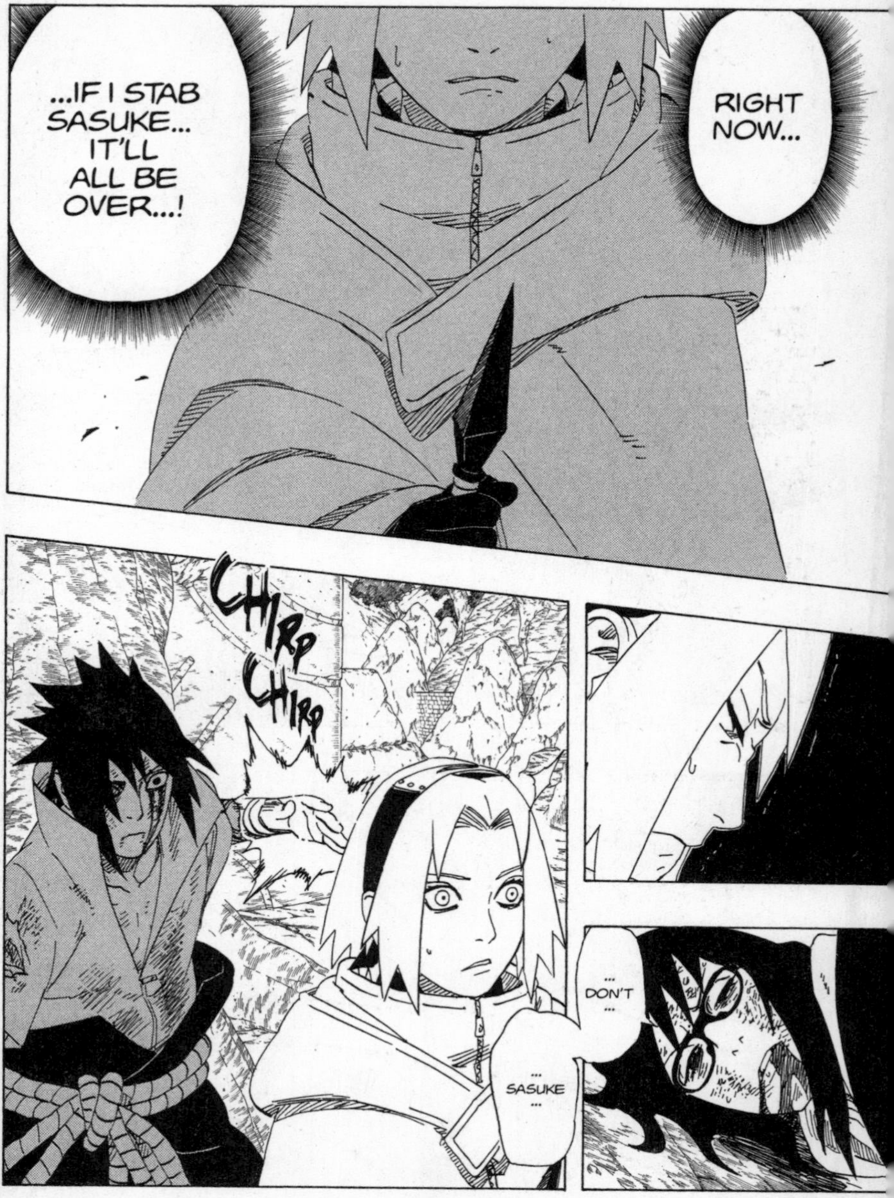
RIGHT NOW...
...IF I STAB SASUKE... IT'LL ALL BE OVER...!
... DON'T ...
... SASUKE ...
CHIRP
CHIRP

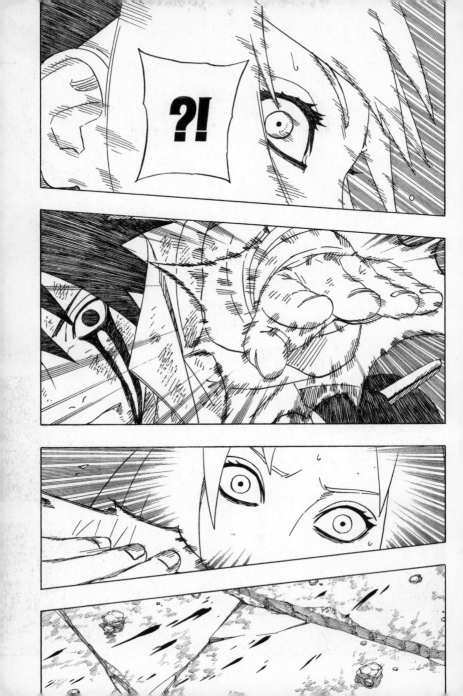

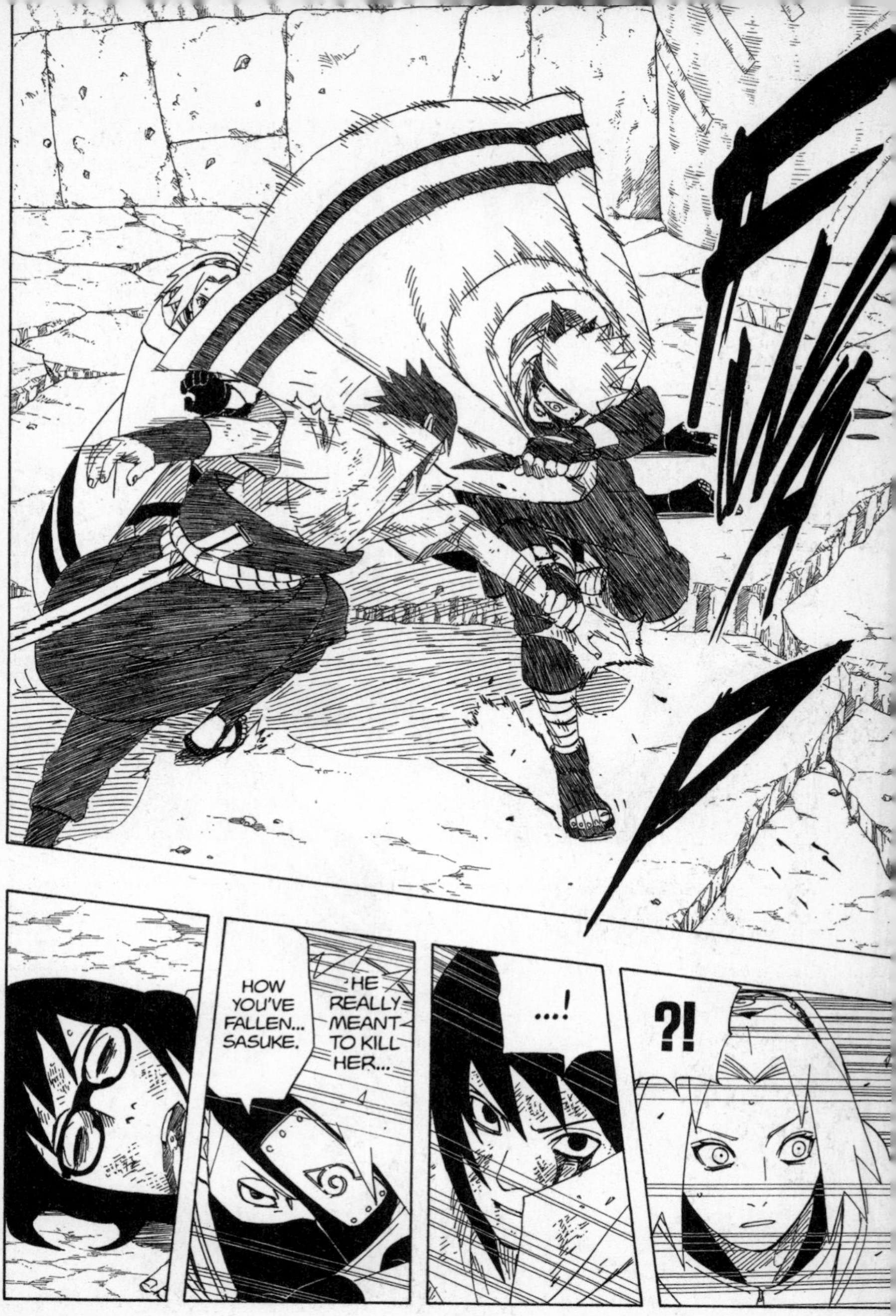
?!
...!
HE REALLY MEANT TO KILL HER...
HOW YOU'VE FALLEN... SASUKE.

READ THIS WAY

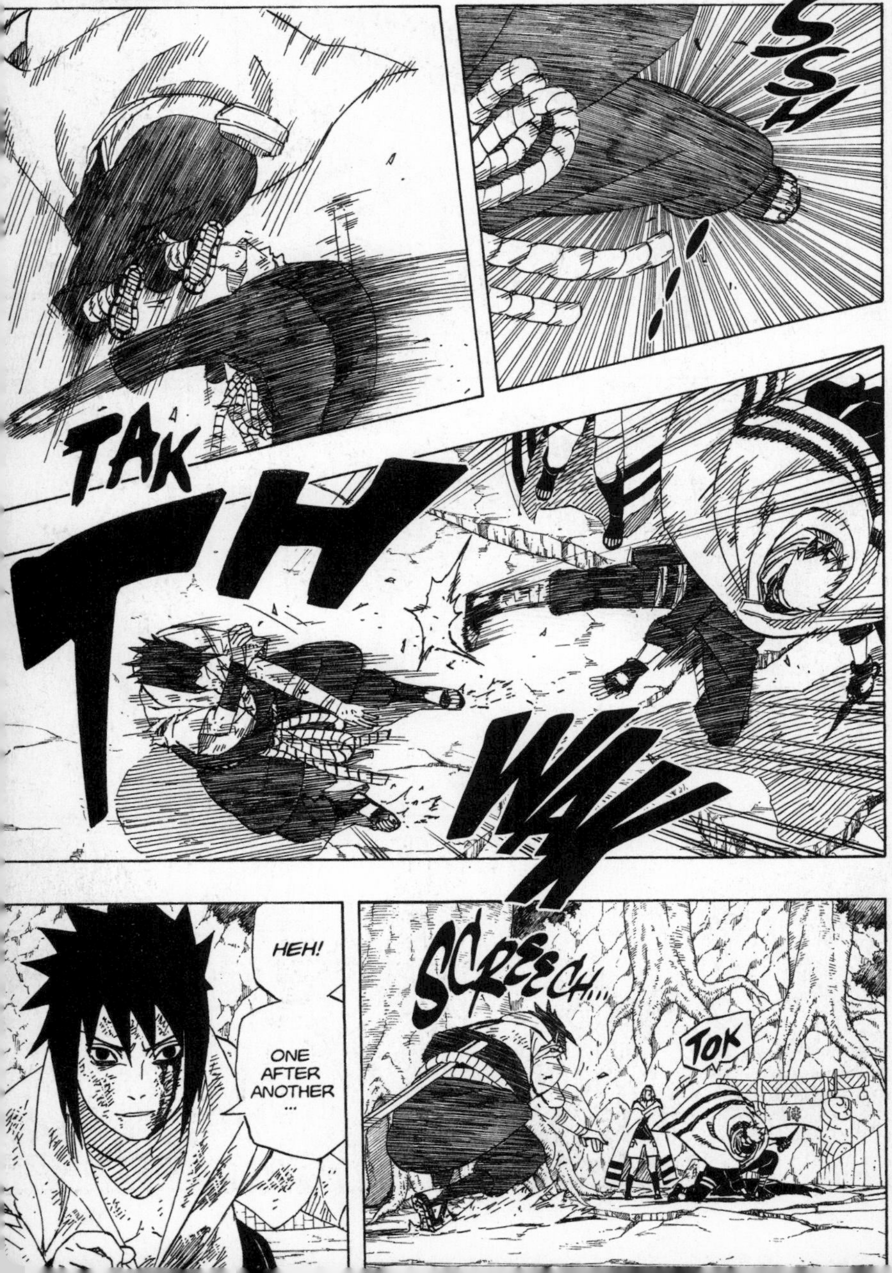

SSH
TAK
THWAK
SCREECH...
TOK
HEH!
ONE AFTER ANOTHER ...

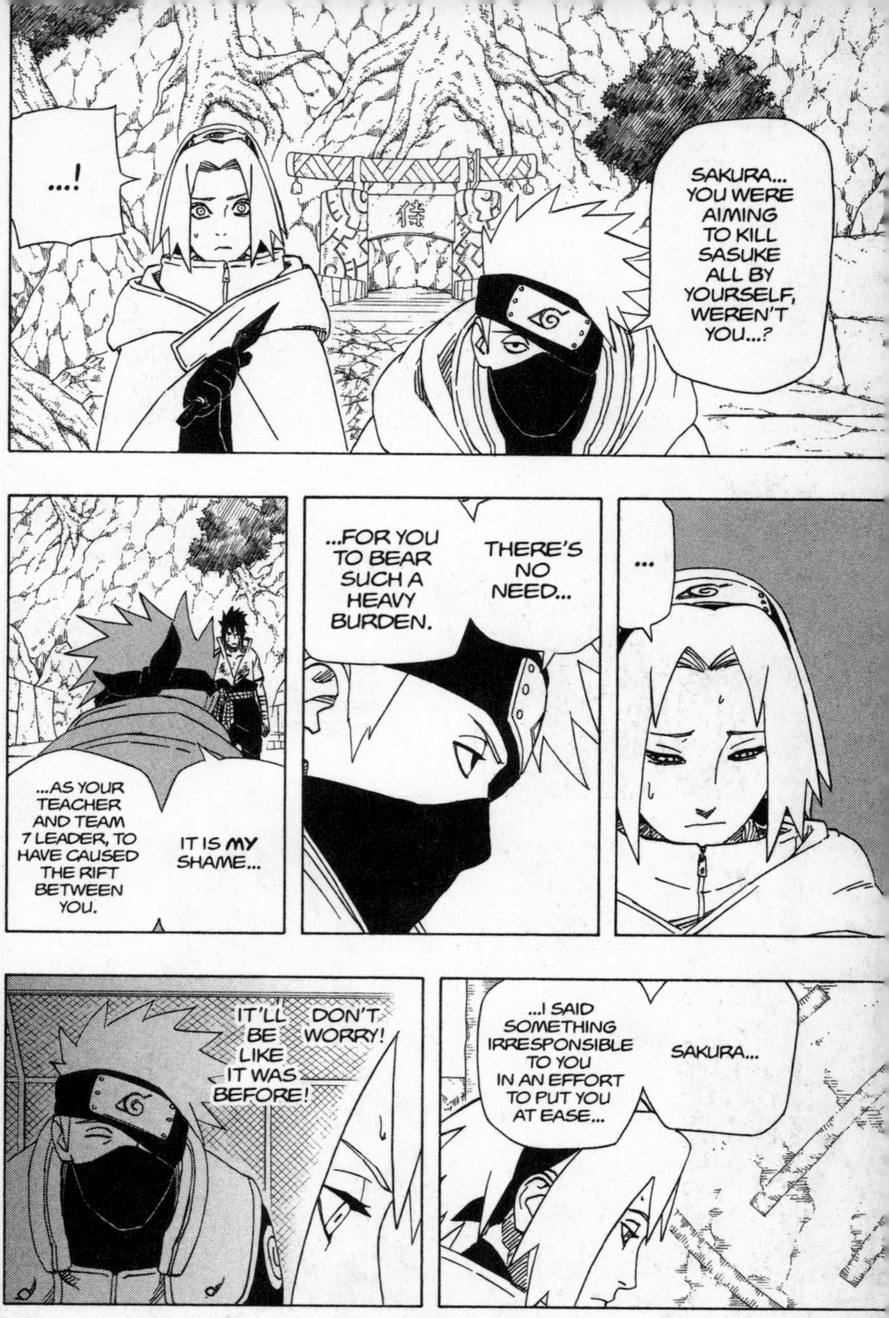
SAKURA... YOU WERE AIMING TO KILL SASUKE ALL BY YOURSELF, WEREN'T YOU...?
...!
...
THERE'S NO NEED...
...FOR YOU TO BEAR SUCH A HEAVY BURDEN.
IT IS MY SHAME...
...AS YOUR TEACHER AND TEAM 7 LEADER, TO HAVE CAUSED THE RIFT BETWEEN YOU.
SAKURA...
...I SAID SOMETHING IRRESPONSIBLE TO YOU IN AN EFFORT TO PUT YOU AT EASE...
DON'T WORRY!
IT'LL BE LIKE IT WAS BEFORE!

READ THIS WAY

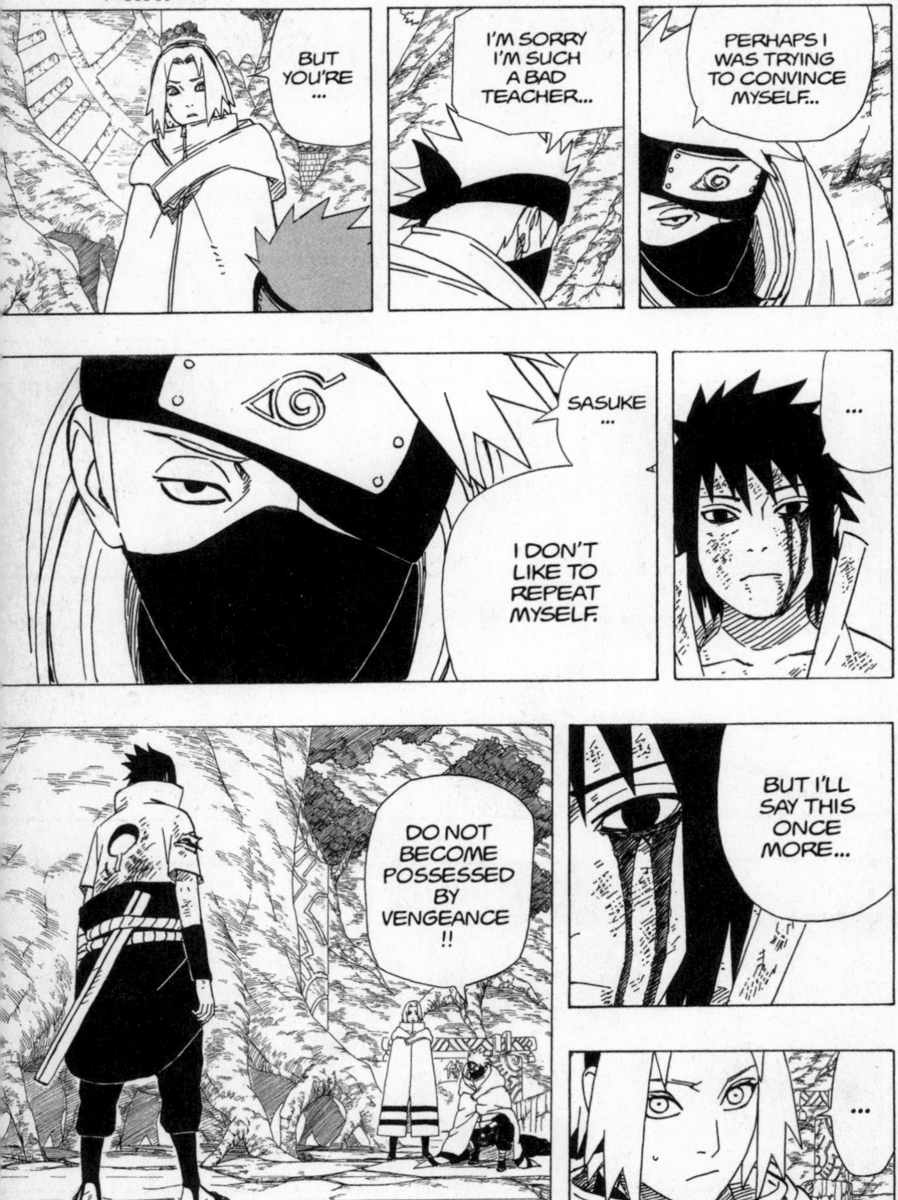
PERHAPS I WAS TRYING TO CONVINCE MYSELF...
I'M SORRY I'M SUCH A BAD TEACHER...
BUT YOU'RE ...
...
SASUKE ...
I DON'T LIKE TO REPEAT MYSELF.
BUT I'LL SAY THIS ONCE MORE...
DO NOT BECOME POSSESSED BY VENGEANCE !!
...

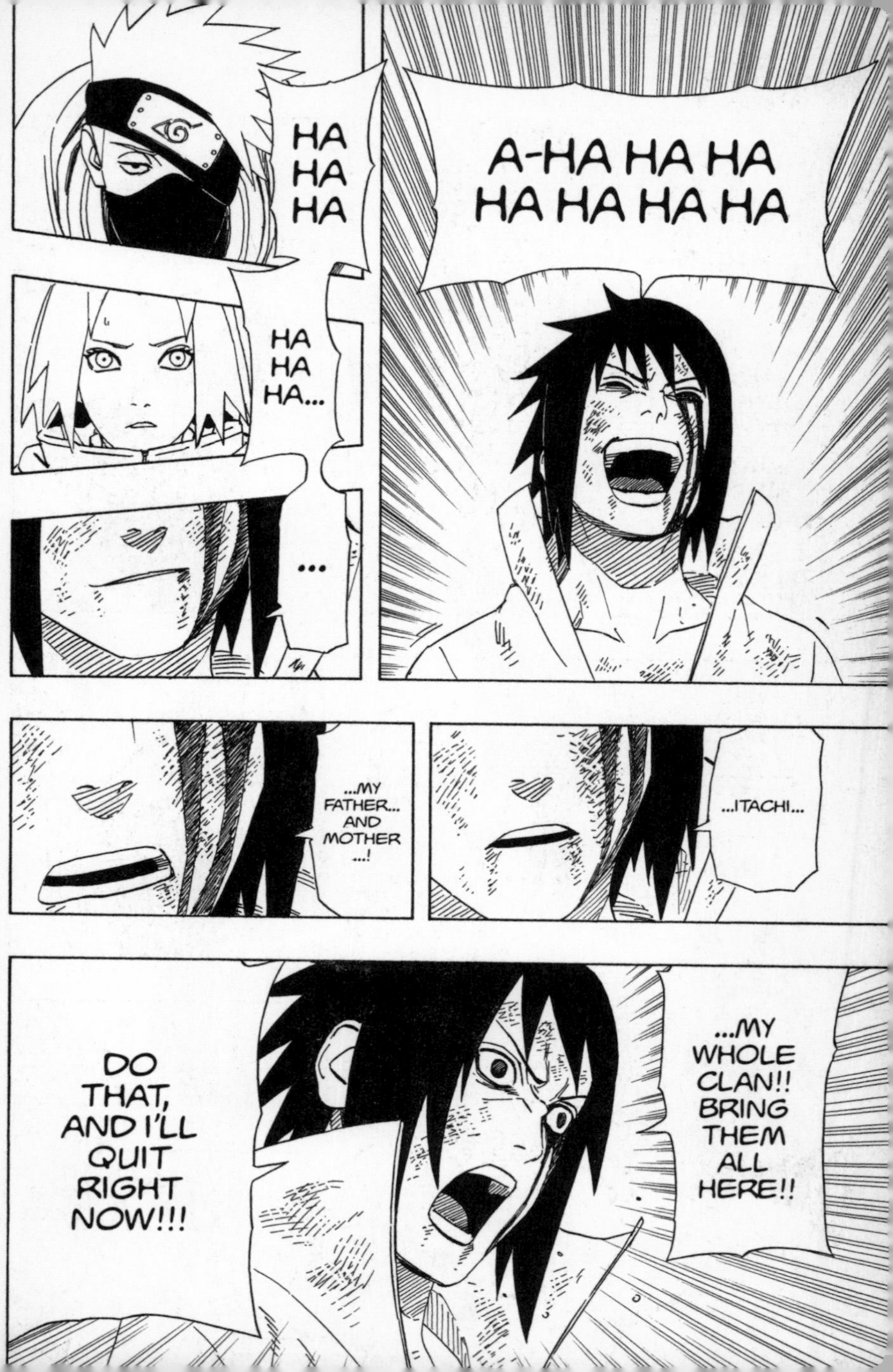
A-HA HA HA HA HA HA HA
HA HA HA
HA HA HA...
...
...ITACHI...
...MY FATHER... AND MOTHER ...!
...MY WHOLE CLAN!! BRING THEM ALL HERE!!
DO THAT, AND I'LL QUIT RIGHT NOW!!!